Visual Basic™ for MS-DOS® By EXAMPLE

que

D.F. Scott

Visual Basic for MS-DOS By Example

Library of Congress Catalog Card Number: 92-61299

ISBN: 1-56529-036-4

95 94 93 92 8 7 6 5 4 3 2 1

Interpretation of the printing code: the rightmost double-digit number is the year of the book's printing; the rightmost single-digit number, the number of the book's printing. For example, a printing code of 92-1 shows that the first printing of the book occurred in 1992.

Publisher
Lloyd J. Short

Associate Publisher
Rick Ranucci

Publishing Manager
Joseph B. Wikert

Development Editor
Jennifer Flynn

Technical Editor
Gordon Arbuthnot

Production Editor
Jodi Jenson

Editors
Charles Hutchinson
Bryan Gambrel
Kezia Endsley

Cover Designer
Jean Bisesi

Book Designers
Scott Cook
Michele Laseau

Production Director
Jeff Valler

Production Manager
Corinne Walls

Imprint Managers
Matthew Morrill
Michael Nolan

Proofreading/Indexing Coordinator
Joelynn Gifford

Production Analyst
Mary Beth Wakefield

Graphic Image Specialists
Dennis Sheehan
Jerry Ellis
Sue VandeWalle

Indexer
Joy Dean Lee

Production
Jeff Baker, Scott Boucher, Jodie Cantwell, Paula Curroll, Michelle Cleary, Brook Farling, Chuck Hutchinson, Bob LaRoche, Laurie Lee, Jay Lesandrini, Cindy L. Phipps, Caroline Roop, Sandra Shay, Linda Seifert, Johnna VanHoose, Lisa Wilson, Phil Worthington

Composed in Palatino and MCPdigital by Prentice Hall Computer Publishing.

Screen reproductions in this book were created by means of the program Collage Plus from Inner Media, Inc., Hollis, NH.

Dedication

To the memory of John J. Anderson, an editor of mine who managed, one way or another, to bring me down a few feet below 40,000.

About the Author

D.J. Scott is an independent technical author, artist, musician, and poet living in Oklahoma City. He was Technical Editor of the *Computer Street Journal*, Contributing Editor of *ANALOG Computing* and *ST-Log* magazines, and a contributor to Computer Monthly. His insights and observations on alternative computing have appeared in Computer Shopper since 1985, where he also served as moderator of the Computer Shopper Information Exchange. He is the author of *Visual Basic By Example* (Que Corporation).

Acknowledgments

Much of the material which appears in this book was printed first in *Visual Basic By Example*. Ideas for many of the programs used in both this book and its progenitor come from Al Meadows. My thanks go to him a second time. My thanks also to Christopher Hood, Steve Yeager (now at NetCom Systems), and the rest of my "support group"—Charles Wagner, Christopher Cook, Richard Kowals, and Tim Grove—at Info 1 Computers in Oklahoma City. Along with two other former employees, Jerrel McWhirter and James Fry, these people help build my personal foundation when I'm under stress, and to maintain my *humilite* whenever that foundation goes off on a tangent. I'd also like to thank Jeffery J. Johnson, my brother in spirit, and his lovely family for helping me through a personal metamorphosis that reared its head sometime between the contract and the deadline. These people listed above form the backbone of my enthusiasm for life. It is strange, though often understandable, that these people are nearly all (incurably) men.

My thanks go again to my friend Kellie, who has been the inspiration for much of the more literary ideas expressed in this book and its progenitor. I neglected, in the previous edition, to mention my mother and my father. During this past year, it has been Mom who has honed my spirit to a fine point, and Dad who has fueled my engine to keep me fighting the good fight.

To Jennifer Flynn, whose name also appears in the credits, go my thanks and my admiration for her persistence and for the good purpose behind it.

Trademark Acknowledgments

Que Corporation has made every attempt to supply trademark information about company names, products, and services mentioned in the book. Trademarks indicated below were derived from various sources. Que Corporation cannot attest to the accuracy of this information.

Finder is a trademark, and Apple, Apple II, and Disk II are registered trademarks of Apple Computer, Inc.

Flight Simulator is a registered trademark of Bruce Artwick.

DEC is a registered trademark of Digital Equipment Corporation.

Intel386 is a registered trademark of Intel Corporation.

IBM and Selectric are registered trademarks of International Business Machines Corporation.

MS-DOS, GW-BASIC, and Microsoft QuickBASIC are registered trademarks of Microsoft Corporation.

Visual Basic, Windows, and QBasic are trademarks of Microsoft Corporation.

Norton Utilities is a registered trademark of Symantec Corp.

Radio Shack TRS-80 is a registered trademark of Radio Shack.

Overview

Contents

III Instructions and Groups

Introduction

Welcome to the art of programming. You are about to become an active participant in a true art form. Programming as art may seem an unusual concept to you, especially if you purchased Visual Basic for MS-DOS and this book with the idea of simply getting some work accomplished.

You may know some people who claim to be art enthusiasts or to be "into" art. For some, being into art means visiting museums regularly or knowing when to use words such as "pointalism" and "impressionism." This author was born in the company of artists. From a true artist's perspective, being "into" art means getting oil paint beneath your fingernails or ink stains on your work jeans.

You also may know some people who are "into" computers. They own every utility package ever published and spend the better part of their work day writing batch files for processes for which no one else has written batch files. This book takes you inside computing—into the thinking and doing part of the process. You won't be talking art here; you'll be doing art.

Much has been accomplished over the last decade in the effort to make computer programs more readily and logically accessible to the common person. This effort shares the spotlight with yet another effort to maintain a reasonable degree of compatibility between older and current versions of software. Where there's friction between two forces in the computing atmosphere, there's thunder—and it was Project "Thunder" which led Microsoft to develop the Visual Basic for MS-DOS (or VB/DOS) programming language. VB/DOS is a hybrid language, a joining together of "QBX"—which was to have become Microsoft's next generation of QuickBASIC—with Visual Basic, the graphically augmented language for Microsoft Windows.

VB/DOS was not engineered to operate in the Windows environment; if it were, it would not be downwardly compatible with older versions of QuickBASIC and Microsoft BASIC PDS, nor would it be compatible with the current version of QBasic for DOS 5. VB/DOS is a bridge, if you will, between two worlds of computing. During the testing stage for the language, Microsoft quite fittingly code-named the VB/DOS project "Escher." The artist M. C. Escher, for whom the project was named, created etchings and engravings which nearly always blended two patterns—be they geometric or realistic—such that one pattern neatly folded into the other. You may be familiar with the famous pattern of fish swimming to the right and, in the spaces where there are no fish, there are perfectly fitted birds flying to the left.

Among M. C. Escher's less noted works include steel engravings which show, in an apparently realistic form of perspective, people marching along apparently realistic paths, which follow staircases and bridges along apparently realistic buildings, and then eventually fold inside out on each other in some totally unrealistic fashion. The eye is challenged to see at what point the path became unrealistic and the people began marching under-neath one another, along what had appeared to be a wall, or beneath something that at first glance seemed to be a window. A thorough examination of these etchings may be of considerable help in warming up for programming in the VB/DOS language. (Some of us were hoping Microsoft would retain the name "Escher" for the language, for architectural as well as aesthetic reasons.)

All programming should be an attempt to make real what on paper appears esoteric, just as M. C. Escher made real pathways that were architectural anomalies. The true path in any program isn't the flow of data within the program itself, but the exchange of data between the program and its user. In all art forms, there is an exchange between the art itself and the participant—not just the artist, but the observer as well. This is why I call programming an art form, categorized alongside etching and music and painting.

Visual Basic for MS-DOS is an elaborate set of resources and tools to be used against perhaps the crudest of canvasses, plain DOS. MS-DOS is a rudimentary structure which is just barely capable of convincing computers with the Intel architectural platform that there are files to be read. As an environment, it is as pleasant as the environment of the planet Pluto. Yet there can be assembled a sort of artificial environment atop DOS that gives users the visual gadgets necessary—the life support systems, if you will—to sensibly operate a program. Visual Basic for MS-DOS is a crude, but effective combination of such elements.

The Creation Process

The objective of this book is to teach you to write computer programs in much the same way a true artist paints. Allow me to switch artists for the time being. When restorers first went to work some years ago on the Sistine Chapel, few people remembered that Michelangelo never applied the final colors of a fresco, or any other work, in one coat. The color you see is layered, a combination of the base coat—which is largely colorless—with a second coat that adds its primary color, and then a series of glazes which give flesh tones and garments their warmth. When restorers removed what they thought was settled dust and junk particles from the surface of the fresco, they, in fact, removed much of Michelangelo's glazes. They then wondered why the revealed color beneath was so flat and lifeless. They had forgotten that the master had mixed together along the very wall itself combinations of rare, even crude elements for his paint, and had not used semi-gloss enamel.

Along those same lines, some books on the subject of programming make it appear that the conjuring of a computer program from the back of one's mind into compiled object code is a one-step process. Many authors seem to believe that if the reader sees how the source code of a program appears when it's fully written and debugged, she will at some time be able to exude source code from her fingertips like the application of a single coat of paint. Such books are concerned with the product of programming. *Visual Basic for MS-DOS By Example* is concerned with the process, the act of mixing elements and the process of discerning whether that mixture is the proper one. It explicitly and exhaustively demonstrates the development of programs and program modules from the perspective of the programmer, showing you what decisions are made—both necessary and arbitrary—that lead to a well-planned, thoughtfully prepared, perfectly executed master work.

Your Programming Studio

The first order of business is to comprehend the mechanics and characteristics of the studio, if you will, where you will produce your programs. In Part I, "The Programming Environment," I take you on an explicitly guided tour of the VB/DOS workspace. Once you're settled in and comfortable, you'll start to concentrate on your objective: learning just what a program actually is and how a VB/DOS program differs from a conventional BASIC program or a C program.

Throughout the book—as its title implies—I show you programs and program modules in various stages of construction, and give you some practice constructing your own modules for real-world purposes. Instead of just showing you a working program or two and saying, "Make yours like mine." Chapter 4, "The Development Process," takes you step-by-step through the construction of a small VB/DOS program, focusing on what goes through the mind of the programmer and what type of goals programmers set for themselves. Any program, no matter what the language, does not manifest itself in complete, flawless source code like some other books might have you believe. Most good programs are the result of bursts of inspiration, separated by several hours of error-trapping and debugging.

When you're comfortable with the setting and the process of programming, you'll then examine, piece by piece, VB/DOS's verbal and graphic elements. As graphically comprehensive as VB/DOS is, a novice programmer might be led to believe there is little or no arithmetic left in the programming process. Such is not the case; arithmetic logic and procedural algebra still comprise the crux of all programming. VB/DOS's arithmetic core is the product of years of redevelopment and refinement, a process which in and of itself may one day be the subject of a book—perhaps a TV miniseries. Still, math in and of itself is not so glamorous a subject. Math can be the most esoteric and paradoxical part of the programming process; so in Part II, "Values and Variables," I carefully introduce you to arithmetic logic and procedural algebra using tangible, real-world terms and analogies.

If you're a veteran of older versions of BASIC, you probably have noticed already how the simple process of printing a line of text has grown from a statement of fact into a complex event of methodology. In Part III, "Instructions and Groups," you examine in detail the reformed syntax of the VB/DOS language. In Part IV, "Modularization," I demonstrate how the overall job of a VB/DOS program is divided and delegated to the various modules and constituent procedures, and I compare the conventional style of BASIC application construction with the more modern styles developed by Microsoft.

The mathematical functions will be explained, using as much glamour as I can muster, in Part V, "Arithmetic Functions." The VB/DOS language contains an automatic system for addressing and maintaining character-mode windows, discussed in Part VI, "Form Design." The remainder of the graphics system is discussed in Part VII, "The Screen." The part of the VB/DOS language which allows the programmer to override the automatic systems provided for recognizing graphic events, is covered in Part VIII, "Event Trapping." The VB/DOS interpreter offers a trial-and-error environment for testing programs. It is quite natural for programs to exhibit errors in the early stages of their development; in fact, one of the major factors in the development of a perfectly formed and executed program is the prior existence of errors. At the end of Part VIII, I introduce you to the fine art of correcting yourself—which is probably what you spend half your time doing as a programmer, even after you become an expert.

Because a primary task of programs that maintain data is to maintain a *database*, it is appropriate that tools for Indexed Sequential Access Management (ISAM) have been supplied within the

VB/DOS language. Of course, because VB/DOS is a derivative of BASIC, the older, more conventional data access mechanisms still abound. The subjects of storing, retrieving, and even *designing* data are covered in Part IX, "Data Management."

How to Use This Book

I assume that you have already used modern computer programs—especially those running under Microsoft Windows or the Apple System—enough that you understand the principles of icons, buttons, and drop-down menus. I also assume that you have already fully installed VB/DOS on your computer, and that it is operating normally. Unless I state otherwise, I assume that you have no prior knowledge or experience with BASIC.

If you're familiar with the language and environment of Visual Basic for Windows, I'd advise that you do *not* skip over parts of the text here that look familiar to you. Microsoft has made efforts to make the two Visual Basics somewhat alike; but in so doing, the differences between the two languages have become rather subtle, and difficult to detect. You will need to familiarize yourself with the specific differences in syntax between the two implementations.

One of the tools I frequently use to show you how the VB/DOS language works is *pseudocode.* In essence, a paragraph of pseudocode states what the program instructions would say if they could state their functions to you out loud, in English. The pseudocode is typeset in *italics,* and a light bulb symbol appears next to the pseudocode.

Actual VB/DOS code appears in this book in a `monospace` font. Placeholders—terms used to represent text that you will supply—appear in *`monospace italic`*. Here are two examples, the first is written in pure VB/DOS; the second is pseudocode that explains the function of the code fragment preceding it.

```
FOR c = 1 TO 5
     Test1.PRINT c
NEXT c
```

Start counting from 1 to 5.
Print the number you just counted.
Go back to where you started counting, and repeat yourself until you counted to 5.

Granted, the preceding segment of pseudocode is a bit verbose, but its purpose not only is to show you what the VB/DOS source code is trying to state for the interpreter, but also at what point in the code it is stated.

Next to many working program modules and fragments is a symbol representing the relative degree of effort and experience required to comprehend the example. A module's size alone is no measure of the extent to which it can be confusing. I hope these symbols help you confirm that, when a particular module is difficult, it was meant to be. The following is a list of the symbols I use for this purpose:

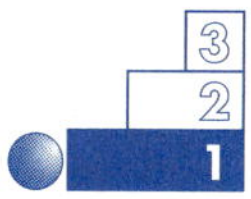
Level 1

Level 2

Level 3

Every once in a while, you encounter a line of VB/DOS source code that is so long, the typesetters couldn't fit it all on one line. In such cases, I've utilized a little rightward-sweeping arrow before the line that continues from the previous line, as in the following example:

```
mainboard$ = STRING$(24, " ") + "   XO     OX   " +
➥ STRING$(24," ")
```

Note also the "Level 3" symbol used next to this example, just to let you know that it's alright to be confused at first by this line of example source code. Believe it or not, by the time you get to the chapter that mentions this very line, you'll be able to understand it just as if it were English—or, at least, English shorthand.

From time to time, I'll focus on a specific VB/DOS instruction and show you how it's phrased. One tool I'll be using is a *syntax line*, which shows the general phraseology of the instruction being discussed. Here's an example:

Syntax:

```
PSET [STEP](pixelx!, pixely!)[, color%]
```

Each syntax line will be specifically marked with the word "Syntax:" so you won't confuse it with a true instruction. In the example above, the italicized words are symbolic of *variables,* or other terms that will be used in their place (also called *placeholders*). The punctuation (such as "!" and "%" refers to the type of symbol that is being replaced. You'll learn what these symbols mean in the chapters to come.

Square brackets around an item or set of items show that the set is optional—you don't need to have these items in the instruction in order for it to work. Any portion of the code—letters, numbers, or punctuation—that does not appear within square brackets and is not italicized, must appear within the instruction in order for it to work.

How the Chapters Are Assembled

In an effort to make every square inch of this book useful to you, I've placed information and diagrams in the margins. If an important new term is being introduced that is a crucial part of the Visual Basic conceptual vocabulary or of the vernacular of computing in general, a definition for that term appears in a *margin note.* Also, where space permits, small *flowcharts* appear to the side of some program examples. These flowcharts have been drawn to help you visualize the flow and throughput of individual procedures.

At the end of most chapters, you are presented with a short series of review questions and, where applicable, exercises that should challenge your comprehension of the information in that chapter. The difficulty-level symbols are used there, too, giving you fair warning as to the difficulty of the questions. You can find the answers to the Review Questions—printed right-side up since I trust you—in Appendix B at the end of the book. For answers to the Review Exercises, turn to the back page of this book to find out how to order the companion disk.

Points of Order

There are a few items concerning English-language syntax worth noting before you proceed. VB/DOS is a derivative of the BASIC programming language. Because BASIC is an acronym standing for Beginner's All-purpose Symbolic Instruction Code, this word appears in all caps *unless* the brand name to which it is associated has the word written normally, as in "Visual Basic." The term BASIC is used to refer to the language genre as a whole. Microsoft has just recently chosen to lowercase Basic when it refers to the language; though in the past, the company has marketed "Microsoft BASIC." In deference to Kemeny and Kurtz who conceived the language as well as its name, however, I choose to leave the acronym as it stands.

In the old days of programming, back when things were simpler to describe (for instance, about 1989), you could print a few pages of source code—pure text and numbers back then—type it all in, and you would have a working program. Times have changed, and now you do not entirely type a Visual Basic program. One of the primary control devices in the VB/DOS environment is the *form.* The programmer creates a form by literally *drawing* it, not typing in its characteristics and parameters as code. When you type one of the programs in this book, it would be unfair for me to simply show you a photograph and say, "Draw your control form like mine." Instead, whenever I give you a complete source code listing, I give you a table showing the name of each graphic object employed in the program, along with the *properties* or characteristics—such as position, size, color, and index number—that have been changed from their default settings. You can then assemble your control form manually using the table as a guide.

All the source code modules, program listings, and property tables in this book are yours to type, manipulate, experiment with, destroy, rebuild, and enhance for whatever purposes you desire. As the original author of these modules, I feel the best way to see how a mechanism—physical or logical—works is to take it apart and put it back together. You shouldn't have to ask permission to experiment with something as basic as BASIC.

With respect to the actions a user makes when operating a program in a graphical environment, I chose to standardize the usage of individual verbs for specific actions. Thus, a menu item is selected, an item from a list box is chosen, data in a form or window is indicated, and a button is clicked. Further, a setting, property, or filename typed manually into a text box is a designation, and a setting or attribute chosen from a list box is an *assignment.* This choice of terms is consistent throughout the book to reduce confusion.

The standard mouse button used for indicating objects on the screen is the left button; however, it is becoming more common to refer to whatever button is used on the mouse or trackball device for the main index pointer as the *index button.* This is especially true for some trackball devices made for laptop computers where both or all three buttons may be on the left. Also, I use the term *cursor* to refer to the blinking vertical line or block that denotes on-screen where text is to appear when it is typed from the keyboard. By contrast, the *pointer* is the arrow that is moved by the mouse.

Finally, I refrain from using the term *user interface,* at the request of an ever-expanding group of engineers and programmers who feel the term *interface* should be limited to mechanical, not visual, devices. I use no poetic synonyms for forms, windows, controls, graphic objects, or devices.

Now that all your tools are in place, you can enter the virtual studio where art is to take place.

Part I

The Programming Environment

1

What a Program Is

In this chapter, you are introduced to the concept of the program, with respect to both Visual Basic for MS-DOS and the art of computing as a whole. This chapter explains what you as a programmer must know about how programs "behave" in a computer so that future users of your programs won't have to worry about this behavior. This chapter introduces you to the elementary concepts of programming with a high-level language. If you're already familiar with what such a language is and what it does, feel free to proceed to Chapter 2, "The Project."

A Programmer's Credo

The objective of all programming is to model or simulate some rationally describable process—whether in the real world or imaginary—as a logical and arithmetic procedure. These processes can be completely mathematical like accounting, geometrical like floor planning, or recreational like starship piloting. If you understand the principle behind the process, you already know what your computer program should contain. What you need to do is reconstruct and reorganize this process as a mathematical model. In other words, you have to find a way to describe absolutely every part of the process mathematically.

Everything about a computer is logical and is composed of numbers and mathematical methods. Therefore, it is relatively easy to conceive an accounting program because the process of accounting is composed of numbers and numerological methods. Consider, however, a program that renders floor plans and landscaping plans. In that instance, geometry plays a role. Some processes that at first may not be viewed as numerological—such as drawing where the trees or shrubbery are to be planted—are simulated with program instructions.

A *database* is a collection of organized records.

Now consider a program that renders routine medical diagnoses for doctors. The part of the program that maintains a list of symptoms, causes, and medications would be the easiest part to create—you might call this portion the *database manager*. A database is a collection of organized records (such as a doctor's list of patients). A database manager is the part of a program that maintains those records, along with the data that defines just what a record is.

It's certainly far more difficult for the programmer to simulate the decision-making process than to maintain the lists of symptoms and medications. If you're not already a doctor, you as a programmer would need to talk extensively with medical doctors and study the concepts and procedures of diagnosis. You would have to read all the introductory material as if you were a medical student. It is important for a doctor to rely to some degree on his gut feelings and intuition when making a clinical diagnosis. Keeping this in mind, you would need to simulate the diagnosis process for the sake of a machine that has no intuition or, for that matter, guts. This task is not impossible. You can let the program simulate just the "memory" functions and let the doctor provide the intuition.

Leaving the doctor's office behind for now, consider writing a chess program. You probably know from experience that a computer *appears* (note the emphasis) to play chess very well. Grand masters like Gerry Kasparov can appreciate how well these programs play the game, although Kasparov still beats them constantly. What you may not know is that no chess program conceives its own strategy for winning the game. The program reevaluates the board, move after move, and the evaluation results are generally discarded after each move is made. When you play chess against a computer, you play human strategy versus a bunch of math. Your job as programmer of a chess game is to conceive the math. Programming a chess game does not require a mastery of chess; however, it does require a mastery of math. You probably should be a reasonably good chess player, but you wouldn't be programming your own strategies into the game because chess programs don't *think.* Instead, you'll define methods for the proper position of the knight 10 moves ahead with respect to all other squares that could be in check by that time.

When conceiving a program that performs work that would otherwise be performed by a human being, it is important that you thoroughly comprehend the fundamentals of the work process and the principles, laws, and mathematics governing that process. It is not necessary for you to master the process itself. In other words, you don't need to be an accountant to write an accounting program or an M.D. to write a clinical diagnosis program. Simply review the fundamentals of the process and *look up the details when you need to.* You should, however, comprehend the jobs of the professionals who will be using your program to a degree that they won't be insulted or aggravated by the way that program addresses them.

When a program is applicable to your business task, that program is an *application.* VB/DOS is a tool for the development of applications. When using it, keep in mind that your objective is *automation*—taking the logical and arithmetic part of a real-world job such as recordkeeping or data analysis and delegating a measure of responsibility for it to the computer. If the applications you write merely invent more work for their users, automation doesn't take place and people will not be compelled to use the applications. An application should take a load off somebody's shoulders, or at least distribute the weight more evenly in the way a word processor organizes documents or a database management system handles records.

Fundamental Terminology

A *program* is the symbolic form of a task.

To comprehend VB/DOS requires more than a modicum of effort; you are trusted to have mastered the mental concept of a *program.* To start you toward this level of mastery, here is a new, broader, but fitting definition for the term *program* in this context: A program is the symbolic form of a task or work process. It is any computing process that is described logically using a fundamental code that is interpretable by both the person reading it and the computer processing it.

Source code is the written text of a program in its native language.

Notice that in the preceding definition of *program* I did not use the term *language.* With a few exceptions, computer programs are written using languages, and the VB/DOS language is not one of the exceptions. Nonetheless, the written text of a program is its *source code.*

An instruction is any complete directive made within a program.

The source code of a program consists of instructions that are executed in sequence. This sequence is not necessarily top-to-bottom or beginning-to-end, but there is a sequence nonetheless. VB/DOS is a *high-level* programming language because the instructions in a VB/DOS program appear to have sentence structure, and the sequence of those instructions communicates to the reader the purpose of the program in a manner more attributable to human language than machine language. Machine or assembly languages, by contrast, are called *low-level* languages because they more closely resemble the logic of the computer than the reasoning of the mind.

Although you use a language to program a computer, the act of programming is not like a conversation or giving orders to an employee or crew member. Unlike communication with a knowledgeable human being, you cannot expect an unprogrammed computer to intuitively understand the meaning behind a complex instruction or have any processing capability ahead of time that's related to the task you're instructing it to perform. If a computer came to you "out of the box" with the capability to do whatever you asked it to do, there would be no need for packaged software.

A machine, scientifically defined, is any device that performs work. A computer is a machine to the extent that it has electronic components that simulate the actions of mechanical ones. A mechanical device such as a watch or a locomotive engine has mechanics that you can assimilate just by looking at it. A computer's mechanics are all electronic. Because you can't see electrons or electric currents, the computer's mechanics must be explained symbolically, both to you as well as the computer. What's different about the computer as a machine is that by changing the arrangement of its symbols, you change its mechanics. This rearrangement is called *programming.*

A *low-level* programming language represents machine code instructions directly.

When you program a computer using the most rudimentary symbols recognized by its central processing unit (CPU), the program is written in *machine language* and the symbolism constitutes a *low-level* program. As a low-level programmer, you could be feeding your computer instructions such as `24, 62, 47` .... Imagine how difficult it would be for you as a rational, intelligent human being to have to interpret the meanings behind these digits day after day.

A *high-level* programming language resembles written words and must be translated into machine code.

This is the reason there is a BASIC programming language. Rational, intelligent people have no time to mess with assembling code that sounds like the emanations from a football quarterback. You have the right to program computers using something more closely resembling human language. BASIC and its descendant VB/DOS both use words as symbols rather than numbers or mnemonics to represent electronic operations logically. This is one reason BASIC is a *high-level* language.

A More Literal Interpretation

An *interpreter* translates high-level linguistic code into low-level numeric code.

An *interpreter* is a program that continually breaks down a program's high-level linguistic symbols into low-level arithmetic symbols. A computer won't execute code until it has been broken down—or *catabolized*—to its lowest level; language of any form is far beyond the capacity of a central processing unit to interpret for itself. Because BASIC instructions must be reinterpreted into machine language before they can be executed, the VB/DOS programming environment contains an interpreter that continually breaks down source code into instructions the CPU can recognize.

If you've programmed a computer using the GW-BASIC or QBasic interpreters supplied with your copy of DOS, you're familiar with the conventional concept of the interpreter. Normally, you supply the BASIC interpreter with a list of instructions using a built-in editor, and the interpreter processes each instruction while the program is being executed.

VB/DOS *interprets* the program as it is written.

With other interpreted languages, the program is translated into machine language one line at a time as the program runs. On the surface, the VB/DOS interpreter appears to be no different from a standard interpreter, except that it performs the interpretation process *while the program is being entered into the editor.* Figure 1.1 illustrates the differences between these processes.

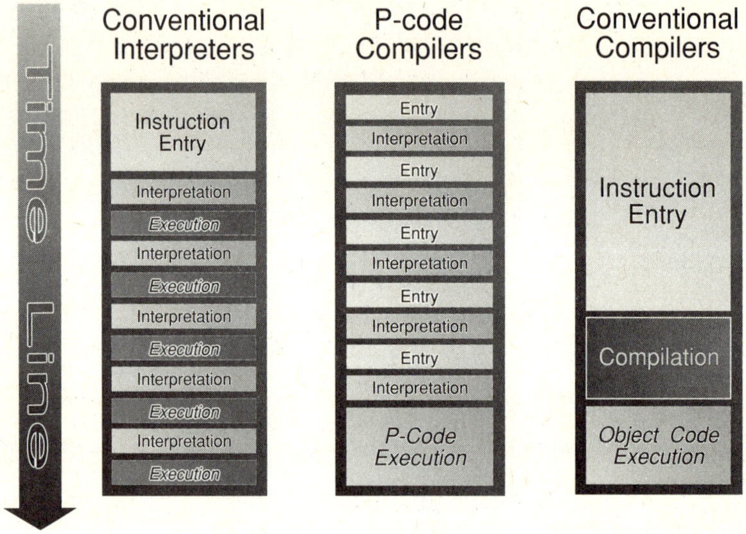

Figure 1.1. Three forms of program generation compared.

Object code (machine code) is composed of CPU instructions that are not symbolized in any way for human interpretation.

VB/DOS does not actually interpret the program fully while it is being written. The code that VB/DOS generates internally (which you never see) is called *intermediate code* or *p-code.* This code rests in memory, awaiting the execution call from the user or programmer. The p-code is then reinterpreted—or interpreted the rest of the way—until it becomes *object code* for the CPU. This code is then executed but is not retained in memory. Instead, the interpreter goes about its business of reinterpreting more p-code.

VB/DOS source code executes quickly in comparison to a standard interpreter because half the interpretation process is already done by the time you give the order to `Run`. The VB/DOS interpreter is provided with the environment for you to be able to test your programs using the trial-and-error method. Because it is the presence of *errors* that helps you steer the course of program development, you'll find the trial-and-error method is by far the most efficient method of programming.

A *compiler* produces a stand-alone executable program file.

In contrast to an interpreter, a *compiler* is a program that takes high-level instructions and translates them all at once into a machine-language executable code file. The VB/DOS compiler, also supplied with the environment, produces object code that is executable (able to be run) without the aid of the VB/DOS interpreter. This code comprises a stand-alone program and needs no other Microsoft program to operate. You can even sell your compiled program; in some cases, however, you may have to give Microsoft credit for part of its content. When you run a compiled program, there is no interpretation process; the compiler has already completely broken the source code into object code. Most programs or applications you'll ever buy or use are compiled in much this way.

Although compilers give you the benefit of generating pure object code without having to supply an interpreter of some form with your programs, the act of programming with a compiler alone generally gives you no room for trial and error. If there's an error in your program, execution generally stops and that's that. Modern compilers, such as those currently sold by Microsoft and Borland, have eliminated this problem by including with their editors separate p-code interpreters (also called *p-code compilers,* perhaps out of confusion). This way you can test your source code to make sure the program works properly before compiling it into pure object code. In the next chapter, you'll study more of the construction of the VB/DOS programming environment.

The Process of Interaction

Information is any symbol or message that is meaningful to people. Data is the carrier of information within a computer.

Earlier, I stated that computing is an *interactive* process. Generally, this term implies the exchange of information between parties. You often hear the misstatement that information can be shared between a person and a computer. It's important that you draw a vital distinction between the terms *information* and *data.* The formal definition of *information* is any symbol or message that conveys meaning to a person or to people. A computer cannot be *informed* of anything; it's not intelligent, and it cannot be taught. Information is imparted from one party to another through a medium. In the field of computing, data is this medium, or what Marshall McLuhan might call the carrier of the message. A computer stores and retrieves only *data,* which may or may not impart meaning to you or anyone else. Data cannot impart meaning to the computer because the computer is not a thing that reasons.

The exchange that takes place between a person and a computer may be informative, and it may even be conversational. Note, however, that this conversation does not really take place between the computer and the user; it is between the *programmer* and the user. The conversation is merely indirect, the symbols used in the conversation are limited, the topic is chosen in advance, and the responses as delivered by the program are, in effect, prerecorded. In the way syllables and phonemes convey meaning when utilized in a conversation between people, instructions and data convey meaning to the person using an application.

To be more specific about this, compare real-world person-to-person interaction with person-to-computer interaction. Assume you are a small-business owner. You deliver your company's transaction data to a professional accountant (or C.P.A.) and give the accountant instructions on what to do. You perform the same role as the user of an accounting program—that of data supplier and process initiator. You wouldn't tell the C.P.A. exactly what to do. You would assume his training would allow him to determine just what he should do, based on the particular data you gave him. You expect the C.P.A. to know the process already.

Switch sides now and assume you're the C.P.A. Your training is based on years of learning and reviewing accounting principles. Along with that, you've gained much business experience. Because of your experience, you know the process of recording this small business' account information after you receive this mountain of data to sift through. The more experienced you are with figuring numbers as an accountant, the more skilled you become.

Still, as a C.P.A. you do *not* perform the role of a computer accounting program. The computer is not an instrument that acquires skill over time or with constant use. The computer's "understanding" of what to do with all this data is constructed beforehand as its program, long before the data is created. The difference between giving a person instructions and giving a computer instructions is that a person has numerous faculties available for *deducing* the proper process. By contrast, you instruct the VB/DOS interpreter using only mathematics, logic, formulas, and comparisons—no specifics and no examples. You cannot construct an accounting program by taking existing business financial data, feeding that data into the program, and having the computer generate formulas from it. Unlike the way you reason, the computer cannot deduce the process that leads to particular results based on the values of those results.

You can, however, take existing business information as an example for yourself and reasonably deduce the formulas that a C.P.A. would use to analyze and record this data. You would, however, remove any part of the formulas that makes them specific to a particular business at a particular time. You replace these specifics with vague references to unknown or arbitrary values, called *variables.* In other words, you remove everything absolute from the example process, leaving in its place only the algebra, which is entirely figurative.

Flying Blind Is Truly Flying

A good analogy for this process—although thankfully not one drawn from the real world—is if you were to use an audio tape to instruct a kindergarten student to pilot a space shuttle. Assume this student is your child; although she's bright and has seen things go up into the sky and come down from it—birds, planes, and kites—she hasn't quite differentiated between them yet. Her current idea of a joystick is something you use to make Mario kick the turtle on the video game.

Your first job as narrator for the Better Daycare Through Astrophysics School for Young Pilots is to define the world for this person. What is space, where is it, and why is it so difficult to breathe there? You'll probably need to explain *g-force*, but you'll probably also need to explain that *g* falls between *f* and *h.* Take note that all the referential information a skilled pilot is naturally aware of has absolutely no bearing upon your child's world for the moment. You not only have to define what all this information is but also define the *world* for your child as well.

Should you introduce into the tape the concept of rocket physics? What makes the thing go in the first place? Arguably, a person might not need to know about the combustion engine to drive a car, but an astronauts' survival might depend on this kind of knowledge. You might be able to tell your young listener something about the universe, the layout of the instrument panel, and the location of certain important valves connected to the flight suit, without necessarily holding true to the absolute facts; and yet, you might impart enough information to your young pilot that she might be able to perform the right procedures at the right time. You don't have to lie to the child, but in the interest of her own safety, you may not want to confuse her by attempting to share all the facts. Perhaps most important of all, because this is an audio tape programmed in advance of flight time, you as narrator cannot assume your pilot has succeeded or failed in her mission. She, therefore, cannot draw any conclusions from experience.

Programming in VB/DOS is not always such an impossible or frustrating task as that invented in the preceding paragraphs. Think of the VB/DOS interpreter as a program that by itself "flies blind." *You* are its vision. You tell the VB/DOS application how to calculate accounting data and generate ledgers without giving it any data except during the testing stage. You mold and develop a solidifying chain of instructions and, with the aid of the VB/DOS compiler, you set it free. In terms of piloting, you're flying by instruments only. Yet being able to fly by instruments makes you a better pilot. To comprehend the work process well enough that you can model it within a computer program not only helps automate your office but also augments your own understanding of how things work.

Concern for the Environment

The *control program* of a computer provides the resources that a program needs to run.

Almost all computers run more than one program at a time. This is not necessarily multitasking; it is merely the result of the division of responsibilities in a computer. In the history of computing, when the job of computer control was first removed from the human operator and handed over to software, as many as two real programs were in operation in a computer system at any one time.

The *control program* (the operating system of the computer) provided input/output, memory, and storage services to the *user program.* In your computer system running the VB/DOS interpreter today, there can be six levels of program operation at any one time, with the program at a lower level providing services to the program above it.

Figure 1.2 depicts the structure of all programs in a computer system at all times while VB/DOS is running. The arrows in this figure depict the provision of services from one level of program to the one above it. The resulting strata of environments forms a sort of computing "atmosphere" in which the richest elements shared between tiers in the structure rise to the top.

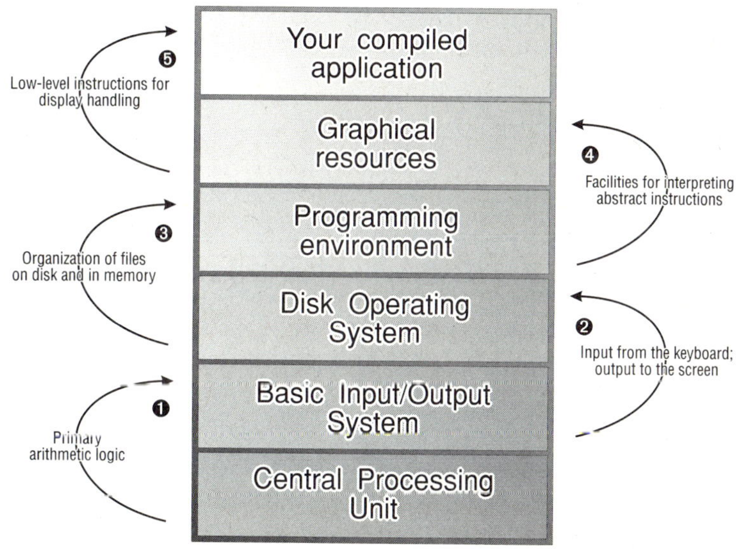

Figure 1.2. The VB/DOS "computing atmosphere."

A *pixel* is the smallest point that can be plotted on-screen at any given resolution.

At the bottom of this structure is the CPU, the core element of any computer system. The primary arithmetic logic of the computer is literally etched into this unit like a drawing. The CPU provides services to the Basic Input/Output System (BIOS), which is officially the lowest-level program in a microcomputer. This part tells your computer that it is a computer and its job is to *poll* (make a request of) the keyboard and other devices for user input and to display characters or pixels on-screen as output. A *pixel* (or picture element) is the smallest point that can be plotted on-screen at any given resolution.

The job of collecting all those characters, pixels, and bytes registered from the BIOS as actual files is delegated to the *disk operating system.* In this particular system, the operating system is some form (or clone) of MS-DOS or PC DOS. DOS takes the stream of meaningless characters and gives them a measure of objectivity by addressing them as files. Yet, DOS is often criticized for being operated through the use of streams of seemingly meaningless characters.

MS-DOS provides the file structure of the storage devices, the memory model of the computer, and the logical port identifiers (for example, LPT1: and COM1) to the VB/DOS programming environment. The VB/DOS environment itself is composed of multiple programs, the two primary ones being the Source Code Editor program VBDOS.EXE and the Form Designer program FD.EXE. The user may invoke either program from the DOS prompt; or, while officially in the environment, he may switch between one program and the other "seamlessly" using a keystroke sequence.

An *environment* acts as the graphical mediator between the user and the program.

Microsoft calls the VB/DOS programming system an *environment* instead of an "editor" or an "interface," or inventing some other term for it. VB/DOS contains graphical facilities (at least, as graphical as plain DOS will allow) that make applications more easily accessible and understandable for new users, as well as comfortable for longtime users. These facilities are resources that VB/DOS provides to the applications you write. Once you compile your VB/DOS program, these resources are compiled into the executable code. In other words, the machine code that defines for the computer what a button is, where the menu goes, and what to do when the mouse pointer enters the list area, is written for your stand-alone program *not by you* but by VB/DOS. More to the point, the object code for these resources is written ahead of time by the programmers at Microsoft; the VB/DOS compiler merely tailors the code for your compiled VB/DOS application.

> **NOTE:** Visual Basic for Windows programmers may remember that VBWin is not capable of producing stand-alone executable code. VB/DOS, by contrast, can produce true .EXE executable files.

The form is one of the resources VB/DOS provides to your applications; optionally, it is a character-based version of the "window" as Microsoft has designed it. Using the Form Designer program supplied with VB/DOS, you will be programming the appearance of form windows by drawing their prototypes onto the screen directly. This type of programming through graphical implication is one of the main selling points of the VB/DOS package. As a VB/DOS programmer, you will spend less time drawing controls and more time conceiving instructions and organizing information as data. The remainder of this book is organized proportionally with respect to what you as a VB/DOS programmer will do with your time and effort.

Summary

The purpose of programming can either be the automation of a real-world process or the simulation of a new process. A VB/DOS program is a mathematical model of a task that people could most likely perform using pencil and paper in the "old world." If the program is no easier to operate than pencil and paper, or if the program does not otherwise add some measure of functionality to the process, the objective of the program hasn't truly been fulfilled.

To achieve automation of a work process within a program does *not* require you to master this process in the real world; in other words, to be the author of a legal assistance database manager, you need not be a lawyer. If you can model just the fundamental principles of a real-world process, that alone will help professionals in their daily business.

The written form of a program is called *source code.* The individual directives within this source code are called *instructions.* A low-level program instruction makes sense to the computer almost instantly, but a high-level program instruction, as in VB/DOS, must first be translated into intermediate instructions or p-code before it can be executed. This is why VB/DOS is called an *interpreted language.* Unlike a conventional interpreter, however, VB/DOS source code is completely interpreted prior to the program's execution. In other words, the program is compiled to memory. Later, VB/DOS can be made to call upon a compiler to produce true object code that can be executed without the aid of the VB/DOS interpreter.

All programs exchange data with their users, but a good program exchanges more information with its user using less data. In information theory, data is seen as the carrier of information, like a sound wave over a phone line is seen as the carrier of the message. A mathematical process cannot be described to the interpreter by example or inference—only through algebra. The form of a VB/DOS program certainly doesn't resemble conventional algebra, although its processes are said to be algebraic. The interpreter makes no assumptions as to how any real-world process works. That process must be described using the vocabulary of VB/DOS in advance of the program's execution before that program can be said to work.

Review Questions

Answers to Review Questions appear in Appendix B.

1. Why is BASIC considered a high-level language?
2. What is a "sentence" within a program's source code called?
3. What is the primary low-level language of any computer called?
4. Which program in your computer provides services to the Disk Operating System?
5. If you were to instruct the VB/DOS interpreter that, for the time being and in the proper context, the letter a would represent the number 6, to what extent can that instruction be considered *informative*?

2

The Project

In this chapter, you are introduced to the methodology by which Visual Basic for MS-DOS programs are organized *visually*. A VB/DOS application contains many on-screen elements called *controls*, around which the linguistic components of the program are constructed. Each control has its own procedure, which is a part of the overall program. You'll learn about the more linguistic elements in Chapter 3; for now, concentrate upon the structural and graphical composition of the VB/DOS project.

The Visual Basic for MS-DOS Project

Armed with the knowledge of interpreters and environments gained from Chapter 1, "What a Program Is," let's dive into the VB/DOS environment. Figure 2.1 shows the VB/DOS Source Code Editor as it appears at startup. This is what you see when you type VBDOS at the main DOS prompt.

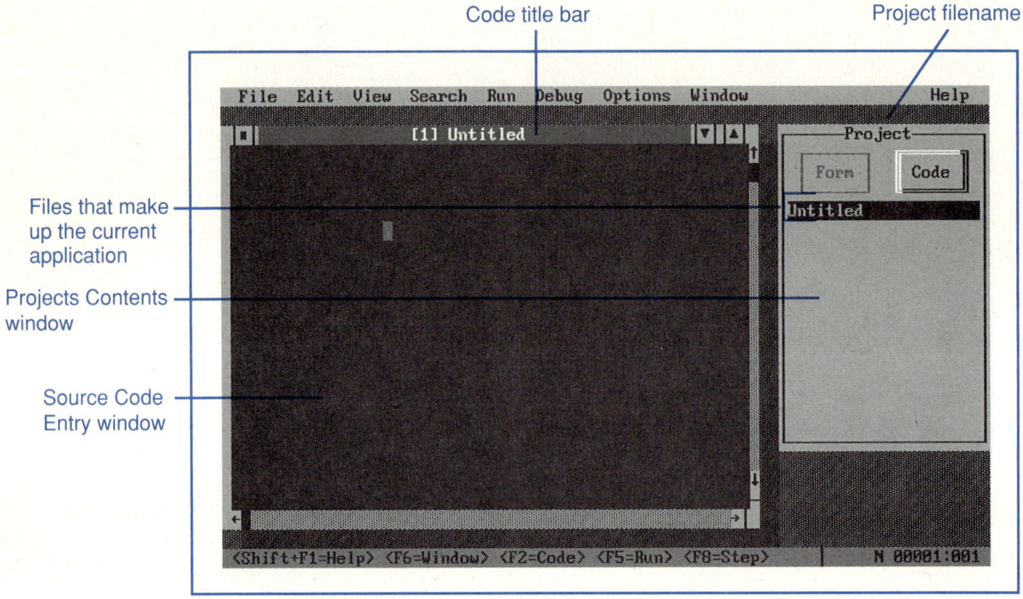

Figure 2.1. The VB/DOS editor environment in its clean, natural state.

If you're looking for a READY prompt like the one you used to rely on if you programmed in BASIC during the '70s and early '80s, you won't find it here—more to the point, you won't find it anywhere in this decade. Instead, the Code Editor screen contains two windows, the leftmost of which begins its life awaiting your input. This is the Source Code Entry window, whose title bar reads `Untitled`. On the right is the Project Contents window, which contains the table of contents for all the files that jointly constitute the VB/DOS interpreted application. The compiled application will be formed using the data supplied to the VB/DOS compiler by these files.

A *form* is a character-mode window that facilitates graphic operation of VB/DOS applications.

The "engine" of VB/DOS is based to a great degree upon the QuickBasic engine; in fact, VB/DOS is designed to be the next step up from QuickBasic. As such, applications written in QuickBasic version 4.5 should be capable of being translated into the VB/DOS environment with little or no problem. With respect to the graphical resources offered in modern programming environments, QuickBasic programs exist in a virtual flatland. When programming in QuickBasic, the primary output device is considered the screen.

If you're accustomed to programming in BASIC, this should seem quite conventional; though in the realm of VB/DOS programming, the *form*—for all intents and purposes, a window—is treated by many instructions as if it were a device unto itself. You may consider these forms as though they were floating above the standard screen device, with the old QuickBasic output region beneath them.

Three or four forms on the screen at one time may be addressed as separate devices, not just output regions, whether or not the forms overlap. If the user of the application moves the form, the VB/DOS interpreter handles the geometry of placing the form contents elsewhere on-screen and revealing whatever lay beneath them previously. These form-handling resources are compiled into the stand-alone VB/DOS application.

A *project* consists of all the files that collectively comprise a VB/DOS application.

While a VB/DOS application is under construction within the interpreter environment, it is called a *project* because the source code of a VB/DOS app (short for "application") is distributed among more than one physical file stored on disk. A VB/DOS project may consist of any of three types of files: namely, a *code module,* which takes much the same form as a standard QuickBasic or Basic PDS program; a *form module,* which contains the "floating" windowed elements of the VB/DOS application along with those instructions pertaining to it; or a *library module,* which contains repetitively executable routines that may or may not be written in VB/DOS.

A *module* is a file that contains some complete portion of executable code and may contain graphic resource data.

The module is the core program component in the VB/DOS language. Each time you develop a new form for your application, a new module is added to the VB/DOS project currently under way. Furthermore, you may write a body of VB/DOS instructions that has no form associated with it; in other words, its primary output device, if it has one, is the standard screen. These instructions also are considered part of a module, saved to disk with the standard extension .BAS.

The Project Contents window, which by default starts life at the right side of the VB/DOS Code Editor screen, contains a list of all module files that are a part of the project currently being edited. This list itself comprises a file; its name appears as the title bar of the Project Contents window. When saved to disk, this title becomes the project filename. This name, like all module address names and filenames, is chosen arbitrarily.

As you take a guided tour of the visual part of the VB/DOS environment, you're invited to follow along on your computer as I show you how to invoke certain facilities and windows. Let's assume you've already started VB/DOS and that your screen looks somewhat like Figure 2.1. A blank code window resides in the left portion of your screen.

A VB/DOS *procedure* is a body of instructions within a module that is addressable by name.

A procedure—as you'll learn in detail in the next chapter—is the secondary program component of the VB/DOS language. A VB/DOS *procedure* is a body of instructions within a module that is addressable by name. In other words, you can write several related instructions within a group that is a part of a program module. By giving this group a formal name, you make it into a procedure to which VB/DOS applies a special program status. The operation of a particular element of the screen may require such a procedure.

Each time you add a graphic object to a form, the VB/DOS interpreter gives that object a default address name. For instance, a command button may be given the name "Command1," until you change it to some other name. (The name of a button and its contents are two separate properties of that button.) The names of graphic objects that comprise a form are saved automatically by Form Designer to a form module; these names are then supplied to the Code Editor.

While programming using the full VB/DOS environment, there are basically two things you'll do (besides staring at the screen and waiting for solutions to come to mind): typing instructions for the program and drawing the contents of the control forms. The Code Editor frequently passes control over to another program called Form Designer, with which you design whatever forms may be appearing within the VB/DOS project. Upon returning to the Code Editor from Form Designer, you'll find the VB/DOS interpreter has made ready for each form module a set of procedure *frames* pertaining to each object you drew onto a form while in Form Designer. Frames in this context are VB/DOS source code instructions that define the beginning and end of the procedures that pertain to each graphic object within the form, as well as the form itself. The instructions within these frames will define what each graphic object will make the program do whenever anything important happens with respect to that object—for instance, the user clicking on it or the arrow pointer entering it. This procedure is given an address name by the VB/DOS interpreter, and that name becomes symbolic of the action or function this smaller group of instructions performs.

Because DOS does not provide much room for the VB/DOS environment to operate as a whole, the Code Editor and the Form Designer are split between two programs. To access the Form Designer program (FD.EXE) from the Code Editor, perform the following steps:

1. From the Code Editor's drop-down menu, select **F**ile. From the menu panel, select **N**ew Form. A dialog box will appear.

2. This dialog box asks you to give a filename to this new form because new forms do not have a default filename. Limit the filename to eight characters; VB/DOS supplies the .FRM extender. For this example, use the form filename `TEST1.FRM`.

3. By default, an "empty project," like the one VB/DOS generates when you first start the code editor program, contains one equally empty non-form code module. If the project contains such a module, and if its name appears within the Project Contents window as "Untitled," it has not yet been saved to disk. In such cases, a dialog box appears, giving you the opportunity to render a name for this module, as well as any other unsaved modules that inhabit the Code Editor workspace. A filename example would be TEST1.BAS. This will not overwrite TEST1.FRM.

4. The current project may not yet be saved to disk. In such cases, a dialog box appears, giving you the opportunity to render a name for this project. At this point, you exit the Code Editor program, and the Form Designer program appears.

The startup screen for Form Designer appears as shown in Figure 2.2.

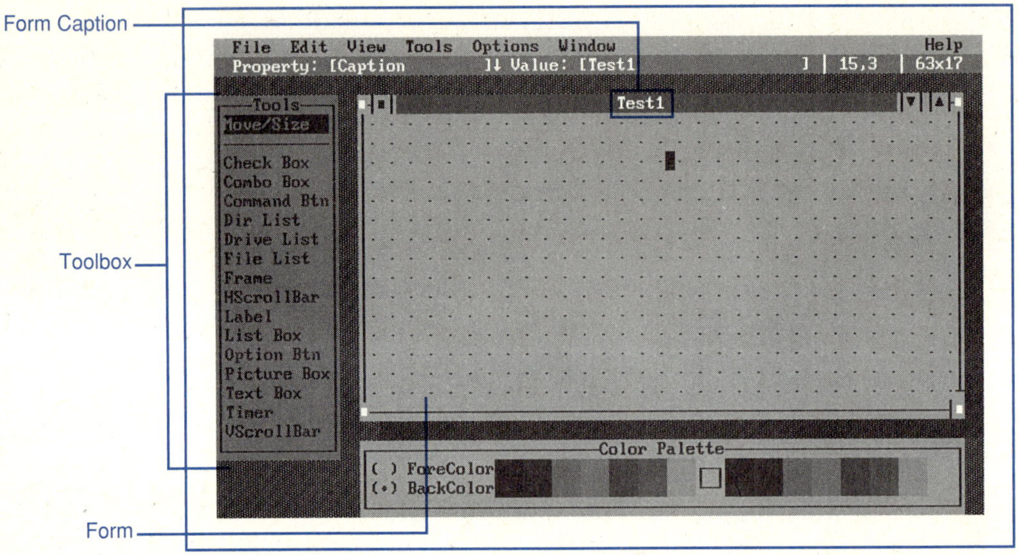

Figure 2.2. The operating table for constructing VB/DOS forms.

You may write an entire VB/DOS application without ever having to construct a form; however, the form is a far more versatile graphic device than the plain DOS output screen for the display of data, especially when multiple data elements or records are to be displayed simultaneously. Whereas the standard screen is like a flat corkboard, the moveable form is like an electronic breadboard, automatically programmed to be sensitive to user input such as text entry onto a line or mouse pointer movement into a region. VB/DOS gives such graphical events names, so you can instruct the interpreter how to react when the named event occurs. This convenience is not available for the standard flat output screen.

Each form in a VB/DOS project, including the one you see now, has a physical file all to itself. Stored in this file is all the information concerning the appearance, contents, and characteristics of the form—the resource data—along with the VB/DOS instructions for maintaining each graphic object that is a part of the form. For instance, if you draw a button on this form, the form file will contain the location of the button relative to the form, the size and textual contents of the button, and instructions for all the events that may pertain to that button—clicking on it, double-clicking on it, moving it over, and so on.

Graphic Objects

The button—or in VB/DOS terminology, the *command button*—is the rectangular device you generally find within dialog boxes, usually containing `OK`, `Cancel`, or some similar directive. The VB/DOS Form Designer program makes such graphic objects as the command button available by means of a moveable list window called the *toolbox*. From this toolbox, VB/DOS "hands" you a button and lets you place it anywhere on the form. The toolbox is a window which may be moved across the Form Designer workspace by clicking and dragging the window's title bar to the new position. If the form you're working on consumes the entire workspace, thus obscuring the toolbox, the same tools are available also from Form Designer's Tools menu.

The general appearance and function of a button is defined and maintained by VB/DOS. Its behavior is part of the resource information that will be compiled along with your completed VB/DOS application. You do not need to program the behavior of the little rectangle itself; in other words, you don't have to provide the interpreter with data depicting the button when it is clicked, or with low-level instructions defining the act of clicking a button in the first place. This is important because programmers of earlier editions of Microsoft's BASIC compilers for DOS often had to provide their applications with such data manually. Now with the VB/DOS toolbox, whenever you need a button for a control panel or dialog box, you can select `Command Btn`, drag a rectangle onto the input form, and give it a new title by typing it from the keyboard. The VB/DOS interpreter thereafter understands that there is a button in this form window and treats it as a graphic object.

By default, the toolbox is located on the left side of the Form Designer screen. Table 2.1 defines the elements listed within the toolbox.

Table 2.1. Contents of the VB/DOS toolbox.

Item	*Definition*
Move/Size	Represents the default state of the mouse pointer. Enables you to manipulate objects already appearing within the form.
Check box	Represents the active or "on/off" state of a single item.
Combo box	Gives the user the option of choosing from the list or entering an option of her own within the attached text box.
Command Btn	Term for button. Will "depress" when clicked. Enables the user to give directives to the VB/DOS application, such as `OK`, `Cancel`, or `Options >>`.
Dirs	Short for directory list box. Displays a list of a device's directories.
Drives	Short for drive list box. Displays a list of the user's active storage devices, such as disk drives, RAM disks, and CD-ROM drives.
Files	Short for files list box. Displays a list of the user's files within a directory.
Frame	Groups related objects together, such as two check boxes.
HScrollBar	Short for horizontal scroll bar. Represents any numeric selection within a range.
Label	A field for the display of noneditable text.
List box	Presents a fixed list of choices to the user.
Option Btn	Stands for option button. Represents the currently active choice in a multiple-choice situation.
Picture box	Displays output text in a more complex manner, using its own self-contained coordinate system.

Item	*Definition*
Text box	A field for the entry and editing of text.
Timer	Allows the form to be timed using a real-time clock. Does not display on a form when the program is run.
VScrollBar	Short for vertical scroll bar. Represents any numeric selection within a range.

To add a button to a form, follow these steps:

1. From the toolbox list, select `Command Btn` by clicking on it once with the index button of the mouse. You do not need to hold down the index button.
2. Move the mouse pointer to the form window; click and hold the index button down on the point that is to be one corner of the button control.
3. With the index button held down, drag the pointer to the opposite corner of the button control area.
4. Release the index button. The button control will appear in the form, containing a default caption, such as `Command1`, that you can change later.

The Big Event

An *event* is some form of user interaction with an active form.

When a VB/DOS application contains forms, any action performed by the user while one of the forms is active—typing text, moving the pointer, clicking a button—can be set to trigger the execution of a code procedure. Each potential trigger is given a term in the VB/DOS vocabulary, which identifies it as an *event*. Event procedures need no instructions that define the behavior or specifications of the event itself; VB/DOS already knows what the act of clicking a button is or choosing an item from a drop-down list or menu.

Using the VB/DOS Code Editor, you can write procedures that pertain to all the graphic objects added to the form or forms thus far. Because a form may act as a control panel, the output device for a document or record, or as a dialog box, the true definition of each form is written using the Code Editor. This means that once you design the form to an adequate extent, you have to make the trip through the "DOS tunnel," back to the Code Editor program.

To begin editing event procedures by way of exiting from Form Designer, perform the following steps:

1. From the Form Designer menu, select Event Procedures from the Edit pull-down menu. A dialog box appears.

2. This dialog box seeks confirmation that you want to exit Form Designer. To proceed, click Yes.

3. If you made changes to any of the forms inhabiting the Form Designer workspace since you entered this program, you will be prompted if you want to save these files. If so, click Yes. Filenames were already apportioned for each form at the time they were initially invoked into the workspace.

4. You exit the Form Designer program, and the Code Editor screen appears.

At this point in your tour, the VB/DOS interpreter has prepared several frames for procedures relating to the button that you added to your form. The dialog box that lists these event procedures appears in Figure 2.3.

The most useful of these event procedures is the one that you invoke when you click the button during runtime. To invoke an Event Procedure window for a graphic object, perform the following steps:

1. In the Event Procedures dialog box in the Code Editor are three lists. The leftmost list contains the filenames of all forms belonging to the current project. From this list, choose the form filename to which the event procedure will belong.

2. The center list contains the control names (not the textual contents) given to each of the controls in the chosen form. The form itself is included because VB/DOS considers it a

graphic object as well. The default control name for a command button is `Command`*n*, where *n* is the accession number of the button in the order of its creation in Form Designer. From this list, choose the name of the control to which the event pertains.

3. The rightmost list contains the standard vocabulary of VB/DOS terms for events pertaining to the chosen graphic object. The procedure you write will be executed once this event occurs. The event for clicking once on a button is simply called `Click`. From this list, choose the event that will trigger the execution of the procedure.

4. To edit the event procedure within the currently active code window, click the Edit in **A**ctive button. To create a new code window for the event procedure, click the Edit in Ne**w** button. As many as nine code windows can inhabit the Code Editor workspace, and you can switch between these code windows on demand.

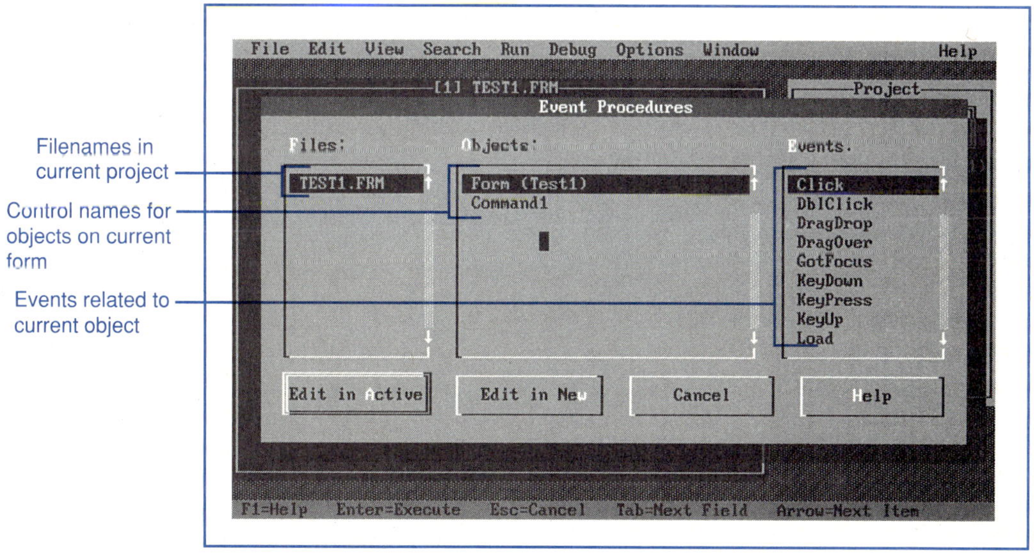

Figure 2.3. A multitude of events awaits you.

VB/DOS uses procedure names consisting of the object name, an underscore (_), and the event name.

After the window appears for the event procedure, the VB/DOS interpreter presents the *frame* of a formal procedure pertaining to the chosen object. This frame awaits further instructions from you. The opening and closing statements have already been entered into the procedure; the blank line between these statements denotes where you type new instructions. VB/DOS buttons are said to direct commands to the application; thus, they are named `Command1`, `Command2`, and so on, by default. The procedure frame showing now is `SUB Command1_Click`, which will contain the instructions to be executed whenever the button is clicked during runtime. The VB/DOS interpreter derived the name for this procedure by combining the name given to the button with the name of the event to which this procedure will pertain, joined with the underscore (_) character.

You can write procedures to be executed on the occurrence of each of the events in the rightmost list. Choosing one of these events from the list brings up its event procedure in the code window. In a sense, you can say the procedures for all the associated events for each object virtually exist, although they remain codeless until you give them instructions.

Many software manufacturers, including Microsoft, are developing standards for phrasing and accessing "objects," such as VB/DOS's graphic objects, within a high-level language. This ongoing standard is referred to as *object-oriented syntax*. With respect to the object-oriented syntax derivative used by VB/DOS, `Click` is an event that acts in this instruction as a verb to the noun `Form`. The `Click` event is the default event for this procedure window. Any instructions you type into this procedure frame will be executed whenever the form—or more to the point, the background area within the form window—is clicked once during the program's runtime.

Think of the Objects list in the Event Procedures dialog box as a display of everything within the form that can have something *done to it,* and the Event list beside it as a display of everything that *can be done.* The object is the recipient of the action in VB/DOS, just as it is in English grammar. Now you have some idea of the general concept of "object-oriented" syntax.

Example

As a test, type the following into the blank line between `SUB Command1_Click ()` and `END SUB`:

```
Test1.PRINT "You clicked on the Command1 button."
```

You have set up a response to an event; namely, whenever the user of your newly constructed program (yes, you've just written a program) clicks the button once during runtime, the text within the quotation marks is printed to the form named `Test1`. Written as pseudocode, here's how your first procedure might appear:

Start this procedure whenever this button is clicked.
Print "You clicked on the Command1 button." to `Test1`.
End this procedure.

After you enter an event procedure for `_Click`, the next time you bring up the Event Procedures dialog box for the project, the `CLICK` event in the rightmost list will be shown in all caps. The VB/DOS Code Editor capitalizes the event names for the list entries of all event procedures that contain real instructions.

Although you can have several forms on-screen at one time (`Test2`, `Test3`, and so on), you can work on only one VB/DOS project at a time. To see the current project in its running state, from the Code Editor's **R**un menu, select **S**tart.

> **NOTE:** If you're a veteran of 1970s BASIC interpreters, the preceding process is the modern equivalent of typing `RUN` at the `READY` prompt. Alternatively, you can press Shift-F5 to run a VB/DOS program that is currently being edited.

When a VB/DOS application runs, the Code Editor workspace disappears, leaving the standard DOS output screen. This is the default output region for data and graphics; if forms are programmed to appear, there should not be any bitmapped graphic on the background screen.

As a test, run the current application and then click the `Command1` button once. Your screen now should look like the one shown in Figure 2.4, with your message in the upper-left corner of the form. Each successive click should place another message beneath the previous one.

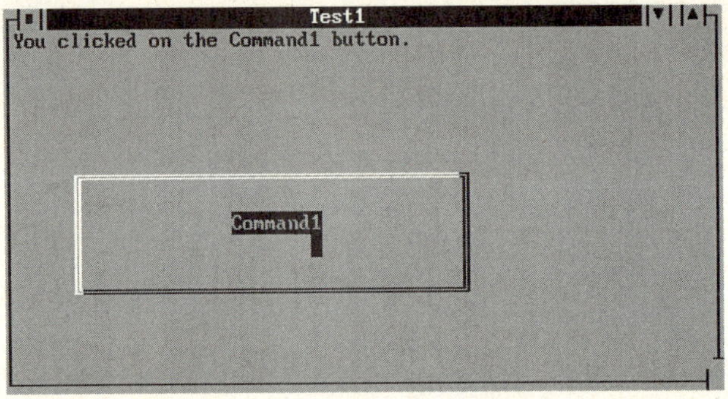

Figure 2.4. Your first running application.

To end program execution at any point, double-click on the close window box in the upper-left corner of the form. After you compile your completed VB/DOS application, you can invoke it from the DOS prompt as if it were a standard application.

This test may not be as exciting as a good game of Asteroids. However, it demonstrates the most important feature distinguishing VB/DOS from its predecessors: The VB/DOS language is almost entirely *event-driven*—most of its procedures won't be executed until the user gives the computer some sign, signal, or other form of input. This sign can be moving the mouse, pressing a key, or making the computer wait for five minutes doing nothing. An *event* is a unit of user input utilizing any of the available devices attached to the computer system and triggering the execution of a procedure.

The VB/DOS interpreter already knows how to wait for an event and how to discern one event from another. As its programmer, you must tell VB/DOS what to do to respond to those events. Event-driven procedures will comprise the majority of almost every VB/DOS application you write.

Property Assessment

A *property* is an attribute of a graphic object that is accessible by name and can be described by a value or term.

As you have witnessed, much of the VB/DOS programming process is accomplished through graphical inference. You place a button on a form not by typing its coordinates into the source code of the program but by drawing the button on the form with the mouse. The position, size, and contents of this button all are defined by VB/DOS, as *properties.*

It is possible to declare these properties using written VB/DOS instructions. I chose not to do so with `Test1`, however, because it was easier at the time not to. The VB/DOS environment lets you place a graphic object on the form by pointing to its location and drawing its outline. The position and size of this object instantly become two of its properties. By using the controls located in the Form Designer window, as depicted in Figure 2.5, you can access each property of a graphic object by name and assign or change its value, setting, or description.

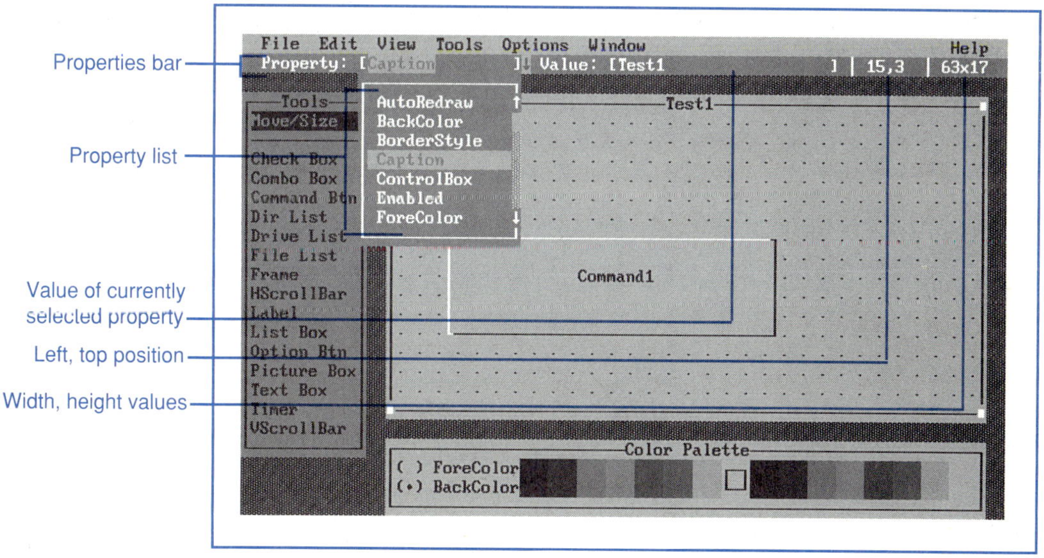

Figure 2.5. The property-setting controls of Form Designer.

Primary Properties— `.Caption` versus `.CtlName`

The `.Caption` property is used to change the text displayed on an object.

One of the more important properties of a button control is its textual contents, or *caption.* After all, the user of this program probably won't be able to make much sense out of a button simply called `Command1`. To change the contents of the `Command1` button in the current `Form1`, change its `.Caption` property to reflect the new contents.

Perform the following steps to change the text of a button control:

1. In Form Designer, indicate the button that is to have its text changed by clicking once on that button. Four *handles* surround the button; these are generally used as controls for resizing the button.

2. From the leftmost drop-down list box marked `Properties:` along the second line down from the top of the screen—called the *properties bar*—choose the property `Caption`. The text line at the center of the properties bar, marked `Value:`, now displays the button's current contents—for this example, `Command1`.

3. Click once within the area of the `Value:` text box to indicate the text to be changed. Pressing the Delete key on the keyboard will delete this text; typing any character key will add letters to the right side of the text. As you type, the text is echoed into the button control.

4. To complete the entry, press Enter. To cancel an entry in progress, press Esc.

The `.CtlName` property is used to identify an object by name in the program code.

It's important to note that changing a button control's contents does not change its name throughout the source code. `Command1` is both the default control name and default caption for the first button in a form. Changing one does not change the other. To change the button's control name from `Command1` to `MainButton`, use the method described previously, but select the property `.CtlName` rather than `.Caption`.

Whenever you change a control's name property, its name for the procedures is changed automatically. Notice that the `_Click` procedure for the former `Command1` now reads `SUB MainButton_Click ()`. You can change a control name at any time, and the interpreter will make the proper changes to the source code of its associated procedures. By contrast, changing a button's caption does not result in any alteration to procedure code.

A property's name is separated from the object name by a period.

Notice that in the terms discussed thus far, an event is separated from an object by an underscore character, as in `MainButton_Click`, whereas a property is separated from its object by a period, as in `MainButton.Caption`. This punctuation helps identify the attribute of the object preceding it as an event or a property.

You can use the properties bar, among other purposes, to designate the size of a control by number, to change the position of that control manually, or to set the color of a control or its background. Throughout this book, you will be continually setting the attributes of properties, setting the stage—at least visually—for each full project you produce. Later in the book, you learn the more conventional predeclaration of values, variables, and functions for the computational portion of the programs, all of which is done with instructions.

NOTE: Although the job of creating controls and designating their properties can be considered programming in the context of VB/DOS, the act of setting a form's initial properties does not involve instructions *per se*, and therefore is not reflected in the source code of the program being constructed. When the source code is executed, the interpreter expects the properties of the graphic objects referred to in the program to have been set beforehand. If you're a BASIC veteran, this may make reading the source code of the program a bit confusing. Most programmers who have programmed in BASIC for a long time have grown accustomed to modeling all the characteristics of a program with written instructions and reading those characteristics as instructions.

Saving Your Work

Follow these steps to save your project to disk for safekeeping:

1. From the **F**ile menu of either the Code Editor or Form Designer, select Sa**v**e Project.

2. If the project hasn't been given a formal filename, a file selector box appears requesting a name for this project. Filenames already have been designated for each of the modules in this project because module filenames are designated upon the creation of each module. Once a filename is given, click OK.

Use the preceding method to save the single-button form project to disk as TEST1.MAK.

Once project development is complete, you can formally compile it as a stand-alone program. To compile a VB/DOS project, follow these steps:

1. From the **R**un menu of the Code Editor, select **M**ake EXE File. A file selector box appears.

2. Type the eight-letter filename for the .EXE file into the text line marked `EXE File Name:`. VB/DOS automatically attaches the .EXE extension to the file. This file will not overwrite any other file pertaining to the project.

3. Make certain the option dot marked `Stand-Alone EXE file` is set. If it isn't, click once between the parentheses beside the label.

4. Click `Make EXE`. You will soon have a stand-alone program file.

Summary

VB/DOS considers several form and code modules collectively as a project. You do not need to provide the VB/DOS interpreter with extensive instructions for the display and handling of graphics controls. When these controls are placed in the control form, you need only tell the interpreter how to respond to the input events attributed to those controls. Each possible event for a graphic object has its own virtual procedure in a VB/DOS program. Each object in a VB/DOS form, including the form itself, has properties attributed to it, the characteristics of which you can set in advance using the properties bar without specifying any instructions in code.

Review Questions

Answers to Review Questions appear in Appendix B.

1. In what type of file does VB/DOS store a collective list of forms and their controls, and modules and their procedures?
2. During the runtime of your application, commands are passed to the application through what graphics control?
3. In a term that joins the object `ClickHere` and the event `DblClick`, what item of punctuation is used between them?
4. In the procedure heading `SUB Form4_Click ()`, what term represents the event?
5. Property settings are assigned through program instructions using what portion of the VB/DOS environment?
6. Property settings are preset before program runtime using what portion of the VB/DOS environment?
7. What would be the three-letter extension of the name of a file that contains the property settings for a form?

Review Exercise

Write a procedure that will print the line `Something has happened!` into a form called `Form7` whenever a button called `BobTheButton` is clicked.

3

Grammar and Linguistics

In this chapter, you study the phraseology of the Visual Basic for MS-DOS program—how its terms and keywords are organized and expressed within the source code. You then begin composing more complex examples of programs than those developed (although perhaps "arrived at" would be the better phrase) in the previous chapters. You then learn about instructions and how they are constructed. You also learn how instructions are executed, organized, grouped, and modularized.

The topics introduced here are covered in greater detail in later chapters, with each topic given a chapter to itself. This chapter presents the major concepts of program construction so that you can see how these concepts relate to each other. Here, I shine a broad spotlight on all the characters of the VB/DOS stage, instead of shining a narrow penlight on one or two parts.

Modern Syntax

A *variable* represents a unit of data that can be altered.

At the heart of every program you write are logical comparisons between unknown and known numeric values. Whatever overall objective you have in mind for your application, the primary business of that application—the stuff that keeps your program busy—is the manipulation of values in memory. As in algebra, unknown values are represented within the VB/DOS syntax by variables. A *variable* is an arbitrarily named term that represents a unit of data in memory that a program can alter.

A *phrase* is a simple instruction.

A value is assigned to a variable with an equality statement, such as `a = 1` or `items = 27`, on a line by itself. When a VB/DOS instruction can be placed on one line, that instruction is called a *phrase*, partly because the syntax of the instruction resembles that of an English-language phrase or, perhaps, a complete sentence. For example, you can deduce the syntax of the instruction `IF a = 1 THEN GOTO More_Help` by using some rules of the English language—if not some rules of English slang. This instruction can rightfully be considered a phrase.

A *statement* is an instruction that specifies a change or deviation in the operating status of the program.

Each VB/DOS instruction has a component structure, in much the same way an English sentence can be divided into component phrases. The preceding instructional phrase consists of three statements, all of which rest on one line. Therefore, this phrase is called a *compound instruction*. A mathematical expression is included in one of the statements: `a = 1`. The words `IF`, `THEN`, and `GOTO` are some of the primary keywords in all BASIC programming languages. `IF-THEN` and `GOTO` are considered *statements* because they specify changes in the state of operation of the program. You'll learn just how they work later. For now, let's concentrate on the fact that a statement in programming is a directive made to the interpreter that tells it how things are changing.

The definition of a statement might be confusing at first. (Frankly, it might be confusing later, so be patient.) If someone told you, "If you're through with your insulting remarks, then leave the room!" you would hardly consider that directive a statement. Just because the inference was made that you should leave doesn't mean that you will leave, and it especially does not mean you have already gone.

In the part-metaphysical, part-sociological structure of modern BASIC programming languages, what appears to be an order or directive to change the state or value of something is actually interpreted as a statement of fact and a report of the current operating status of the program. In the statement `GOTO Away`, the line marked `Away` is someplace else in the program. Telling the interpreter to *go to* that part in the program, from the interpreter's point of view, is as good as saying it *is* at that point in the program now. You've written what looks like a command, but from the standpoint of the logic of the computer, you've made an unconditional statement.

Suppose, however, that you add a condition to that statement. For instance, assume the VB/DOS interpreter comes across the phrase `IF count > 1000 THEN GOTO Away`. Here `count` is a *variable* or symbol that represents a numeric value, standing in place of that value in the text. For this example, the interpreter first evaluates the variable `count` to determine whether its value is indeed greater than 1000. The two parts of this phrase `IF` and `THEN` constitute one statement, which is called the `IF-THEN` statement. It tells the interpreter to make an evaluation—in this case, to see if the value represented by the variable `count` is greater than 1000. The result of this evaluation is logically considered to be "true" or "false." In pseudocode, the statement's general framework might appear as follows:

If what's being said here is true, then execute the statement immediately thereafter.

In this case, if the expression `count > 1000` evaluates true, the interpreter suspends execution and then resumes at the point of the program marked `Away`. The phrase `GOTO Away` is interpreted as a statement only if the expression is true. Otherwise, the interpreter never sees the statement. `IF-THEN` in this instance appears to be a "command." In earlier versions of BASIC, it was categorized as such. Yet given the understanding that commanding the interpreter to do something is really a metaphorical way of *stating* that it is done already, realistically you can and must consider `IF-THEN` and `GOTO` as statements.

A *binary state* is the minimum unit of value in a computer and can be described as either true (–1) or false (0).

All computer processes are the result of logical evaluations. Such evaluations are called *binary* because their results can have either one or two states—true or false, or in VB/DOS values, –1 or 0 (negative one is simply how that bit of "true" data is interpreted within a byte by VB/DOS). The purpose of logical evaluation in the real world is to eliminate "gray areas." Nothing, once it is logically evaluated, is "for the most part true." Within the computer, there are no gray areas to begin with. Absolutely everything retained in memory, stored on disk, or undergoing processing within some evaluator chip is describable in its rudimentary form or forms as a *binary state.*

Because there is no "in-between" state in a logical evaluation and because logical evaluation is all the computer actually does, the computer cannot understand "change." The concept of one state becoming another state is foreign to the computer; there is simply no logical way to represent it, just as in real-world evaluation there is no way to logically represent gray. The VB/DOS language makes it appear that you tell the interpreter to change something by giving it instructions that appear to be commands, when in fact you actually restate the operating conditions for the computer at the present time. The syntax of the language gives you a more tangible and perhaps more realistic method of communication with the computer. In the real world, things change all the time, so it might help you to understand what's happening in the computer if things appear to change—in other words, if things within the computer behaved more like things in the real world. If you were a computer, however, you would believe that nothing ever changed.

A Matter of Expression

The computer can "think" using only on/off *binary states*, represented by ones and zeros.

In the preceding example, one of the statements within the `IF-THEN` compound instruction was an expression: `count > 1000`. This expression compared an unknown value to a known value and evaluated the result of that expression. Logically, there can be only two possible results, which may only be expressed as binary states.

An *expression* is the assigning of or the comparison between two variables.

Whenever an unknown value or variable is compared to a known or unknown value—as in `count > 1000` or `liquidity_ratio = (assets / liabilities)`—the statement of that comparison is called an *expression.* An expression is any of the following:

- An arithmetic comparison between two values, having a result that is expressed logically as a binary state
- One or more values or variables arithmetically joined by functions or functional operators
- An assignment of value to a variable using another value, variable, or another expression

Under the first definition, `count > 1000` is an expression of comparison. If the value of `count` is greater than `1000`, a Boolean value of *true* (–1) is returned to the interpreter that may trigger the execution of a process. Under the second definition, `a + b * c` and `4 * (n - 3)` are expressions of combination, resulting in a numeral value that can be assigned to a variable. Also under the second definition, `6` is officially an expression—a rather boring one but an expression nonetheless. Under the third definition, `x = a + b * c` and `liquidity_ratio = (assets / liabilities)` are expressions of assignment, in which the results of the arithmetic combinations are actually stored as variables.

An *equation* is often a statement of equality that assigns a value to a variable.

You could place `liquidity_ratio = (assets / liabilities)` on a line by itself, in which case the expression would be both a statement and an *equation* that assigns the value of `assets` divided by `liabilities` to the variable `liquidity_ratio`. You would then say the preceding expression assigns a value to the variable `liquidity_ratio` using two other variables.

A *binary operator* is a symbol that represents a mathematical function combining, comparing, or equating two values.

In the preceding equation, the slash (`/`) is used as an *operator* designating division between the two values it separates. You use operators within BASIC expressions like the function buttons on a calculator.

When an equality expression is listed on a line by itself, that expression is considered by the interpreter as an assignment of value to a variable. The equal sign in that statement would be considered the *assignment operator.* If you were to state on a line by itself `x = 6` and then later invoke the statement `TextBox.Print x`, the number `6` would appear in the text box. By contrast, when an expression is part of an instruction—as in `If x = 6 Then...`—that expression is treated as a comparison of `6` to `x`, the result being a Boolean value of True (–1) or False (0). The equal sign in a comparison is the *comparison operator*. The negative sign (–) preceding the 1 is called a *unary operator* because it concerns only one value, not two.

Intrinsic Functions

A *function* returns a value in a single variable.

For arithmetic operations that cannot be described by symbols or operators, VB/DOS maintains a broad vocabulary of intrinsic *functions* that perform arithmetic operations on values or expressions enclosed in parentheses. A function is an arithmetic operation performed on a value, variable, or expression, resulting in an explicit value returned within a single variable.

A function in VB/DOS has the following syntax:

```
FUNCTION_NAME(expression)
```

The expression in parentheses is evaluated first so that the function may operate upon one rational value—something more closely resembling `67.5` than `(x + 6)`. There may be more than one expression within the parentheses; in such cases, they will be separated from each other by commas. The specified function is then performed on the value or values between the parentheses.

An *intrinsic function* is a VB/DOS keyword that represents a VB/DOS arithmetic function.

An *intrinsic function* is a term that is built into the VB/DOS vocabulary (a *keyword*). You can program other functions and add to the functional vocabulary within the scope of a VB/DOS project.

Intrinsic functions are actually quite simple. For instance, `SQR(9)` represents the square root of `9`, so the function is said to *return* a value of `3`. `INT(3.1415927)` returns the value of the expression in parentheses converted to an integer by rounding to the nearest whole number—in this case, `3` again. If the variable `g` has the value `6`, the function `ABS(g - 10)` would return the value `4`, because `g` is `6`, `6 - 10 = -4`, the absolute value of –4 is 4, and thus `ABS(-4) = 4`.

Groups, Subgroups, Subsubgroups, and So On

Over the decades that the BASIC programming language has been developed and redeveloped, those programmers who have been lucky enough to become part of the development process have also managed to break BASIC constructs into an increasing number of parts. You may already be familiar with reading sets of instructions including steps that read, "Repeat last step." In VB/DOS, as with every other version of BASIC, you write such instructions into your source code—in fact, GOTO is one of those instructions. You'll often find yourself telling the VB/DOS interpreter to execute those three or sixty-three instructions that were executed a minute ago.

Because BASIC instructions are executed so repetitiously by nature, grouping instructions were added to the vocabulary to make certain passages—or *routines*—executable merely by addressing its group by name. In the earliest versions of BASIC, there were *subroutines*, identified by the number of the line where each began. Today, instruction groups have their own enclaves that behave as if they were complete programs in and of themselves. One subprogram passes control to another subprogram, like the flow of energy through the wheels of a Swiss watch.

Figure 3.1 depicts the interlocking order of the components of a VB/DOS application.

A *module* is a complete set of instructions stored within a single file.

The entire source code of a VB/DOS application is considered the *program*. The primary component of a program is the *module,* which is, in effect, any complete body of VB/DOS instructions. Like a good novel, a module has a beginning, a middle, and an end. It may contain "hooks" that lead or pass control to some other module, but on the whole a module describes a task for the computer completely.

The chief reason for modularizing BASIC code is to give it added legibility for the human reader. When Kemeny and Kurtz were first designing BASIC, they set forth a principle early on that when a question arose whether to design for human legibility or computer interpretability, the BASIC designers should work toward the former. Back in the '60s, however, BASIC source code resembled, to some extent, the grocery receipts for a family of twelve. To the BASIC programmers of that day, however, this was certainly preferable to reading a bunch of holes punched in a seemingly infinite deck of cards—which was what the first programs were, literally.

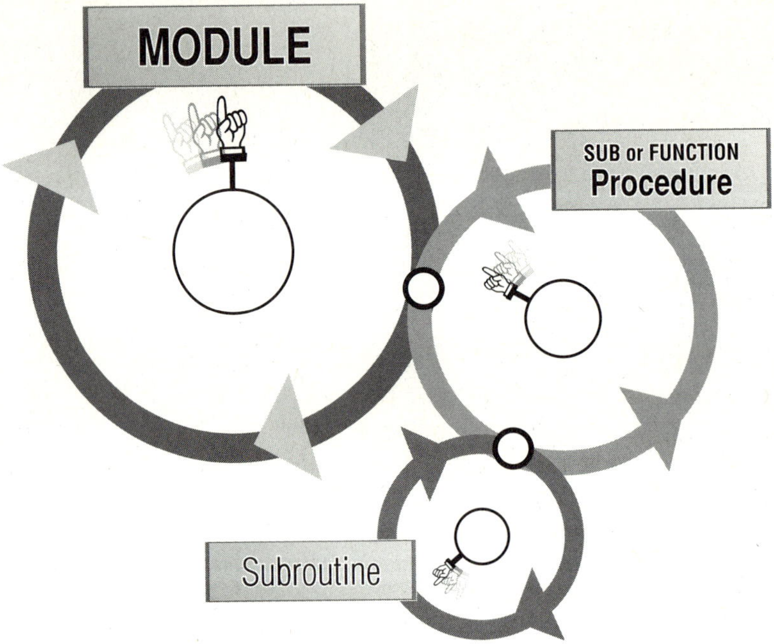

Figure 3.1. The VB/DOS code component machinery.

A *procedure* models at least one repetitive task or function.

A VB/DOS module, by its design, breaks down into tangible elements the multiple tasks represented symbolically within a program. Not only does this make the instructions more understandable, it gives them a structure that allows them to be used as interchangeable parts. A module may contain procedures for the display of a dialog box and the acquisition of user input. Each time the program needs to display a dialog box, there may be subtle differences in the contents of that box, but the general contents are often the same. A *procedure* is a reusable component within a module that contains instructions that represent a whole task but allow for variations.

When you start adding instructions to the VB/DOS application, using the code window that is at first marked `[1] Untitled`, the interpreter at first assumes the instructions are being added to the *startup module* for the application. The startup module sets the itinerary for the entire program; it declares the variable names of all the values represented, states what the program's primary components are, and denotes what values are shared between those components. Furthermore, the startup defines the order of execution of each component in the application.

An application can include the following three types of modules:

> The *trunk module,* when present, contains the main body of instructions pertinent to the application, not including any instructions belonging to forms or procedures. When there is a trunk module, it is the startup module.
>
> A *form module* contains the data that describes the appearance and contents of a form window, along with those procedures that instruct the interpreter how those controls will function. When there is no trunk module, a form module may be declared the startup module.
>
> A *procedure module* is an independent file that contains a set of reusable procedures, which may or may not pertain to any forms or graphic objects.

At the "front" of a module is generally a set of instructions that declare the procedure components of that module, along with the names of variables whose values are to be shared throughout that module. Let's call this "front" area the *declarations area.* It is important here to point out that the trunk module is the only component of a VB/DOS application that may contain nondeclarative instructions outside of a procedure.

When you edit procedures using a Code Editor window, that window will only show one procedure at a time. The name of the procedure appears within the window's title bar just to the right of the module name, separated from it by a colon (:). The procedure name also appears within the window itself, beside a statement that begins with either the `SUB` or `FUNCTION` statement. This statement acts as the *procedure heading*. Within the declarations area of the procedure's encompassing module will be a *procedure declaration* that begins with either the `DECLARE SUB` or `DECLARE FUNCTION` keyword pair; VB/DOS places this instruction there automatically.

The *context* of a procedure defines its relative pertinence to the rest of the program.

The procedure declaration not only defines that procedure for the rest of the VB/DOS application, but it also helps define the *context* of that procedure—what values and variables it shares with the rest of the program. The context of a procedure is the understanding the interpreter has of which variables and functions pertain only to the procedure, which values and variables are exchanged between this procedure and the one that called it, and which variables and functions pertain to the program as a whole.

A *parameter* is a value or variable passed to a procedure.

The way a `SUB` or `FUNCTION` procedure is structured enables it to accept variables and values as input from the body of the program that called it (in VB/DOS, another procedure) and perform computations using those values. These passed values are called *parameters.*

Any variables created or declared within a procedure are specific to that procedure alone, unless otherwise specified with statements. In other words, each procedure has a variable context all its own, called the *local context.* When the procedure is exited and some other procedure is being executed, the variables within the local context are deallocated. Likewise, any variables created or declared within a trunk module are local to that module, unless a broader context is otherwise specified.

Example

As an example, here is a procedure that draws an unfilled rectangle on-screen, given four parameters.

```
SUB rect_draw (x AS INTEGER, y AS INTEGER, w AS INTEGER,
  h AS INTEGER)
    LINE (x, y)-(x + w, y)
    LINE (x + w, y)-(x + w, y + h)
    LINE (x + w, y + h)-(x, y + h)
    LINE (x, y + h)-(x, y)
END SUB
```

So that you can get a better feel for what the program is doing, here is the preceding procedure translated into pseudocode:

Procedure for drawing a rectangle with its upper-left corner at (`x,y`)*, a width of* `w`*, and a height of* `h`*:*
  Draw a line from the upper-left to upper-right corners of the rectangle.
  Extend the line to the lower-right corner.
  Extend the line to the lower-left corner.
  Extend the line back to the origin point.
End of procedure.

The coordinates for the upper-left corner of the rectangle are accepted as `x` and `y`. The width and height of the rectangle are accepted as `w` and `h`. Here is a procedure with the sole purpose of calling procedure `Rect_Draw`:

```
SUB Form3_Click ()
    Rect_Draw 10, 10, 500, 500
END SUB
```

Notice that the four variables mentioned previously don't exist within the context of procedure `Form3_Click`. Instead, there are four explicit integral values, designated in the same *order* as the variables listed as parameters for `Rect_Draw`. Whether these values are numerals or variables, by invoking the name of the procedure, these parameters are passed to it. Procedure `Rect_Draw` then accepts parameters in the order in which they were given and utilizes those parameters within its own context only. This way variable `w` can refer to *width* in the context of `Rect_Draw` and perhaps to *water level* within some other procedure. When `Rect_Draw` is exited, variables `x`, `y`, `w`, and `h` no longer exist; but if `Form3` is clicked, the rectangle remains.

A variable's *scope* is its pertinence to the rest of the program.

Within the preceding procedure, the individual variables invoked pertain only to that procedure. The way it is written now, when the procedure is exited, the values of `x`, `y`, `w`, and `h` are discarded. The names can be used again when the procedure is reentered. This is one example of a set of variables with *local scope;* their meaning pertains only to their local procedure. The scope of a variable is the degree to which that variable pertains to the rest of the program; a variable's scope can be broadened to encompass an entire module or the breadth of the VB/DOS application.

Example

A function passes a value in its own name.

Another form of procedure is the `FUNCTION` procedure, which is structured like a `SUB` procedure, except it passes a value *back* to the procedure that called it. Here is a function example that finds the future value of an annuity, given three parameters.

```
FUNCTION Fvalue (pvalue, interest, nper AS INTEGER)
    Fvalue = pvalue * ((1 + interest) ^ nper)
END FUNCTION
```

Notice how `Fvalue` is not only the name of the `FUNCTION` procedure but also a variable to which the computed value is assigned. Here, `pvalue` is the present value of the annuity or loan, `interest` is the rate of interest per annum, and `nper` is the number of payment periods remaining. Here is the procedure which calls this function:

```
SUB Future_Click ()
    FutVal1.PRINT Fvalue(1000, .1, 3)
    FutVal2.PRINT "Computation complete."
END SUB
```

Here is the procedure written in pseudocode:

Procedure for clicking the Future button:
Execute the procedure `Fvalue` *for a $1000 annuity paid off with a 10 percent interest rate over three years, and print the result within the picture box called* `FutVal1`.
Print the message "Computation complete." within the picture box called `FutVal2`.
End of procedure.

In VB/DOS, a display (picture) box acts like a miniature terminal screen; you can tell the interpreter to print to the display box in much the same manner you'd tell it to print to the screen, except that the display box is addressed directly. For a button having the control name `Future` and for two picture boxes with control names `FutVal1` and `FutVal2`, procedure `SUB Future_Click ()` will place the future value of a $1000 annuity at 10 percent interest over three years—assuming annual payment periods—into picture box `FutVal1`. The call to `Fvalue` looks and acts like an intrinsic function in the regular VB/DOS vocabulary.

Note that function `Fvalue` will be executed in its entirety *before* the instruction to print the message in picture box `FutVal2` is executed. This is an example of program control being passed between procedures. Further execution of procedure `Future_Click` is suspended when the call to `Fvalue` is made. When `Fvalue` is done, execution of `Future_Click` resumes with the instruction immediately following the call.

Subsubsubdivisions and So On

Informally speaking, a grouping of instructions from a procedure is called a *routine.* On occasion, I may use as an example a portion of a large procedure, without the headings. If the instructions within that portion perform some whole function or task, I refer to the excerpt as a routine.

In the previous two examples, you saw program control being passed from procedure to procedure. As noted before, instructions within modules are not necessarily executed from top to bottom. Within the confines of a procedure, program control can be commanded to branch to another point designated by a *label.* A label is a noninstruction set to a line by itself and succeeded by a colon (:), designating a branching point.

Formally speaking, a *subroutine* is a series of instructions within a procedure—especially a long one—that can be branched to by calling its label by name. A subroutine allows for automatic branching back to the instruction that follows the one calling the subroutine.

A long instruction broken apart and distributed over several lines is called a *clause.* A clause is a compound instruction containing one or more subordinate instructions distributed in a single group over more than one line.

A *clause* contains one or more instructions that are treated as a group.

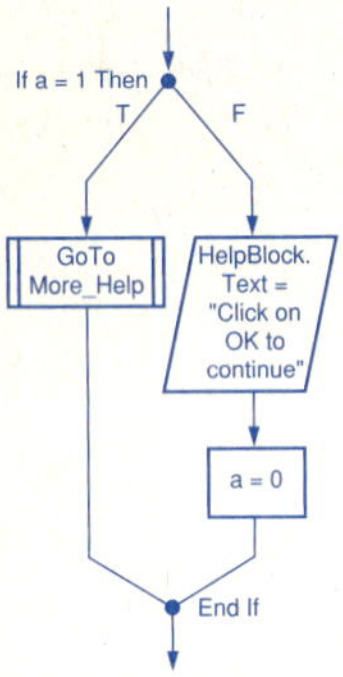

Here is an example of a small clause:

```
IF a = 1 THEN
     GOTO More_Help
ELSE
     HelpBlock.Text = "Click on OK to continue."
     a = 0
END IF
```

To be honest, there really is more than one instruction here. All three lines that are inset a few spaces are legitimate instructions by themselves. At the same time, they are part of a greater conditional instruction that tells the VB/DOS interpreter, "Either execute *this* group of instructions or else execute *that* group." These inset phrases are called *nested* instructions. The act of embedding instructions within a clause in this manner is called *nesting*. Still, `IF-THEN...ELSE...END IF` is treated as a single instruction, and more categorically, as a statement.

A *loop* is a sequence of instructions that is repeated either a specific number of times or until a condition is true.

The next most common type of clause after the conditional clause is the loop clause. A *loop* is a sequence of instructions that is repeated either for a specified count or until a condition is evaluated true.

Example

Often, you find you need to execute a set of instructions a certain number of times; or to evaluate functional series, you need to accumulate values using a loop clause. Here's an example loop that uses an array variable and uses its own running count to create an exponential series:

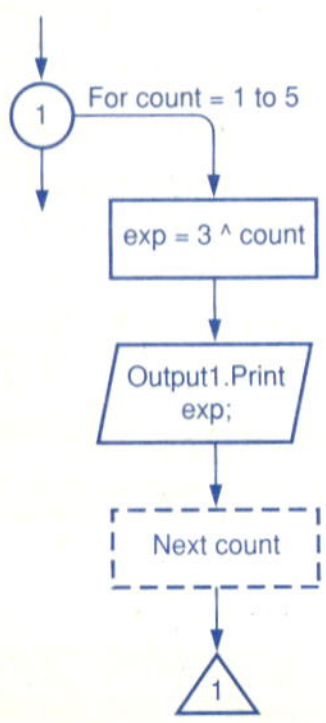


```
FOR count = 1 TO 5
   exp = 3 ^ count
   Output1.PRINT exp;
NEXT count
```

Count from 1 to 5, and for each count, do the following:
Assign the value of 3 raised to the power of the count to the stated variable.
Print the value of this variable within this output region.
Count the next number and execute all instructions between the beginning and end statement of the loop.

The primary loop clause statement in any BASIC language is the `FOR-NEXT` loop. Within the loop clause invoked in the preceding example, the variable `count` is created and its value is initially set to 1. The program continues execution in sequence. First, the value of `3 ^ 1` (three to the first power) is evaluated and stored in the variable `exp`. The value of the variable `exp` is then printed to the output region named `Output1`. On reaching the instruction `NEXT count`, the interpreter increments (adds 1 to) the `count` variable and branches back to the instruction following the `FOR` statement.

This repetition continues until `count = 5` and `NEXT count` is reached. At that point, `count` is no longer to be incremented, and execution continues with the instruction following `NEXT count`. The result is a text region that contains the exponential series `3`, `9`, `27`, `81`, and `243`.

Summary

A large percentage of all instructions within the source code of a VB/DOS application will consist of comparisons between known and unknown values. The unknown values are represented, as in algebra, by variables. The instruction that compares such values can be classified, among other instructions, as a statement.

The phraseology of a BASIC-language statement is borrowed from English syntax, though more from the syntax of an English command rather than an English statement. An VB/DOS statement may appear to be a command to the computer to change some value or some operating component of the program; but from the point of view of the interpreter, the would-be command states the present value of a variable or the present state of the component, and for this reason directive instructions are called statements.

The portion of a statement that actually compares the two values to each other is called an expression. An expression is arithmetically reduced by the interpreter to the most fundamental logical value in computing, that being a true/false binary state. A complex statement that assigns a value to a variable is a formula. Within formulas, common arithmetic functions may be symbolized by VB/DOS function terms, which contain an abbreviation of the function's name followed by a value or expression that the function will operate upon.

An VB/DOS project consists of at least one module, which is by default the startup module. Modules generally consist of self-contained procedures; though any module that contains active, nondeclarative instructions outside of a procedure is considered the trunk module. A form module contains not only source code but also the graphic appearance and behavior of a form window to be used within the VB/DOS application. A general module contains a set of reusable procedures that may or may not pertain to a form window. A procedure describes or models at least one work task, or performs at least one mathematical function.

Within the boundaries of a procedure, a subroutine in VB/DOS is a set of instructions that may be executed repetitively. This repetition is accomplished by branching to that set and then branching back to the instruction following the one that called the subroutine. A more common method of repetitive execution is the loop clause.

Review Questions

Answers to Review Questions appear in Appendix B.

1. Write the part of the instruction `IF f = 6 THEN GOTO Outahere` that is an *expression.*

2. Write the part of the instruction `Total = INT(a + b + c)` that is a *function.*

3. Write the part of the instruction `IF quality > 10 THEN good = 1` that is an *expression of assignment*.

4. If `x = 5` and `y = 2`, the function `SQR((x - y) ^ 3)` returns what integral value?

5. The instruction `IF coins >= too_many THEN RETURN` ends what type of instruction grouping?

4

The Development Process

This chapter begins by explaining how the source code for Visual Basic for MS-DOS applications is presented throughout this book. Then, you can follow along, type the examples, and experiment with some working programs. You also learn how a programmer conceives and develops a VB/DOS application as you take a tour of the development process and see a VB/DOS application being written.

Instructions on Instructions

Throughout this book, I highlight individual VB/DOS instructions and demonstrate their best use within the context of the language. Each instruction being introduced is preceded by a half-page summary of its construction and purpose. Toward the beginning of each summary is a line or paragraph devoted to demonstrating syntax for the instruction. In the sample syntax frame, the regular parts of the instruction appear in `monospace` type to simulate computer output. Placeholders—words that represent the "parts of speech" that appear in a VB/DOS application—appear in `monospace italic` type. Here is an example using the `SELECT CASE` statement clause:

```
SELECT CASE variable
    CASE [IS] comparison1a [TO comparison1b]
        instruction block1
    [CASE [IS] comparison2a [TO comparison2b]]
        [instruction block2]
        .
        .
        .
    [CASE ELSE]
        [instruction blockn]
END SELECT
```

Here, the words that appear in square brackets represent optional terms that you do not necessarily have to type for the instruction to operate. The italicized words, along with their enclosing brackets, stand in place of real terms and denote the types of terms that would be used in their place. For the preceding example, here is what the italicized words represent:

variable	Any term that can be interpreted as a variable, not as a keyword. For instance, `x` or `items`.
comparison	The value to which a variable is being compared for equality, such as `6` or `x`.
instruction block	Any number of interpretable instructions.

When more than one term of the same type appears in a syntax example, digits differentiate the terms, as in *variable1* and *variable2*. This way, if the same term appears twice within the same syntax, the matching numbers enable you to spot where the terms match as well. Also, when a vertical line separates two or more terms within braces—as in `{either | or}`—only one of the terms within the braces appears in that position. In the syntax example of a clause, a *vertical ellipsis* (three dots, each on its own line, as in the preceding `SELECT`

CASE example) stands in place of any number of interpretable instructions. Finally, punctuation such as brackets ([ ]), braces ({ }), or ellipses (. . .) are not actually typed into the instruction or clause.

Entering Code Listings into the Interpreter

In just about every other book on programming, it would be easy for the author to present you with a source code example and ask you to type it verbatim, from front to back. Such listings are not possible with VB/DOS for the following reason: The VB/DOS form module contains graphic elements and property settings that were defined within the Form Designer program. Properties are descriptive elements of graphic objects, defining some manner in which the objects appear or behave. Among the properties mentioned are the objects' contents and control names. These property settings were not made with VB/DOS instructions but by drawing the controls onto the form and setting their properties through a drop-down list box. Because these settings are not instructions, they are not listed along with the instructions in the source code listing.

In order to show the property settings for each object, a table precedes the source code for each form module and shows the property settings for each graphic object in the form. The property settings for the form itself are listed first. As for the other properties, the table shows only those properties in which settings are changed from their default values.

To enter property settings from the listings, perform the following steps:

1. In Form Designer, if a window for the form mentioned in the "Object type" column is not present, select **N**ew Form from the **F**ile menu.

2. Find and choose each form property listed in the "Property" column from the leftmost drop-down list box in the properties bar, beneath the menu bar.

3. Enter the setting for that property in the center text box in the properties bar. If the setting is textual, type it directly in the box. If the down-arrow button is available (if the arrow is black rather than gray), click it to see the list of current setting choices for that property.

4. For each graphic object that is a part of the form, click the term associated with the object type in the Form Designer toolbox. Draw or place the object somewhere within the form for the moment, preferably not overlapping another object. Use the properties bar to set the properties for the object, in the same manner as in the preceding step.

For your convenience, the `.CtlName` and `.Caption` or `.Text` properties are listed first, followed by other properties that have been changed from their default values.

The project listing concludes with the source code for the general code modules (those not related to a specific form), again arranged in order of importance. Procedures within those modules are arranged in order of their relevance or by their frequency within the source code of the program.

Crawling Before You Walk

An application is conceived in stages and written in layers, with the heart of the program—the calculation part—written first and the various frills and eccentricities added to it later. You may not yet understand many of the structural details of programming; the rest of this book is devoted to that subject. Still, to understand what you're learning, you need to see a program being built.

You don't learn to paint a portrait with oils by first studying how to hold the paintbrush, then memorizing the chemical composition of the oil paints and the resilience of different brands of canvas, and finally by counting the number of brushstrokes to be made per minute. You learn to paint by watching an artist at work. You don't teach your child how to speak to you by force-feeding him parts of speech—"Look, son, a ball. *Ball* is a noun. Can you say *noun*?" He learns by listening to you talk. Programming can be as natural for you as speech—or as playing the clarinet, or tennis, or anything else you enjoy.

Programming is a science to the extent that it is studied, analyzed, and theorized on. Programming can be an art inasmuch as it can be practiced, cultivated, and appreciated. You are about to witness a VB/DOS application under construction. If this application were a drawing, it would be a thumbnail sketch. Still, by observing the principles of the programming process being applied, you may be able to obtain a greater understanding of the meaning behind each individual part of the program when you study it in detail.

To give you an idea of how the VB/DOS programming process works, here's how I went about programming a special type of scientific formula calculator that I call the Expressor. For some time, I've wanted a scientific and financial hand-held calculator from which I could retrieve a formula; type the variables into specific windows that showed me not only each variable I typed, but what it represented with respect to the formula; and see the result of the formula in a separate window. (*Window* was, at one time, what the LED registers on calculators were called.) Generally, when you operate most scientific and financial calculators (sci/fi?), by the time you reach the result of your formula, you lose track of your input parameters because they are no longer visible.

All "sci/fi" calculators have a storage bank of "memories" that holds values you typed in at one time or another. The Expressor is to have five of those "memories" visible, set apart from the main register, and labeled with terms that relate them to the formula on which you're working. This allows you to calculate the values for the memory parameters independently from the main formula calculation. One input parameter, for instance, may be the sum of several items added together. With the Expressor design, you can calculate the inputs separately and let the Expressor take care of the main formula.

Figure 4.1 is a diagram of the Expressor in its conceptual stage. Programming is a process of trial and error. Many books paint a picture of a logically rosy world where programs can be compiled and executed on the first try. This is simply an unrealistic viewpoint; the better you are at programming, the more errors you will make per program. The reason is that the better you are, the bigger and more cumbersome your programs will be.

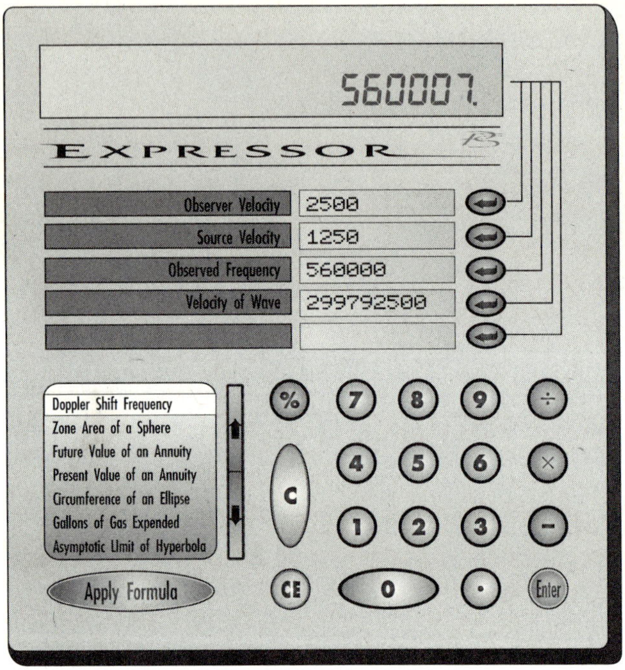

Figure 4.1. A sketch of the Expressor.

Here's how the Expressor works: The calculator portion of the program behaves like a standard RPN four-function calculator. By pressing one of the arrow buttons, the value currently appearing in the readout is copied into the "memory slot" next to the button. If the user wants to solve a formula for a set of given values, she selects the name of a formula from a list in the lower-left corner of the device. The names of various parameters for this formula then appear beside each memory slot. Values can then be copied into the memory slots by making the input parameters appear in the readout, either through calculation or direct entry, and then clicking the arrow button beside the appropriately labeled slot.

When the text for the parameters accurately describes the values that have been inserted into the slots, the user clicks the Apply Formula button. The Expressor then immediately solves the formula for the parameters given and displays the result in the main readout. This method of entry reduces the possibility of error and makes the entry process more fluid and efficient.

The most difficult part of writing a program is the act of translating those first ideas into logic. Rather than first imagining the initial line of source code, I visualize a potential end product. When I've decided on a partway-feasible goal (and my goals tend to be just that, partway-feasible), the final part of the conception process is in creating the beginning of the program.

For the Expressor, my goal was to write a program the user could operate like a hand-held device. One of Microsoft's design goals is to provide an environment in which programs appear to operate like real-world devices with buttons and gadgets. It is tempting at this point in the VB/DOS programming process to start drawing buttons and gadgets on the screen—to first plot how the user sees the program and later decide how the computer will see the program. The real-world term for this method of programming is *procrastination.* To construct a program in any language, you do not organize the user-control elements (the *shell*) first and try to fill that shell with the yolk of the program later. The first task of a programmer is to determine which elements of the program can be represented numerically as values.

When looking at the Expressor sketch, what do you see beneath the obvious that can be represented numerically as values? If you've ever used a programmable calculator, you know that the specific key you press—whether a numeral or function key—is represented numerically. A calculator arithmetically combines the value previously entered into its main window with the one currently being entered, so there are two important values there. The number being typed is different from the one that will be entered into the arithmetic combination, so there is a third important value. The number of digits appearing in the main window is another important value because you can't enter a number of characters that flows past the leftmost edge of the display.

For the sake of the Expressor, there are five "memory" values held in separate text boxes for use later as parameters for the chosen formula. The formula name appears in a drop-down list box. Which formula is chosen also can be considered a value. The VB/DOS interpreter "thinks" in terms of numbers, not gadgets or things. So when you plan a program, you should think in terms of numbers as well.

An *event procedure* is executed once a graphical event is recognized by the system.

You may think that a VB/DOS form appears to be a set of chunky character-mode objects on-screen that react to events in a programmed way. But at the core of the system, an object has properties that are described numerically; beneath that surface, events are merely the results of continual comparisons of numbers to each other until an expected result is reached. These numbers concern the position of the object, the position of the pointer with relation to the object, the color values within the object, and so on. Objects are not the quanta—or indivisible constituent units—of VB/DOS any more than atoms—as learned from the discoveries of subatomic particles, quarks, superstrings, gluons, and so on—are the building blocks of matter.

When you determine what can be represented as values, your next step is to estimate which values will be important throughout the entire program. To explain: Your VB/DOS program will be composed of numerous *event procedures*, such as those that respond to the user pressing a button, those that apply arithmetic functions to the input values, or the one that stores a displayed number in a "memory slot." Each event procedure awaits a certain event that will trigger its execution. When the procedure starts, it needs to be shown those values that are important to its operation. Otherwise, the procedure doesn't know what's going on in the program. Think of the event procedure as being asleep until an event wakes it. When the procedure is awake, it suffers from the logical form of insomnia until it has a chance to be briefed concerning the current status of the program.

So that the program never forgets its purpose, I declared the most important values the program uses throughout as module-level variables. The place in the program to make these declarations is the *general declarations area* of the module. Figure 4.2 shows how this area looks within the Code Editor window. (With DOS, I'm limited to an eight-letter filename, so I purposefully removed one S to derive the project's filename.)

You may not be able to read the contents of this window in detail, so here are the contents of EXPRESOR.FRM's general declarations area:

```
DECLARE SUB assess_readout ()
DECLARE SUB ClearAll_Click ()
```

```
DECLARE FUNCTION surf_area_rccyl! (r!, h!)
DECLARE FUNCTION volume_rccyl! (r!, h!)
DECLARE FUNCTION zone_sphere! (r!, h!)
DECLARE FUNCTION force_att! (me!, mb!, r!, y!)
DECLARE FUNCTION dopp_shift! (vo!, vs!, fo!, c!)
DECLARE SUB Clear_Params ()
DIM SHARED label$(15, 4), p(4)
DIM SHARED readout_value AS SINGLE, combine_value
   AS SINGLE, solution AS SINGLE
DIM SHARED ready AS INTEGER
CONST PI = 3.1415927#
CONST GRAV = 6.6732E-11
```

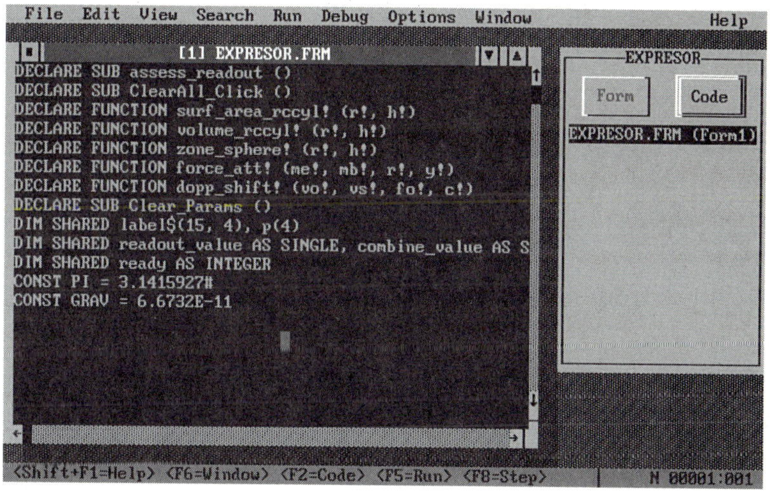

Figure 4.2. The Expressor's main variables and declarations.

The value of a *local variable* is restricted to the procedure that invoked it.

The first eight statements in this area were added automatically by the VB/DOS interpreter at the time I created each of the general procedures they declare. A *general procedure* is any procedure that is *not* an event procedure. It is not "attached" to any form or graphic object and, therefore, must be declared separately using the DECLARE SUB or DECLARE FUNCTION statements. The symbols within the parentheses represent the variables that each procedure will use to accept values rendered unto them from outside; the values passed to these procedures will be maintained within these variables. Unless otherwise declared, these will be *local* variables; that is, variables whose scopes are restricted to the boundaries of their respective procedures, and whose values are discarded once the procedures are exited.

The three `DIM SHARED` statements in the program fragment declare those variables that are pertinent to the program as a whole. They are, respectively, an array for a list of phrases that describes the Expressor's formulas, an array that contains the parameters for an Expressor formula, the current value in the calculator's "readout" window, the value with which it is combined, and the number of digits currently displayed in the window. I named these variables arbitrarily, as every BASIC programmer has the right to do. I decided to call the window where the main number appears the *readout*, rather than the *window* or the *display*—two words with synonyms that may be confusing for another person to read. I decided to call the values I attributed to the readout `readout_value` and `combine_value`. The underscore character is not part of a VB/DOS convention, but it is instead a replacement for a space, making the variable name easier to read.

In determining which values are modular in scope and which, by contrast, are local, one consideration is what values compose the objective of your program—the sum totals, the statistics concerning the records being kept, and the product of the analysis. Another consideration is which values, unseen by the user, most likely will be shared among several procedures. For the Expressor, the number of digits in the readout is one such value. I named its variable `ready` because it refers both to the readout and to the state of readiness for the readout to receive more digits from the button panel.

Does Function Follow Form?

When planning your program, start with the most important *operational* elements.

When writing a program from the beginning, you do not simply know, clairvoyantly, the procedural interrelationship, draw the framework of that interrelationship into the program, and fill that framework with immaculate source code. The technique I use is to select some procedure of the program, make that function work well, and then orient the rest of the procedures around that one. This might not necessarily be the main procedure of the program, although it can be.

With the Expressor, I chose to make the digit buttons operational first. I could have written the formula-solving routines instead, but to test them out in their running state I would need a number entered into the readout. Here is one rule of programming you generally do not learn from a book: The most important *purposeful* elements of a program are not necessarily the most important *operational* elements. Each procedure of a program is like the gear of a mechanism, such as a watch. When you lay out a program using the layered technique, the main gear is "wound" first. This becomes the "engine" of the program, in a sense. When the engine is running, it provides the power for the rest of the program, including those gears that perform the true purpose of the program.

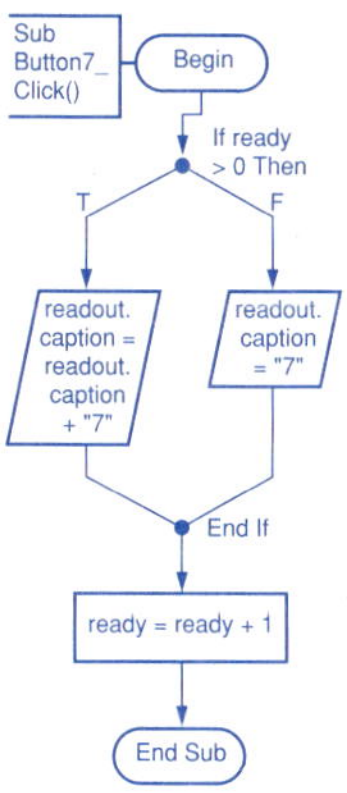

The Expressor project is one good example of this principle in action because the actual formula-solving part of the program was added toward the end of the project. The first stage in the process was to make the digit buttons work. The method I chose in the beginning (albeit a naive one) was to draw the first 11 buttons (digits 0 through 9 and the decimal point), write the procedural source code for one button that would echo its contents into the readout, and copy that code into the procedures for the remaining buttons. I wrote the code for the 7 button and then copied it into the other procedures, replacing 7 with the appropriate digit. Here's how the procedure looked:

```
SUB Button7_Click ()
IF ready > 0 THEN
     readout.caption = readout.caption + "7"
ELSE
     readout.caption = "7"
END IF
ready = ready + 1
END SUB
```

Here's the preceding procedure explained as pseudocode:

Procedure for clicking on the 7 button:
If the tally of digits in the readout is one or more,

Add a "7" to the end of the readout,
Otherwise,
Make the readout just say "7" and nothing else.
End of condition.
Add 1 to the number of digits in the readout tally.
End of procedure.

A *control array* is a group of similar objects (such as command buttons or text boxes) addressed jointly within a single procedure.

Notice that this procedure starts to mimic the way a pocket calculator works. When clear, the readout always reads `0`, and the first digit typed always replaces that 0—unless you type a decimal point or press the 0 key. In the process of writing a program, you gradually realize what all the exceptions are and add them layer by layer as you go.

The second major principle you learn—and continue to learn—as a programmer is that the simplest code to produce is not necessarily the most efficient. The most efficient BASIC code is generally the most compact. The preceding source code example may look compact, but multiply it by eleven and you may begin to wonder whether one big gear runs better than a handful of smaller ones.

VB/DOS allows for a structure of graphical controls to be established, called a *control array*. Such an array can contain several controls, each accessed using the same control name and all referenced within the same `Sub` procedure. Each control in an array, however, is distinguished by its `.Index` property. To initiate a control array, the first object of the array is placed in the form. After indicating that object and selecting **C**opy from the **E**dit menu, the Code Editor responds by asking you if you want the copies of this object to form a control array. You respond by clicking the Yes button. At that point, VB/DOS sets the original object's `.Index` property to `0`, and each clone thereafter to `1`, `2`, `3`, and so on.

Here's how a programmer thinks: The `.Index` property of elements of a control array is a number. The purpose of each button in this particular array is to pass a digit—which is a number, after all—to the readout. If that number is always a single digit, you can write a generic procedure for the entire control array. The procedure will pass some distinct value, whatever it is, to the readout whenever one of the buttons in the array is pressed. You don't need several separate-but-equal procedures to define the pressing of buttons when one procedure does the job just as well. The one element of distinction here is the `.Index` property of each button, so if you make each `.Index` equal to the number being passed, you can program the procedure to pass the `.Index` to the readout.

The third thing you learn to do as a programmer is to say, often, "On second thought...." As stated previously, the 0 and decimal point buttons operate differently on a calculator than the rest of the digit keys, so you can't include these two wayward buttons in the control array. The 1 through 9 buttons are functionally identical, however; so you can include those buttons with positive-valued indices in a control array. Here's the code for the new procedure, rewritten from the 7 button version presented previously:

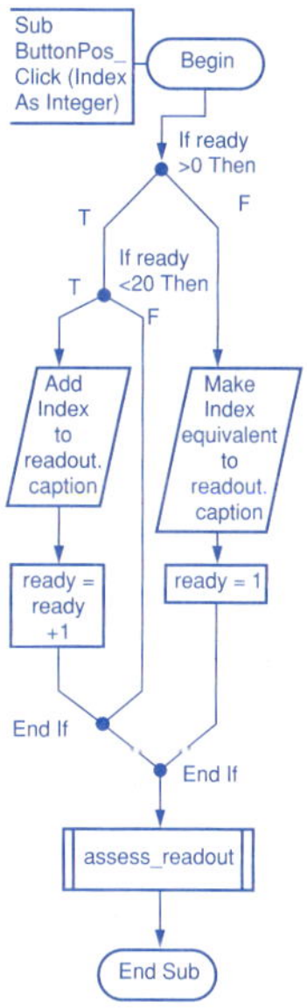


```
SUB ButtonPos_Click (Index AS INTEGER)
IF ready > 0 THEN
    If ready < 20 THEN
        readout.caption = readout.caption + RIGHT$(STR$(Index), 1)
        ready = ready + 1
    END IF
ELSE
    readout.caption = RIGHT$(STR$(Index), 1)
    ready = 1
END IF
assess_readout
END SUB
```

Notice how this procedure has evolved. Because this procedure belongs to a control array rather than to one control, the `Index` of that control is automatically passed to the procedure through the parentheses within the initial `SUB` statement. `Index` is the parameter passed to the procedure when the user clicks on a positively numbered button. Think of the parentheses within the `SUB` and `FUNCTION` statements as a slot through which values—here called *parameters*—are passed.

The function `RIGHT$(STR$(Index), 1)` converts the numeric value of `Index` to textual contents. VB/DOS stores alphanumeric text and real numbers differently; the text may happen to have numbers in it, but VB/DOS still cannot evaluate that text. To give numeric text value, it must be converted to a value using the function `STR$()`. The function that, in this instance, encloses that function, `RIGHT$(..., 1)`, removes the leading space character—another bit of alphanumeric text.

Here are the instructions for the new and improved procedure, written as pseudocode.

For all positively numbered buttons, receive
the index for the particular button pressed.
If the tally of digits in the readout is one or more,
Then if this tally is less than 20,
Add the numeric form of the index to the readout
and add one to the tally of digits.
End of this condition.
Otherwise (if there's only one digit in the readout),
Place the numeric form of the index into the
readout and make the tally equal 1.
End of the main condition.
Execute the procedure that assesses the readout value.
End of procedure.

Within the "memory bank" portion of the Expressor form, the groups of five value registers, descriptive text boxes, and value-loading buttons were each created as control arrays.

I programmed the four-function calculator portion of the Expressor using Reverse Polish Notation (also called H.P. or Hewlett-Packard notation) primarily because it is easier to implement. If you've ever used a Texas Instruments (T.I.) calculator or one that uses T.I. notation, you know that you enter each element of an arithmetic expression the way it would appear on paper in algebraic notation. Thus, *two times three divided by six* is entered in T.I. notation as `2 * 3 / 6`, where `*` is the multiplication operator and `/` is the division operator.

The downside of T.I. notation is that the previous arithmetic function is implemented whenever the next one is entered. For instance, in `2 * 3 / 6`, 2 will actually be multiplied by 3 when the division key is pressed. Subsequently, the division operation takes place when the `=` key is pressed. To implement this notation in a VB/DOS program, the previous arithmetic function has to be remembered—which means creating another variable and giving each function its own arbitrary index.

For Reverse Polish Notation, the same formula is entered as `2 [Enter] 3 * 6 /`. This looks backward on paper—thus the name *Reverse*—but it's easier to implement in a program. Each arithmetic operation takes place at the time its operator is pressed. You can then program the Expressor's function buttons to execute the operation the moment the button-pressing event is triggered.

Here's the source code for the procedure that handles the pressing of the multiplication button:

```
SUB Times_Click ()
    assess_readout
    readout_value = readout_value * combine_value
    combine_value = readout_value
    readout.caption = STR$(readout_value)
    ready = 0
END SUB
```

Here is the same procedure written in pseudocode:

Procedure for clicking on the "Times" button:
Execute the procedure that assesses the value of the number in the readout.
Multiply that assessment by the combination value—previous value entered into the readout.
Make the combination value the current value, in the event of future button presses.
Place the textual form of the mathematically combined value into the readout.
Pretend there are no digits in the readout, so that the next digit button pressed will clear it.
End of procedure.

Notice the next-to-last statement in the procedure. The way the digit buttons work, a digit replaces the contents of the entire readout if the register of the number of digits, `ready`, is equal to `0`. You know that the solution value in the readout is not likely to be 0. You also know, however, that the next digit button pressed should not add a digit to the solution but should instead replace it. Therefore, I set the digit-number tally to 0. The real-world term for this form of process-triggering is *lying*.

This is the point in the discussion of the art of programming where I admit to you that I am a "code-as-you-go" programmer. I don't devise the inner schematics of my BASIC programs beforehand. In fact, most of my grand solutions to procedural dilemmas come to me by accident. The setting of `ready` to `0` when there were clearly digits in the readout is one case in point. I could have prepared another variable to act as a register that sets itself to 1 whenever a function button is pressed and then had my digit button procedures check to see if `register = 1` before proceeding. I would, however, have had to add another comparison to my conditional statements. Furthermore, why make two registers perform similar purposes when one does the job just as well, if not better? When programming, be prepared to abandon at any time whatever process or method you originally *thought* would work in favor of a better way. This really is the way to program.

Summary

Here is an outline of the principles of programming introduced in this chapter, which are utilized throughout the book:

1. When conceiving a program in your mind, start with the end product and work backward toward the beginning.
2. Your first task as a programmer is to determine which elements of the program—graphical or logical—can be represented numerically as values.
3. The second task is to determine which values are important to the entire program and which are necessary only within their own local procedures.
4. Make one whole procedure of the program work first and then write the other procedures to work around it.
5. The most compact code may be the most difficult for a person to read—or, for that matter, write—but it is probably the most efficient code for the interpreter to execute.
6. Prepare to rewrite entire procedures as you discover new methods that work better. You will probably keep less than 30 percent of the original draft of your source code, regardless of how well-written it is.

7. Accept new solutions that come to mind along the way, even if they are devious and the apparent product of a scheming mind.

The Expressor program is far from complete at this point in the development process. In upcoming chapters, however, you will learn more about the initial programming process, as well as the revision process. The entire source code for the final version of the Expressor appears in Appendix D.

Review Questions

Answers to Review Questions appear in Appendix B.

1. In the Expressor program, why were the 0 and period keys not part of the same control array as the keys 1 through 9?
2. Reverse Polish Notation is easier to implement in a computer program for what primary reason?

Part II

Values and Variables

5

Definition and Declaration

This chapter introduces the concept of the variable, which is the logical container for values and text in Visual Basic for MS-DOS and all other variations of BASIC. You will learn the different categories of variables and experiment with placing values within each type. You will also construct mathematical expressions using variables as components.

Variables and the Universe as We Know It

Every VB/DOS instruction you write manipulates the contents of the computer's memory in one way or another. Even the single-statement instruction STOP—which suspends the program's execution—alters the contents of memory. The STOP statement, however, does not impart to its human reader just what contents are being altered at the time. You as programmer, therefore, are manipulating the computer indirectly. As the user, you see only the cause of the program's suspension—the "command" STOP—and its seemingly immediate effect. What you don't see are all the values in memory being manipulated, which result in the appearance of stopping the VB/DOS application. If you were inside the computer, you would discover that by saying STOP, you actually started a myriad of internal processes—for instance, processes that turn control back to the VB/DOS control program or to DOS. These processes are invisible, so the VB/DOS interpreter doesn't appear to be guilty of insubordination; in other words, it really does respond to the "command" as directed.

A *variable* represents a unit of data.

A direct statement such as STOP is, in fact, an indirect method of manipulating values in memory. In all BASIC language forms including VB/DOS, the direct method of manipulating values in memory is to represent those values as *variables.* A variable is an arbitrarily named term that represents a unit of data in memory that the program can alter.

In the history of the English language, few scientific formulas have ever become cliches. Perhaps the best-known of these formula catch phrases is $E=mc^2$, the formula that explains one of the primary principles of relativity theory. Many people who know this catch phrase have no idea what it means; however, many of these people seem to know that the three letters of this formula represent values of some sort—although they may not be sure just what those values are.

At the time this formula was conceived, *c* represented what appeared to be a *constant*—that is, an unchanging value. Namely, this value is the speed of light. But recently, physicists have determined that this value is not, in fact, constant at all. Therefore, the three letters in the famous formula are all variables that represent values that are subject to change. The very fact that fewer people know what values are represented by these variables than know that they are variables underscores the principle of using variables to represent values: Variables are often *unknowns.*

When writing a program, you constantly deal with unknowns—more specifically, with unknown values. For instance, you may write a program that at one point tells the interpreter to solve for the velocity of a jet airplane traveling at so many thousand feet through some level of atmospheric density with the throttle at some percentage level. You do not know the specific attributes of this flight, but you do know the *relationships* between those attributes. In the relativity formula, the particular level of mass (*m*) is not specified, and the speed of light is no longer specifiable as a constant. Still, the formula denotes what is perceived to be the proportional interrelationship between mass, light, and energy. Formulas specify relationships; now you know why it's called "relativity" theory.

A *formula* states the relationship between known and unknown quantities.

A *formula* is an algebraic expression of equality that states the relationships between qualities, quantities, or other such values, whether known or unknown. This definition holds true in common conversation as well as with respect to VB/DOS.

I Declare!

An *expression* can be a comparison between values, a formula, or an assignment of value to a variable.

VB/DOS recognizes variables as unique combinations of alphanumeric characters up to 40 characters long. (You probably will use a 40-character variable only on extremely rare occasions.) When the VB/DOS interpreter starts executing a program, no variables at all exist for that program. In other words, the interpreter maintains several values for the program even at first, although you have not yet explicitly claimed any of them. To stake your claim on a variable using the informal method, you use that variable for the first time in a mathematical *expression* of equality.

An expression is any of the following:

- An arithmetic comparison between two values, having a result that is expressed logically as a binary state
- One or more values or variables arithmetically joined by functions or functional operators
- An assignment of value to a variable by way of another value, variable, or expression

In BASIC, a variable is *declared* whenever it is first invoked within the source code.

Whenever you use a variable for the first time within a program, that variable is *declared.* A declaration of a variable is the first statement in a program to assign a legitimate value to that variable.

Example

Here is perhaps the simplest variable declaration:

```
x = 1
```

The preceding declaration is a mathematical expression that creates the variable x and assigns to it the value 1. From this point on, whenever x appears in the program, the interpreter evaluates it to be 1 until some instruction explicitly changes the value of x to something else.

The best way to experiment with variables is to invoke a pair of windows from the Code Editor: the *Immediate window* and the *Output window*. Once open, they appear as depicted in Figure 5.1.

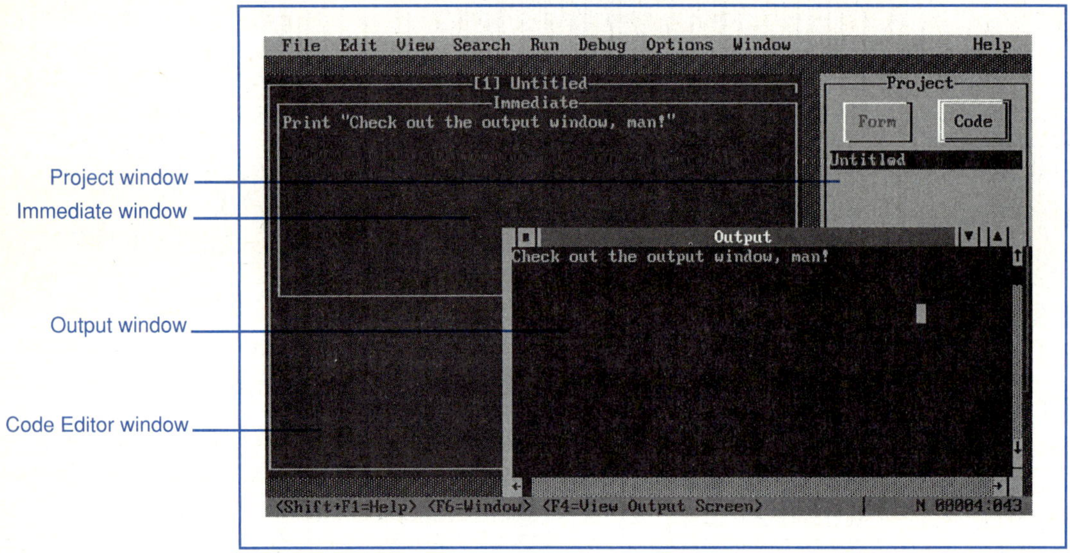

Figure 5.1. The VB/DOS interpreter in action.

The Immediate window contains a command-line interpreter—a prompted line like the DOS prompt—in which you type direct statements as commands. This is the descendant of the READY prompt from the old BASIC interpreters. The Output window is truly a window in the more traditional definition. When invoked from the Code Editor menu, the Output window provides a partial view of the VB/DOS main output screen, or the *application workspace*. When used in conjunction with the Immediate window, the Output window is capable of responding to direct BASIC-language commands placed through the Immediate window. The effect is like having a two-way conversation with your computer.

To invoke the Immediate and Output windows, perform the following steps:

1. From the Code Editor's **W**indow menu, select **I**mmediate. A blank window titled `Immediate` appears. By default, this window is blue.

2. Next, select **O**utput from the **W**indow menu. A blank window titled `Output` appears. If a VB/DOS application is currently running in suspension (if you ran an application and pressed Ctrl-Break to stop it) and that application runs in the DOS character mode, you'll see a portion of that application in the Output window. If no application is currently running, you'll see a blank window that is black by default.

3. Click once within the upper left corner of the Immediate window to begin operating it.

Each instruction you enter here is interpreted immediately, hence the window's name. You can enter `x = 1` into this window and start your variable-manipulating career at once.

To test the effectiveness of dynamic instructions, enter `PRINT x` at the Immediate prompt. The Code Editor screen disappears for now, and the screen responds with a `1` at the upper left corner. Upon pressing any key, the Code Editor screen returns, and its Output window displays a `1` on a line by itself. Likewise at this point, if you enter `PRINT y`, the screen and Output window should respond with `0` because no real value has yet been loaded into a variable `y`. All variables that have never been officially declared are "virtually" equal to `0`; in other words, if a variable is invoked in a formula that has never had a value assigned to it, the variable is evaluated as `0`.

The statement `x = 1` is an expression of assignment, in that the value `1` is assigned to `x`. It is also a declaration of the existence of `x` only if the expression is the first instruction within the VB/DOS program to use `x`.

We Hold This Truth to Be Confusing

The fact that a program is made workable by continually assigning and reassigning values to variables is not self-evident—in fact, little in the art of programming is ever self-evident. I could stop here in the text and say, "Now that you've made `x` equal to `1`, you know how to make value assignments," and then skip merrily away to the next topic. Such methods of explanation through assumption lend themselves to such widely read and underappreciated works as the Federal Budget.

As stated previously, an expression of equality—an *equation*—specifies the relationships between values as well as their proportions, ratios, and limits. The VB/DOS application is, in the purely logical sense, a mechanism that utilizes equations as instructions for the construction and assembly of a product. This product is not the program but the data "manufactured" by that program. The data are always, in their root form, a set of numbers. In its tangible form, the product of a program is a record of names, a graph, a mathematical series, or the destruction of the Xamphoid Empire. Whatever its guise, the product of any program is really a bunch of numbers.

For the mechanism to work, the instructions to be interpretable, and the final product to be manufactured, at some point you must draw out your parts list. These elements are *seeded* into the formulas and procedures, and, when they are combined, produce solutions. Lo and behold, these parts are a bunch of numbers. If you're beginning to get the impression that all a computer program does is take one group of numbers and reconstitute it with formulas so that it is another group of numbers, you're beginning to think like a programmer.

Example

Here's an example of this principle in practice. Suppose there is a formula you use in your business to determine whether the price you charge for an item is excessive. You figure your cost for the item is equal to the actual wholesale cost you paid for it as a retailer, plus your costs for shipping, employee man-hours of maintenance, and time the item spent consuming your shelf space. This formula is fixed, but your percentage of markup over your costs varies, perhaps by the day.

Here's how your formula might appear, written within a VB/DOS SUB procedure:

```
SUB Analyze_Markup (sale_price, shipping, manhours,
  shelf_time, markup_ceiling)
total_cost = shipping + manhours + shelf_time
ratio = (sale_price / total_cost - 1) * 100
IF ratio > markup_ceiling THEN
     too_high = 1
END IF
END SUB
```

Here is the task the VB/DOS interpreter is being instructed to perform, rendered as pseudocode:

Procedure for analyzing the fairness of the markup value, taking into account the current sale price, costs for materials shipping, production hours, shelf time, and the current markup ceiling:
Calculate the total cost of producing the item as equal to the shipping cost for raw material, plus the number of production man-hours, plus the time the item will rest on the shelf.
Calculate the percentage ratio of sale price to this total cost.
If this ratio is higher than the maximum allowable markup ceiling, then
Set the "too high" flag.
End of condition.
End of procedure.

There are three value assignments in the preceding procedure. You add all the operating costs and expenditures to arrive at the total cost per item. The next procedure is a formula that determines the percentage of price markup. The third procedure, which is executed conditionally, is the simplest of all. It assigns a value directly to a variable, as a flag, in case the markup is too much.

Suppose that before you execute this procedure, in lieu of acquiring inputs from a form, you *seed* the formula with the following statements appearing in the midst of another procedure:

```
.
.
.
shipping = 2.90
manhours = (av_salary / no_boxes) * 8
shelf_time = .25 * no_days
markup_ceiling = 33
.
.
.
```

You can interpret these statements as a sort of parts list for the "assembly manual" that is `SUB Analyze_Markup ()`. These statements, or some such assignment of value to these variables referred to in `SUB Analyze_Markup ()`, are essential to the operation of the program. Otherwise, the VB/DOS interpreter is not able to execute the procedure. The variable `total_cost` cannot be allowed to equal 0 because the interpreter will "error out" if it attempts to divide another value by 0.

Because some of the preceding ingredients are, in fact, formulas, you could take this seeding process one step further with the following initial statements:

```
av_salary = 6.50
no_boxes = 1300
no_days = 5
```

As stated before, the programming process sometimes works best backward. Direct assignment statements act as the fuel for the arithmetic engine of the program. You can easily change the values within these statements.

Degrees of Precision

A standard *byte* is composed of eight binary digits.

When the VB/DOS interpreter sees a variable for the first time, it allots a space for that variable in memory. Computers do not "think" in terms of decimal numbers (numbers in the base 10 numeral system). Therefore, the interpreter does not place into memory numbers like the kind you are accustomed to using. A unit of memory, as you learned in the preceding chapter, is a byte—the primary memory storage unit for all forms of data in a computer system. A byte is composed of eight binary digits (bits).

Each eight-bit byte can hold any absolute integral value between 0 and 255 and any signed value between –128 and 127.

As you've seen, variables can have fractional values. Bytes, however, do not have fractional values; so when apportioning space for a variable that may at some time become fractional, the VB/DOS interpreter, by default, apportions extra memory for both fractional and whole-number values to be maintained for each variable.

A *floating-point* value may or may not be fractional.

In fractional value storage, the interpreter maintains a separate register for each value that could possibly be fractional. This register specifies the placement of the decimal point in the binary, or base 2, form of the number. The whole-number and fractional parts of the number are then translated into base 10 separately. This type of number is referred to as a *floating-point* number. The term *floating-point* refers to the storage format for a value that is possibly fractional, where the position of its decimal point is stored as a separate value.

Table 5.1 shows the five numeric precision types that VB/DOS supports and the number of bytes apportioned for each type. The table also shows the special characters used for addressing these different classes. These characters are placed immediately following the variable name to denote the variable's precision type throughout the source code.

Keep in mind that a *kilobyte* (K) is equal to 1,024 bytes and that a *megabyte* (M) is equal to 1,024 *kilobytes*. With the amount of a computer's installed memory now being measured commonly in megabytes rather than in multiples of 16K, it might seem out of fashion to consider conserving memory for variable usage two bytes at a time. Those people who concur that it is out of fashion may very well be the authors of the programs that do less with two megabytes than some late-70s applications did with 32K.

Table 5.1. Numeric precision types.

Variable Type	*Symbol*	*Memory Usage*	*Fractional Value Storage*
Integer	%	2 bytes	None
Long Integer	&	4 bytes	None
Single-precision floating point	!	4 bytes	Includes 2 bytes of fractional value storage
Double-precision floating point	#	8 bytes	Includes 4 bytes of fraction value storage
Currency	@	8 bytes	Includes 2 bytes of fractional value storage

The degree to which you conserve memory when writing programs should not be dictated by the deflating dollar value of memory on the open market. Furthermore, if you've ever tried simultaneously to write a book with a huge word processor, test programs with a high-level interpreter, and run background utilities all in the same environment, you most likely have come to appreciate small, efficient programs.

An *integer* is any whole number that has no fractional value.

One way to tighten the object code or threaded p-code of a program is to eliminate the "trailing zeros" from unnecessarily decimalized integers, or whole numbers with two or four bytes of decimal values all set to zero. Another might be to determine which variables always are described as whole numbers—for instance, the number of man-hours expended in the earlier example—and declare those variables as integers rather than as floating-point (possibly fractional) variables.

Example

Here's the last group of assignment expressions, edited, in the interest of conserving space, to specify their new variable type:

```
av_salary@ = 6.50
no_boxes& = 1300
no_days% = 5
```

For those values you know will never be fractional—for instance, any variable that represents a number of units—you should consider using the % integer symbol to use two bytes for the variable instead of four, or the & long integer symbol for anything you keep in stock that may number in the billions.

Live and Let Live

Optionally, you can write a statement of assignment or an informal declaration as a formal VB/DOS statement using the keyword LET, as introduced here:

[LET] **Statement**

Syntax:

```
[Let] variable = expression
```

The interpreter first evaluates the expression on the right side of the equation. If that expression evaluates to be a rational arithmetic value, that value is assigned to the variable stated. If that expression evaluates to be a legal textual string, that string is assigned to the string variable stated. If the expression can be evaluated rationally and the statement of the variable is the first instance of that variable within the code of the procedure, the stated variable is considered officially declared, either as a single-precision number or a string, with its scope set to local.

Example

Here are the three values of assignment revised again to appear as formal LET statements:

```
LET av_salary@ = 6.50
LET no_boxes& = 1300
LET no_days% = 5
```

Using LET gives your instructions more of a sentence-like structure. Beyond that, the term does nothing more of importance for the instruction; for that reason, I tend to avoid using it. In the 1960s versions of BASIC, LET was a mandatory term to be used before statements of assignment. Perhaps because there is no word LET in algebra, usage of the term was dropped in the mid-70s. In deference to those who prefer the older structures, LET is maintained in VB/DOS as an optional keyword. Almost no other part of BASIC looks like it did in 1964, so consider the LET statement the syntactic equivalent of your own body's appendix.

In upcoming chapters, you'll learn about textual strings and variable scopes.

Summary

A computer program of any type, written with any language, works by manipulating values in memory. The result of this value manipulation is the production of data. In the VB/DOS language, values used within a program that are not subject to change are represented using numerals and are called *constants*. Values that are subject to change are represented using alphanumeric characters and are called *variables*.

In VB/DOS, a value is automatically assigned to a variable once that variable is invoked within a program, even if that value is zero. When a variable is formally declared, its initial value is zero. A variable may be informally declared by means of its invocation within a formula. Such a formula assigns a specific value to a variable, whether by means of direct assignment or calculation.

The primary program element used to assign a value to or assess the value of a variable is the *expression*. In an expression, a variable on the left side is compared to a variable or value on the right side. If one value is being compared to another within an expression for equality, the equal sign (=) is used between the two.

Review Questions

Answers to Review Questions appear in Appendix B.

1. The result or solution of an expression of comparison is described logically as what?
2. The `PRINT` instruction to the Immediate window falls under what category of instruction?
3. If one instruction sets the value of `y` to `12`, what type of instruction is required to set it to some other value?
4. How many binary digits (bits) are there in a long integer variable?
5. Estimate why an unsigned byte can hold a value between 0 and 255, but a signed byte can hold a value between –128 and 127. Why not between –256 and 255? Why is the positive maximum value odd?

Review Exercises

1. Write five instructions that set the variables `prime1`, `prime2`, and so on, equal to the first five prime numbers.
2. Write expressions of assignment for arbitrarily named variables. Assign the following values to those variables. Use symbols for those variables that direct the interpreter to allocate the least number of bytes feasible for each value.

   A. 17.725

   B. 1 3/8

   C. –16

   D. 0.176470588235294

   E. $56.25

   F. 152,587,890,625

6

Formulas

In this chapter, you experiment with equations and formulas that involve values and arithmetic functions. You learn how values are derived from elsewhere in the program and assigned to a variable with an expression of assignment. You also study the order of evaluation of simple arithmetic functions and begin to incorporate more complex, intrinsic Visual Basic for MS-DOS functions into formulas.

The Function of Formulas

Although VB/DOS uses procedural algebra to encode its own applications, it really doesn't use algebra to its full extent in evaluating mathematical expressions. Algebraic equations deal primarily with unknown values. As you saw in the previous chapter, no variable in VB/DOS has an unknown value. Even if a variable was never declared and you asked the interpreter to print its value to a form, VB/DOS would respond with 0—a known value.

An *equation* is a statement that assigns a value to a variable.

If you've studied algebra, you know that each algebraic statement is an equation. Likewise, each statement of value assignment in VB/DOS is an equation. An *equation* is a statement of equality that assigns a value—whether it is a numeral or an arithmetically derived value—to a variable.

The elementary syntax of a VB/DOS equation is as follows:

```
variable = value1 [[operator1] [value2]...]
```

When you assign a value to a variable, through direct specification (as in `x = 1`) or through indirect reference by way of other variables (as in `x = y + 1`), you use an equation. Here are some valid VB/DOS equations:

```
a = n + 1
lifeboats = crewmen / 15
Energy = mass * light_speed ^ 2
sphere_volume = (4/3) * 3.1415927 * r ^ 3
```

Notice that in the preceding expressions the left side of the equation is always a single variable. Arithmetic functions are placed on the right side of the equation. It would be invalid, therefore, to state `n + 1 = x / 6` and expect the interpreter to solve for `n`. Although VB/DOS uses algebraic notation, it is not so figurative in its evaluation. In other words, the interpreter does not simplify algebraic terms in the way the equation $6y^2 = 3y$ is simplified to $2y = 1$ and then to $y = 1/2$.

> **NOTE:** The solution to a VB/DOS equation is always a known value and is always assigned to a single variable by itself on the left side of the equation.

An *operator* is a symbol (+, –, *, /) that represents a mathematical function.

In the preceding VB/DOS equations, the variables and numbers were each separated by arithmetic symbols. You probably recognize some of these symbols; however, there are some you may not recognize if you're a newcomer to BASIC. These symbols are called *operators,* and their purpose is to represent simple arithmetic functions. A *binary operator* is a symbol that represents a mathematical function that combines, compares, or equates two values.

Table 6.1 lists operators used in VB/DOS expressions. The third column of this table lists solutions to the expression `2 operator 3`, where `operator` is replaced with the specific arithmetic operator to the left of each solution.

Table 6.1. Arithmetic functional operators.

Operator	*Function*	`2 operator 3`
^	Exponentiation (raising to a power)	8
*	Multiplication	6
/	Division	.66666666
+	Addition	5
-	Subtraction	-1

The Order of Evaluation

In Table 6.1, the operators are listed in the order of their evaluation in a formula. When you type numbers and functions into a pocket calculator, the evaluation generally takes place as you press each button, so the order of evaluation—also called the operator *precedence*—is generally front-to-back.

Example

With VB/DOS, the entire expression is stated within an instruction before evaluation takes place. A VB/DOS expression is, in many ways, a restatement of an algebraic formula or equation. To understand why the order of evaluation in VB/DOS is the way it is, examine an equation stated in pure algebraic notation, followed by an equivalent VB/DOS expression:

$$c = y^3 + \frac{5y^2}{4}$$

c = y ^ 3 + 5 * y ^ 2 / 4

In algebra, a variable raised to an exponent—such as y^3—is considered to be one term rather than a function relating y to 3. Thus, if the entire equation is to be solved rationally, "y to the third" is solved first. If the term is to be multiplied by a whole number, that number is the term's coefficient. In algebra, "5 y squared" is rarely stated as "5 *times* y squared" although it would be correct to do so. Multiplication of this nature is generally presumed in algebra to exist almost by default, so the function has taken on a virtual priority just below exponentiation.

In the preceding algebraic equation, "5 y squared over 4" is considered to be a fraction. Fractional values in VB/DOS are stated as functions of division, as in "5 times y raised to the power of 2 *divided by* 4." Nonetheless, a fractional term in algebra is one term, rather than two terms separated by a division symbol. Therefore, to maintain the algebraic hierarchy, division operations are performed at the same time as multiplication.

Addition and subtraction symbols separate terms in algebraic notation. Because they do, those functions are evaluated last. To understand why, take the first part of the preceding VB/DOS equation: `c = y ^ 3 + 5`.... Logically speaking, the solution for just this part of the equation should be the same if instead you state it as `c = 5 + y ^ 3`.... If addition were to be performed first rather than exponentiation, then in the first example, `3 + 5` is evaluated first. The solution for the first three VB/DOS terms would be the value, algebraically speaking, of y^8 rather than y^3—y to the eighth power (the `3 + 5` power) rather than y to the third.

In the second example, if addition were to be evaluated first, the solution would reflect the value of $(5+y)^3$ rather than $5+y^3$. In other words, y and 5 would be added together and then the result would be cubed, instead of the cube of y being added to 5. There would be a discrepancy of 120 in the final solution.

In Praise of Parentheses

A *delimiter* separates elements of an expression from each other.

If you want to evaluate the value of `5 + y` added and cubed, just as in the algebraic instance in the previous paragraph, place parentheses around the part of the expression you want the interpreter to evaluate before the other parts. You would therefore write `(5 + y) ^ 3`. In such an expression, the parentheses act as *delimiters* for the interpreter. A *delimiter* is a punctuation mark used to distinguish or separate elements of an expression from each other.

Example

Here's an example of a real-world formula in which parentheses are necessary. A formula for depreciation of the monetary value of an asset over a given period follows:

```
dep@ = ((init_value@ - prior_dep@) * factor%) / life%
```

Figure 6.1 depicts a "parenthetical mountain" for this formula. At the summit of this mountain is the smallest enclosure of terms within parentheses. Evaluation of this formula starts at the summit and works its way toward the foot of the mountain. Notice that I included the type designators (such as `@` and `%`) beside each variable. I didn't have to include them, but the formula now consumes less memory.

Figure 6.1. A mountain of depreciation.

The first order of business for this formula is to subtract any depreciation of the asset `prior_dep@` from the initial value of that asset `init_value@`. The remainder is multiplied by the factor at which the balance declines `factor%` before it is divided by the life span of the depreciation in equivalent periods `life%`. The solution is rendered to the depreciation variable `dep@`. Variable `dep@` is a currency value, so the result is limited to four decimal places.

Here is an example session—a "conversation"—using the Immediate and Output windows of the code. In the remaining text, conversations of this nature will be typeset with the instructions typed into the Immediate window in standard `monospace` type and the response from the Output window in **`bold monospace`**. You can test this formula without having to devise an entire project for it.

```
init_value@=2400
prior_dep@=500
factor%=2
life%=12
dep@=((init_value@-prior_dep@)*factor%)/life%
?dep@
 316.6667
```

Occasionally, you will use the Immediate window to test formulas. BASIC formulas have been tested and proven this way for years, and there is no reason for that to change now. I've left out the spaces between terms, operators, and delimiters in the preceding code. VB/DOS does not require these spaces, especially within the Immediate window.

CLI (*command-line interpreter*) is another name that can be used for VB/DOS' Immediate window.

The first four lines seed the variables for the formula in the fifth line. The statement `?dep@` is on the sixth line. Here, the `?` is an abbreviation for the `PRINT` statement. Since the '70s, `?` has stood in place of `PRINT`, primarily because in conversations with the *command-line interpreter* (*CLI*) such as the preceding one, `?` is easier to type when you're in a hurry and you're "quizzing" the interpreter. Hereafter, I refer to the Immediate window as the CLI. Take note, however, that `?` does not substitute for the `.PRINT` method in a procedure window when used with respect to a graphic object in a form.

In the first six lines of the conversation, the CLI does not type a response. Only after the quizzing statement does the CLI respond with `316.6667`. In the text of such conversations, the CLI adds a leading space to distinguish its responses from your statements.

Example

For the next example, you construct a working VB/DOS project concerning coordinate geometry. Its objective is to allow you to figure the distance between two points with Cartesian (x, y) coordinates—such as (0,0) or (16,5)—on a plane. Figure 6.2 shows the form for the two-dimensional Cartesian calculator, along with a graph that shows two points on a Cartesian plane and the distance between them.

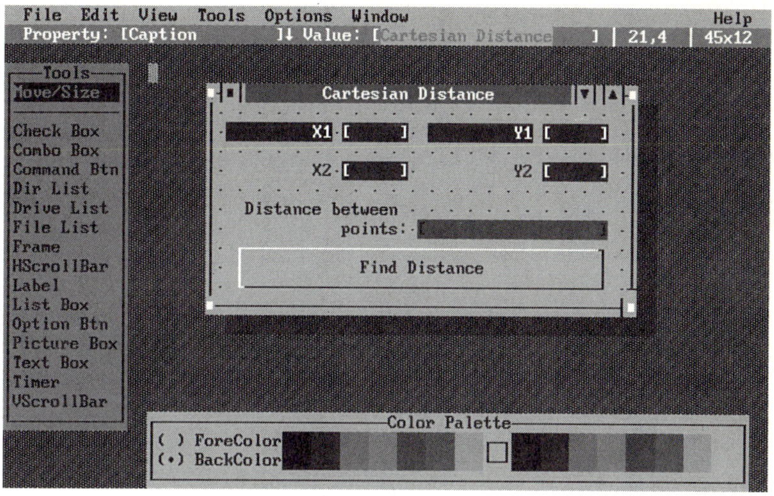

Figure 6.2. The Cartesian calculator.

Again, to add controls and graphic objects to a form, click on the name for that control where it appears within the Form Designer's toolbox and move the pointer to the form area. Click and hold down the index button, and drag the pointer from one corner of the control to the opposite corner. After you release the button, the object appears on the form. You may alter its shape or position by dragging any of the eight indicator nodes that surround it. You can change properties such as textual contents using the combo box in VB/DOS' main properties bar.

Using Figure 6.2 and the following table as guides, draw five text boxes, five labels, and one command button on the form. Change the properties of each object as indicated. Here is the extended listing for the two-dimensional calculator:

2D Cartesian Coordinates Calculator

Project name: 2D_DIST.MAK
Constituent file: 2D_DIST.FRM

Object Type	*Property*	*Setting*
Form	.Width	45
	.Height	12
	.Caption	Cartesian Distance
Text box	.Left	1560
	.Top	240
	.CtlName	Box_x1
	.Text	(blank)
	.TabIndex	0
Text box	.Left	4080
	.Top	240
	.CtlName	Box_y1
	.Text	(blank)
	.TabIndex	1
Text box	.Left	1560
	.Top	600
	.CtlName	Box_x2
	.Text	(blank)
	.TabIndex	2
Text box	.Left	4080
	.Top	600
	.CtlName	Box_y2
	.Text	(blank)
	.TabIndex	3
Label	.Left	2520
	.Top	1080
	.CtlName	Distance
	.Caption	(blank)
Label	.Left	120
	.Top	240
	.Caption	X1
	.Alignment	1 - Right Justify

Object Type	Property	Setting
Label	.Left	2640
	.Top	240
	.Caption	Y1
	.Alignment	1 - Right Justify
Label	.Left	120
	.Top	600
	.Caption	X2
	.Alignment	1 - Right Justify
Label	.Left	2640
	.Top	600
	.Caption	Y2
	.Alignment	1 - Right Justify
Label	.Left	120
	.Top	1080
	.Caption	Distance between points:
	.Alignment	1 - Right Justify
Button	.Left	240
	.Top	1440
	.CtlName	Go
	.Caption	Find Distance

To enter the following procedure, double-click the Go command button in the newly drawn form and type the following:

```
SUB Go_Click ()
x1 = VAL(Box_x1.Text)
x2 = VAL(Box_x2.Text)
y1 = VAL(Box_y1.Text)
y2 = VAL(Box_y2.Text)
d# = SQR((x2 - x1) ^ 2) + (y2 - y1) ^ 2)
Distance.Text = STR$(d#)
END SUB
```

To help you understand what's going on, here is the preceding procedure written in pseudocode:

Procedure for clicking on the Go button:
  Retrieve the four values from their respective text boxes.
  .
  .
  .
  Calculate the zone of the given sphere using the specified coordinates.
  Place the result in the text box called `Distance`*.*
End of procedure.

This program has only one formula to maintain and one procedure to execute. After you click the Find Distance button given the control name `Go`, the alphanumeric contents of the four text boxes are converted to real numbers using the VB/DOS function `VAL()`. Four variables are derived from this process, which are referenced in the formula for variable `d#`. The formula solves for `d#`—a double-precision floating-point number. Then the solution is converted back to text using the VB/DOS function `STR$()`. The string is then placed in the text box named `Distance`.

When examining a formula with multiple sets of parentheses, you should try to imagine it in three dimensions, as a terraced platform seen from above. Visualize each parenthesis as a stairstep, with the left parenthesis leading up towards you and the right leading down away from you. If you can project a complex formula that way, those parts of the formula that solve first should telescope themselves toward you, perhaps in breathtaking CinemaScope.

Put on your 3-D glasses now and stare closely at the preceding Cartesian distance formula. The two expressions `(x2 - x1)` and `(y2 - y1)` solve first because they appear to jut out furthest toward you. Geometrically speaking, these two expressions each represent the difference between coordinates along one axis. So the difference between the x-coordinates and the difference between the y-coordinates are solved separately. The solutions to those two expressions are squared and then added to each other in the part of the equation that solves next. *Squaring* a value, geometrically speaking, gives it form or dimension.

Along the final tier, the base platform of the equation, the sum of the two squares is then "rooted" once more back to a linear value, using the square-root function `SQR()`. This value is the distance between two points along a Cartesian grid, which is assigned to the double-precision variable `d#`.

The distance-finding formula can be used for the coordinate systems of any two points appearing on a map. Compare the VB/DOS version of the formula to the algebraic version that appears here:

$$D = \sqrt{(x_2-x_1)^2 + (y_2-y_1)^2}$$

Summary

Values are assigned to variables in VB/DOS by way of equations. In equations that arithmetically combine values, simple arithmetic functions are represented by operators, and complex functions are evaluated using intrinsic VB/DOS function terms. A VB/DOS equation is an expression of assignment and, therefore, it has only one term on the left side of the equation, that being the variable receiving the solution value to the equation. The solution is always a known value.

The simple arithmetic functions in VB/DOS equations have a natural order of evaluation that is based on the way terms are evaluated in algebra. This natural order can be overridden through the use of parentheses as delimiters in an equation. These delimiters reestablish the precedence of terms' evaluation; offsetting an expression in parentheses raises its precedence.

Review Questions

Answers to Review Questions appear in Appendix B.

1. Predict the solution values to the following equations:

   A. x = 4 + 6 ^ 2 / 5 * 6

   B. x = (4 + 6) ^ 2 / (5 * 6)

   C. x = (4 + 6 ^ 2) / 5 * 6

2. Convert the following algebraic expressions to VB/DOS equations:

   A. $v = \frac{1}{3} \pi r^2 h$ (where $\pi = 3.1415927$)

   B. $P = \frac{F}{(1 + i)^n}$

Review Exercise

Using 2D_DIST.MAK as a framework, revise the project so that it displays the distance between coordinates in three-dimensional space. As a guide, here are the formulas for distances in two-dimensional and three-dimensional space:

$$D_2 = \sqrt{(x_2 - x_1)^2 + (y_2 - y_1)^2}$$

$$D_3 = \sqrt{(x_2 - x_1)^2 + (y_2 - y_1)^2 + (z_2 - z_1)^2}$$

7

Logic

In this chapter, you dive directly into the heart of all computer operations, exploring those functions that result in true or false (–1 or 0) values. First, you explore how logic constitutes every part of a computer's operation, both numerically and mechanically. Next, you construct expressions of comparison that have solutions that are true or false values. You then learn about Boolean logical operations, separating "black" from "white" using truth tables.

Boolean Logic and Pinball

A *bit* can only be true (1 or ON) or false (0 or OFF).

The only function a computer performs is to compare two binary digits and render the state of that comparison as another binary digit. This is the basis of all logic. As stated in Chapter 2, the logic of a computer is such that it can interpret only states; more to the point, it evaluates the presence or absence of electrical current in its own integrated circuits. A binary state represents the presence or absence of current as the simplest digit within a computer—a bit. The term *bit* is short for *binary digit,* which is the elementary unit of value within a computer, which represents a logical state of true (1 or ON) or false (0 or OFF).

A current, electrically speaking, is a constant change or flux. The computer does not know this, however, because it looks only for the presence of this flux. This presence is treated as if it were a physical object in the machine.

Imagine the central processor of the computer as a converted upright pachinko machine, with slots for eight marbles positioned along a horizontal chute at the top of the machine. A lever is pulled that releases the marbles from the chute all at once. As they drop, they hit various pins, dampers, and levers, which flip up on one end as marbles strike them on the opposite end. As the levers move, they can cause other marbles to change course and roll in some other direction. When struck, some levers open gates through which other marbles can pass. Others open traps that cause marbles to become stuck. At the bottom of the machine is a series of collector slots that catch the marbles that survive the obstacle course.

Suppose the operator of this machine loads marbles into the top eight slots at random. She may fill some slots and leave others blank as she wishes. In other words, she selects the pattern in which the marbles are loaded into the chute. After she releases the marbles, she keeps track of which marbles were accumulated in the slots at the bottom. Assuming the following things:

The pachinko machine remains upright at all times

The machine is bolted to something firm

The marbles have identical mass, shape, and weight

The various levers and gates are all set to their starting positions

Gravity remains a constant

it should follow that for each particular random marble-loading pattern, there should be one predictable falling pattern as a result. To restate, as long as you maintain identical conditions for the machine, each loading pattern must result in only one falling pattern.

A *byte* is composed of eight bits.

Suppose the woman at the pachinko machine attributes a specific number to each pattern. There is an easy way to do this: Each slot in the loading chute either contains a marble or it doesn't; the same holds true for the accumulator at the bottom. Each slot can therefore be described by a binary digit—1 for presence and 0 for absence. The opening chute and closing slots can thus be described by eight-digit binary numbers—by bytes. In computing, a *byte* is the primary memory storage unit for all forms of data in a computer system and is composed of eight binary digits (bits).

Here's how each pattern is enumerated: You're familiar with the decimal system of numbers (also called base 10), in which digits from 0 through 9 each have their own place—or slot—in the number. The value of each place is described by increasing powers of 10 (10^0, 10^1, 10^2, 10^3, and so on). Thus, there is the *ones* place followed by the *tens* place, *hundreds* place, *thousands* place, and so on.

There are 10 digits in the decimal system, thus the alternate name *base 10*. In the binary number system, or base 2, there are two digits (0 and 1). Each place is described by increasing powers of 2 (2^0, 2^1, 2^2, 2^3, and so on). Thus, there is the *ones* place, followed by the *twos* place, *fours* place, *eights* place, and so on by powers of two.

Figure 7.1 depicts a potential marble-loading pattern, represented as an eight-digit binary number. The powers of two for each place are listed beside each slot so that you can better comprehend the arithmetic behind the conversion of a binary number to a decimal number.

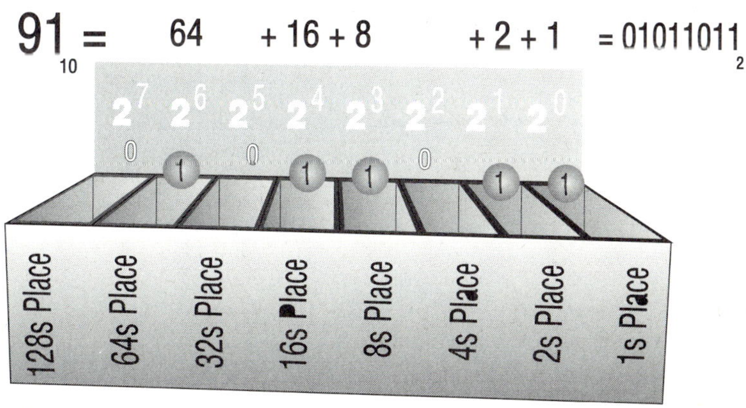

Figure 7.1. A somewhat overbearing view of a byte.

Suppose the marble-loader pays careful attention to the starting position of the devices—the pins, levers, gates, and traps—before loading marbles into the chute. She could give each setting pattern its own number as well. Conceivably, therefore, for each particular pattern of loaded marbles and for each particular pattern of device settings, there is one predictable fallout pattern of marbles in the bottom accumulator. Resetting the devices' loading positions by their pattern numbers would have a direct, perhaps measurable, effect on the outcome of the fallout pattern. The term for this type of device-resetting by pattern number is *programming.*

For all intents and purposes, you have just witnessed what a computer and its programmer actually do, except that the marbles are really electric currents, the various devices are actually logic gates, and both the loading chute and the fallout accumulator can be described as memory. An instruction in machine language is literally a device-setting pattern. The sequence of these patterns is a program. If you consider patterns to be instructions and you give each pattern a number corresponding logically to the construction of that pattern, every logical arrangement of those patterns yields a predictable result. This is how a computer works.

Higher-Level Comparisons

In Visual Basic for MS-DOS, the results you have in mind for your program are complex. The tools you use to achieve those results are complex as well. This complexity is necessary for you to be able to program with instructions like `IF-THEN` rather than `00101101`. Still, the most fundamental tools of programming—logical comparisons between two states—are at your disposal in the VB/DOS vernacular.

VB/DOS assumes true to be equal to –1 and false to be equal to 0.

Let's begin with arithmetic operators of comparison, which are used in expressions of comparison to derive logical results. Think of these operators as the high-level language version of pins, traps, gates, and levers. As you've learned, VB/DOS recognizes the values –1 and 0 to be true and false, respectively. An expression of comparison always results in a true or false value.

Table 7.1 shows VB/DOS' logical operators of comparison. Beside each operator is the logical solution to the expression `6` *`operator`* `3`.

Table 7.1. Comparison operators.

Operator	*Function*	6 operator 3
=	Equal to	0 (False)
>	Greater than	-1 (True)
<	Less than	0 (False)
>=	Greater than or equal to	-1 (True)
<=	Less than or equal to	0 (False)
<>	Not equal to	-1 (True)

You can swap the order of the symbols in both <= and >=; so you can state =< and => just as easily, and the VB/DOS interpreter won't mind.

Example

For the first example of comparison operators in action, go to the CLI in the Immediate window. Here's a sample conversation that evaluates the logic of b = 4. Again, the response from the Output window appears in bold monospace type.

```
b=4
?b=4
-1
```

It might seem odd at first to use the equality operator = in an expression that is not an equation, but you'll soon get used to it. After setting b to 4, I quizzed the CLI whether b = 4. The CLI's response was -1, which means that it is true.

If you quiz the CLI whether b < 3, you get the following response:

```
?b<3
 0
```

Zero is the response for false.

Understand that –1 and 0 are not just the CLI's way of saying *yes* and *no;* these are the evaluated values of the expression and are real numbers. Thus, this dialog:

```
?(b=4)-1
-2
```

Now, `-2` is not a symbol for *more true than true.* By subtracting 1 from –1—the value of `(b = 4)`—you made the expression part logical and part arithmetic. The parentheses in this expression are important. Look what would happen if you removed them:

```
?b=4-1
 0
```

The CLI evaluated `4 - 1` first, derived `3`, and compared `b` to `3` rather than to `4`. The traps were set in the wrong order.

While we're on the subject of order of evaluation, can truth be evaluated for the presence of truth? This bit of dialog proves that it can be done. Remember that `b = 4`.

```
?b=4=-1
-1
```

Yes, there can be two equality operators within a single expression, just as long as you realize it's not an equation. The value of `b = 4`, which you already know to be –1, was compared next to –1 for equality. Naturally, the result was nothing but the truth: `-1`. Suppose you change the order of evaluation, however, by placing the latter comparison in parentheses, as in:

```
?b=(4=-1)
 0
```

The first thing the CLI did this time was compare `4` to `-1` for equality. The result, of course, was `0`, which was compared to the value of `b` (`4`) for equality, and that too was false.

I realize that the preceding comparison of 4 to -1 was, to borrow a phrase, "stupid," and not something you'd ever want to write during the course of a real program. However, it did prove the point about the importance of ordinance in a compound logical comparison. If you ever used the expression `b = (c = d)` in a program, and `c = 4` and `d = -1`, the result of that expression would still be `0`, and this time it might not be so stupid. I simplified this expression by using real numbers so that you can understand the role of the operators in the instruction.

Making Logic Do Something

In VB/DOS, you use comparison expressions most frequently within the IF-THEN comparison clause statement. Here, an expression is evaluated for truth. A set of instructions following the term THEN is executed if the result of the expression is logically true. Alternatively, another set of instructions that may follow the term ELSE can be executed if the result of the expression is logically false.

Example

You'll study the construction of conditional clauses in greater detail in Chapter 15. For now, concentrate on the logical part of the IF-THEN statement. Assuming `b` is still equal to `4`, give a conditional instruction to the CLI:

```
if b=4 then ?"Works for me."
Works for me.
```

The bottom line is the CLI's response to the instruction on the top line. First, the interpreter evaluates the expression `b = 4` for truth. As you've already learned, the value of that expression at present is `-1`. The interpreter executes the instruction following the term `then` if the result of the expression is `-1`. This is proven by the following test instruction fed to the CLI:

```
if b=3 then ?"Probably won't see this line again."
```

The prediction is correct because, as you can see, the CLI did not make any visible response to this instruction.

Truth and/or Fiction

A *Boolean operator* compares one binary value to another.

The second category of logical operators in VB/DOS is *Boolean operators*. These are terms used to compare one binary value to another and to derive a single binary value as a result.

The purpose of Boolean operators is to evaluate expressions comparing two values that are already binary in nature. For instance, `-1 AND -1 = -1`, while `-1 AND 0 = 0`. Here, `AND` is the Boolean operator; it is capitalized where it appears in a paragraph in the remaining text to distinguish it from the everyday word "and." The result of the expression `x AND y` is true only if `x` is true *and* `y` is true; otherwise, the result is logically false.

Example

As an example, here is yet another dialog with the command-line interpreter:

```
x=3
y=5
?x=3 and y=5
-1
```

First, I seeded variables `x` and `y` with the nonbinary values `3` and `5`, respectively. On the third line is the compound logical comparison. Here, the values of `x = 3` and `y = 5` are obtained first. They are both `-1`, which satisfies the conditions for the `AND` comparison to equal `-1`, as printed on the fourth line by the CLI. In the preceding quizzing statement, it is important to leave spaces around the Boolean operator so that the interpreter won't confuse it with just another variable.

Example

Assuming you leave x and y as they are, you can apply the preceding compound logical expression in a conditional execution clause:

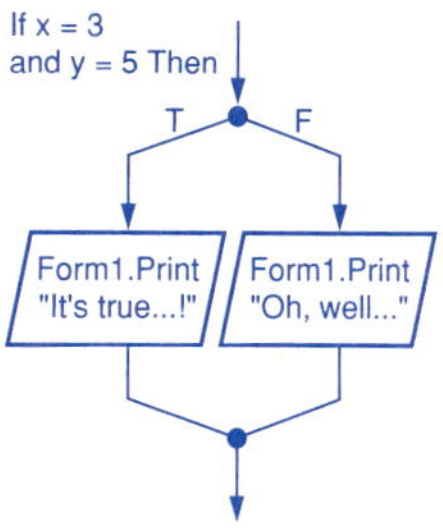


```
IF x = 3 AND y = 5 THEN
     Form1.PRINT "It's true!  It really is!"
ELSE
     Form1.PRINT "Oh, well, forget it."
END IF
```

The logical expression is evaluated and its result triggers the execution of one or the other set of instructions in the `IF-THEN` clause. `IF-THEN` really does not evaluate the expression. In truth, all it is looking for is a –1 or a 0. One way or the other, a logical expression simplifies to one of those two possible values. When that's done, `IF-THEN` takes off.

By introducing the Boolean operator `OR`, you now can have a logical expression that has a true result (–1) if one or the other value is true.

Example

As usual, the best way to test a function is through a dialog with the CLI:

```
x=4
y=10
?x=4 or y=9
-1
```

Obviously, the result can be true if one of the compared values is true. As a quick test, see if it works if both comparisons are true:

```
?x=4 or y=10
-1
```

The result is still true. The only way you can obtain a false value is if both comparisons are false:

```
?x=3 or y=9
 0
```

Example

A related Boolean operator XOR (exclusive-or) returns a true value if one or the other comparison evaluates true, but not both. In other words, the compared values can't match. Leave x = 4 and y = 10 for a moment and retry a few of the preceding evaluations, using XOR instead of OR.

```
?x=4 xor y=9
-1
?x=4 xor y=10
 0
?x=3 xor y=9
 0
```

Notice that when both comparisons evaluated true, the result of the XOR comparison was false. An exclusive-or comparison really does want one or the other to be true.

Example

Combining the ANDs and ORs and taking advantage of what you know about the usefulness of parentheses, examine a complex logical comparison, first using the CLI:

```
x=6
y=7
z=9
?(x=6 and y=3) or z=9
-1
?(x=6 or y=3) and z=9
-1
?(x=6 and y=3) or z=10
 0
```

The values within parentheses, as always, are evaluated first. The result of that comparison is itself compared using another Boolean operator to the expression outside the parentheses. When you integrate one of these compound comparison expressions into the source code sample you created a few pages back, you have the following:

```
IF (x = 6 AND y = 3) OR z = 9 THEN
     Form1.PRINT "It's true!  It really is!"
ELSE
     Form1.PRINT "Oh, well, forget it."
END IF
```

If the two compared values of a Boolean expression are not binary, the Boolean operators compare the bitwise values of each bit of both values in their respective places and render their results in the same place of the solution variable. In other words, the binary value of the third binary place in one variable (representing 23) is compared to the value in the third binary place in a second variable, with the binary result rendered in the third binary place of the solution to the expression.

Summary

Logic is the basis of all computing operations. In VB/DOS, logical operations are comparisons between two binary states, the result of which is rendered as a binary state. Logical operations can be compounded by means of further operators and the inclusion of parentheses; however, the result of the expression of logical comparison is still a binary state.

Review Questions

Answers to Review Questions appear in Appendix B.

Given x = 5, y = 9, and z = –1, assess the binary truth value of the following:

1. (x = 5)
2. (x < y)

3. ((x + z) >= y)
4. (x = 5) AND (x < y)
5. ((x < 5) AND (z < x)) OR (y = 9)
6. (x < 5) AND ((z < x) OR (y = 9))
7. ((x <= 5) AND (y = 3 ^ 3)) XOR z

8

Strings

In this chapter, you learn about string variables, which are containers for groupings of alphanumeric characters—letters, words, or entire sentences. You witness how alphanumeric contents of graphic controls are assigned to strings, using what appear to be arithmetic expressions. You then study how patterns of binary numbers form the patterns that comprise alphanumerics.

Next, you see how expressions are used to manipulate the contents of string variables, using the + arithmetic operator as well as intrinsic Visual Basic for MS-DOS functions. Finally, you see how properties of graphic objects in VB/DOS forms are treated as string variables.

Value Versus Content

Up to this point, you have learned about the manipulation of data in memory as values—numbers you can use in calculations or substitute for variables in formulas. A value is one way VB/DOS translates data. As you've seen, a byte of data is, at its lowest level, just a sequence of 1s and 0s. *Value* is, in essence, a higher interpretation of data, in the way that 81 is a higher interpretation of 01010001.

The other common way to interpret data is as text. This form of data in VB/DOS is assigned to string variables. A *string* is a sequence of any number of bytes that are interpreted jointly as text or alphanumeric characters.

A *string* is a sequence of alphanumeric characters.

A sequence of characters is assigned to a string variable with an expression of assignment, as in the following example:

```
a$ = "Q"
```

Assuming the variable `a$` wasn't declared beforehand, this statement creates it and assigns it the contents `Q`. A simple expression of assignment for a string variable is stated as an equation, using the following syntax:

```
variable$ = "alphanumerics"
```

The dollar sign (`$`) is used to distinguish string variables in the way the percentage sign (`%`) is used to distinguish integer variables.

> **NOTE:** The reason `$` was chosen so many years ago for strings is that it looks like an *S* without being one. The currency category for variables was created long after 1964. The `$` already had a job, so it couldn't be used to represent money. Thus, Microsoft chose the `@` character to distinguish currency variables.

In the preceding expression, the text to be assigned to the string variable is enclosed in quotation marks. These quotation marks do not become part of the string; they are merely used as delimiters to mark where the string begins and ends. The following are some valid string variable assignments:

```
x$ = "Valid."
alert$ = "RED"
full_name$ = "Hubert H. Humphrey"
sale_price$ = "359.95"
```

Using this syntax, any character can be assigned as part of a string variable, the sole exception being a quotation mark, which is reserved for marking the beginning and end of the string. The contents of `sale_price$` appear to be numeric. Like the three examples preceding it, however, the contents are actually textual. In other words, `sale_price$` is six bytes long, beginning with the character representation for 3, followed by that for 5, and so on.

Of ANSI, ASCII, and Other Such Acronyms

When I refer to *character representation,* I mean the pattern of bits in a byte that stands for an alphanumeric character. The decision of which pattern belongs to which character is not exactly arbitrary. If this decision were left to the individual manufacturers, however, you would be left with dozens of incompatible codes. Imagine what would happen if Microsoft's *Q* was Borland's *&*.

Some time ago, the American National Standards Institute (ANSI) devised a coding scheme for the most-used characters in computers and teletype machines. A subset of that code exists today as the American Standard Code for Information Interchange (ASCII, often pronounced *as'-key*). The ASCII code is the most widely used method for transmission and storage of alphanumeric data in a bitwise form within or between computers. "True" ASCII code represents numerically the most common 256 characters (letters, numbers, and symbols) shared between computers. Some computers' BIOS make their own additions to this code and still call it ASCII. Modern industry-standard (ISA) computers (such as yours) use what is called the IBM Extended Character Set, though even this set is referred to in VB/DOS by a function that was designed to pertain to true ASCII.

In the ASCII code, the letter *Q* is represented by the binary form of decimal value 81. Table 8.1 shows the word *quantum* as it appears in its binary form.

Notice that no consideration is made for place or value because you're not dealing with storing a number.

ASCII is a binary code like Morse Code. Both use two symbols interchangeably (*on* and *off,* or *dot* and *dash*) to create patterns that stand for characters. The trouble is, Morse Code was not meant for use with a computer. Although Morse Code is binary, its sequence of dots and dashes do not follow a binary pattern. If a dot was 0 and a dash was 1, for instance, the code for *E* (one dot alone) would be *0* and would fall first in line before the rest of the alphabet. Furthermore, Morse Code does not have a set number of symbols per character; ASCII uses a constant number of symbols per character—

eight. A listing of the ASCII character codes used by Microsoft with DOS and VB/DOS appears in Appendix A.

Table 8.1. The mechanics of *quantum*.

Alphanumeric Characters	*ANSI*	*Binary*
Q	81	01010001
U	85	01010101
A	65	01000001
N	78	01001110
T	84	01010100
U	85	01010101
M	77	01001101

Example

For the first example, I start a dialog with the VB/DOS Immediate window CLI.

```
quantum$="Niels Bohr"
?quantum$
Niels Bohr
```

Notice that the syntax of the `?` (`PRINT`) statement doesn't really change when referring to a string rather than a numeric variable. The expression of assignment (also known as the `LET` statement) is one of the few in which string variables and numeric variables are interchangeable. The CLI's response to the `?` on the bottom line is precisely the contents between the quotation marks in the assignment equation.

Example

Strings can also be used in place of values in equations that appear to involve addition, as shown in the following dialog:

```
first_name$="Niels"
last_name$="Bohr"
full_name$=first_name$+" "+last_name$
?full_name$
Niels Bohr
```

Concatenation is the process of joining strings together.

The third line of the preceding dialog constitutes a formula that consists of three elements—two string variables and an explicit string consisting of one space to separate the first name from the last name. The + operator here is used for *concatenation*—joining strings together. This is the only operator symbol allowed in string variable formulas. The minus sign doesn't work here because it wouldn't be reasonable to try to "subtract" the contents `Bohr` from `Niels`.

Example

Certainly the most common practical use of string variables is as containers for people's names and vital information. This test involves the skeleton of a record-entry system. A VB/DOS form acts as the receiver for the individual elements of each person's vital information. A recordkeeping system might have to sort each record by the person's last name; when you print these names to envelopes, however, the first name should come before the last name. Such a system that maintains a database, by the formal definition, would need to be capable of resituating elements of data, such as the parts of a person's name, in a list or reference.

Figure 8.1 is a picture of the `NameForm`, which is the form for the skeletal recordkeeping system. For now, examine one particular procedure from this form, which is shown in Figure 8.1.

Use Figure 8.1 and the following table to construct the `NameForm` form. Be sure to adjust the properties of objects as needed.

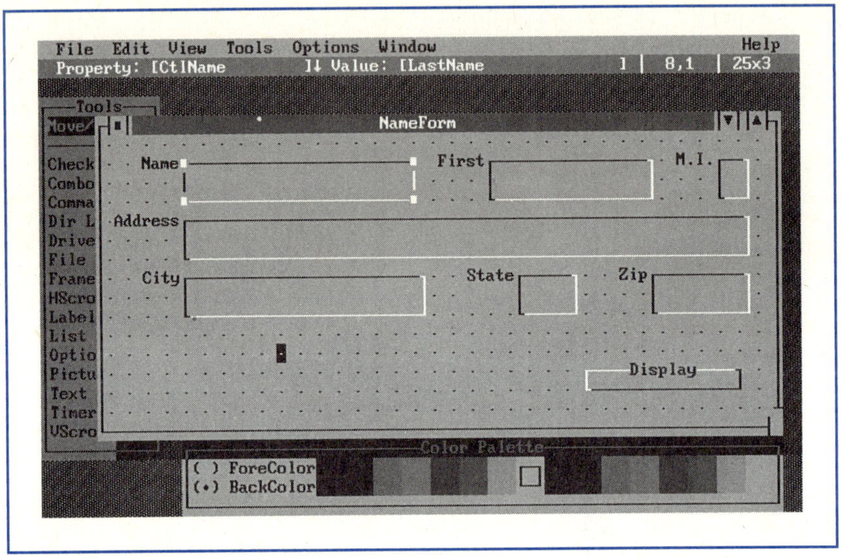

Figure 8.1. The rudimentary NameForm.

Name-Only Record-Entry System

Project name: NAMEFORM.MAK
Constituent file: NAMEFORM.FRM

Object type	*Property*	*Setting*
Form	`.Left`	`6`
	`.Top`	`4`
	`.Caption`	`NameForm`
Text box	`.Left`	`960`
	`.CtlName`	`LastName`
	`.Text`	(blank)
Text box	`.Left`	`4440`
	`.Top`	`360`
	`.CtlName`	`FirstName`
	`.Text`	(blank)

Object type	*Property*	*Setting*
Text box	`.Left`	`7080`
	`.Top`	`360`
	`.CtlName`	`MidInit`
	`.Text`	(blank)
Text box	`.Left`	`960`
	`.Top`	`960`
	`.CtlName`	`Address`
	`.Text`	(blank)
Text box	`.Left`	`960`
	`.Top`	`1560`
	`.CtlName`	`City`
	`.Text`	(blank)
Text box	`.Left`	`4800`
	`.Top`	`1560`
	`.CtlName`	`State`
	`.Text`	(blank)
Text box	`.Left`	`6240`
	`.Top`	`1560`
	`.CtlName`	`Zip`
	`.Text`	(blank)
Label	`.Left`	`360`
	`.Top`	`240`
	`.Caption`	`Name`
	`.Alignment`	`0 - Right Justify`
Label	`.Left`	`3960`
	`.Top`	`240`
	`.Caption`	`First`
	`.Alignment`	`0 - Right Justify`
Label	`.Left`	`6600`
	`.Top`	`240`
	`.Caption`	`M.I.`
	`.Alignment`	`0 - Right Justify`

continues

Object type	*Property*	*Setting*
Label	`.Left`	`120`
	`.Top`	`840`
	`.Caption`	`Address`
	`.Alignment`	`0 - Right Justify`
Label	`.Left`	`360`
	`.Top`	`1440`
	`.Caption`	`City`
	`.Alignment`	`0 - Right Justify`
Label	`.Left`	`4200`
	`.Top`	`1440`
	`.Caption`	`State`
	`.Alignment`	`0 - Right Justify`
Label	`.Left`	`5760`
	`.Top`	`1440`
	`.Caption`	`Zip`
	`.Alignment`	`0 - Right Justify`
Button	`.Left`	`960`
	`.Top`	`2160`
	`.CtlName`	`Display`
	`.Caption`	`Display`

After entering the contents from the preceding table into the form, switch from Form Designer to the Code Editor by selecting Event Procedures from the **E**dit menu. Respond to the `Exit to Programming Environment?` dialog box by clicking OK. The dialog that follows lets you know the form file has changed. Tell Form Designer you want to save the form file by clicking Yes. If you haven't yet given the form a name, another dialog box appears. In this case, type `NAMEFORM.FRM` within the text line marked `Filename:` and click OK. Form Designer is exited, and the Code Editor window appears. Figure 8.2 shows the resulting dialog box.

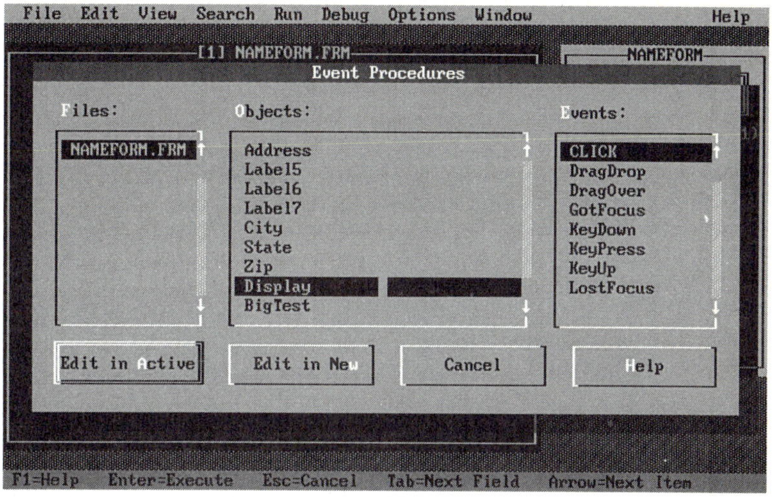

Figure 8.2. The Event Procedures dialog box.

This application consists of the only one file it will ever require, NAMEFORM.FRM. If you click around in the Objects list, you'll note the list of events associated with each object changes. The act of actually typing text into an object such as `LastName` or `Address` is not really an event; however, `_GotFocus` is an event that occurs whenever the user clicks its antecedent text box or presses Tab until the cursor block rests within that box.

NOTE: The events listed in the Event Procedures choice box are not presented with preceding underscore (_) characters, although event terms in this book are typeset with such characters. This is to help distinguish certain keywords as events because only event terms in VB/DOS are separated from antecedent graphic objects by an underscore character.

The only event within the `NameForm` test application that has any real meaning for it at the moment is the act of clicking the Display command button. The program collects the data from the form when this button is clicked and, within a separate dialog box, displays that data as it might appear on an envelope label. The event this application is most interested in, therefore, is `Display_Click`. The most convenient way to structure this application is to write the data processing instructions within the event procedure `SUB Display_Click ()`.

If you entered each graphic object in the order in which it is presented (unless you altered the `.TabStop` properties for any of the graphic objects in the form, to be discussed later), then `Display` is the very last item in the Objects list. To reach it, drag the scroll box for that list all the way to the bottom. To bring up the code frame for this event procedure, click `Display` once. When the Events list changes for that object, click once on `Click` at the top of that list. Next, click `Edit in Active` to place the event procedure frame within the active code window `[1]`. You exit the Event Procedures choice box, and the code window appears with the first and last instructions in the procedure already entered in.

Now edit the procedure window so that it reads the following:

```
SUB Display_Click ()
  FullName$ = FirstName.Text + " " + MidInit.Text + " " +
    LastName.Text
  StreetAddress$ = Address.Text
  Residence$ = City.Text + ", " + State.Text + "  " +
    Zip.Text
  Next_Line$ = CHR$(13) + CHR$(10)
  Envelope$ = FullName$ + Next_Line$ + StreetAddress$ +
    Next_Line$ + Residence$
  MSGBOX Envelope$
END SUB
```

Here is the procedure rephrased as pseudocode:

Procedure for clicking the Display button:
The person's full name is the equivalent of his first name plus a space, plus his middle initial plus a space, plus his last name.
Take his street address out of the address box.
The location where the person lives is phrased as the city plus a comma and space, plus the state plus two spaces, plus the ZIP code.

The code for "next line please" is a carriage-return character plus a line-feed character.
The name that appears on the envelope is the equivalent of the full name, next line please, his street address, next line please, plus the locale in which he lives.
Place this data into a message box.
End of procedure.

The property `.Text` is applied to each text box in the form. Therefore, when you refer to the contents of a text box, the name of the box is stated first, followed by `.Text`. Think of this reference as pulling the text that the user typed from the form without placing it in a variable. Although considered a reference to an element of text in formulas, object properties such as `FirstName.Text` are not considered string variables; so for many statements, the `.Text` property of an object will not suffice when an explicit string variable is required.

In the first line following the `SUB` statement, a string variable `FullName$` is created that contains the three parts of a person's name—assuming that all people have middle initials. These parts are added using the `+` concatenation operator. Notice, however, that I've separated the elements with `" "` spaces. There is exactly one space between the quotation marks, so the words in the string are set apart from each other. Concatenated strings do not space themselves, and for good reason. Suppose you had `part1$ = "Washi"` and `part2$ = "ngton"` in the course of a procedure. If you were to join the two with `+`, you would not want an automatic space between them. Therefore, when you need a space, VB/DOS has you insert it yourself.

In `SUB Display_Click ()`, the variable `Residence$` is created on the fourth line. Notice that a comma and space together are used to separate the city from the state. As a result, you don't have to make a comma part of every `City` *datum* (unit of data) to make the address appear properly in print.

On the fifth line, `Next_Line$` is created purely as a signal string to tell the interpreter to invoke the carriage return (with `CHR$(13)`) and to feed one line down (with `CHR$(10)`). The term `CHR$()` is an intrinsic VB/DOS function that returns the specific ANSI-code character having the number that falls between the parentheses. For example, `CHR$(81)` returns the letter *Q* and `CHR$(51)` returns the digit 3. `CHR$()` follows the standard intrinsic function syntax *`function(expression)`*.

Control characters are handled in memory like regular letters and numbers although their purpose is—or rather, was—to send some signal to the computer, such as to delete the previous character or end the current line. Control characters comprise part of both the ANSI and ASCII codes, though in much of the DOS character set (also called the "IBM Extended Character Set") what were originally control characters were instead utilized as graphics characters, such as those that form the button borders for VB/DOS buttons and the happy-face character for one of VB/DOS' desktop wallpaper backgrounds.

> **NOTE:** Carriage returns (`CHR$(13)`) and line feeds (`CHR$(10)`) work well when displaying text within VB/DOS message boxes and picture boxes. These special characters by default do not work within text boxes; instead, they generate, respectively, a sixteenth note and a black option dot, which act neither as carriage returns nor line feeds. This problem can be eliminated within a text box by setting its `.MultiLine` property to True. Also, within a picture box, `CHR$(10)` and `CHR$(13)` appear to perform the same purpose. Within a text box whose `.MultiLine` property is True, however, both characters are necessary for text to proceed down to the beginning of the next line.

In `SUB Display_Click ()`, the next-to-last line `MSGBOX Envelope$` invokes a message box that displays the contents of `Envelope$`. A *message box* is a small window that contains just a message, often with an accompanying symbol such as a big exclamation point or question mark, and one OK button. In the preceding procedure, `Envelope$` is created in the line above the `MSGBOX` line by joining all three lines of the person's formal address and separating those lines with `Next_Line$`—the special string that forces the carriage return with the line feed.

The results of this first effort at concatenation are shown in Figures 8.3 and 8.4. Figure 8.3 shows the fully-filled form, and Figure 8.4 displays the contents of this form reorganized as the information would appear printed on an envelope. This application is not extremely functional just yet; through the course of this book, however, you will add functionality to it.

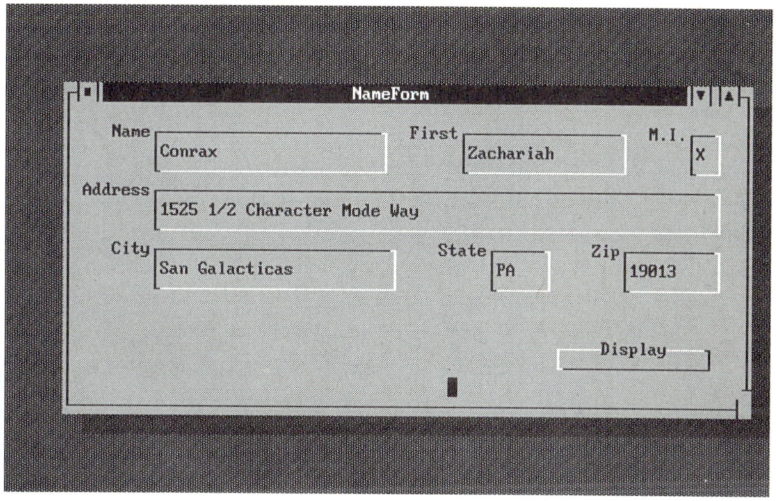

Figure 8.3. NameForm before processing.

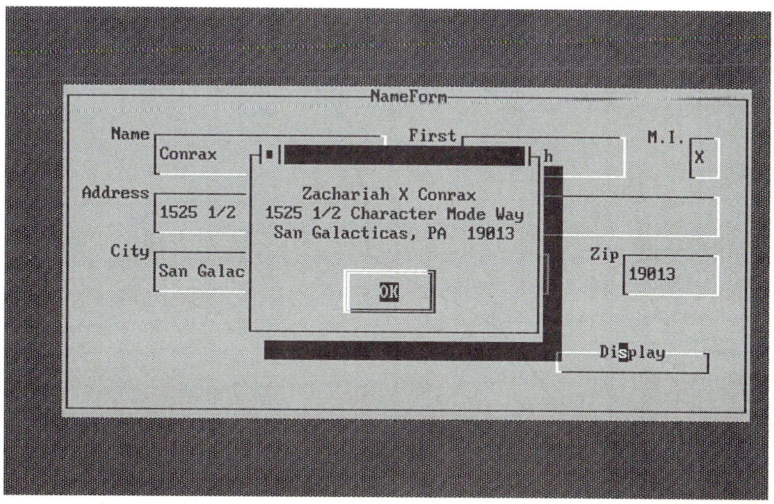

Figure 8.4. NameForm after processing.

Summary

A string is a group of alphanumeric characters that are to be considered as text rather than values. Characters in the computer are patterns that have code called ANSI or ASCII code. This code consists of logically derived bitwise patterns for the most necessary 256 characters in standard communication between computers. Each character in this code is stored in one byte.

A string variable is an arbitrarily named term used to represent text groupings in an expression. The contents of such a variable are set with an equation, in which the contents to be assigned to the variable are enclosed in quotation marks. String variables are identified within source code by the symbol `$`, which is not used here to represent currency. Strings can be joined in an expression with the `+` concatenation operator. Textual properties from user input forms can be assigned to string variables. Names chosen for string variables must not conflict with names chosen for any other string or numeric variables within the same context of the source code.

Review Questions

Answers to Review Questions appear in Appendix B.

Figure 8.5 shows the form from the `NameForm` procedure in this chapter, filled with vital information for a fictitious person (don't attempt to write to this person for assistance).

Using the property table and the procedure `SUB Display_Click ()` printed in this chapter as a guide, determine the contents of the following:

1. `LastName.Text`
2. `Zip.Text`
3. `FirstName.Text + LastName.Text`
4. `StreetAddress$`
5. `Residence$`
6. `Envelope$`

7. `FullName$ + Next_Line$ + Next_Line$ + Residence$`

8. `"Mr. or Ms. " + FullName$`

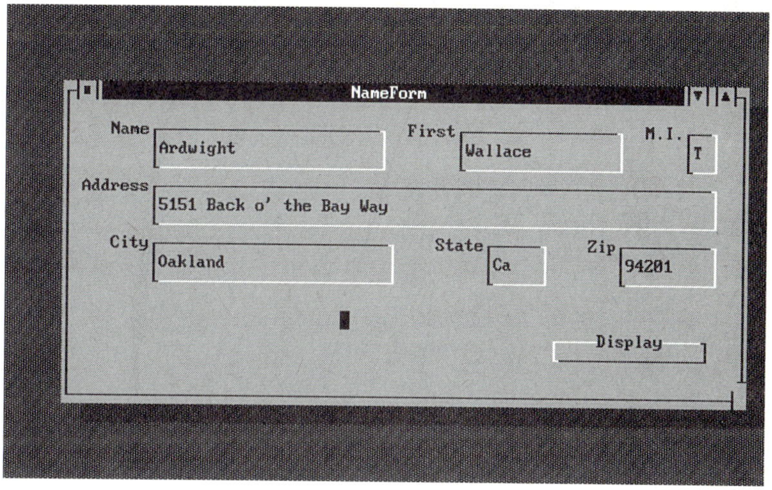

Figure 8.5. NameForm filled with fictitious information.

Review Exercise

Using the `NameForm` example program as a guide, modify the line that prints the person's name so that the last name is printed first and is separated from the first name by a comma.

9

Arrays

In this chapter, you will see how Visual Basic for MS-DOS processes lists of items in the form of arrays. First, you experiment with generating simple item-by-item lists. You then progress to processing values that reside in two-dimensional tables.

The Purpose of Arrays

An *array* is a list of related values that are referred to by a common term.

In almost every VB/DOS application you write, you find yourself composing a formula or procedure that processes a list of values that each have the same purpose or fulfill the same role individually in a formula. For instance, you might have a formula that returns a value for *a1* and then at some other time for *a2* and *a3*. Or you may compose a record-keeping routine that tells the interpreter how and where to print the last name, the first name, and the middle initial—and there will certainly be more than one name on this list. The primary tool you use for referring to lists of values that are somehow related is the *array variable.*

As an example, one array variable may contain the names of the 50 United States in alphabetical order. You could then have `us$(1) = "Alabama"`, `us$(2) = "Alaska"`, `us$(3) = "Arizona"`, and so on until `us$(50) = "Wyoming"`. Another procedure in the program might be used to figure the state sales tax on an item printed on an invoice for a company that does business in all 50 states. Instead of having 50 forms, you can program one form that contains "holes" for any state's sales tax. The print line might appear as follows:

```
Form7.PRINT us$(state); " State sales tax:",tax_pcnt(state)
```

In effect, what you're telling the interpreter to do is this:

Print to `Form7` *the name of the state having its number currently kept by the variable state, followed immediately by the words "State sales tax:," followed thereafter by a tab and then that state's sales tax value.*

A *subscript* is the position within an array that holds a particular value.

Suppose you want to put the tax percentage for Maine on this line. Maine, on the alphabetical list, is the 19th state; at some point in the program the value of the variable state would be set to 19. The value 19 becomes important because it now stands for Maine in any array variable within this program that pertains to the states. It is as if 19 were equal to Maine. Of course, it can't be in the logical sense although it can in the symbolic sense. The number 19 is now representative of Maine. Representation in this manner is part of the role of an array variable's subscript. A *subscript* is an integral value or variable within an array variable that represents the place or position of a value in the array's list or table.

You're Traveling into Another Dimension

A standard variable in VB/DOS with one associated value can be informally declared by its mere invocation in a formula. As you've seen, you can write `state = 19` and, by writing `state` for the first time, you've made that variable exist for the sake of the program. An array variable, on the other hand, cannot be invoked in this manner. Obviously, you couldn't have a statement `us$(19) = "Maine"` as the first instance of `us$()` in a program and expect the interpreter to know that you want 50 of these things.

BASIC has always handled the matter of declaring array variables with the `DIM` statement. `DIM` does not refer here to a low level of light, but rather it is short for *dimension*. In the vernacular of BASIC, the word *dimension* has been used rather liberally—and geometrically, for that matter—as a verb. As a result, to *dimension a variable* is to declare an array and thus make a unit into a list the way you make a point into a line. In geometry, by drawing a line and understanding it as a sequence of points, you give that line dimension; likewise, extending that line into a plane gives it another dimension. Dimensioning is therefore used analogously in VB/DOS to add a sequential level to a variable.

The conventional syntax and definition for the `DIM` statement follows.

DIM **Statement**

Simple one-dimensional syntax:

```
DIM variable(integer)
```

Multivariable one-dimensional array syntax:

```
DIM [SHARED] variable1(integer)[, variable2(integer)
   [AS type]...variable60(integer)][AS type]
```

Complex two-dimensional syntax with specified subscript ranges and declared types:

```
DIM [SHARED] variable1(integer [TO integer]
[,integer [TO integer]])[AS type][, variable2
(integer [TO integer][,integer [TO integer]])
[AS type],...variable60(integer [TO integer]
[,integer [TO integer]])[AS type]]
```

The `DIM` statement declares at least one array *variable* to be a list or table of values or string contents that are each addressable by number. This number is an *integer* (whole number) and is used as an address to represent the place of a datum in the list. A one-dimensional array, or *list*, is generally declared using one integer (or integral expression) between the parentheses. This integer represents the highest address in the list. Optionally, a one-dimensional array can be declared using two integers, which represent the lowest and highest addresses, respectively, in the list and are separated by the term TO.

A two-dimensional array, or *table,* is declared using two integers between the parentheses, separated by a comma. These integers represent the references, or *axes,* of the table, as in a table's x- and y-axes. Both integers represent the highest address along their respective axes, unless the term TO is used to distinguish the lowest and highest addresses along either or both axes. A three-dimensional array, or three-axis table, is declared in the same fashion, using three sets of integers separated by commas.

Unless otherwise specified, a variable bearing no type symbol is dimensioned as single-precision floating-point. A type can be established for each variable in the dimension list either by attaching a type symbol to the variable or by stating the type as an optional term following the word *As.* You can declare up to 60 variables within a DIM statement, for up to 10 dimensions per variable.

When the DIM statement appears on the module level (that is, outside of a procedure) and the term SHARED is included as a qualifier, this instructs the interpreter to apply all dimensioned variables within the instruction to every procedure within the module. The value of any variable, single-value or array, dimensioned with DIM SHARED at module level is therefore maintained as program control passes between procedures and module-level code within that module.

When the DIM statement appears within a SUB or FUNCTION procedure without any qualifying terms, this instructs the interpreter to apply all dimensioned variables within the instruction only to the procedure containing the DIM statement. When DIM appears within a procedure with the qualifier SHARED, this instructs the interpreter to apply the specified variables to that procedure, giving them the values or contents of variables with the same names informally declared at the modular level. Further information on variable scope appears in Chapter 12, "Value Management."

Example

For the first example, here's how an array for the 50 states would be dimensioned:

```
DIM us$(50)
```

The minimum address in any array dimensioned in this way is (0); consequently, the preceding statement makes room for 51 states (reserving room, perhaps, for Puerto Rico). Still, it might not make sense at times to refer to states 0 through 49, or to Alabama as the 0th State (it's doubtful that Alabama would appreciate that distinction, anyway). You may choose simply to allocate strings for addresses 1 through 50 and leave address 0 blank.

Example

Here's a simple two-dimensional array being dimensioned:

```
DIM chessboard%(8,8)
```

This statement would be useful within a chess program, perhaps to establish what piece rests on the board at any one time. The array variable `chessboard%` is integral and would symbolize the type of piece that rests on a specifically addressed square. A 0 value would represent an open square; likewise, 1 would represent a pawn, 2 a rook, and so on. At opening position with the upper-left corner square considered to be (0,0) (assuming that you played white and the x-axis (file) is to be represented first and the y-axis (rank), second), `chessboard%(4,8)` would be your white queen.

Example

Here's a compound declaration for a set of array variables I have found myself dimensioning often in my programming career—some might say too often:

```
DIM klingons(299), starfleet$(15), sector_map(7,7)
  AS INTEGER
```

Perhaps the two most well-known games ever originated in BASIC (or so says legend) are both called *Star Trek*, after the original television series. One version is played on an eight-by-eight grid that is sometimes called a *short range sensor map* or a *sector map*. There are several of these maps in the game—generally 64.

In the example dimensioning, I pay closer attention to the type of variable being declared, as well as the number of units. The variable `klingons` may represent the current energy level given the maximum number of enemy ships in the game—300 of them, numbered 0 through 299. When a ship's energy level reaches 0, it's considered conquered. The energy level may have fractional value. So, knowing that the default setting for a dimensioned array variable is single-precision floating-point—just what I want—I added no extra symbols or type declarations to `klingons`.

The string array `starfleet$` can contain the names of 16 (numbered 0 through 15) friendly starships in the game. The two-dimensional integer array `sector_map` is an eight-by-eight grid (again, remember the number system starts with 0) within which the identities of the individual game pieces (friendly ship, enemy ship, star, planet) are represented. This time I used the keyphrase `AS INTEGER` to specify that I wanted whole numbers only; there's no need to have a variable that has a default value that is roughly 0.00000000 when 0 does just as well. I could have dimensioned `sector_map%` instead. Using `AS INTEGER`, however, you can refer to `sector_map` without the accompanying symbol and still have it represent an integral value.

Controlling Arrays

Consider some future possibilities for the `NameForm` application. Suppose that at some future date you have this program save and load its data as disk files. When reloading a saved file into memory, you want the contents of the old file to be erased. This can be accomplished with the `ERASE` statement.

ERASE **Statement**

Syntax:

```
ERASE array[, array...]
```

The ERASE statement clears the values and contents of all specified arrays in the statement. Parentheses are not used in the specification. If a specified array being erased is static, then the upper and lower bounds of the array are not affected. If a specified array being erased is dynamic, the upper and lower bounds of that array are abolished and may later be redimensioned.

When referring to a *static array,* you mean a standard (default) array variable whose upper and lower bounds are fixed at the time the array is dimensioned.

Example

Suppose you're writing the routine in the NameForm application for loading a new file into memory. Here's how the ERASE statement for that application would appear:

```
ERASE LstName$, FrstName$, MdInit$, Adress$, Cty$,
  Stat$, Zp$
```

Now the contents are clear for entry of new data.

Next, suppose you don't want every file you create to be exactly 1,000 records long. VB/DOS has provisions for allocating array variables dynamically; in other words, it has ways for the program itself to change the variables' sizes on demand.

REDIM **Statement**

Simple syntax:

```
REDIM variable(integer)
```

Complex syntax:

```
REDIM [SHARED] [PRESERVE] variable1(integer
  [TO integer][,integer [TO integer]])[AS type]
  [, variable2(integer [TO integer][,integer
  [TO integer]])[AS type],...variable60(integer
  [TO integer][,integer [TO integer]])[AS type]]
```

The `REDIM` statement is used to declare a list of array variables to be dynamic arrays, capable of having their upper and lower bounds as well as their contents cleared at any time during program execution. If an array variable specified within the `REDIM` statement has not been dimensioned previously using `DIM` or `REDIM`, then the `REDIM` statement performs the initial declaration of that array variable, in the same manner as the `DIM` statement only for dynamic allocation. If an array variable specified by `REDIM` has already been dimensioned for dynamic allocation using `DIM variable()` or `REDIM`, then the statement may be used to clear or respecify the upper and lower bounds of the array, using the same general syntax as the `DIM` statement.

If the term `SHARED` is stated when `REDIM` appears within the module-level code of a module, then the scope of the redimensioned variables will apply to all procedures contained within that module. If the term `PRESERVE` is stated and if `ERASE` has not been invoked, the previous contents of the array are preserved as much as possible. If the upper or lower boundaries have been changed, certain cells within the preserved array may lose their contents.

The size of a *dynamic array* may be changed on demand.

Dynamic allocation allows the VB/DOS application to declare an array of any length required at the time by the program. Redeclaration of the variables specified by the `REDIM` statement is possible in three cases:

1. If the array variables are first allocated dynamically, with the statement `DIM variable()` in precisely this syntax, without any expression specified within the parentheses.

2. If the array variables are first allocated dynamically, with the statement `REDIM` *`variable(bounds)`*, in which case the *bounds*, whatever they may have been set to be initially, are dropped during redimensioning.
3. If the default declaration type of the interpreter has been changed to dynamic using the `$DYNAMIC` metacommand, described in Chapter 12, "Value Management."

Example

Suppose you implement within the NameForm application a routine that allocates as many units for each array variable as there are records within the file being loaded into memory. This way there aren't several null and void records residing in memory following the last one loaded. Within the general module, you would first need to declare the arrays in this manner:

```
DIM LstName$(), FrstName$(), MdInit$(), Adress$(),
  Cty$(), Stat$(), Zp$()
```

When the file is loaded into memory, the first value recognized is a value that sets the length, in records, of the entire file. This value is then assigned to the variable FileLength. The loading procedure would then contain the following statement:

```
REDIM LstName$(FileLength), FrstName$(FileLength),
  MdInit$(FileLength), Adress$(FileLength),
    Cty$(FileLength), Stat$(FileLength), Zp$(FileLength)
```

As a result, each array in the program would be exactly as long as the loaded file.

By default, arrays are dimensioned by the VB/DOS interpreter to be *static*.

Establishing Bounds

One problem that might come up when you are dimensioning an array variable for a variable amount, or when you are dimensioning an array dynamically, is that a procedure may not know at any one time just where the array starts and ends. Conventionally, when a list array is dimensioned, one integer is specified within the parentheses, representing the upper limits or *bounds* of the array. The lower bounds are assumed to be 0, or 1 if the statement `OPTION BASE 1` appears at the top of the general or global module. Using the term `AS`, two integers are declared between the parentheses, which specify both the upper and lower bounds of the array. If you allow both bounds to be variables themselves, the possibility of losing track of that array doubles.

So that a procedure might be reminded how big the arrays are, VB/DOS provides you with two functions suited to the purpose: `LBOUND()` and `UBOUND()`.

`LBOUND()` — **Function**

Syntax:

```
variable% = LBOUND(array[, dimension])
```

`UBOUND()` — **Function**

Syntax:

```
variable% = UBOUND(array[, dimension])
```

These two functions return the lower and upper bounds, respectively, of the specified array. If the array is multidimensional, to return the bounds for a dimensional level, the number of that level is specified as the second parameter of the function. The name of each array is stated without parentheses.

Example

Using the existing NameForm program, the following function would return the value 1,000 in the variable FileMax:

```
FileMax = UBound(LastName$)
```

Summary

An array is a list or table of values or text. In VB/DOS, arrays are referred to through the use of array variables, which contain integral subscripts enclosed in parentheses. Each subscript in an array variable acts as the address for a value or string contained within the array. Each subscript in an array variable gives that array an added dimension, or an added axis of a table.

When an array is dimensioned using the DIM statement, it is given upper bounds, or the address of the highest element in the array. The lower bounds are by default assumed to be 0, unless lower and upper bounds have been specified in the dimension statement using the TO term. The type of a variable can also be declared using DIM paired with the AS term. The REDIM statement may be used to allocate dynamic arrays, whose upper and lower bounds can be changed on demand. You may also use REDIM to change the specifications of an array that has been allocated dynamically using DIM with empty parameters. The ERASE statement clears the contents of a dimensioned array without changing its dimensions or type. Upper and lower bounds of a dimensioned array can be returned using the UBOUND() and LBOUND() functions, respectively.

Review Questions

Answers to Review Questions appear in Appendix B.

1. Using what you know about the structure and dimensioning of array variables, and using the first example as a guide, what would be the contents of the variable us$(27)?

2. In the second example, assuming you are playing black, what piece occupies the square that has its value represented by chessboard%(6,8)?

3. Assume that the general procedure of your form contains the statement `DIM GridValue(255, 400 To 1200)`. If `GridHigh = LBOUND(GridValue, 2)`, what is the value of `GridHigh`?

4. Which of the following three valid statements allocates the dynamic array?

   A. `DIM Aspen AS DOUBLE`

   B. `DIM Aspen() AS DOUBLE`

   C. `DIM Aspen(30) AS DOUBLE`

Review Exercise

Write just the procedure for the `NameForm` application that would accept numeric input from a text box and interpret this number to be the upper bounds of all the array variables used in the program, assuming they were dimensioned dynamically. Have the procedure redimension the array to the upper bounds specified when you click a button. If possible, reconfigure the right scroll bar so that the lowermost point of its thumb represents the upper bounds of the array.

10

Number Systems

In this chapter, you are given further insight into how a computer counts, thus becoming reacquainted with the number systems of mathematics. You then construct an application that utilizes the primary principles of number systems to convert any decimal number to a number system from base 2 to base 36.

Touching Base

You normally count using the *decimal*, or base 10, numeral system.

The reason the common system of counting is called *decimal* is because *deci-* is a Greek prefix meaning *ten.* Some people have a tendency to call fractional values *decimal numbers,* perhaps only because such numbers force you to use the *decimal point* to divide the whole-number side of the number from the fractional side.

The number *1495* is a decimal number because you trust it to be written in base 10. At least you assume it is a decimal number because there is nothing to tell you otherwise. You have a natural tendency to trust numbers for what (you think) they are. Unfortunately, as you become a programmer, you start to lose some of that trust, replacing it with a sort of natural, rational skepticism which, if not controlled carefully, can creep into your entire way of thinking. When you regulate your skepticism, however, you'll be more able to detect how something or some system—mechanical or interpersonal—works and operates, just from observation and logical deduction.

To understand how computers count is to understand the inspiration behind their invention. The concept of modern computing began to take shape in 1854, when British mathematician George Boole wrote a treatise called *Investigation of the Laws of Thought.* In this work, Boole attempted to equate the sciences of mathematics and psychology by theorizing that strictly binary logical processes may be the primary constituents of all reasoning in the human mind. Boole believed—at least at that time—that absolutely all thought could be *catabolized* (broken down) into comparisons of one binary state to another. It is for him that Boolean logic is named.

Charles Babbage generally receives credit for inventing the mechanism of the computer, but the concept was actually brought forth, in large part, by a Hungarian physicist named John von Neumann. In the late 1930s, von Neumann studied Boole's works thoroughly and, employing a natural skepticism for which the world will be forever thankful, bent Boole's logic so that it applied not to mental processes but to *physical* processes—as in quantum physics and mechanics. Along the way, von Neumann discovered that sequences of electrical currents—as you learned in Chapter 7—can replace mechanical devices such as wheels and levers in a calculation mechanism. The first stored-program computers, for precisely that reason, were called *von Neumann machines.*

Without question, John von Neumann was one of the masters of logical analysis and proofs. One of the things he managed to "prove," using the very types of logic you're starting to deal with now, is that there is no common, everyday world at all—that "ordinary" objects do not exist by ordinary definition. To some extent, von Neumann proved that you as an individual *create* everything you see just by thinking about it, or by being conscious of it. In other words, the world in which you live is in great measure created within your own mind and soul. Should you ever want to read von Neumann's proof, it appears in his 1932 book *The Mathematical Foundations of Quantum Mechanics (Die Mathematische Grundlagen der Quantenmechanik).*

If you are (or will be) a good mathematician or programmer, you may at some time, in the midst of a daydream, start disproving the existence of anything and everything. Certainly the only thing that changes by doing so is your perspective. The world continues to exist, no matter how you choose to define *existence.* When you see some principle proven mathematically, yet you still wholeheartedly disagree with it, even if you're the creator of it you begin to realize that belief—or faith, if you prefer—is actually somewhat stronger than proof. If you realize that, however, you fall right into von Neumann's trap.

There's a Place for Us

This section on places, bases, and powers may cover old ground from your point of view. If it does, I beg your indulgence for just a few pages. One of the things you rely on in the everyday world is the ability to count and to know what a number means when you see it. When you write 1495, you expect the number to mean *one thousand four hundred and ninety-five.* If this number is written in base 16, however, that isn't what this number means. The 9 is no longer in the tens place but is instead in the sixteens place.

A *bit* (binary digit) is a single binary state within a computer, which can be described as either on (1) or off (0).

Computers have a difficult time with decimal, or base 10, numbers because computers are naturally binary and have an easier time dealing with anything that is a factor or multiple of 2. Computers have an easier time with base 16, or *hexadecimal,* numbers because 16 factors out to *2 times 2 times 2 times 2.* A computer can easily interpret anything you can describe as a power of 2. The number 10 factors out to *5 times 2* and stops there because 5 is a prime number. Computers, at their heart, interpolate (arithmetically interpret) only two states—0 and 1—so 5 is as much a mystery to a computer as a 10-dimensional universe would be to you.

The number 5 is best represented within a computer as a combination of three binary states—three being the number of binary digits, or *bits,* required to represent 5.

When written in base 2, or binary, 5 appears as 101. In other words, there's a 1 in the fours place and a 1 in the ones place. What determines the place in any number system is the base of that number system, raised to the number of the place counting from the right toward the left, starting with the zeroth place. Table 10.1 demonstrates this principle in action using the number 1495 (base 10). The \ operator used in Table 10.1 is similar to the regular division (/) operator, but returns an integer without any fractional remainder.

Table 10.1. Finding your place in the world.

Conversion of 1495 base 10 to a base 2 number						
1495	=	1495	\	1024	=	1
– 1024	=	471	\	512	=	0
	=	471	\	256	=	1
– 256	=	215	\	128	=	1
– 128	=	87	\	64	=	1
– 64	=	23	\	32	=	0
		23	\	16	=	1
– 16	=	7	\	8	=	0
		7	\	4	=	1
– 4	=	3	\	2	=	1
– 2	=	1	\	1	=	1

In any number system, there are as many digits as stated in the base of that system, ranging from 0 to the base minus one. In the decimal system, there are 10 digits ranging from 0 through 9. In octal (base 8), there are eight digits ranging from 0 through 7. In hexadecimal (base 16), however, there are more digits than there are numerals available. Thus, the digits for 10 through 15 are represented by the capital letters *A* through *F*. Where no digit (0-9) can represent the value within a place, capital letters are used.

Making Spaces for Places

To put what you know about number systems into action, I present an application that takes any base 10 number and converts it to any specified number base from 2 to 36. I picked 36 because it is equal to the number of digits (10) plus the number of letters in the alphabet (26). The form appears as shown in Figure 10.1.

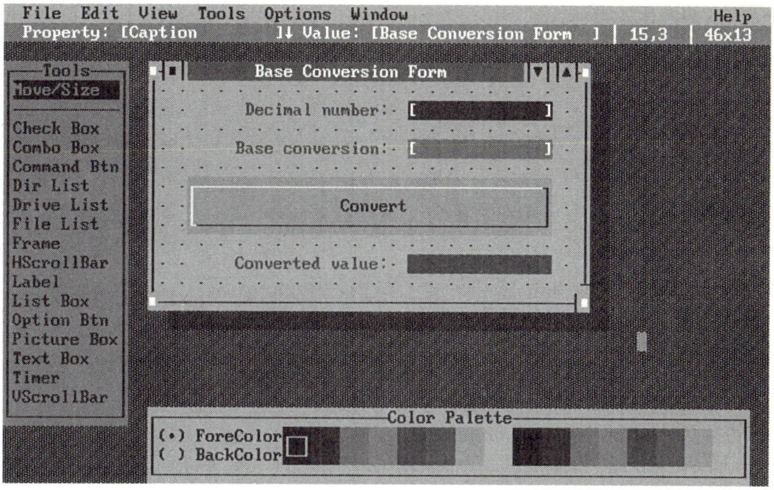

Figure 10.1. The base conversion form.

The objects and property settings for the form shown in Figure 10.1 are provided in the following table.

Numeric Base Conversion Form

Project name: CONVBASE.MAK
Constituent file: CONVBASE.FRM

Object type	*Property*	*Setting*
Form	`.Width`	`46`
	`.Height`	`13`
	`.FormName`	`ConvBase`
	`.Caption`	`Base Conversion Form`
Text box	`.Left`	`26`
	`.Top`	`1`
	`.CtlName`	`Decimal`
	`.Text`	`(blank)`
	`.BackColor`	`9 - Bright Blue`
	`.ForeColor`	`15 - Bright White`

continues

Object type	*Property*	*Setting*
Text box	.Left	26
	.Top	3
	.CtlName	BaseNum
	.Text	(blank)
	.BackColor	2 - Green
	.ForeColor	15 - Bright White
Text box	.Left	26
	.Top	9
	.CtlName	Total
	.Text	(blank)
	.BackColor	12 - Bright Red
	.ForeColor	15 - Bright White
Button	.Left	3
	.Top	5
	.CtlName	ConvertButton
	.Caption	Convert
	.BackColor	6 - Brown
Label	.Left	3
	.Top	1
	.Caption	Decimal number:
	.ForeColor	4 - Red
	.BackColor	15 - Bright White
Label	.Left	3
	.Top	3
	.Caption	Base conversion:
	.ForeColor	4 - Red
	.BackColor	15 - Bright White
Label	.Left	3
	.Top	9
	.Caption	Converted value:
	.ForeColor	4 - Red
	.BackColor	15 - White

CONVBASE.FRM

General declarations area:

```
DECLARE FUNCTION Convert$ (convValue!, convBase!)
```

Don't worry about typing in the preceding line; the Code Editor will place it into the code automatically after you type in the following general procedure:

```
FUNCTION Convert$ (convValue, convBase)
Find_Top:
comp = convBase ^ expn
IF comp < convValue THEN
    expn = expn + 1
    GOTO Find_Top
END IF
FOR spot = expn TO 0 STEP -1
    digit% = convValue \ (convBase ^ spot)
    convValue = convValue MOD (convBase ^ spot)
    IF digit% < 10 THEN
        cvt$ = cvt$ + RIGHT$(STR$(digit%), 1)
    ELSE
        cvt$ = cvt$ + CHR$(65 + (digit% - 10))
    END IF
NEXT spot
IF LEFT$(cvt$, 1) = "0" AND LEN(cvt$) > 1 THEN
    cvt$ = RIGHT$(cvt$, LEN(cvt$) - 1)
END IF
Convert$ = cvt$
END FUNCTION
```

Because this procedure is the largest you've worked with thus far, I explain it in detail. This is a `FUNCTION` procedure that accepts two values: the base 10 value being converted (`convValue`) and the base to which it's being converted (`convBase`). The converted number will be expressed as `Convert$`, an alphanumeric string, because it may contain "digits" such as `A` and `F`. The function will "compose" a string of these digits called `cvt$`, and at the end, it will assign the contents of `cvt$` to `Convert$`, the string variable for which the `FUNCTION` procedure is solving.

An *implied loop* starts at the point marked `Find_Top`. The purpose of this loop is to determine the number of digit places in the number `convValue` after it is converted to the base specified in `convBase`. The point of this loop is to keep adding power exponentially to the variable `comp` until its value becomes greater than that of the number you're converting (`convValue`). Each time you add power to `comp`, you increment (add 1 to) variable `expn`; so `expn` is counting the number of places in the converted number that will be `cvt$`. When `comp` becomes greater than `convValue`, you know you've gone too far and have counted enough places. You now know there are as many digits in `cvt$` as have been counted by `expn`.

The loop that follows is a conventional `FOR-NEXT` loop, wherein you start with the *leftmost* place in `cvt$` and work backward (`STEP -1`) to the right toward the ones place. The countdown is kept within the variable `spot`. When `spot = 0`, the loop is complete and the number is nearly converted. You're figuring the value of `cvt$` one digit at a time, starting from the left. For the first iteration of the loop, the leftmost digit is equal to the number of times the value being converted, `convValue`, goes evenly into the place value being considered (`convBase ^ spot`). That number is the first `digit%` of `cvt$`.

Having converted one digit, the procedure *shaves* the amount of the converted digit from `convValue` using *modulo arithmetic*. In other words, you take the *remainder* from the division equation `convValue / (convBase ^ spot)` and put it back into `convValue`. This remainder is evaluated during the next iteration of the loop. Until then, a conditional `IF-THEN` clause appears evaluating the value of `digit%`. The value of the converted `digit%`, from 0 to 9, is made into an alphanumeric character using the function `STR$()`, and the leading space VB/DOS attaches to positive values is trimmed from it using the function `RIGHT$()`. If, however, the value of `digit%` is 10 or greater—as in cases of hexadecimal numbers where upper case letters starting with `A` are used in place of numerals—the `CHR$()` function is used to determine which letter in the ASCII sequence of characters is used, starting with #65 ("`A`"), adding the value of `digit%`, but subtracting ten. These intrinsic VB/DOS functions are covered in detail later in the book.

The final instruction before `END FUNCTION` assigns the final contents of `cvt$` to the all-important `Convert$`, the solution string. The way VB/DOS `FUNCTION` procedures work, such solution assignments should be made only once, preferably toward the end of the procedure.

Here's the only event procedure necessary for this application:

```
SUB ConvertButton_Click ()
dec = VAL(Decimal.Text)
bn = VAL(BaseNum.Text)
Total.Text = Convert$(dec, bn)
END SUB
```

This procedure performs the "housework" for this application. It will execute the moment `ConvertButton` is clicked, as the `SUB` procedure title makes obvious. Two value variables, `dec` and `bn`, are informally declared and "absorb" the numeric value of the textual contents of the two text boxes `Decimal` and `BaseNum`. VB/DOS' value conversion function is `VAL()`. The `.Text` contents of text box `Total` will contain the converted numeral; those contents are assigned by way of referencing `Convert$()`, which is a call to the `FUNCTION` procedure you typed in earlier. These three instructions are all that's necessary to maintain the form; the VB/DOS interpreter handles all the other aspects. Now, perhaps, you understand a bit more about the construction of small graphical applications.

As a test for your new application form, assume `convValue` is the base 10 number 1495 from the previous table and `convBase` is 2—meaning that you're converting to base 2. The initial `Find_Top` loop will determine that the base 2 form of 1495_{10} is an 11-digit number. At the end of that loop, `expn = 10`—the power that 2 is raised to at the 11th digit. The `spot` loop counts down from 10 to 0. During the first iteration, `spot = 10`. The value of 2^{10} is 1024, and that goes into 1495 once. This makes 1 the first digit in `Convert$`. The remainder 471, equal to `1495 - 1024`, is derived using the `MOD` modulo arithmetic function, which returns the remainder of a division—in this case, of `1495 \ 1024`. The value 471 becomes the `convValue` for the next iteration of the loop. After the final iteration, `Convert$ = 10111010111`. Figure 10.2 demonstrates this solution.

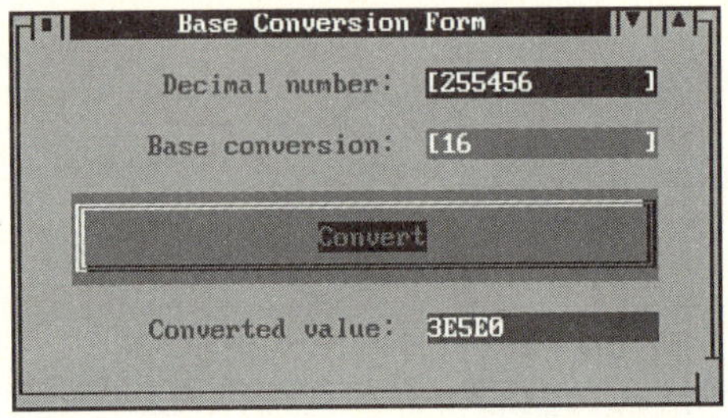

Figure 10.2. The systematic disassembly of the numeral system.

NOTE: In VB/DOS, hexadecimal (base 16) values, when written into source code or displayed on-screen, are preceded by the symbol `&H`. Thus `&HFF` is equal to 255.

Summary

The native number system of a computer is binary (base 2). Often certain variables used by the system are expressed as hexadecimal (base 16) because its numbers are shorter, and 16 is a multiple of 2, making conversion between the two bases easy. By comparison, conversion between binary and decimal (base 10) numbers is difficult for the computer. A representation of the digit-by-digit conversion procedure was the example program for this chapter.

Review Questions

Answers to Review Questions appear in Appendix B.

Respond to the following questions using Table 10.1 and the `FUNCTION` procedure presented in this chapter.

1. The fifth digit from the left of `Convert$` represents 2 raised to what power?

2. When `(convBase ^ spot)` does not divide into `convValue`, what is the value of the `digit%` at the current `spot`?
3. If `convValue` is integral, will there ever be a case in which `Convert$` is a fractional number?

11

Scope and Context

A *module* is a complete set of instructions stored within a single file.

In this chapter, you see how variables are formally declared in Visual Basic for MS-DOS using explicit statements rather than equations. You learn about the scope of a variable, which is the extent to which the value contained within a variable pertains to the various modules of the program. You see how VB/DOS statements are used to define the scope of variables, and in so doing define the context of the procedures in which they reside.

Structured Programming, Such as It Is

BASIC is believed to be the first high-level programming language in which variables can declare themselves. Time after time, this book has presented source code examples containing equations such as `a = 1`, where there was no `a` before. BASIC always has been smart enough to play catch-up with you as the programmer; if you say `a` not only exists but also equals 1, it must exist.

The patchwork quilt that has become modern BASIC is composed of many elements of FORTRAN, PL/I, Pascal, and C. In each of these languages, a variable is declared formally before a value is assigned to it or before the variable is used in a formula. In other words, the variable is formally introduced to the program with a statement.

> **NOTE:** In a BASIC program, a declaration of a variable is the first statement to assign a legitimate value to that variable.

For years after BASIC's inception, the only real way to declare a variable was simply to assign a value to the variable, as in `a = 1`. At first, this method of declaration was seen as a true advance in the art of high-level programming. As time passed and more low-level programmers added new structures to BASIC, absolutely every variable of every type could be declared before it was utilized. This capability was seen immediately as an advance in the art of high-level programming.

You will find, after being a programmer for a number of years, that this business has certain fashion trends. One trend concerns the structure of your source code. A frequent argument among programmers is whether to include comment lines. Another debate, although perhaps not as frequent, is whether to declare variables before values are assigned to them.

At the time of this printing, the fashion is to declare variables before a value assignment. You will notice in Microsoft's own source-code examples that most major variables are declared in advance for type and scope, although even Microsoft occasionally invokes a "utility variable" for a simple loop or a temporary value container. No law states that you should predeclare every variable you use; I certainly don't. Often, in writing a loop clause, I need a quick utility variable to keep the count from 1 to 5 so that the program performs some set of instructions five times. I don't care what the count variable is, as long as its name is not in use. Sometimes I give it a name from out of the blue, as in the statement `FOR ralph = 1 TO 5`. I'm not about to go out of my way to declare `ralph` in a separate statement (such as `DECLARE ralph AS INTEGER`) just so that `ralph` can count for me.

As you read more about programming, you undoubtedly will come across the subject of *structured programming*. Modularity in source code, conservatism in choosing variable type categories, and explicit variable declaration are three products of discourse and argument on this topic. Structured programming is one of the great, redundant statements to come from the computing industry; all programs are, to some degree, structured. In the interest of preserving structured programming, some programmers would argue that you should write source code in a specified style. Imagine how such proponents would be received if they applied their arguments to architecture, poetry, or music.

The most conventional definition of structured programming is source code that is legible to humans, executes relatively quickly, and compiles to a reasonably small size. Since compilers and languages change every year, the most desired structures in programming generally change with them. John Kemeny and Thomas Kurtz, the inventors of BASIC, believed that a "structured program" consisted of source code that was highly legible and readily interpretable to the *human* reader. Yet, it is BASIC that is perhaps most criticized for its tendency to be "unstructured." Those who argue against the natural course of BASIC code structures generally program in a lower-level language that either resembles or *is* assembly language. Yet it is this class of language that is criticized by high-level language (such as BASIC) proponents for being "destructuralized"—that is to say, allowing its purpose to be obfuscated by its design. In another realm of art, the work of Salvador Dali has been criticized for not having structure, whereas the work of R. Buckminster Fuller has been criticized for not having style. Both structures, artistically and even functionally, *work*; and it is my belief that *workability* should be the chief criteria for judging the quality of any device or program.

When you program, you should strive for conservative use of memory, efficient use and exchange of values, and an appearance that makes the user want to understand what she's reading. Style is a consideration that comes later, when you start developing a style for yourself. Never allow style to be dictated to you by something that calls itself "the norm." Remember that Hewlett and Packard, Jobs and Wozniak, and Gates and Allen all developed the tools that reshaped this industry partly in defiance of "the norm."

A Variable's Scope of Existence

The *scope* of a variable defines at what level in the program its value is remembered.

When you create a variable by expressing it within an equation for the first time, the implied declaration for this variable gives the variable a local scope. The *scope* of a variable is the extent to which that variable applies across the various divisions of the program's source code.

Example

A variable with *local scope* applies only to the procedure in which it is declared, whether it is a specific declaration or an inference from an equation. Here's an example from the two-dimensional distance-calculator project, 2D_DIST.MAK:

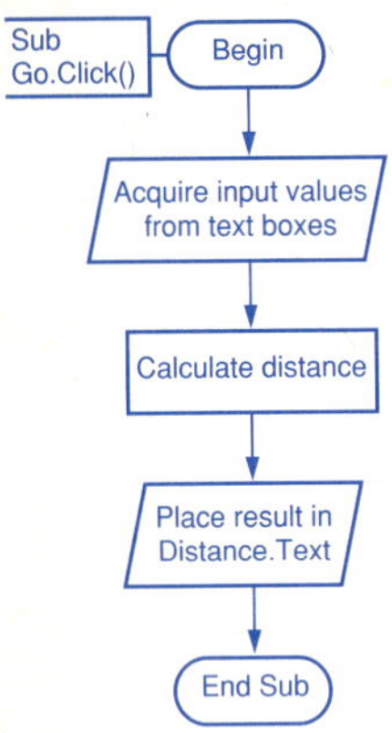


```
SUB Go_Click ()
x1 = VAL(Box_x1.Text)
x2 = VAL(Box_x2.Text)
y1 = VAL(Box_y1.Text)
y2 = VAL(Box_y2.Text)
d# = SQR(((x2 - x1) ^ 2) + ((y2 - y1) ^ 2))
Distance.Text = STR$(d#)
END SUB
```

Here I invoked five variables: `x1`, `x2`, `y1`, `y2`, and `d#`. The purpose of these variables is to reach a result that could be displayed as `Distance.Text`. None of these variables has any purpose beyond the context of this procedure. The *context* of a body of source code is the extent to which the values generated within that body, and the statements made within that body, relate to the rest of the program.

If I had wanted to be more formal about introducing variables to the reader of this source code, I could have added the following after the `SUB` procedure declaration:

```
DIM x1 AS SINGLE, x2 AS SINGLE, y1 AS SINGLE, y2 AS SINGLE
DIM d AS DOUBLE
```

The *context* of a body of source code describes its relationship to the rest of the program.

Frankly, not much would have changed about the program, except that I wouldn't have had to use the pound sign (`#`) following variable `d` to identify it as a double-precision variable. The true convenience of using `DIM` to declare non-array variables within a procedure is to help define the "world" for this procedure, for the benefit of some other person who may happen to be reading this source code later.

The View from the Gallery

High-level programs such as BASIC are broken down into modules for almost the same reason that books such as this one are broken into chapters. Segmentation is necessary for any long work, whether it's written in English or in VB/DOS. Modern BASIC is even more similar to written language than its predecessors, not only because it represents instructions as sentences, but also because the instructions can be coordinated together as groups. Each group defines for the interpreter or the system an *action*, giving it a term you can use repetitively. You don't have to redefine the action every time you perform it.

The process of programming, therefore, resembles more and more the process of teaching. Imagine that you are a tour guide for a group of foreign-exchange students from Russia who are visiting the New York Stock Exchange. Looking down at the trading floor from the gallery, these students don't see anything that quite resembles the barter system in their hometown, so they're bewildered. In an attempt to reach these students, to educate them, where do you start?

Because your primary tool is language, you might start by pointing out the trading centers on the floor, the trading specialists who work for the Exchange, and how to spot a transaction between a trader and a specialist. "Okay, but what are they trading?" someone asks. "Naturally, stock in a public corporation," you respond. "And what is stock?" "Oh, boy," you say to yourself with a sigh. "Stock refers to a pool of shares in a company's assets." Someone asks, "Is the value of these assets divided evenly into shares, with each share having a set value?" "Now you're getting the picture," you respond. "Then why is everyone trying to change the value of these shares higher or lower if they're supposed to represent a set fraction of the assets' value?"

The preceding conversation could go on forever. The further you go, the more you break down a complex process into graspable, logical components. In a sense, this breaking down is what you do as a programmer. Where would the concepts of *scope* and *context* fit in with the tour-guide analogy? When you show the students where the trading posts are and where the exchange counters and the communications centers are, you break down the larger "stage" into smaller *contexts*. Mind you, there are no "walls" on the NYSE floor that demark where one trading area stops and another begins, but the traders certainly know where they are.

Now that you have modularized the trading floor into hazy though interlocked components, you can discuss each component as though it were its own little world. Within this world, each action or transaction has its own laws. These laws may or may not hold true outside this world. The amount or the extent of each transaction here is, in effect, the scope of that transaction. If you were writing a computer program that simulated the goings-on of the NYSE, you might now have a clearer picture of how you would organize and group the instructions and arrange the values and variables therein.

Modular variables are declared in the general declarations area.

A procedure is, for the sake of the VB/DOS application, a subdivided miniature world. The scope of certain declared variables within a program, therefore, may be modular or procedural (local); that is, they may pertain to the larger frame of reference or to the smaller frame. Variables declared to have modular scope pertain to all the procedures within that module. The place for declaring modular-scope variables is in the general declarations area of the module's Source Code window. You can spot this window by its lack of markings; that is, if the window number and module name appear alone within the code window's title bar, you are looking at the general declarations area for that module. This area may contain instructions other than declarations only if it is going to be declared as the startup module.

Take a closer look at how you can use `DIM` to declare non-array variables within a procedure and why you would want to use it in the first place.

DIM **Statement**

Non-array declaration syntax:

```
DIM [SHARED] variable1 [AS type][, variable2
  [AS type],...variable60 [AS type]]
```

With this syntax, as many as 60 non-array variables can be declared and given type specifications. By itself, `DIM` is used to declare variables with a scope local to the procedure or module containing the `DIM` statement. If `DIM` appears within a `SUB` or `FUNCTION` procedure, the variables declared within `DIM` are assumed to have local scope to that procedure. If `DIM` appears within module-level code, the variables declared within `DIM` are assumed to have local scope to that module—which means that no procedures are given access to those variables unless those procedures so request.

A special qualifier term, SHARED, may be used at the modular level to declare that all variables listed within the DIM statement are to be applied to all procedures within the module, as well as to module-level code. Variables so declared are modular in scope. Declared variables are assumed, by default, to be single-precision floating-point variables unless a type is specified using the optional AS qualifier.

A reasonable person might ask, what does it matter whether a procedure has access to certain variables? Wouldn't it be easier for the value of variable `a` to be the same throughout the source code and not have three or four different `a` variables scattered about the program?

It might be easier if the program you were writing were guaranteed to be one complete, swiftly performed task from beginning to end. As you will learn, however, programs that work well are those composed of several small functions working in conjunction with one another. Suppose that your VB/DOS application had to "know" a lot about the laws of geometry. When you look at a geometry reference and see the formulas for finding the surface areas and volumes of differently shaped solids, the formula for finding each area or volume uses commonly accepted variables such as `r` for radius, or `w` and `h` for width and height, respectively. When you look at a set of such formulas, you know automatically that `r` for the radius of a sphere and `r` for the radius of a cylinder are two different `r`'s altogether; yet you allow the same term to stand for a shared concept. Mathematicians don't choose different letters every time they run across a different shape.

If every variable you declared in a BASIC or VB/DOS program were global in scope—the way they used to be—each time you wanted to define an important function, you would have to create a new and original name not already being used. You would have several different variables for all forms of radii. The computer would not be confused, but you would be.

To reduce the amount of confusion that developed from perpetually global contexts, the re-architects of BASIC found it beneficial to the human reader to place limitations and restrictions on the use of symbols, partly because there probably will be far more symbols in your program than there are letters in the alphabet. The use of unreserved words or character strings as variables is relatively new to BASIC; the original BASIC variables were single letters.

A good synonym for "scope" with reference to VB/DOS variables would be "domain," as demonstrated by the map, appearing as Figure 11.1.

This map shows the six statements for variable declaration in the VB/DOS vernacular (one statement, `DIM`, appears in two places.) Here's how to read this map: Assume the two dark blocks represent two modules of VB/DOS source code. Within each module block is a smaller block that represents a procedure. Along the perimeter of each of the rectangles within the module blocks is one of the declarative statements. Each statement appears within the type of block where it is allowed to appear; for instance, the `STATIC` declaration is only legal within a procedure, as denoted by its sole appearance within one of the procedure blocks.

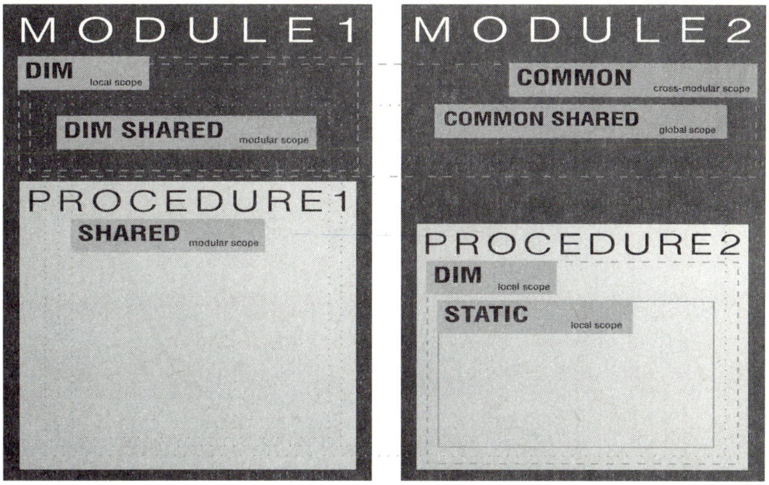

Figure 11.1. An overhead view of the territorial boundaries of VB/DOS.

Table 11.1 lists and defines the categories of variable scope introduced in the map.

Table 11.1. Scope categories of variables.

Category	*Declarative*	*Definition*
local	`DIM`	Pertaining only to the procedure in which the variable is first invoked or declared, and whose value is cleared when the procedure is exited.
static	`STATIC`	Pertaining only to the procedure in which the variable is first declared, although whose value is maintained after the procedure is exited in case of possible reentry to that same procedure.

continues

Table 11.1. Continued.

Category	*Declarative*	*Definition*
shared	`SHARED`	Pertaining to the procedure in which the variable is re-declared, as well as to the module-level code of the module where the variable was first declared.
modular	`DIM SHARED`	Pertaining to the module-level code as well as all procedures within a module.
cross-modular	`COMMON`	Pertaining only to the module-level code of all modules in the application but not to any procedures contained within those modules.
global	`COMMON SHARED`	Pertaining to the entire source code.

To declare a variable with static scope requires a `STATIC` statement.

STATIC — Statement

Syntax:

```
STATIC variable1[(integer [TO integer]
  [,integer [TO integer]])][AS type][, variable2
  [(integer [TO integer][,integer [TO integer]])]
  [AS type],...variable60[(integer [TO integer]
  [,integer [TO integer]])][AS type]]
```

The `STATIC` statement is used in place of `DIM` to declare all of a procedure's local unit and array variables whose values are to be maintained by the interpreter after the `END SUB` or `END FUNCTION` statement is executed for that procedure. With the exception of the main term itself, STATIC's syntax is the same as the syntax of the DIM statement when invoked within a procedure.

Example

You may remember the following procedure from the Expressor application:

```
SUB Button_Point_Click (Index AS INTEGER)
STATIC point_lock AS INTEGER
IF point_lock = 0 AND ready < 20 THEN
    readout.caption = readout.caption + "."
    point_lock = 1
    ready = ready + 1
END IF
assess_readout
END SUB
```

Here, the variable point_lock is declared STATIC because I want it to remember whether the user clicks the decimal point button of the calculator. This way, the decimal point won't appear in the readout twice. This procedure will be exited and reentered several times; it is crucial that every time the procedure is entered, it knows whether a lock has been placed on the point key. This fact is not at all pertinent to any procedure or code outside of SUB Button_Point_Click (), so I chose to declare point_lock within the procedure as STATIC, giving the variable just as much scope and pertinence as it needs.

There is one more term for declaration at the procedural level: SHARED.

SHARED **Statement**

Syntax:

```
SHARED variable1[()][AS type][, variable2
  [()] AS type,...variable60[()][AS type]]
```

The SHARED statement is used within a procedure to redeclare those variables previously declared on the module level using DIM, as pertaining to the procedure containing the SHARED statement. The DIM declaration initially declaring these variables must appear within the same module as the procedure sharing the variables. If any of the redeclared variables is an array, it is marked with opening and closing parentheses but with no upper or lower boundaries stated. If a variable type was declared at the modular level using DIM, that type must be stated again within SHARED using the AS qualifier. If AS was not used in the DIM statement, any descriptive type symbols (% for integer, # for double-precision, and so on) used with respect to the variables in the DIM statement must appear likewise with the variables in the SHARED statement. The order of variables in the SHARED statement need not match or follow that in the earlier DIM statement.

The purpose of SHARED is to extend the scope boundaries of a select group of variables to specific procedures. It's crucial to note the differences between SHARED and DIM SHARED: The purpose of DIM SHARED is to extend the scope boundaries of certain variables to any and all procedures in the module. This is why DIM SHARED appears on the modular level, outside of procedures. You don't need to redeclare variables using SHARED once you've invoked DIM SHARED. Furthermore, DIM SHARED works like the DIM statement as well, declaring variables on the modular level. When DIM is used all by itself on the modular level, then SHARED is required within each procedure that will share variables with the module.

Example

Suppose, for instance, you placed the following line within the declarations area of a module:

```
DIM SHARED assets AS CURRENCY
```

Any time you invoked variable assets within a procedure, it would equal the same amount as it did when assets was last invoked in some other procedure, or within the module-level code. Suppose instead you placed this line in the declarations area of your module:

```
DIM assets AS CURRENCY
```

The next `SUB` or `FUNCTION` procedure to utilize the variable name `assets` would see it as an entirely new variable, with an initial value of 0. This new variable doesn't have any bearing or effect upon the modular `assets`; from the point of view of the interpreter, it's a different variable entirely. Suppose, however, you want a particular procedure to share `assets` with the module. In such an instance, you could redeclare `assets` within the procedure as follows:

```
SHARED assets AS CURRENCY
```

Now the modular variable `assets` has its own particular boundary that crosses over into the procedure. Some other procedure may use the term `assets`; unless the procedure includes the `SHARED` statement, however, that new variable will be an entity unto itself.

> **NOTE:** Another way for modules and procedures to share variables and/or values with each other is by means of parameter passing. Some programmers find this process (for good reason) far more powerful, if not just far more palatable. Parameter passing is, however, a one-way transfer. Scope extension is a much broader, more controllable, although more complex, method of exchanging values between bodies of code. You'll learn more about this method in Chapter 20, "Parameter Passing."

The Search for Common Ground

Despite all this effort in boundary setting, there may be cases in which you want certain variables to be applicable throughout the entire application. In such instances, within the general declarations area of the main (startup) module, the `COMMON SHARED` declarative statement is available.

COMMON SHARED **Statement**

Syntax:

```
COMMON SHARED variable1[(integer [TO integer]
  [,integer [TO integer]])][AS type][, variable2
  [(integer [TO integer][,integer [TO integer]])]
  [AS type],...variable60[(integer [TO integer]
  [,integer [TO integer]])][AS type]]
```

The COMMON SHARED statement is used within the general declarations area of the main (startup) module of an application to declare those variables that will have global scope, and that will apply to all parts of the application. The values of the declared variables will be maintained as program control passes between all modules and procedures in the application.

Example

Suppose you're writing a bookkeeping application for your business. A handful of the variables therein—annual earnings, real stock value, stock trading value—will be utilized by most of the procedures in the application, or at least enough that it wouldn't be convenient for you to pass these variables as parameters every time you place a procedure call. To declare these reference variables as having global scope, you can use the following statement:

```
COMMON SHARED perannum AS CURRENCY, realstock, tradestock
```

The latter two variables will be declared single-precision by default because you didn't include AS qualifiers.

As discussed previously, the context of a procedure or other body of code is the extent to which that code relates to the rest of the program. Variable scope plays a major role in defining contexts, due especially to the *de facto* boundaries established by the multitude of supported variable scopes.

In previous Microsoft editions of BASIC—most notably, the latest editions of QuickBasic and QBasic—the keyword `COMMON` was used to declare variables as having cross-modular scope. If you look back at the map in Figure 11.1, you will note that the boundaries for `COMMON` declarations extend across modules but not into the procedures. It made lexical sense to combine the `COMMON` declaration for cross-modular scope with the `SHARED` declaration for module-to-procedure scope to form `COMMON SHARED` for global scope declarations.

The march of progress has a tendency to tromp right over yesterday's bold new path. The new contextual model of the VB/DOS language is composed mostly of procedures. With the exception of the startup module, module-level code is restricted to declarations only. The startup module's nonprocedural code therefore acts like a `main()` procedure as in the C language, or like the optional `Sub Main ()` procedure in Visual Basic for Windows. The difference is that the VB/DOS startup module has its own all-encompassing context, allowing you to divide major variables in the front of the module from minor ones within the procedures. As you'll see later, the structure also allows you to divide the module-level code into the more conventional routine/subroutine structure of early BASIC, making older programs more compatible with the newer structure.

VB/DOS' new advances in modularization nearly made obsolete the `COMMON` statement, whose original purpose was to bridge the modular-level code between two or more modules. In VB/DOS, module-level code (with the exception of declarative statements) exists only within the startup module. There would be no purpose in extending the scope of a set of variables into what had become, for all intents and purposes, a dead-end street. To give `COMMON` a purpose in modern BASIC, it became necessary to alter the syntax of the statement. You may now use the statement to declare lists of *values*, by way of variables, as being shared across modules. You may give each set or block of values its own name, for identifying it in future `COMMON` statements. This makes possible a form of *context portability*, as introduced in the following section.

COMMON **Statement**

Syntax:

```
COMMON [/blockname/] variable1[(integer [TO integer]
  [,integer [TO integer]])][AS type][, variable2
  [(integer [TO integer][,integer [TO integer]])]
  [AS type],...variable60[(integer [TO integer]
  [,integer [TO integer]])][AS type]]
```

The COMMON statement is used within the general declarations areas of multiple modules to declare those variables whose values are to be shared between the modules. Sharing these values is restricted to module-level code; procedures do not automatically have access to these values. The primary purpose of the COMMON statement in VB/DOS is to transfer variable values between selected modules, acting as a link in a bridge between the main module and the SUB and FUNCTION procedures in selected subordinate modules. The bridging process works as follows:

- COMMON is used within the general declarations area of the main startup module to declare those variables whose values will be shared with other modules, at the modular level.
- COMMON is then used again within the general declarations area of those subordinate modules that will be receiving the shared values.
- Finally, SHARED is used within the declarations portion of each of the subordinate modules' procedures sharing the values. A select group of procedures within a remote module, using this process, may be given access to module-level variables from the startup module.

Using the standard syntax of COMMON, variable scopes are transferred between modules in name as well as content. Thus, a variable w declared COMMON in one module is considered the same variable w when declared COMMON in another module. Using the optional syntax, a block of values represented by variables may be given a collective name, written between two forward slashmarks (/). This name may then be used in future invocations of COMMON to refer to the listed values. A variable list must always follow the block name, although the names of variables used to contain the shared variables from another module may be chosen arbitrarily. Thus, a variable declared `COMMON /overall/ w` in one module will transfer its value and identity to another variable declared `COMMON /overall/ width` in another module, by virtue of their having been declared with the same block name `/overall/`. Any changes to `width` in one module are automatically reflected in `w` in the other.

Example

If you're used to paragraphs making sense when you read them the first time, then the preceding text may have assaulted your sensibility. Hopefully, the following three-part example will put things back in order. Here's a portion of the module-level code for an application that plots and examines two-dimensional shapes:

```
DECLARE SUB boxplot ()
COMMON /testblock/ originx AS INTEGER, originy
  AS INTEGER, boxwidth AS INTEGER, boxheight
  AS INTEGER
.
.
.
originx = 100
originy = 50
boxwidth = 50
boxheight = 50
CALL boxplot
PRINT originy
```

A *subordinate module* is one whose procedures are called by the main startup module.

Here, you see the `COMMON` statement used to declare a list of four values with cross-modular scope. These values help form the context of this module; now that they have been declared within value block `/testblock/`, they will help form the context of another module as well. This second module—a *subordinate module*—contains the following statement:

```
COMMON /testblock/ x AS INTEGER, y AS INTEGER,
  w AS INTEGER, h AS INTEGER
```

The /testblock/ is the same here, although the four variables have different names. Nonetheless, the *values* declared earlier in the main module will be transferred here, in the order in which they were declared. Variable w in this subordinate module will have the same value as variable boxwidth in the main module; more to the point, variable w will also share *identities* with variable boxwidth as well. If the subordinate module's procedure changes the value of w, once execution proceeds back to the main module, boxwidth will reflect that change.

The "pipeline" has yet to be completed, so now bring the values from /testblock/ down into a procedure. Here's a procedure from the subordinate module:

```
SUB boxplot ()
SHARED x AS INTEGER, y AS INTEGER, w AS INTEGER,
h AS INTEGER
  SCREEN 10
LINE (x, y)-(x + w, y + h), 15, BF
END SUB
```

Notice here that the SHARED variables are declared as explicitly as they were in both of the previous COMMON declarations. Once you've started the trend of declaring AS INTEGER, your shared variable redeclarations must follow in turn. The preceding procedure will take the four values that have (finally) been handed down to it and use them to plot a filled white box to the screen.

You might not necessarily want to have different names for the same variables used in two different modules; when looking at constructing an application from the ground up, it might not seem there's a valid reason for renaming the same variables. The real reason that different names are accommodated in VB/DOS is so that code modules can be constructed that have meaning or purpose with regard to many different possible applications. To add the functionality of a code module to a new project, the module may be ported into that project by selecting **File/Add Project** from the Code Editor menu. The old module will fit seamlessly into the framework and context of the new project because you don't have to make all your new variable names fit the old terms, nor do you have to edit all the old terms to fit your new choices. All you need to do is remember the block value name you chose for your `COMMON` statements; the interpreter or compiler will handle the job of transporting values between the modules, regardless of what name you originally gave the variables for those values.

Summary

A variable in VB/DOS may be declared by inference, which means stating it within an expression for the first time within the source code of the program. Variables declared by inference are assumed to have local scope and single-precision floating-point type unless otherwise specified. Formal declaration for local variables with either procedural or restricted-modular scope is accomplished with the `DIM` statement. Variables with static scope, which are local to procedures but have values that are constantly maintained, are declared on the procedure level with the `STATIC` statement. Variables with global scope are declared using the `COMMON SHARED` statement.

Variables that are to be shared between module-level code and all procedures within that module are declared using the `DIM SHARED` statement at the module level. Variables that are to be shared between module-level code and *selected* procedures within that module are declared first using the `DIM` statement at the module level and then by redeclaring them using the `SHARED` statement at the procedure level. Variables that are to be shared between modules are declared in both modules using the `COMMON` statement. Blocks of values may be given names using the `COMMON` statement so that related values may be given different variable names for each module.

Review Questions

Answers to Review Questions appear in Appendix B.

1. Only one statement may be used to declare new variables either for local scope within modular-level code or for local scope within a procedure. Recall the statement.

2. If a procedure is executed more than once and a `STATIC` statement is the first instruction in the procedure, will the variables listed within the `STATIC` statement be cleared?

3. Why does the `COMMON SHARED` statement not have an option for declaring a block name for a list of values, as does the `COMMON` statement?

Review Exercise

Take the source code for the `NameForm` application (project name NAMEFORM.MAK) and list on paper each variable invoked, along with the type and scope for that variable.

12

Value Management

In this chapter, you'll experiment with declaring certain terms that stand for unvarying values as formal constants. Next, you'll explore some of the terms used in the Visual Basic for MS-DOS vernacular to overcome the scope and context boundaries defined in the preceding chapter.

A thorough discussion of these issues compels me to introduce the topic of *metacommands*. Metacommands are instructions to the VB/DOS interpreter, rather than the VB/DOS application, that are embedded in the source code. The primary purpose of metacommands is to attach *include* files to a project. Many of the include files you can attach concern the declaration of constants and the establishment of customized scopes and contexts.

Constants

A *constant* is a term that stands in place of a single value.

Throughout the source code of VB/DOS applications, arbitrary terms that aren't keywords or instructions can be declared as constants. A *constant* is a term that stands in place of a single, unvarying value in an expression. A constant's value is set only once.

The CONST declarative statement for constants is as follows.

CONST **Statement**

Syntax:

```
CONST name = expression[, name = expression...]
```

The CONST statement is used to declare a term to represent a fixed (nonvariable) value for use in expressions. The scope of a constant is determined by the position of its declaration in the source code. A constant declared within a SUB or FUNCTION procedure has local scope. A constant declared within the general declarations area of a module has modular scope, and will be recognized by any of the procedures included in that module. Constants may not have global scope.

Example

Here is perhaps the most common use for constants within a program:

```
CONST TRUE = -1
CONST FALSE = 0
```

Now, tests of logical expressions can be read more clearly; for instance, `IF Form1.Visible = TRUE THEN....` (The constants in this example were capitalized, although they aren't required to be.)

Example

Following is a revised general declarations area for the Expressor:

```
DIM label$(15, 4), p(4)
DIM readout_value AS SINGLE, solution AS SINGLE
CONST PI = 3.1415927
CONST GRAV = 6.6732E-11
```

Here, two universally recognized constants appear: the value of pi and the gravitational constant `GRAV` that is so important to Newtonian laws.

Declaring constants may prove to be a convenience in cases where it's easier for you to remember a word than a number. For instance, you may prefer to set a control's `.BackColor` background color property to `MAGENTA` rather than use the color look-up table number for magenta. In such a case, simply declare `CONST MAGENTA` equal to the table number one time, and you won't find yourself looking up color tables in the middle of late-night programming.

I Never Metacommand I Didn't Like

Microsoft's programmers prefer to use constants rather than numerals when programming in C or BASIC, for nearly any value that can be found within a look-up table. Because of this, Microsoft included a special file with the VB/DOS package called CONSTANT.BI for inclusion within your VB/DOS application. The .BI filename extension stands for "Basic Include file," or any file containing VB/DOS language code that may be attached by the VB/DOS interpreter to the front of a module.

The file CONSTANT.BI contains a set of CONST statements for declaring commonly used numerals from commonly referenced look-up tables as formal constants. Among the constants declared in this file are the following:

```
CONST KEY_NUMPAD0 = &H60
CONST KEY_NUMPAD1 = &H61
CONST KEY_NUMPAD2 = &H62
CONST KEY_NUMPAD3 = &H63
CONST KEY_NUMPAD4 = &H64
CONST KEY_NUMPAD5 = &H65
CONST KEY_NUMPAD6 = &H66
CONST KEY_NUMPAD7 = &H67
CONST KEY_NUMPAD8 = &H68
CONST KEY_NUMPAD9 = &H69
```

The &H symbols before the numerals tell the interpreter that they represent hexadecimal (base16) values. The preceding table relates the key scan codes for the number keys on your numeric keypad, as constants. This way, when you're writing an event trap procedure that checks to see if a keypad key has been pressed, instead of looking at a scan code table for the proper value, you can recall the constant term from memory using this conditional statement:

```
IF KeyCode = KEY_NUMPAD9 THEN PRINT "9";
```

To write this statement, you didn't have to find &H69 someplace in a book. You did, however, have to include the CONSTANT.BI file in your application using a metacommand. This is a directive to the VB/DOS interpreter itself, not really a program statement. A metacommand can, however, make alterations to the application's environment. Perhaps the most often-used metacommand in VB/DOS is $INCLUDE.

$INCLUDE **Metacommand**

Syntax:

```
{REM ¦ '} $INCLUDE: filename
```

where *filename* is any legitimate body of VB/DOS code saved in a file generally bearing the .BI filename extension.

The $INCLUDE metacommand directs the VB/DOS interpreter to attach the body of code contained in the stated file to the front of the current project. The metacommand is written in that point of the source code where the attached body of instructions would appear if it were written there directly. $INCLUDE, when written on a line by itself, must be preceded by a remark statement; however, it may be preceded by another metacommand. A colon is used to separate the metacommand term from the filename.

Before going on, here's a bit about the syntax of metacommands. Because they are not VB/DOS language instructions *per se*, they do not follow the standard VB/DOS syntax. This partly explains why metacommands are set off from the rest of the VB/DOS code by a remark statement, either REM or ' (apostrophe). The REM statement is a real VB/DOS statement, and it is generally used to instruct the interpreter to ignore the rest of the current program line. This way you can include comments in the midst of your source code, such as "General Ledger formatting section," or "Let's see if this works," or one of my personal favorites, "Dave Loves Bea."

In the case of metacommands, however, the part of the VB/DOS interpreter sees the REM (short for "remark") and goes about its business, but the interpreter itself sees the dollar sign, $, and knows something else is afoot. It then identifies the metacommand, puts aside regular program execution for a moment, and executes the metacommand. You can have more than one metacommand in a remark line, just as long as each term is preceded by a dollar sign.

Example

The metacommand for including the CONSTANT.BI file within your application would appear as follows:

```
REM $INCLUDE: CONSTANT.BI
```

While on the subject of include files, here's how you can use the VB/DOS Code Editor to make your own .BI file for later inclusion in any of several future projects.

To edit and save a Basic Include file, follow these steps:

1. From the Code Editor menu, select **F**ile/**N**ew Project. If an unsaved project currently inhabits the workspace, a dialog box will appear asking if you want to save the project files. After you make a decision there, the project window will be reset, and all open and minimized code windows will be cleared of their contents. They will, however, remain in the same position and size as they were.

2. Select **F**ile/New **M**odule. A dialog box will appear.

3. Within this box is a set of option dots designating the module file type to be edited. Set the option dot marked Include File [*.BI].

4. Type a filename for the include module in the uppermost text box; VB/DOS includes the .BI extension by default.

5. To avoid cluttering the workspace with any more code windows, click `Edit in Active`. The code window for the include file will soon be visible.

6. When the include file is ready, select **F**ile/**S**ave File. If all is well, no dialog boxes should appear, and the include file will be saved.

> **NOTE to BASIC veterans:** Many of you use the REM statement to temporarily disable or "comment out" an instruction for the purpose of testing, or so that you can delete something without forgetting what it was that you deleted. Since REM is also used to identify a metacommand, in order to "comment it out," you may place a lower-case x before the $, as in REM x$INCLUDE.

'Dis Array and 'Dat Array

In Chapter 9, "Arrays," you were introduced to the concept of static arrays versus dynamic arrays. You may remember that a static array is one that retains its upper- and lower-dimensioned bounds after it is cleared of its contents by the `ERASE` statement. By contrast, a dynamic array is one that discards its bounds after it is cleared by means of `ERASE`. By default, the `DIM` statement declares static arrays. This default state can be altered by means of the `$DYNAMIC` and `$STATIC` metacommands.

$DYNAMIC
$STATIC

Metacommands

Syntax:

```
{REM ¦ '} $DYNAMIC
{REM ¦ '} $STATIC
```

The `$DYNAMIC` metacommand is used to change the default array declaration mode from static to dynamic. By contrast, the `$STATIC` metacommand places the interpreter in static declaration mode.

Other Options

Microsoft has historically used `OPTION` statements rather than metacommands to change some operating mode of the interpreter or compiler. In the VB/DOS vocabulary, only two such statements are in current use: `OPTION BASE` and `OPTION EXPLICIT`.

OPTION BASE — **Statement**

Syntax:

```
OPTION BASE {0 ¦ 1}
```

The `OPTION BASE` statement, invoked within the general declarations area of the main module of an application, establishes whether the starting address of an array variable is to be 0 or 1. This value is specified in the accompanying integer and can be no other value. The default lower-bounds value of array variables is 1.

Example

A good place for `OPTION BASE` to appear is at the top of the general module area in the `NameForm` application:

```
OPTION BASE 1
DIM LstName$(1000), FrstName$(1000), MdInit$(1000),
  Adress$(1000), Cty$(1000), Stat$(1000), Zp$(1000)
DIM SHARED RecordNo AS INTEGER
```

This statement can come in handy if you'd like the first element of your arrays to be element #1 rather than element #0. If you plan to use two-dimensional geometric arrays, however, in which an origin point is element `(0, 0)`, you'll want to leave the `OPTION BASE` at 0.

Finally, for all of you "realists" in the art of programming, `OPTION EXPLICIT` is a statement that makes it illegal to declare variables implicitly.

OPTION EXPLICIT — **Statement**

Syntax:

```
OPTION EXPLICIT
```

The `OPTION EXPLICIT` statement is used within the general declarations area of the main module to change the operating mode of the VB/DOS interpreter so that variables may not be invoked within the source code without a prior declaration. A `DIM` statement or some other declarative would be necessary to declare any array or non-array variables to be used anyplace within the program before they may be used in any equations or expressions within the program.

In Chapter 11, "Scope and Context," we discussed the issue of style in programming with respect to whether variables should be declared before they are used in an equation or expression. By placing `OPTION EXPLICIT` at the front of the startup module, you allow the interpreter to restrict your usage of variables to those you have explicitly declared. For some, this statement helps restrict redundant variables that a programmer may allocate for similar purposes, and helps reduce memory consumption. For others, this statement can be irritating.

Summary

A term can be declared as representing a fixed value within a program by means of the `CONST` statement. Multiple `CONST` declarations, among other instructions, can be added to a Basic Include (.BI) file. Such files are attachable to a module by means of the `$INCLUDE` metacommand.

A metacommand is a directive to the VB/DOS interpreter that generally changes the operating mode of the application. Besides `$INCLUDE`, two other metacommands are `$DYNAMIC` and `$STATIC`, which change the default array declaration mode. The operating mode can also be changed by means of `OPTION` statements. `OPTION BASE` is used to set the initial count number in an array to 0 or 1. `OPTION EXPLICIT` is used to force variables to be formally declared and to disallow informal or implicit ("on the fly") declarations.

Review Questions

Answers to Review Questions appear in Appendix B.

1. If an application contains a conditional expression `IF status = FALSE THEN...`, what instruction must have been either invoked or included within the general declarations area of the main module?

2. If an array variable was declared dynamic and its contents were erased during redeclaration using the `REDIM` statement, is an `ERASE` instruction really necessary before invoking `REDIM`?

Part III

Instructions and Groups

13

Primary Program Operation

This chapter is a quick examination of the statements that affect the execution of some defined portion of the application or the execution of the program as a whole.

The End

With every complete procedure or multiple-instruction clause listed in this book thus far, I've closed the instruction set with some form of the END statement. The program itself can end after the last statement is executed, but for the sake of formality as well as legibility, you can use END to end it all.

END **Statement**

Syntax:

```
END [{FUNCTION ¦ IF ¦ SELECT ¦ SUB ¦ TYPE}]
```

On a line by itself, the END statement, when executed, terminates the current program. When used in conjunction with another term, the statement specifies the closing portion of a clause or procedure. There can be only one END statement per clause or procedure.

One member of the original BASIC vocabulary that survives in Visual Basic for MS-DOS is the STOP statement.

STOP **Statement**

Syntax:

```
STOP
```

Executing the STOP statement suspends program execution, provoking the same response from the interpreter as if the user had pressed Ctrl-Break on the keyboard. If the program is being run from the interpreter, the Code Editor will be visible after STOP is executed. If the program has been compiled, execution is suspended, and the controlling application or system should resume control. Program execution may later resume at a procedure or line label specified within a statement that the user must issue through the Immediate window CLI.

Because you can END a clause or procedure only once, VB/DOS provides you with a sort of "back door" statement with which you can terminate execution of a particular instruction set: EXIT.

EXIT **Statement**

Syntax:

```
EXIT {DO ¦ FOR ¦ FUNCTION ¦ SUB}
```

Execution of the EXIT statement immediately terminates execution of the current procedure or loop clause. In the case of loop clauses, execution of the program resumes with the instruction following the clause closure instruction. In the case of a SUB or FUNCTION procedure, execution resumes with the instruction following the instruction that placed the call to the procedure. If forms are currently running on-screen and the procedure was not called by another instruction, execution suspends pending the occurrence of a recognized user event.

Example

Here is an excerpt from a procedure appearing within the Expressor application introduced in Chapter 4, "The Development Process," slightly revised for this chapter to utilize all three of the preceding statements properly:

```
SUB ApplyFormula_Click ()
FOR in = 0 TO 4
p(in) = VAL(param(in).text)
NEXT in
ndx = CalcList.ListIndex + 1
IF ndx = -1 THEN EXIT SUB
ON ndx GOTO f1, f2, f3, f4, f5
MSGBOX "Trouble processing your request."
STOP
f1:
solution = surf_area_rccyl(p(0), p(1))
GOTO display_result
.
.
.
f5:
solution = dopp_shift(p(0), p(1), p(2), p(3))
display_result:
readout.caption = STR$(solution)
END SUB
```

Here is the preceding procedure written as pseudocode:

Procedure for clicking on the Apply Formula button:
Start counting from 0 to 4.
Place the value of the input parameter in the memory slot currently being counted into the stated array variable.
Keep counting.
The number of the formula just chosen is equal to the index of the formula listed in the list box, plus one to account for the fact that the first item is #0.
If no formula appears to be chosen, then get out of here.
Depending on the index value of the chosen formula, branch to the point in the code corresponding in the list to the index value.
If there was no branch, notify the user that something's wrong.
Then stop the program.
Branchpoint #1:
Go solve the surface area of a cylinder.
Display the result.

.

.

.

Branchpoint #5:
Solve for the Doppler shift equation.
Result-displaying branchpoint:
Place the solution value from the function procedure just executed into the readout.
End of procedure.

If you look closely, you find the instruction `IF ndx = -1 THEN EXIT SUB`. This instruction exits the procedure by itself if there is no formula selected within the drop-down list that the procedure can process. If, for some reason, the `ON ndx GOTO` multiple branch statement fails to work, a message box is displayed to that effect and `STOP` is executed. This works like a break command issued from the keyboard. If the Code Editor is running, execution may resume if the user invokes the Immediate window and tells the CLI to `GOTO display_result`.

Chain Stores

VB/DOS provides you with two methods for starting a new VB/DOS application from within the current application. The first is arguably the oldest statement in all of BASIC: `RUN`.

RUN **Statement**

Syntax:

```
RUN "[filename$]"
```

The `RUN` statement resets the operating state of the VB/DOS interpreter or the system running the current compiled program. If no *filename$* is specified, the current application is run again from the first instruction. If a *filename$* is specified and if that file refers to a VB/DOS application, that application is run from the first instruction. The *filename$* can include DOS path data and must be included within quotation marks. By default, VB/DOS searches for a .BAS source code file although the *filename$* can have any of the following extensions:

.BAS Basic source code module, without an included form

.MAK Uncompiled VB/DOS project file

.FRM VB/DOS form module

Once compiled, the `RUN` statement will allow .EXE files to be run, as long as they are compiled VB/DOS applications.

Another instruction in the VB/DOS vocabulary, `CHAIN`, is extremely close to `RUN`, except for one important difference, as outlined in the following text.

CHAIN **Statement**

Syntax:

```
CHAIN "[filename$]"
```

The `CHAIN` statement resets the operating state of the VB/DOS interpreter or the system running the current compiled program. If no *filename$* is specified, the current application is run again from the first instruction. If a *filename$* is specified and if that file refers to a VB/DOS application, that application is run from the first instruction. The *filename$* can include DOS path data and must be included within quotation marks. By default, VB/DOS searches for a .BAS source code file although the *filename$* can instead refer to a .MAK or a .FRM file.

If the module containing the `CHAIN` statement has declared any `COMMON` module-level values within named blocks, using the `COMMON /blockname/` syntax, then the program being chained to might declare, in its main module, the same */blockname/* using the `COMMON` statement. When execution passes to the new program, the variables declared in that program's `CHAIN` statement will pick up the values and contents of the variables with the same names in the previous program. The effect resembles a sort of "passing of the baton" between programs. VB/DOS is the first edition of Microsoft BASIC to offer this feature.

With the advent of VB/DOS, values within BASIC applications now have *cross-application scope,* by means of the `CHAIN` statement. This broadening of the scope boundaries has some far-reaching implications. Suppose you're writing a general accounting system for your business. The preferred accounting system model generally uses several interrelated programs that are often called "modules" but, unlike the VB/DOS definition of the term, they really are separate programs. You could rig each program in the accounting set to save its data file to disk before transferring control to the next program, which would load that file back in from disk. With the new functionality of `CHAIN`, however, you could simply store your primary variables outside of the database in memory blocks by way of declaring them with the `COMMON` statement, giving each block an appropriate name. You can then use `CHAIN` to transfer control between programs in the set without any added parameters. VB/DOS knows to keep the declared `COMMON` value blocks intact while the new program is being loaded in.

Finally, there's one statement in the VB/DOS vocabulary that passes control, for the time being, to an .EXE or .COM file: `SHELL`.

SHELL **Statement**

Syntax:

```
SHELL filename$
```

The `SHELL` statement temporarily suspends the execution of the current VB/DOS application, whether in interpreted or compiled mode, and passes control to the stated .EXE, .COM, or .BAT file. Generally, this file constitutes a DOS extension command whose associated file is located in the default DOS subdirectory. After execution of the file is complete, control is passed back to the VB/DOS application.

Summary

In VB/DOS, a conditional clause or procedure is terminated using the `END` statement. This statement acts as the bottom part of an instruction set enclosure, or nest. A loop clause or procedure is exited using the `EXIT` statement, without having to execute the statement that closes the clause or procedure. At any time, you can suspend execution of the program with the `STOP` statement.

Another VB/DOS application can be run through an instruction from the running VB/DOS application, using either the `RUN` or the `CHAIN` statements. The two statements are similar, except that `CHAIN` leaves intact any values declared within a memory block using the COMMON statement. Control can be passed at any time to an .EXE, a .COM, or a .BAT file using the SHELL statement.

Review Questions

Answers to Review Questions appear in Appendix B.

1. What is the difference between the END SUB statement and the EXIT SUB statement?
2. What is the difference between the END statement and the END SUB statement?

14

Phraseology

This chapter is a review of Visual Basic for MS-DOS' many "parts of speech." In the course of this review, I expand on many of the principles introduced in Chapter 3, "Grammar and Linguistics." You are then introduced to the principles of object-oriented syntax, which is relatively new to BASIC. Object-oriented syntax may not be entirely new to you, however, because you've been using it since Chapter 2.

Programming Versus the Real World

When you write instructions for another person to follow—for instance, how to construct a filing cabinet—each individual written instruction is generally a complete sentence. Each sentence represents a step in the construction process. For the moment, assume that there is only one way to build a filing cabinet given the tools and materials you've specified that your reader must have ready in order to begin. You have one specific objective or product in mind, for which there is only one design and one method of construction, without variance.

You expect each step in the construction process to follow the previous one in a natural sequence. It's highly unlikely that you'll ever find yourself specifying special cases for what to do if the screws are twice as long as they should be; what action is required if the side panels have been sawed to one-half the width of the shelf panels; or how to drive a nail into a shelf panel if the panel happens to be made of aluminum rather than oak. You don't expect to have to write such "conditional" instructions because you assume your reader has acquired precisely the tools and materials you specified and wishes to construct exactly the filing cabinet you have in mind. You assume your reader's objective is definite.

When writing instructions for a VB/DOS program, you as a programmer cannot assume that anything related to the user is definite. Suppose you're writing an index card filing program. Your intention is for the user to be able to define the data fields, field labels, and contents for each index card. In effect you're programming a flat-file database manager. Whenever you give the user choices—either in terms of how the user inputs data or how the user manipulates the program—you cannot make assumptions or even predictions as to what that choice will be.

You instead could have written a program that keeps, in a specified format, records concerning some absolute subject, such as baseball cards. It would probably be an easier program for you to write because you wouldn't have to devise a system by which the user could manipulate the record storage format. In making things more definitive and more manageable for yourself as a programmer, you in turn limit the degree of choice the user has, which makes your program less applicable. From a marketing standpoint, you'll have fewer users.

To make your program more applicable to more people, you must write instructions that take possibilities into account. The more generalized you make the purpose of your application, the foggier your view of its intended user becomes. You do not see the world where this user resides, and you aren't sure of what his job really is. Because of this, as programmer you often have to place yourself in the role of several users, anticipating what each user can possibly do with your application. There is some measure of hypothesis, after all, in programming.

Subjective Reasoning Versus Objective Reasoning

A *statement* is an instruction that specifies a change.

A *function* is an arithmetic operation that returns a single value.

The two primary types of VB/DOS instructions are statements and functions. A *statement* is an instruction that specifies a change or deviation in the operating status of the program.

By contrast, a function is an abbreviated form of an expression or mathematical formula. A function often appears in a formula itself. A *function* is an arithmetic operation performed on a value, variable, or expression, having a result that is returned as a single value.

The two types of instructions are quite distinguishable from each other. In short, a statement performs operations on the computer or the program, whereas a function performs operations on a value or on data. You undoubtedly have noticed that when I formally introduce each instruction term or keyword to you, to the right of the keyword is its "part of speech," or type. To this point, I have introduced many statements, some functions, and the only four internal variables in VB/DOS.

An *object* is a data structure that combines the data contents and attributes with the encoded form of its function.

With the advent of Visual Basic for Windows, from which VB/DOS is partly derived, Microsoft has added object-oriented syntax to the BASIC language, particularly with regard to the wide array of graphic objects supported by the interpreter. In the conventional BASIC vernacular, changes are made to some part of the program or to some value by stating the results of those changes as facts. In object-oriented syntax, in contrast, changes are made to some part of the program by specifying the nature of the change.

A *handle* is used by a true object-oriented language to manipulate objects.

This concept is confusing, so here's some more detail. A true data object actually contains the part of the program that states what should be done with the data. More to the point, the structure of a true object defines how that structure is to react or be changed when an action is applied to it. For instance, a true object-oriented sentence (although not in VB/DOS) might be `object1.move`. Part of the program for moving is called when the move action is invoked; however, just how the object is moved is defined by the data object itself. In doing so, the object gives the computer a type of *handle* with which it can be operated.

VB/DOS is not an object-oriented language in the true sense of the word. It does, however, give the appearance of true object orientation by utilizing its syntax to some degree in VB/DOS instructions. Figure 14.1 depicts the interlocking nature of terms in VB/DOS' implementation of object-oriented syntax.

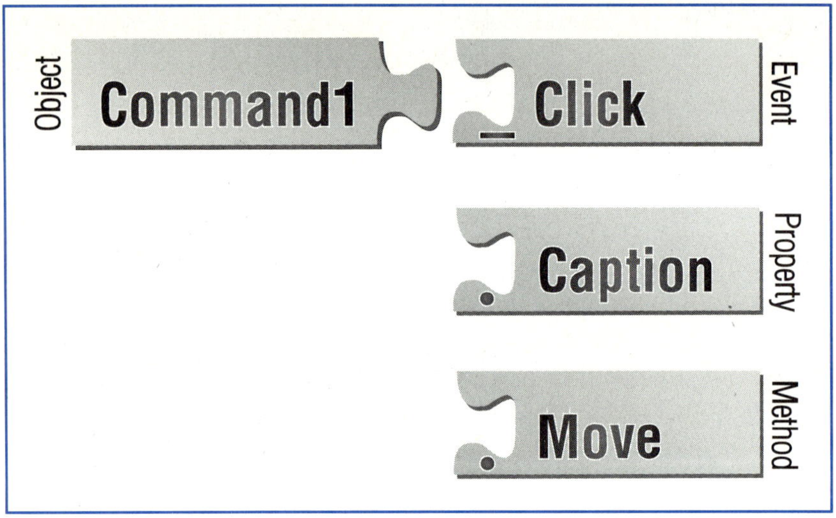

Figure 14.1. Object orientation can be puzzling at first.

A Visual Basic for DOS *graphic object* either receives input or displays data.

The only data objects supported by VB/DOS are *graphic objects.* Many people argue that these are not really objects by the definition subscribed to by the Object Management Group, a coalition of software manufacturers cooperating to define language standards. Microsoft is a member of this group. A graphic object in VB/DOS is a data structure that is representable visually and that behaves to some degree as a device which either receives user input, displays results, or does both.

A *method* is an instruction that directs the interpreter to perform a programmed action on a graphic object.

Each VB/DOS graphic object has been given a predefined set of actions that are applicable toward that object, which are called *methods.*

The syntax of a method instruction is as follows:

```
object.method [parameters]
```

Like an objective-case noun in Latin, the object is stated first, separated from the name for the method—the verb in the Latin sentence—by a period. The BASIC `PRINT` instruction, which is one of the language's original statements, has two syntaxes in VB/DOS. In addition to the standard statement syntax, VB/DOS has added the *method* syntax. The new syntax appears in such instructions as `Form1.PRINT "One more method under way."`.

Properties are the attributes of graphic objects that can be changed.

By entering the programs listed here into the interpreter, you gain a modicum of experience in manipulating the properties of graphic objects. A *property* is an attribute of a graphic object that has values or contents that can be established or reassigned in the manner of an expression of assignment.

Here's a piece of one of the property tables from a revised version of `NameForm`:

Object Type	*Property*	*Setting*
Vertical Scroll Bar	.Top	71
	.Left	0
	.Width	1
	.Height	14
	.CtlName	RecordShown
	.LargeChange	10
	.SmallChange	1
	.Max	1000

These properties can alternatively be set with source code instructions, as follows:

```
VScroll1.Top = 71
VScroll1.Left = 0
VScroll1.Width = 1
VScroll1.Height = 14
VScroll1.LargeChange = 10
VScroll1.SmallChange = 1
VScroll1.Max = 1000
```

As you can see, the syntax of property assignments is as follows:

```
object.property = "setting"
```

A *setting* represents the state, appearance, or some aspect of a graphic object.

An *event* is used to trigger the execution of a procedure.

Notice how strings are assigned to object properties by enclosing the string within quotation marks, just as if you were assigning the contents to a string variable. The values or contents assigned here are called *settings*.

As the beneficiary of user input, each graphic object can be the recipient of what object-oriented syntax calls *events*. An *event* is a type of user input applied to a graphic object, which is often used to trigger the execution of a procedure.

By now you're familiar with the syntax for attributing an event to a graphic object:

```
object_event
```

The event is separated from the object by an underscore character, as in `Command1_DblClick`.

One Final Remark

Before you start breaking new ground again, I'd like to introduce you to one statement that is used primarily to add things that are not executed by a program: `REM`.

REM — **Statement**

Syntax:

```
{REM ¦ '} [metacommand_set][remark]
```

When the interpreter encounters the `REM` statement on a line, it ignores the remainder of the contents of that line and skips execution to the next line. This enables you to type anything into the source code at random, generally for use as comments. The apostrophe (') can alternatively be used in place of the term `REM`. All metacommands entered into the source code of an application must be preceded by the `REM` statement or an apostrophe.

Example

Here's an example of `REM` in use as the anchor for a bannerhead along the top of the general declarations area of the main module of Expressor Mark II:

```
'-----------------------------------------------------------------
'¦ Expressor Mark II                                              ¦
'¦   by D. F. Scott for Visual Basic for MS-DOS By Example        ¦
'¦                                                                ¦
'¦----------------------------------------------------------------¦
COMMON SHARED readout_value AS DOUBLE, combine_value
➥ AS DOUBLE
COMMON SHARED ready AS INTEGER
```

Notice the apostrophes on the far left side of the nonexecutable lines. These characters make room for you to place your signature on your program. What better use for a remark than as a way to promote yourself?

Example

The other major use for remarks is as explanations for people who read your program and would like to know what you're talking about. Here's a revised procedure from the Expressor:

```
SUB Times_Click ()
'Find out what the readout says.
assess_readout
'Multiply the readout by the compared value...
readout_value = readout_value * combine_value
'...and swap values.
combine_value = readout_value
'Display the result.
readout.caption = STR$(readout_value)
'Make the next digit pressed clear the readout.
ready = 0
END SUB
```

Before every instruction in the preceding code is a relatively long comment explaining what's happening. Such comments are not unlike writing pseudocode.

Summary

The two major types of instructions in BASIC and VB/DOS are statements, which operate on elements of the program, and functions, which operate on elements of data. Microsoft has added object-oriented syntax to VB/DOS. In the process, it has classified graphic controls in VB/DOS applications as graphic objects. A stated action to be performed on a graphic object is a method. An attribute an object affects or changes somehow by such an action is a property. An element of user input involving a graphic object is an event. Each of these three "functions" of graphic objects is invoked using its own particular syntax.

Review Questions

Answers to Review Questions appear in Appendix B.

1. If the term `REM` appears before a legitimate VB/DOS instruction on a line, will that line be executed?
2. In the instruction `PRINT "Goodbye, Old World!"`, is `PRINT` being used as a statement or a method?

Review Exercise

The following is a procedure from CONVBASE.FRM, the application introduced in Chapter 10, "Number Systems." Using what you know about the various types of VB/DOS instructions, write this procedure on paper. Beside each instruction write its type.

```
FUNCTION Convert$ (convValue, convBase)
Find_Top:
comp = convBase ^ expn
IF comp < convValue THEN
```

```
    expn = expn + 1
    GOTO Find_Top
END IF
FOR spot = expn TO 0 STEP -1
    digit% = convValue \ (convBase ^ spot)
    convValue = convValue MOD (convBase ^ spot)
    cvt$ = cvt$ + RIGHT$(STR$(digit%), 1)
NEXT spot
IF LEFT$(cvt$, 1) = "0" AND LEN(cvt$) > 1 THEN
    cvt$ = RIGHT$(cvt$, LEN(cvt$) - 1)
END IF
Convert$ = cvt$
END FUNCTION
```

15

Conditional Clauses

A *condition* is the test of whether an instruction will be executed.

In this chapter, you learn about the mechanism that makes the execution of a set of Visual Basic for MS-DOS instructions dependent on the results of a test. The test that must be passed for this instruction set to be executed is called a *condition.* When the test is passed, the set of instructions is executed conditionally. The specific set of instructions that is executed based on the results of the test, or the state of some value in memory, is called a *clause.*

You will construct VB/DOS clauses based on expressions of comparison, which execute sets of instructions based on the results of that comparison. The two major conditional clause statements in VB/DOS are IF-THEN and SELECT CASE. You use both statements in this chapter.

The Construction of a Clause

A *clause* is a set of instructions whose execution is in some way dependent upon the value of a variable.

As you become more familiar with VB/DOS, you'll hopefully grow more comfortable with the various ways of referring to sets and sequences of instructions. VB/DOS has many different conventions for referring to instruction sets, some more formal than others and some less formal. A clause is an informal way of referring to an instruction set, although most of the source code of a VB/DOS application can be divided into clauses. A *clause* is any set of instructions having its execution dependent on the value of a variable in a mathematical expression.

When you read VB/DOS source code instructions from top to bottom in sequence, each clause is bound at its beginning and end by two parts of a clause statement. The following pseudocode shows the general construction of an ordinary clause:

Clause statement part1 [expression]
Instruction1
Instruction2
.
.
.
Instructionn
Clause statement part2

The dependent instructions between both parts of the clause statement are *nested.* When nesting instructions within a clause, many programmers choose to indent them a few spaces or, in VB/DOS, with a tab. This form of typesetting helps clauses stand out and makes them more easily identifiable, although the indention is not necessary for the clause to be executed. The instructions in a clause can all be flush against the left margin without affecting the program.

When the clause contains a mathematical expression for evaluation, it appears within the first part of the clause statement. For the most part, expressions are stated outright in the manner you've learned thus far. In a few cases, however, parts of the expression are actually implied within the statement governing the clause, as you'll see later in this chapter.

Example

Following is an ordinary conditional clause the way it might normally appear in a VB/DOS program:

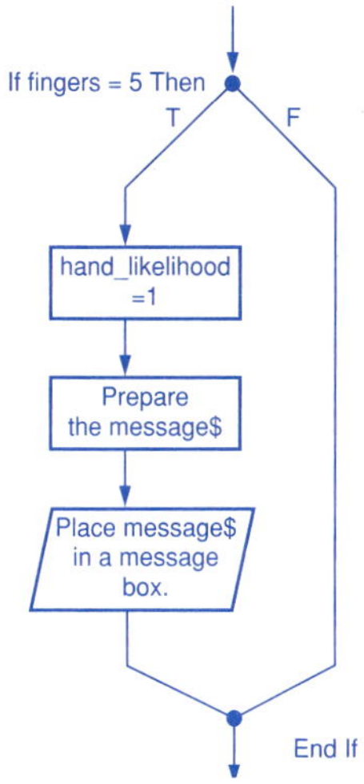


```
IF fingers = 5 THEN
   hand_likelihood = 1
   message$ = "Five fingers. . . could be an
     ordinary hand."
   MSGBOX message$
END IF
```

The purpose of this somewhat fictitious code fragment is hopefully self-evident. Suppose you have a program with the purpose of evaluating data pertaining to a sentient being, to determine whether it's human. The preceding fragment is a whole clause because it is bordered at the beginning and end by two parts of an `IF-THEN` statement. The mathematical expression being tested is `fingers = 5`, where `fingers` is an arbitrarily named variable. The three dependent instructions within the clause will be executed only if this sentient being's data shows that it has five fingers. Within those dependent instructions, a flag variable is declared and a message is displayed to that effect. Here is a detailed description of the statement:

`IF... THEN... [ELSEIF... THEN] [ELSE... ]... END IF` Statement

Syntax 1:

```
IF expression1 THEN
   instruction block1
[ELSEIF expression2 THEN
   instruction block2]
.
.
.
[ELSE
   instruction blockn]
END IF
```

The `IF-THEN` statement tests a mathematical expression to see if it is true. If it is, execution continues with the first dependent instruction below the expression. If the expression is not true, execution skips down to the first instruction outside of the nest. If that instruction is ELSE, the dependent instructions below it will be executed. If that instruction is ELSEIF, another mathematical expression is evaluated in the same manner as the first. The clause is terminated when END IF is reached.

An alternate syntax for this statement that is used in cases warranting extreme brevity is Syntax 2:

```
IF expression THEN instruction1 [ELSE instruction2]
```

The preceding syntax is reserved for single-instruction clauses and can be written all on one line. Notice that the END IF is excluded from this syntax.

IF-THEN is the fundamental conditional statement of the BASIC programming language. The statement can be described as a mechanism having a trigger that is a mathematical expression. The result of this expression is a Boolean logical value somewhere in memory, which can be interpreted as true or false (–1 or 0). If the expression is true, the first set of instructions in the clause is executed in sequence.

Should there be another set of instructions in the IF-THEN clause following the term ELSE or ELSEIF, that set will be executed in sequence if the original expression beside the term IF is false. Written in pseudocode, here is how the general mechanism of a fully developed IF-THEN statement appears:

If this expression evaluates true, then
  Execute this set of instructions;
Otherwise, if this other expression evaluates true, then
  Execute this set of instructions instead;
If all else fails to be true, then
  Execute this set of instructions as a last-ditch measure.
End of clause.

The mechanism of IF-THEN is flexible; think of it like an adaptable logical switch. In the conventional structure of IF-THEN, you can use this switch to have the program either perform a process or leave things as they are. The mathematical expression being evaluated throws this switch one way or the other. Therefore, any process of instructions that can be described as "one way or the other" or "one way or nothing at all" can be modeled by `IF-THEN`.

Example

Suppose you have an input form on your screen containing two option buttons marked `Active` and `Inactive`, describing the state of some process. You want the users of your program to click `Active` if they want the process to take place. `IF-THEN` can be used to trigger a process if the `Active` button on the form is set. Here is how the conditional clause might appear:

```
IF ActiveButton.Value = -1 THEN
   process$ = "Active"
END IF
```

Here the value `-1` represents the Boolean *true* logical value as defined in Chapter 7, "Logic." If the `.Value` property of `ActiveButton` is set to true (–1), the contents of string variable `process$` are in turn set to read `Active`. Otherwise, execution of the program skips to the instruction following `END IF`. A word of caution here: If the variable `process$` was never formally declared before this clause was executed and if the state of `ActiveButton` is *false* (0), `process$` will not exist as a variable. This may result in an error with any evaluation of that variable later in the program.

The `IF-THEN` statement itself is not "cognizant" of the complexity of the mathematical expression being evaluated. In other words, `IF-THEN` is not performing the actual evaluation. What the interpreter actually does first is take the included expression and reduce it logically to a –1 or 0, a true or false. Regardless of how many terms you include in your expression of comparison, `IF-THEN` only operates as if you wrote `-1` or `0` in place of that expression.

Example

Suppose a list box on your form is to contain a series of over-the-counter stock issues that have attractively high price-to-earnings ratios and are worth your consideration for investment. Here's how an IF-THEN clause might appear that enters the name of an attractive company to the list:

```
IF price(stock) / earnings(stock) > 10 THEN
   OTCStock.ADDITEM ticker_symbol$(stock)
END IF
```

In the preceding clause, the subscript variable stock was used as an index number for each informal record of stock offerings in the list. Variable stock is thus the *key* to each array. For instance, if you're evaluating a stock with index number 143, at some time prior to the execution of this clause the value of stock would be set to 143. The variable is then used as an index for the three array variables in the example. In English, the clause might read: "If the price of stock #143 divided by the earnings of stock #143 is greater than 10, add the ticker symbol of stock #143 to the list of OTC stocks to consider."

IF-THEN as a Two-Sided Argument

If the IF-THEN clause can be likened to a sandwich, when ELSE is included it becomes the Big Mac of clauses—with IF-THEN and END IF on both sides and ELSE acting as the thin slice of bun in the middle. When ELSE is included in an IF-THEN clause, it acts as a partition between the true part of the instruction set and the false side. IF-THEN is used in such cases to have the interpreter execute either one or the other set of instructions, depending on the reduced logical value of the expression (–1 or 0). Figure 15.1 demonstrates this point, by breaking an ordinary clause into two "either/or" segments.

Example

Suppose there is a number box in the form and you need it to register a value only if it is positive. If the value is negative, you want the box to be left blank or else made blank. Here is a clause for that purpose:

```
IF balance >= 0 THEN
   num_box.Text = STR$(balance)
ELSE
   num_box.Text = ""
END IF
```

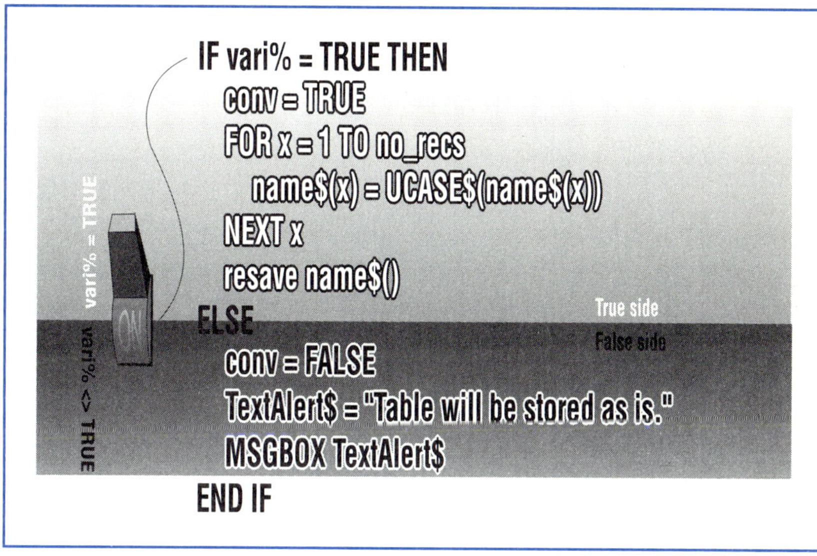

Figure 15.1. Point/Counter point.

The clause will set the number box named `num_box` to the textual form of the value of the variable `balance` if the value of `balance` is greater than or equal to 0 (in other words, if `balance` is positive). If the expression contained within `IF-THEN` evaluates true, the expression preceding `Else` is executed. When `ELSE` is reached, execution skips to the instruction following `END IF`. If the initial expression evaluates false, execution skips to the first term outside of the instruction nest immediately below. In this case, that term is not `END IF`, but it is instead `ELSE`. This tells the interpreter that there is a set of instructions to be executed in the event of falsehood. In this case, the text of `num_box` is set to a null string (made blank). Graphic objects cannot receive numeric values as output assignments—only text or string contents.

Example

The mathematical expression being tested within IF-THEN can be divided into parts by Boolean logical operators. As long as the expression reduces to logical true or false, any operator is allowed within the expression. For instance, imagine that your program is a game that branches to the end if the player has run out of money or if time has expired. The clause that triggers that branch might read as follows:

```
IF money <= 0 OR time = 0 THEN
   GOTO no_win
END IF
```

The preceding clause is one example of a *conditional branch,* which jumps the program to the statement beneath the label specified in the GOTO statement only if the condition evaluates true. Here, the condition will evaluate true if the player has beaucoup bucks but no turns left, or if the player has several moves to go but is bankrupt.

NOTE: Although the clause is written like a sentence, the term IF is never stated twice—so `IF money <= 0 OR IF time = 0` would be erroneous.

Example

The syntax of a mathematical expression within the first line of the IF-THEN clause is not restricted to that of an expression of assignment; the left side of the equation does not have to be a single variable. It instead can be an expression, as demonstrated by the following amendment to the no-more-money conditional branch:

```
IF money + account <= 0 OR time = 0 THEN
   GOTO no_win
END IF
```

Suppose a second variable account comes into play in this game, representing an amount the player has stashed away in savings. The player is considered bankrupt if he has no money in his pocket + no money in his account.

CAUTION: In expressions of comparison in VB/DOS, values or contents can be combined on both sides of the equation. Keep in mind that this is not true for all versions of BASIC.

Natural Selection

The IF-THEN statement is used frequently in this book because it comprises a huge portion of all BASIC and VB/DOS programs. There is another conditional clause that is used far less frequently but has a form that makes it especially functional in cases of multiple evaluated states, and not just one or two. This multiple-evaluative clause is SELECT CASE.

SELECT CASE... CASE... END SELECT — Statement

Syntax:

```
SELECT CASE expression
   CASE [IS] comparison1a [TO comparison1b]
      instruction block1
   [CASE [IS] comparison2a [TO comparison2b]]
      [instruction block2]
.
.
.
   [CASE ELSE]
      [instruction blockn]
END SELECT
```

The SELECT CASE statement compares the value or text contents of an initial expression to that of one or more other expressions for equality. The statement contains several expressions of comparison for equality, although the element being compared is written only once as the initial expression, at the front of the clause. This initial expression can consist of a variable by itself or even a number by itself; however, it can also contain any number of elements specified or implied, and combined by arithmetic operators.

For each equality comparison, in the event (or CASE) one of the comparisons between expressions evaluates true, the set of instructions below CASE is executed. When the next CASE or END SELECT is reached, execution skips to the instruction immediately following END SELECT.

The purpose of SELECT CASE is to give the program a way of assessing options. Written in pseudocode, here's the general mechanism of SELECT CASE:

The following clause concerns the logically reduced
value of this expression:
    In case the reduction equals this amount,
        Execute this set of instructions;
    On the other hand, in case the reduction equals
     this amount,
        Execute this set of instructions instead;
    If all else fails and the reduction equals nothing
     mentioned thus far,
        Execute this final set of instructions.
End of clause.

The phrase *logically reduced,* with respect to arithmetic, refers to the act of obtaining the solution value to an expression. For instance, if `a = 5` and `b = 3`, the expression `5 - (a - b)` logically reduces to `3`. Similarly, the expression `(a > b)` logically reduces to `-1` (true). At the present time, `5 - (c - b)` logically reduces to `8` because you haven't assigned `c` a value yet; `c` is assumed to equal `0`, and `5 - (0 - b)` = `5 - (-b)` = `8`. As you can see, expressions that contain variables that haven't been formally declared still reduce logically to real-number values.

> **TIP:** There are no symbolic, imaginary, or irrational values for variables in any computer language, as there are in algebra. Every VB/DOS expression, therefore, must logically reduce to a real number value.

The most common type of SELECT CASE comparison concerns an integer variable having a value that represents one of a handful of possible states. This state could be as simple to comprehend as which button was pressed, the user's selected expert level, or which planet in the solar system is being evaluated for orbital characteristics. Conceivably, you might have several unique sets of instructions for each option; for instance, the formula for sideways orbits applies only to Uranus. The sets of instructions for each option can be included within the SELECT CASE clause, with each option specified following the word CASE.

Example

For the first example of SELECT CASE, imagine you're programming a board game with three expert levels (0 = novice, 1 = intermediate, 2 = expert). You need your program to set specific conditions based on which number the user selects. Here's how the code sample might appear:

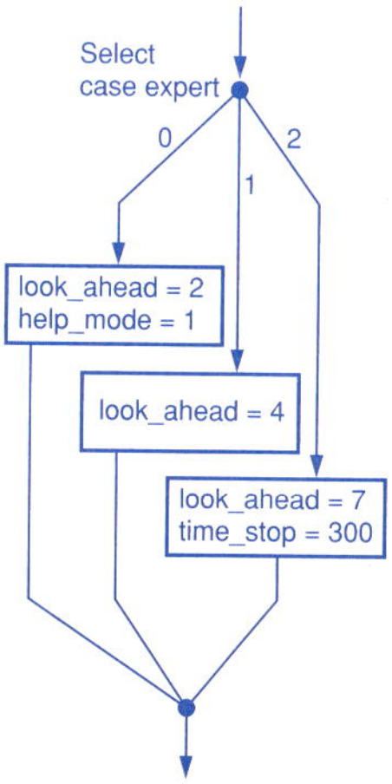


```
SELECT CASE expert
   CASE 0
      look_ahead = 2
      help_mode = 1
   CASE 1
      look_ahead = 4
   CASE 2
      look_ahead = 7
      time_stop = 300
END SELECT
```

There are three comparisons taking place here: `expert = 0`, `expert = 1`, and `expert = 2`. In each of these cases, however, the equality operator = does not appear. The CASE term implies that you're comparing the value beside CASE with the value beside SELECT CASE for equality.

Example

The same logical mechanism of SELECT CASE can be applied with respect to string variables. Here's an example that creates a currency conversion factor based on the contents of a string variable:

```
SELECT CASE currency$
   CASE "pound sterling"
      conv_fact = 1.76
   CASE "franc"
      conv_fact = .87
   CASE ELSE
      conv_fact = 1
      currency$ = "dollar"
END SELECT
```

I could have been more worldly and added more cases; a SELECT CASE clause can handle significantly more cases than three. The preceding clause declares by inference a currency conversion factor conv_fact and assigns to it a value based on the contents of a string variable currency$. Notice the final condition in the clause, headed by CASE ELSE. This final case takes care of the conversion factor in the event that the contents of currency$ aren't anything the program recognizes. You can use CASE ELSE for setting default values or initial conditions for your program if those conditions cannot be set or determined logically.

In Search of the Pneuma

The key to comprehending a high-level programming language is in recognizing its mechanisms of logic. Oftentimes, the more linguistically complex a language such as BASIC becomes, the more difficult it is to discern its logical mechanism from its mesh of phraseology. This is the primary danger in using "fourth-generation" languages, or "graphically-objective" languages such as VB/DOS or Visual Basic for Windows, to perform logically-intensive tasks. Perhaps the primary secret to programming well in VB/DOS is being able to look beneath the phraseological and graphical *phenomena*, and operate first and foremost with the logical mechanism of the language—the soul of any programming language, or what the Greeks call the *pneuma*.

Figure 15.2 depicts the logical mechanism of the SELECT CASE clause. Notice how, in the same way ELSE acts as a partition between the true and false side of the IF-THEN clause, CASE acts as a partition between multiple potential solutions. It's easy to spot the *phraseological* difference between SELECT CASE and IF-THEN. Recognizing the *logical* difference between them, however, can make both simpler for you to use. Think of IF-THEN and SELECT CASE as two ways of posing questions as on a written test, in which case the two types of clauses are like two categories of questions: IF-THEN is like a true or false question, whereas SELECT CASE is multiple choice.

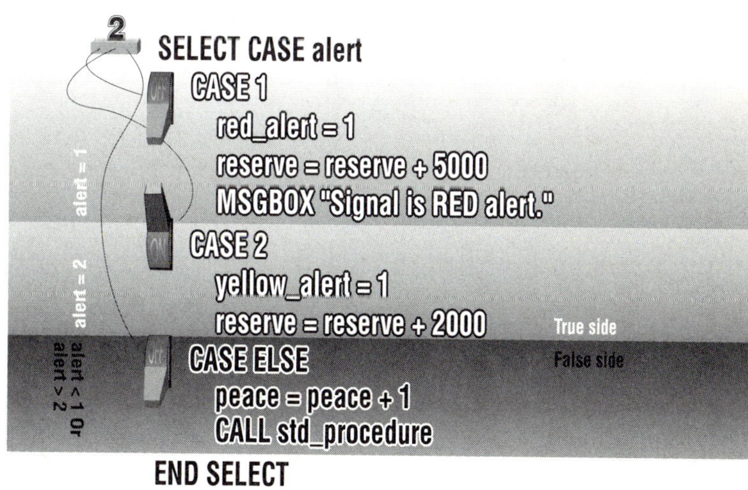

Figure 15.2. The mechanism of SELECT CASE.

The way SELECT CASE is designed, the interpreter's mission is to compare the reduced value of two expressions for equality. You can fool this mechanism so that it evaluates one expression to see if its value is greater than or equal to the reduced value of several other expressions. Assume you have a variable `fuel_level#` having a value that tends to drop over time below three set stages—from *optimal* to *nominal,* then below *marginal,* and then below *critical.* You could establish `CASE` ranges for what fuel levels are nominal and what are critical. But for a double-precision variable, you'd have to specify range values to within 308 decimal places. In other words, you couldn't specify `0 TO 299` and `300 TO 499` as ranges and expect a fuel level of 299.349834923 to fall within one of those ranges. You have to have some way of saying "over and above this level" rather than merely specifying ranges and allowing for borderlines to form virtual blind spots.

Example

Here's a way of defeating the "equality only" restriction of the `SELECT CASE` clause:

```
SELECT CASE -1
   CASE fuel_level >= 1000
      alert = 0
      status$ = "Optimal"
   CASE fuel_level >= 600
      alert = 1
      status$ = "Nominal"
   CASE fuel_level >= 200
      alert = 2
      status$ = "Marginal"
   CASE fuel_level >= 0
      alert = 3
      status$ = "CRITICAL"
END SELECT
```

`SELECT CASE` compares two expressions for equality, though the depth of these expressions is unlimited. Thus, `-1` is an expression and, as you know, –1 stands for logical truth in VB/DOS. Each expression of comparison beside the `CASE` term is reduced to a logical value of either –1 or 0. All `SELECT CASE` has to do is keep making comparisons until `-1 = -1`—until the reduced value of the expression is equal to logical true. When that happens, the instructions following CASE are executed until either the next CASE instruction or END SELECT is reached. You now have multiple ranges with discernible borderlines, and you have also defeated the equality restriction of SELECT CASE. If you had used the instruction CONST TRUE = -1 in the global module, the first line of this clause could read SELECT CASE TRUE and make even more sense to the human reader.

You could have used an IF-THEN clause to achieve much the same results as the SELECT CASE clause did previously. In fact, in the interest of full disclosure, here's the substitute clause:

```
IF fuel_level >= 1000
   alert = 0
   status$ = "Optimal"
ELSEIF fuel_level >= 600
   alert = 1
   status$ = "Nominal"
ELSEIF fuel_level >= 200
   alert = 2
   status$ = "Marginal"
ELSEIF fuel_level >= 0
   alert = 3
   status$ = "CRITICAL"
END IF
```

There's one less line in this clause, and the logical mechanism is much the same. Theoretically, SELECT CASE should execute more quickly; however, the difference in speed may be so marginal that it isn't noticeable. Your choice of instructions may be one of style.

Summary

Sets of VB/DOS instructions can be executed conditionally by placing them within clauses. Each conditional clause is contingent on at least one expression evaluating true. Those instructions that are dependent on this expression are called *nested instructions.* In the IF-THEN clause, the crucial expression is one of comparison. Such expressions are said to logically reduce to a value of –1 (true) or 0 (false). In the complex form of IF-THEN, the statements preceding ELSE are executed if the expression is true, and the statements following ELSE are executed if the expression is false.

In the SELECT CASE clause, the logically reduced values of several expressions are compared with one expression for equality. Several sets of dependent instructions can be nested within SELECT CASE, each set being bound by a contingent expression evaluating true. Only one set of instructions is executed within a SELECT CASE clause.

Review Questions

Answers to Review Questions appear in Appendix B.

The following fragment of code is designed to test your brain. Without using your computer, execute the instructions in your mind. Respond to the following questions by estimating the value or contents of the variable shown at the time the last instruction in the list is executed.

```
x = 15
y = 5
throughput$ = "Go"
logic = -1
IF x > 8 THEN
   SELECT CASE logic
      CASE (x / y) = 3
         logic = 0
         y = 3
      CASE (x / y) = 5
         throughput$ = "Stop"
         x = logic
   END SELECT
ELSEIF x > 1 THEN
   SELECT CASE y
      CASE 5
         throughput$ = "Caution"
      CASE 3
         caution$ = "Negative"
   END SELECT
END IF
```

1. `x`
2. `y`
3. `throughput$`
4. `logic`
5. `caution$`

Review Exercise

A variable `velo` represents the velocity of a test rocket-powered automobile. The maximum velocity projected for this vehicle is 305 miles per hour. On the other end of the scale, the minimum safe velocity for the car at maximum power is 120 miles per hour. The VB/DOS automobile simulator will light a yellow alert light when the velocity of the car is within 20 percent of its maximum or minimum speed, and a red light when it is within 10 percent of its maximum or minimum speed. You can say `alert$ = "yellow"` or `alert$ = "red"` to stand for this light. Write a routine that sets `alert$` to its proper contents for any value of `velo`.

16

Loop Clauses

In this chapter, you see how Visual Basic for MS-DOS interprets instructions that are to be executed a set number of times with the loop clause. A loop is a set of instructions to be repetitively executed in a cycle. This cycle continues from the top of the clause to the bottom of the clause and back to the top again, generally until some condition is met—until a logical expression evaluates true. If the loop has no condition, execution continues in a cycle indefinitely until the loop is exited manually or the program ends. At the end of this chapter, you'll understand why you would want to repeat yourself so often.

To Loop or Not To Loop

Following is the high-level language definition for the term *loop*. If you read it carefully, loops may not be as repetitious as they seem.

A *loop* is a set of instructions that generally repeat as long as a condition holds true.

A *loop* is a set of instructions executed repetitively until an expressed mathematical condition is met or until the loop is exited manually.

What VB/DOS instructions are worthy of being executed several times in succession? Suppose you assigned a value to a variable, as in `spare_tires = 15`. Making that assignment five times in succession would result in the value of spare_tires being 15—which is what it would have been had you made the assignment only once.

An *iteration* is one cycle of execution of the instructions in a loop clause.

In cases of small clusters of instructions, the point of establishing loops must not be for the sake of pure repetition. The secret to the operation of the loop is in repeating the same instructions without evaluating the same values each time. Loops are generally constructed so that a separate variable maintains the current count of the number of *iterations* made thus far in the loop.

In the FOR-NEXT loop, a variable is maintained by the enclosing statement that is changed with each iteration. Generally, 1 is added to the variable (the variable is *incremented*) unless some other value is specified. In any event, the count variable changes. This change is reflected in the instructions within the loop. So a FOR-NEXT loop, although a repetition of the same instructions, is not a repetition of the same interpretations.

FOR...NEXT — Statement

Syntax:

```
FOR count = startval TO endval [STEP addval]
   instruction block1
   [EXIT FOR]
   [instruction block2]
   .
   .
   .
NEXT [count]
```

The FOR-NEXT clause encloses a set of instructions that are to be executed repetitively. At first, the variable *count* is assigned an initial value specified by *startval*. Execution of the clause then proceeds in sequence and can be exited on reaching the statement EXIT FOR.

At NEXT *count*, a value is added to variable *count*. This value is generally 1, unless otherwise specified as *addval* beside the optional term STEP. If the augmented value of *count* is less than or equal to *endval* specified at the top of the clause, execution jumps to the instruction immediately following the `FOR` line. If *`count`* is found to be greater than *`endval`*, the loop is terminated and execution proceeds to the instruction below `NEXT` *`count`*. If no `FOR-NEXT` clause exists within this `FOR-NEXT` clause, specification of *`count`* following the term `NEXT` is optional.

Here's the general construction of a `FOR-NEXT` loop, as expressed in pseudocode:

Start counting between this initial value and this maximum value, keep track of the count, and be prepared to add this amount to the count value.

Execute this block of instructions.

Now add the stated amount to the count. If the result is equal to or less than the maximum value, go back to the beginning of the loop.

As you can see, `NEXT` *`count`* speaks volumes. Figure 16.1 shows the `FOR-NEXT` statement in more visual terms.

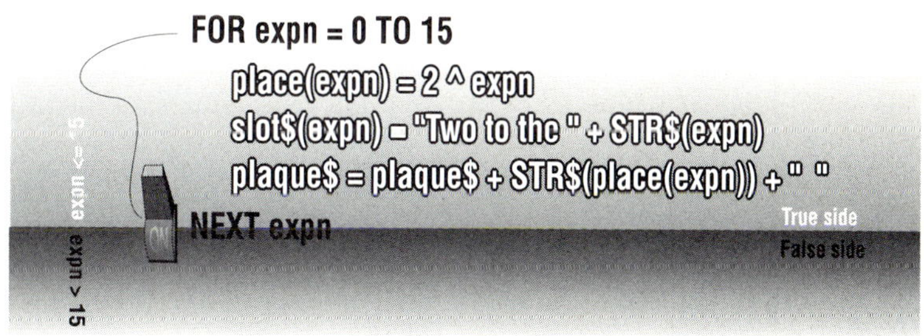

Figure 16.1. The true and false sides of a loop clause.

Example

For the first demonstration of a reasonable loop, you see how with each passing iteration the evaluation should change, whereas the instructions remain the same:

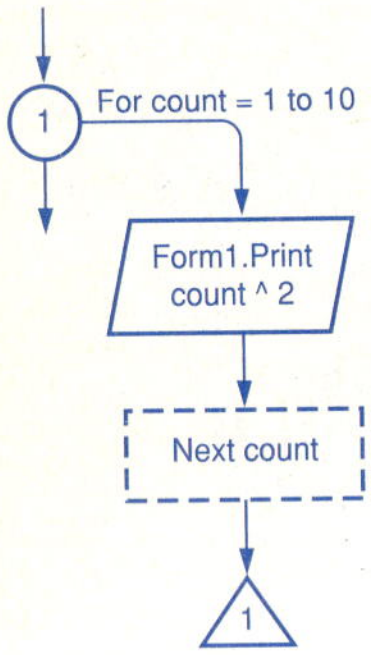


```
FOR count = 1 TO 10
   PRINT count ^ 2
NEXT count
```

The result of this loop is a list of the first 10 squared integers. Notice that `count` is referred to within the loop nest itself. Because `count` is continually incremented by `NEXT count`, each time the expression `count ^ 2` is encountered, the result is always different. In almost every `FOR-NEXT` loop you'll write, the variable expressed just after `FOR` plays a role in the expressions within the nest of the clause.

Example

Perhaps the most common use for loop clauses is as a way to address elements of an array in sequence. Here's a loop that writes the contents of one array to a file one datum at a time:

```
FOR c = 1 TO recno
   PRINT #1, dat$(c)
NEXT c
```

Here `recno` is a variable containing the number of records in memory. On the first iteration, the `PRINT #` statement writes the contents of `dat$(1)` to channel `1` because `c = 1`. (Channel 1 is a logical path to a disk file.) After the first instance of `NEXT c`, variable `c` is incremented, the loop is reexecuted, and the contents of `dat$(2)` are written to channel `1`. This process goes on until the contents of `dat$(recno)`—the last record in the array—are written. Execution then drops to the instruction below `NEXT c`.

Example

Suppose you have a variable `resp()` that contains one aspect of a patient's electroencephalographic response level to external stimuli over time. For each second of time, a new reading is taken. These readings of responses over the passing seconds are entered into the `resp()` array. You want to plot these readings to a chart so that you can see the rises and falls in response levels. Here's the loop that would plot these levels as vertical lines emerging from the x-axis of the chart for some defined segment of time:

```
SCREEN 12
FOR sec = min TO max
   LINE (sec, 479)-(sec, 479 - resp(sec))
NEXT sec
```

The preceding `LINE` statement plots a series of pixels between two pairs of screen coordinates listed within parentheses. The statement assumes a current VGA screen mode of 12, which means the graphics screen is active at a resolution of 640 pixels horizontal to 480 pixels vertical, with a 16-color palette. The uppermost y coordinate is 0; the lowermost, 479. Each vertical line plotted by the preceding `LINE` statement will start at line number `sec` and work its way line-by-line to the right. Assuming `sec`'s initial value `min` is preset to `0`, the loop would draw lines starting at (0, 479), working to (1, 479), then (2, 479), and so on until the final value of `sec` is reached (`sec = max`).

Each new line is plotted to the right of the previous one and is drawn from the bottom (pixel number 479) up toward pixel number `479 - resp(sec)`. This array variable holds the E.E.G. response for each second of testing. Loop variable `sec` here establishes the relationship between the line being plotted and the response value being tested.

Example

Suppose you want a less precise chart—perhaps a bar chart—that shows the patient's reaction over 10-second intervals. The array variable still contains reaction levels over one-second intervals. Here's how the code fragment could be modified:

```
FOR sec = min TO max STEP 10
   LINE (sec, 479)-(sec + 8, 479 - resp(sec)), , B
NEXT sec
```

Notice that the `LINE` statement now draws a box (the capital `B` at the end of the statement). By adding `STEP` to the end of the `FOR` instruction, you change the additive value from 1—the default—to 10. Now when `NEXT sec` is executed, the interpreter adds 10 to `sec`. In so doing, the origin point of the graph line is moved 10 pixels to the right rather than one. The box being plotted is eight pixels wide, which accounts for the `sec + 8` in the second pair of coordinates.

Example

The next example of FOR-NEXT comes from the Expressor. If you recall, this formula calculator has up to five parameter lines for formulas selected by the user. When the user chooses a formula, a text line appears beside each parameter to describe its purpose in the formula. Here's the procedure that makes those descriptor lines appear:

```
SUB CalcList_Click ()
FOR n = 0 TO 4
    ParamText(n).Caption = label$(CalcList.ListIndex, n)
NEXT n
Clear_Params
END SUB
```

The event that triggers this routine is clicking the drop-down list of formulas called `CalcList`. The value of the property `CalcList.ListIndex` represents the formula chosen with the index of the formula name as it appears in the list.

The five descriptor lines called `ParamText()` in the Expressor form comprise a *control array,* which is a sequential grouping of graphic objects that have the same purpose. Graphic objects in a control array can be addressed by number, using a subscript in the same manner as with an array variable. The first object in a control array is object `0`, so the loop `FOR n = 0 TO 4` starts there and counts to 4. Variable `n` here acts as a *loop index,* keeping count of the number of iterations performed thus far. The string array variable `label$` is two-dimensional; it maintains a set of parameter descriptor strings for each formula and line in the form.

When the loop instruction undergoes its first iteration, `n` is equal to `0`. Therefore, the loop index pertains to the first descriptor line. Within the array variable `label$`, `CalcList.ListIndex` points to the chosen formula name, and `n` points to the first descriptor line (line #0). So the contents of `label$`, for whatever `.ListIndex` number chosen by the user, is assigned as the setting of property `ParamText(0).Caption`. At the next loop iteration, loop index `n` points to the second descriptor line (line #1), and so on.

The last line in the procedure before `END SUB` is `Clear_Params`, which is a call to yet another looping procedure:

```
SUB Clear_Params ()
FOR pl = 0 TO 4
    param(pl).text = ""
NEXT pl
ClearAll_Click
END SUB
```

At this point, you should be able to recognize the loop mechanism at work, even without indentations to demarcate the nest. The control array `param()` consists of the five parameters for the chosen formula. The property `param(pl).Text` (not to be confused with `ParamText()`) refers to the textual form of the parameters because text boxes within a form can contain only what VB/DOS recognizes as text.

TIP: Two quotation marks next to each other—two enclosures that enclose nothing—signify a null string. Setting the textual property of a graphic object to "" clears that object of its contents.

The preceding procedure clears objects in the `param` control array, numbered 0 through 4, in sequence. The program then continues to the procedure, which clears any calculations in progress.

When invoking a count variable for a loop clause, the name you choose for that variable is often not very important; what is important is that you keep whatever name you choose consistent throughout the loop. In the preceding routine, for instance, I could have named the variable `pl` something else—such as `place_where_the_numbers_will_appear`—and the operation of the routine would not have been affected in the least. For small loops, the variable name you choose can be arbitrary. I find myself using `n` or `x` when I'm in one of my pensive moods, and `triumph` or `indomitable` when I'm feeling more literary.

Example

A loop clause can easily be embedded within another loop clause, in which case the embedded clause is repeatedly executed itself. Here's an example that creates a textual chessboard:

```
FOR file = 1 TO 8
   FOR rank = 1 TO 8
      chessboard$(file, rank) = man$(square_val(file, rank))
   NEXT rank
NEXT file
```

Assume `man$()` is an array that contains symbols representing chessmen. Variable `square_val()` maintains the numeric value of the chessman seated on each square in a two-dimensional array, where pawns are 1s, rooks are 2s, and so on. The preceding equation assigns the symbol for each chessman to its proper position in the array `chessboard$()`. As a result, the following double-embedded loop displays a symbolic chessboard:

```
FOR file = 1 TO 8
   FOR rank = 1 TO 8
      PRINT chessboard$(file, rank); "   ";
   NEXT rank
NEXT file
```

This is perhaps the oldest way to symbolize chess pieces in computer programs, especially in machines that didn't have graphics or used printers as their main output devices. In both preceding examples, the loop clause for variable `rank` is executed eight times because of its inclusion in the greater loop clause for variable `file`.

Example

Here's an example that tests both the FOR-NEXT loop and SELECT CASE clause structures: Suppose you're keeping records of clients that are sorted in order of their last names. These files are to be stored on disk; however, all the records together would comprise too unmanageable a file. You want to separate the records into four files, with each file designated its own quarter of the alphabet. Before you can perform an alphabetic sort, you'll need to assign a file division to each record and then sort each resulting file within its respective division. Following is a routine for establishing this division:

```
FOR recno = 1 TO maxrec
   SELECT CASE LastName$(recno)
      CASE "Aaa" TO "Fzz"
         division = 1
      CASE "Gaa" TO "Mzz"
         division = 2
      CASE "Naa" TO "Szz"
         division = 3
      CASE "Taa" TO "Zzz"
         division = 4
   END SELECT
   LNDivided$(rec(division), division) = LastName$(recno)
   FNDivided$(rec(division), division) = FirstName$(recno)
   .
   .
   .
   rec(division) = rec(division) + 1
NEXT recno
```

Here is the preceding procedure written in pseudocode:

Start counting from the first record to the last record.
For all possible cases of the current last name:
Should the name fall between A and F, assign the name to division 1.
Should the name fall between G and M, assign the name to division 2.
Should the name fall between N and S, assign the name to division 3.
Should the name fall between T and Z, assign the name to division 4.
End of possibilities.
Add the next last name for the previously assigned division to the current list for that division.

Add the next first name for the previously assigned division to the current list for that division.

.

.

.

Increment the current subscript number for this division.

Count the next record.

VB/DOS recognizes alphabetic ranges as valid textual expressions. Thus, `"A" TO "F"` would be a range that includes "Aaron," "Ezekiel," and "F." "Fenchurch," however, would not be included because, in an alphabetic sort, "Fenchurch" falls after just plain "F." Because of this, you must establish ranges for the preceding procedure with lowercase `a`'s and `z`'s to include all the pronounceable proper names that may fall within the range. "Sycyznyk" would therefore fall between `"Naa" TO "Szz"` where it would not fall between `"N" TO "S"`.

In the preceding `FOR-NEXT` loop clause, the variable `maxrec` represents the number of the final record to be processed. The loop counts from 1 to this number, with the count kept in the variable `recno`. There are four files being created within this clause, with each file given its own number addressed by the variable `division`. Each created "drawn and quartered" file has its own independent count of the number of records stored within it, which is kept in the array variable `rec()`. Each time a record is added to a quartered file, the independent count is incremented by 1. In the meantime, the count of records currently being processed by the loop clause is maintained in `recno`, apart from the independent counts. The statement `NEXT recno` increments that variable by 1 and sends execution to the top of the loop to process the next record in the main list.

The way the `SELECT CASE` clause works, variable `LastName$()` is an array that contains the surnames of everyone in the list. Variable `recno` is the key variable here, establishing the sole relation between `LastName$()` and similar array `FirstName$()`, as well as those that are addressed in the area represented by the ellipsis. When the contents of `LastName$()` fall within one of the `CASE` ranges, a file division number is drawn from one of the four *slots.* Execution then skips to the instruction following END SELECT, where the current record contents are assigned to a two-dimensional array in four partitions.

Erstwhile

FOR-NEXT is the primary loop clause in the BASIC vernacular, and so it is with VB/DOS. As you've seen, the instructions within the FOR-NEXT clause are executed as long as a condition holds true. The clause enclosure term NEXT, however, plays a role in making the condition eventually test false. Two other clause instructions in VB/DOS, which are related to one another, allow for repetitious execution of sets of instructions within a clause. Unlike NEXT, however, which changes the outcome of the conditional evaluation, these statements don't affect the condition of execution whatsoever. The instructions within these clauses must alter the outcome of the condition so that, eventually, the clause can be exited.

The first of these independent enclosure clauses has its origins in Pascal; the other, which you'll see later, in the old ALGOL pseudocode of the '60s.

WHILE...WEND **Statement**

Syntax:

```
WHILE [expression]
     [instruction_block1]
     [EXIT WHILE]
     [instruction_block2]
WEND
```

The WHILE-WEND statement acts as the enclosure for a conditional loop clause. The instructions within the clause are executed in sequence as long as the stated mathematical *expression* beside the WHILE term evaluates true. In such instances, if the term WEND is executed, execution proceeds back to the WHILE statement, where the `expression` is reevaluated. If `expression` evaluates false, execution skips to the instruction following the `WEND` term. If during clause execution, an `EXIT WHILE` instruction is reached, execution of the instructions within the loop clause is terminated, and the course of the program proceeds immediately to the instruction following `WEND`.

Example

Suppose you're accumulating a string for a message box to be composed of words extracted from an array. A message box cannot contain more than 255 characters, so you have to know when to stop adding words to the box. Here's how the routine for adding as many words in sequence as will fit might appear:

```
WHILE LEN(Message$) + LEN(word$(count)) + 1 < 255
    Message$ = Message$ + word$(count) + " "
    count = count + 1
WEND
MSGBOX Message$
```

Here's the preceding code fragment translated as pseudocode:

While the length of the current message
 added to the length of the next word, plus one
 for a space character, is less than 255 characters,
  Add the word to the current message, plus a space.
  Add one to the tally of words added.
End of loop.
Place the current message in a message box.

Variable `Message$` contains the contents to be displayed in the message box. The VB/DOS intrinsic function `LEN()` returns the length of any string appearing within the parentheses, so `len("firefly") = 7`. The array `word$()` contains the list of words to be added to the message.

The expression tests to see if the current length of the message, plus the length of the next word to add plus 1 (accounting for the space between words), adds up to less than 255, the maximum length. If it does, execution of the dependent set proceeds. If not, execution skips to below WEND. In any event, the message is displayed immediately thereafter using MSGBOX.

Example

The implied loop that appeared in the CONVBASE.MAK numeric converter application could have been stated as a WHILE-WEND loop clause, as follows:

```
WHILE cb ^ expn < ConvValue
    expn = expn + 1
WEND
```

Obviously, the preceding clause is much shorter and more efficient than the implied variety used the first time.

Because the instructions in the VB/DOS vocabulary—like the words in the English language—all have different origins, their syntax is often governed by the need to preserve history rather than to maintain standards. The end statement in an IF-THEN clause is END IF. Likewise, in a SELECT CASE clause it is END SELECT, and in a TYPE clause it is END TYPE. Because WHILE-WEND was introduced to BASIC with WEND as its ending statement, it has never been changed to "end while," nor is "end while" accepted as a closing to this clause.

Everybody's Doing It

The other form of loop clause supported by VB/DOS is the DO-LOOP clause.

DO [WHILE ¦ UNTIL]...
LOOP [WHILE ¦ UNTIL] **Statement**

Syntax 1:

```
DO [{WHILE ¦ UNTIL} expression]
   instruction block1
```

```
[EXIT DO]
   [instruction block2]
   .
   .
   .
LOOP
```

Syntax 2:

```
DO
   instruction block1
[EXIT DO]
   [instruction block2]
   .
   .
   .
LOOP [{WHILE ¦ UNTIL} expression]
```

Syntax 3:

```
DO
   instruction block1
[EXIT DO]
   [instruction block2]
   .
   .
   .
LOOP
```

The DO-LOOP clause repetitively executes the set of instructions enclosed within it. Execution of this set may or may not be dependent on an optional conditional expression. If a condition is expressed, execution of the set can be terminated. If a condition is not expressed, the loop is considered endless and can be exited only with an EXIT DO statement.

Under Syntax 1, a conditional expression is made at the beginning of the clause, following DO. If the expression is preceded with WHILE, execution of the instructions within the clause proceeds in sequence as long as the expression evaluates true. If the expression is preceded with UNTIL, execution proceeds in sequence as long as the expression evaluates false—in other words, when the expression is true, the clause is terminated. If the WHILE expression is false or the

UNTIL expression is true, execution skips to the instruction following LOOP. If this is the first iteration of the loop and execution skips to LOOP, the instructions within the clause will never be executed.

Under Syntax 2, a conditional expression is made at the end of the clause, following LOOP. The rules governing use of WHILE and UNTIL are the same as for Syntax 1. Under Syntax 2, execution of the instructions within the clause proceeds following the DO statement *unconditionally.* The expression will be evaluated when LOOP is reached. If the loop is to proceed, execution skips to the instruction following DO. Otherwise, the loop is terminated and execution proceeds normally.

Under Syntax 3, no conditional expression is made at all, and the loop clause is considered unconditional. Execution of the instructions proceeds in sequence from the DO statement until LOOP is reached, when execution immediately proceeds to the instruction following DO. In this syntax, the only escape from this unconditionally repetitious loop is with the aid of the EXIT DO statement, which allows execution to skip to the statement immediately following LOOP. EXIT DO may appear within a subordinate conditional clause, such as IF-THEN.

Example

DO-LOOP can be used interchangeably with WHILE-WEND; in fact, here is the converted implied loop after being given the syntax of DO-LOOP:

```
DO WHILE cb ^ expn < ConvValue
    expn = expn + 1
LOOP
```

Absolutely no logical change has been made to this clause in converting it from WHILE-WEND to DO-LOOP. The only true logical difference in syntax between WHILE-WEND and DO WHILE-LOOP is that the DO clause has the option of being exited using the statement EXIT DO. There is no equivalent "exit while" statement.

Example

Suppose you have a list in memory of people or organizations who have contributed to your client's political campaign. The names are accompanied by the amount contributed and are arranged in the order in which the contributions were made. You want to extract from this list the names of contributors of the first $25,000 to your client's campaign for inclusion in a newsletter. Because everyone contributed variable amounts, the only way your application can know when to stop extracting names is by keeping a running tally of contributions as each name is extracted and evaluating that tally each time to see if $25,000 has been exceeded.

Here's the routine that performs the name extraction:

```
DO
   first$(listno) = contrib$(listno)
   famount(listno) = camount(listno)
   tally = tally + camount(listno)
   listno = listno + 1
LOOP UNTIL tally >= 25000
```

Here the variable `listno` maintains the current count of which record is being extracted and written to. The array `first$()` will contain the first contributors extracted from array `contrib$()`. Likewise, `famount()` will contain the amounts they contributed as extracted from `camount()`. Variable `tally` contains the running amount, which is evaluated at the end of the clause to see if $25,000 has been met or exceeded.

If you're a veteran of other recent editions of BASIC, you may be accustomed to writing `DO` loops that end not with `LOOP`, but with `UNTIL` or `WHILE` whenever conditions are expressed. In VB/DOS, the term `LOOP` is mandatory when closing a `DO` loop, whether or not a condition is expressed immediately following the `DO` loop.

The keywords `WHILE` and `UNTIL`, when used with the `DO-LOOP` clause, are terminological opposites of each other. They enable you to determine whether the clause exists on the true side of the "logic table" or the false side, as Figure 16.2 demonstrates.

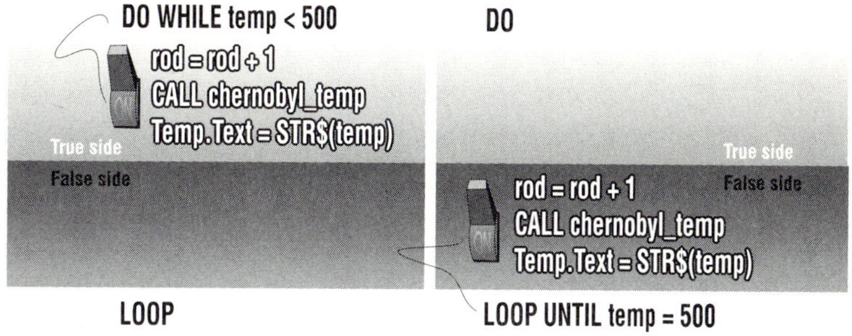

Figure 16.2. The good, the bad, and the unconditional.

Summary

A clause that executes instructions repetitively is called a loop clause. Each repeated execution of instructions in a loop clause is called an iteration. The primary BASIC statement that governs loop clauses is the FOR-NEXT statement. This statement is dependent on a count variable, which has its value updated each time the NEXT instruction is executed. Generally, 1 is added to the count variable unless a different update value is specified beside the optional STEP term.

Another loop clause supported by VB/DOS is DO-LOOP. The DO-LOOP clause can be far more versatile as a conditional loop clause, allowing conditional expressions to be evaluated either at the beginning or end of the loop, and for either truth or falsehood. The DO-LOOP clause also allows the loop to be exited manually, if necessary, using EXIT DO.

Review Questions

Answers to Review Questions appear in Appendix B.

Of these types of loop clauses, FOR-NEXT, DO WHILE-LOOP, and DO-LOOP UNTIL, which is best suited for the following routines?

1. Plotting the trajectory of a moving target for each second of movement.
2. Plotting the trajectory of a moving target for each second until the target travels beyond a specified range.
3. Plotting the trajectory of a moving target for each second while the target travels within a specified range.

Review Exercises

Write loop clause routines that you feel would be the best-suited to perform the following jobs. You can name your variables according to your personal preference.

1. Counting the number of people in a list whose last names begin with *S*.
2. Tallying the first 25 people in a list whose last names begin with *S*.
3. Tallying the first 25 people in a list whose last names begin with *S* until there are no more names left in the list.
4. Tallying the first 25 political contributors in a list whose names begin with *S*, as long as the total of their contributions doesn't exceed $50,000.

17

Arbitrary Instruction Clusters

In this chapter, you learn more about *branching*. Branching enables you to manually and unconditionally make execution of a Visual Basic for MS-DOS application jump from one instruction to a distant one. You'll see how the line labeling system works and how it is used to mark the specific landing point of a manual jump. You then examine how a subroutine works and find out how VB/DOS knows to jump back to the instruction just below the one that called the subroutine.

A Branch of Archaeology

When BASIC was first conceived, there were two ways to perform a direct branch: with the GOTO "command" and with the GOSUB "command." Then, each instruction line within the entire program was given its own number in one running sequence, as you saw in Chapter 3, "Grammar and Linguistics." To force a branch, you would "command" BASIC to GOTO a specific line number. Generally, a programmer would number each line in increments of 10; the first line might be line 10, followed by lines 20, 30, and so on. To add several lines to the middle of a program, the programmer often had to change the numbering sequence of the program entirely. If, by some stroke of bad luck, the programmer had to add one instruction between lines 17 and 18, he would have to find some way of moving lines 18, 19, and 20 down one number. Then the programmer would have to edit all those GOTO commands that branched to line 20, making them branch instead to line 21.

Luckily, in VB/DOS you aren't forced to worry about this ongoing, often nightmarish sequence. Computing has progressed to the point that you do not have to reteach computers how to count day after day. Line numbers, though they are acceptable by the VB/DOS Code Editor, have been replaced for the most part by *labels*. A label, with respect to elements of source code, is a noninstruction that appears on a line by itself and is followed by a colon (:). The label designates a branching point.

Branching causes the program to jump to some other specified point.

In VB/DOS, line labels are used as jumping points for branch statements. To *branch* is to direct the interpreter to suspend execution of the normal sequence of instructions and to resume the sequence at some other specified point.

Some programmers argue that, along with the passage of time, the GOTO and GOSUB statements should also pass into antiquity. Indeed, many fully functional modern BASIC programs contain neither statement anywhere in their source code. The main reason for the recent exclusion of these once-staple elements of BASIC programs is that you can usually make execution of instructions pass seamlessly from procedure to procedure without them. Any point the interpreter might jump to can be the start of a formal SUB procedure. Conceivably, every possible use for GOTO and GOSUB can be duplicated by some other clause instruction or procedural declaration.

The statements remain, however, and this language with which you write programs still contains the word *Basic* in its name, albeit now in lowercase. The role these two statements play in VB/DOS programs today is greatly reduced. They can be used only to branch execution to some other point within their own procedure and not outside of it. The exception to this new rule occurs in cases of event trap-driven branches such as ON ERROR GOTO. You may or may not choose to use GOTO and GOSUB in your programs, but they still work, and people who have programmed in BASIC for decades still have a tendency to invoke these statements by nature or out of habit. As long as your applications operate efficiently, the matter of your personal programming style should not be argued.

Following is the explanation of the GOTO statement.

GOTO — **Statement**

Syntax:

```
GOTO label
```

On being executed, the GOTO statement causes the interpreter to suspend execution and resume with the instruction within the same procedure immediately following the *label* specified in the statement. The label must appear on a line by itself and must be followed by a colon.

Example

Here's a demonstration of the manual jump mechanism. What follows is a fragment from a procedure that has its initial conditions set at the beginning. The branch point for the main body of the procedure follows the setting of those conditions.

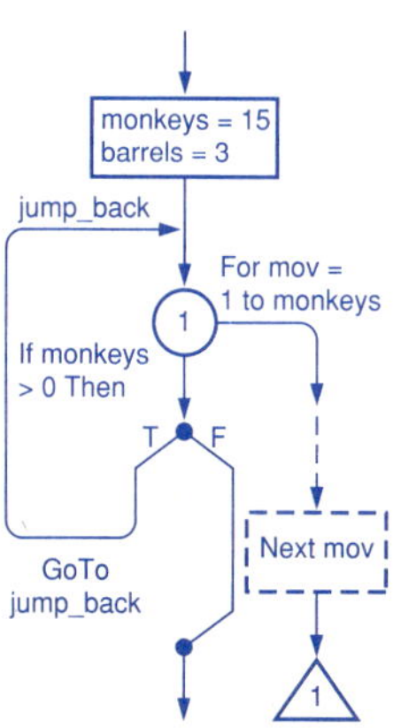


```
monkeys = 15
barrels = 3
jump_back:
FOR mov = 1 TO monkeys
    .
    .
    .
NEXT mov
IF monkeys > 0 THEN GOTO jump_back
```

Forgive my hypothetical cruelty to animals, but the preceding routine branches back to the instruction immediately following the label `jump_back` as long as there are monkeys left to manipulate (`monkeys > 0`).

> **NOTE to BASIC veterans:** In single-statement conditional branches, you no longer have the option of omitting the `GOTO`. For the preceding example, stating `IF monkeys > 0 THEN jump_back` would be illegal. It is acceptable, however, to state `IF monkeys > 0 GOTO jump_back`, omitting the `THEN` term.

Example

Here's another valid use of `GOTO`: You have a main procedure that simulates the actions and conditions of a race car on a hot day in Indy. The order in which the procedures are generally executed is maintained within a loop clause. Execution branches to each procedure and returns from it back to the main procedure in the order specified within that loop clause. What if, however, the car were to stop for some reason? You need to exit the main loop and enter a damage control routine that executes corrective procedures based on the current track conditions.

But what routine do you execute? If you use the normal `EXIT DO` statement for emergency exit from the main loop, regardless of the condition of the car, execution branches to only one point: the instruction immediately following the `LOOP` clause-closing instruction. This would be the same instruction that executes when the car comes to an intentional stop or crosses the finish line under the checkered flag. You would prefer in cases of emergency that the program go someplace else.

Here's a skeletal model of the main procedure, concentrating mainly on the elements of damage control and how the main loop is exited conditionally:

```
Up_top:
DO
   full = Fuel_System (gas, temp, velo)
   cool = Cooling_System (water_level, temp, velo)
   intact = Body_Structure (integrity, momentum, velo)
```

```
   .
   .
   .
   IF velo = 0 THEN
      IF full < 50 THEN GOTO CheckFuel
      IF cool > 300 THEN GOTO OverHeat
      IF intact < 20 THEN GOTO DidWeCrash
      .
      .
      .
   END IF
LOOP UNTIL miles = 500
GOTO GoodFinish
CheckFuel:
   .
   .
   .
GOTO Status
OverHeat:
   .
   .
   .
GOTO Status
DidWeCrash:
   .
   .
   .
Status:
   IF okay >= 10 THEN GOTO Up_top
Totaled:
   CLS
   PRINT "Damage is beyond repair."
   .
   .
   .
   END
GoodFinish:
   CLS
   PRINT "You finished in ";place$(p);" place."
   .
   .
   .
   END
```

Here's the preceding fast-paced circuit written in "encapsulated pseudocode" (EP):

Top of main loop.
Copy the main values from the global arrays into some local variables.

.
.
.

If there's no speed in this car anymore, then
If the car is low on gas, go to the fuel-checking routine.
If the car appears to be overheating, then go to the heat-checking routine.
If the car seems to be falling apart today, then go to the crash-detection routine.

.
.
.

End of condition.
Keep up the main loop until the car has traveled 500 miles.
At the end, go to the Good Finish routine.
Here are the branchpoints for all those diagnostic routines introduced earlier.

.
.
.

At the end of each diagnostic routine, go check the car's overall status.
Overall status checkpoint:
If the car still runs, then go to the top of this procedure and resume execution there.
Evidently if we're executing this instruction, the car's a heap of junk, so clear the form.
State the hopelessness of things.

.
.
.

End of program.

Good Finish branchpoint:
Clear the form.
State how the car finished overall.
.
.
.
End of program.

A *routine* is any arbitrarily bounded sequence of instructions within source code.

The preceding model shows three of the many possible conditional exit points in the main `DO-LOOP` clause that would cause execution to branch out of the loop to a specific instruction. This instruction is marked by a label that designates the beginning of the damage assessment routine. A *routine* is any arbitrarily bounded sequence of instructions within a body of source code.

There really isn't any formal structure of source code called routine that is maintained by the VB/DOS interpreter. When you want to refer to some working set of instructions, however, you should refer to it as a routine.

In the preceding skeletal model, the `DO-LOOP` clause first places calls to `FUNCTION` routines (not shown) that return the operating status of certain parts of the car. When these functions are executed, the `IF-THEN` clause checks to see if for some reason the speed of the car has become 0. If it has, several embedded `IF-THEN` statements check to see if any variables have fallen below the critical level, indicating a possible need for corrective action. If action is necessary, execution branches to the specified routine. You can (unofficially) refer to a portion of a procedure that is bounded by a line label and a terminating statement as a routine.

The corrective action routines fall below the `LOOP` statement that terminates the main loop. To ensure that the interpreter doesn't execute one of these routines by accident when the car reaches the finish line (`miles = 500`), another `GOTO` statement is added that branches to a routine called `GoodFinish:`. Thus, you can avoid the program's diagnosing the car at the end of the race.

Each diagnostic routine starts with a line label. Two of the three routines end with—of all things—`GOTO` statements, which take the program to a single routine called `Status:` that decides whether it's safe to continue running the car. The routine called `DidWeCrash:` doesn't need to branch to `Status:` because it falls immediately below the routine anyway. If `Status:` determines 10 reasons or more why it should continue—as indicated by the variable `okay`—execution will branch to `Up_top:`, which is the start of the main `DO-LOOP` clause.

At the end of this procedure are two terminating routines called `Totaled:` and `GoodFinish:`, both of which end with `END` and that together represent the extreme worst-case and best-case scenarios as far as the interpreter is concerned.

As you've probably already determined, when you "let in" the `GOTO` statements, they start to swarm like sparrows in a barnyard. VB/DOS' syntactic structure is based not on the manual tracing of execution paths like old BASIC, but on the natural flow of data between formal procedures. When you add manual branching to a routine, you actually introduce something somewhat foreign to the scheme of things, not unlike damming a river. When you redirect the course of the river, you suddenly become responsible for where the water goes.

When you look even more closely at the rather long fragmentary code example, perhaps you'll noticed something about its architecture: The fragment represents the work that would be accomplished by the entire program. It's entirely self-contained, much like the system of politics in Washington. The assessment, logical, error-trapping, and reporting routines take place inside the beltway. There doesn't appear to be any reliance upon routines on the outside to share any part of the workload. Generally, when the workload is more evenly distributed, the program becomes more modular, and statements such as `GOTO` and `GOSUB` are used less frequently.

CAUTION: If you're new to programming, you may want to be cautious in your use of manual branch statements. If you're a veteran of BASIC, however, you have nothing to fear by using `GOTO`. VB/DOS allows you to use it only under the confines of local procedures.

Wherefore the Subroutine?

A subroutine is a set of instructions within a procedure that branches back to the instruction just past the one that called it.

The first formal subdivision in the long history of BASIC source code was in the creation of the *subroutine.* A subroutine is a set of instructions within a procedure that is repetitively executed, can be called by name, and whose end forces a branch back to the instruction just after the one that called it.

The first subroutines had no absolute beginning; a branch to a subroutine was performed by addressing a line number, as in `GOSUB 2900`. The end of each subroutine was supposed to be more definite, defined with the `RETURN` "command," but such commands could be applied in conditional statements such as `IF A > 15 THEN RETURN`. As a result, subroutines had fuzzy boundaries on both sides—they had no marked point of entry and many possible points of exit.

GOSUB **Statement**

Syntax:

```
GOSUB label
```

On execution of the `GOSUB` statement, the interpreter branches to the instruction immediately following the specified label. While execution proceeds in sequence, the interpreter keeps track of the location of the instruction that performed the branch. On executing the `Return` instruction, the interpreter branches back to the instruction immediately following the `GoSub` call.

Example

Suppose your application sends its output directly to your printer. Periodically, you need the program to send the page footer and page eject code to the printer. Here's how you can do this using `GOSUB`:

```
SUB PrintTotals ()
LPRINT "Monthly Totals for Period Ending ";date$
.
.
.
LPRINT "Totals thus far: ";total(pageno)
GOSUB NextPage
LPRINT "Advertising Expense Projection"
.
.
.
LPRINT "Totals thus far: ";total(pageno)
GOSUB NextPage
LPRINT "Maintenance Expense Projection"
.
.
.
EXIT SUB
NextPage:
   LPRINT "    Page"; pageno
   pageno = pageno + 1
   Printer.NEWPAGE
RETURN
END SUB
```

As you can see, you can place more than one GOSUB call within the same procedure to the same subroutine. Notice that no parameters are passed; this is true for all GOSUB statements. In VB/DOS (unlike some other, more obscure BASIC dialects) no data is exchanged during the branch to a subroutine. Such an exchange isn't really necessary because the context of a subroutine is identical to the procedure in which it resides; in other words, it shares variables with its procedure. Because all variables belonging to the procedure belong to the subroutine, parameter passing is entirely unnecessary.

Notice that the RETURN statement closes the subroutine.

RETURN **Statement**

Syntax:

```
RETURN
```

When the RETURN statement is processed, a branch is made to the instruction immediately following the most recently executed GOSUB statement.

Example

Using subroutines, you can modify the Indy automotive simulator procedure so that multiple diagnoses can be performed on the same accident. You can rewrite the branch statements to the diagnostic routines as follows:

```
IF velo = 0 THEN
IF full < 50 THEN GOSUB CheckFuel
IF cool > 300 THEN GOSUB OverHeat
IF intact < 20 THEN GOSUB DidWeCrash
.
.
.
END IF
```

Each diagnostic routine branches using a GOTO statement to a single point called Status, which you can update as follows:

```
Status:

   IF okay >= 10 THEN RETURN
```

Now, if something is wrong when velo = 0 (the car isn't moving), the branches to each of the diagnostic routines are all GOSUB statements. The labels of the individual routines have not been altered. The end of each diagnosis routine still branches to Status: using GOTO statements. At the end of the Status: routine, however, is a `RETURN` marking the end of not only one but all the diagnosis routines. The interpreter knows to branch back to the instruction following the `GOSUB` statement that called it, wherever that is. In this procedure, the `RETURN` branch could be to another conditional `GOSUB` branch, which could start this cycle all over again.

Sequential Branching

In the previous example, you saw how a single `RETURN` can cause a branch back to any of multiple calling points. VB/DOS continues to use a variation of both `GOTO` and `GOSUB` for branching from the calling point to any of multiple locations specified in a sequence.

ON...GOTO
ON...GOSUB

Statements

Syntax:

```
ON expression GOTO label0, label1[, label2,. . . label255]
ON expression GOSUB label0, label1[, label2,. . . label255]
```

Placing `ON` *`expression`* before a `GOTO` or `GOSUB` statement converts that statement into a sequential branch to any of the labels specified in the list following the keyword. Branching is dependent upon the value of *`expression`*. Generally, *`expression`* consists of one variable by itself. The logically reduced value of *`expression`*, when rounded to the nearest integer, must equal between 0 and 255, inclusive. This value is equivalent to the place in the list of the *`label`* that will be the destination of the branch. If the statement placing the branch is `GOSUB`, the branch will be treated as a regular call to a subroutine; on processing `RETURN`, execution will proceed to the instruction immediately following `ON...GOSUB`.

Example

You may remember seeing `ON...GOTO` used in the Expressor application to branch to any one of the five routines for processing formulas. The branch appeared within `SUB ApplyFormula ()`:

```
ON ndx GOTO f1, f2, f3, f4, f5
```

Variable `ndx` in this routine contains the index of a formula selected from a drop-down list box. If a formula was indeed selected, `ndx` should be equal to an integer from 0 to 4. This makes the list box control a perfect candidate for being evaluated with `ON...GOTO`. In essence, the preceding statement is like making five statements all on one line: `IF ndx = 0 THEN GOTO f1`, `IF ndx = 1 THEN GOTO f2`... and so on.

CAUTION: Line labeling can be a messy business. Although a standard `GOTO` or `GOSUB` statement may not effectuate a branch outside of a `SUB` or `FUNCTION` procedure, or between module and procedure levels, all line labels within a VB/DOS application must have unique names. For instance, if within a procedure you have an `ON` *`expression`* `GOTO` statement that branches at one point to a line `branchpoint4:`, and `branchpoint4:` exists outside of the procedure, VB/DOS will render a `Label not defined` error. On the other hand, if you place `branchpoint4:` within the procedure and fail to change or remove `branchpoint4:` from outside the procedure, VB/DOS will render a `Duplicate label definition` error.

Summary

VB/DOS allows for manual branching to other points in a procedure marked by line labels. You can identify these labels by their solitude on an instruction line and by the colon (:) that follows them. The primary statement for performing a manual branch is `GOTO`. The area of instructions within a procedure that is the recipient of a branch can be called a routine, although no such structure formally exists in VB/DOS.

A subroutine is a portion of a procedure that is branched to using the GOSUB statement. After a subroutine is completed, execution branches back to the statement immediately following the previously executed GOSUB after processing the RETURN statement. Subroutines are informal structures and often do not have absolute beginning or ending statements. Many subroutines can be closed with a single RETURN statement. The instructions comprising a subroutine need not be adjacent to one another within the context of a procedure.

A conditional sequential branch is possible using ON *expression* before a GOTO or GOSUB statement. Such a statement branches to any label within a list delimited by commas, having a place in the list that is equal to the rounded value of the *expression* stated beside the ON term.

Review Questions

Answers to Review Questions appear in Appendix B.

1. Speculate: The interpreter comes across a RETURN instruction within a procedure without having processed a GOSUB instruction. What happens?

What VB/DOS loop clause structure substitutes for the conditional branch used in the following routines?

2.
```
top_loop:
c = c + 1

.
.
.
IF c < 4 THEN GOTO top_loop
```

3.
```
top_loop:
IF c = 4 THEN GOTO out_loop

c = c + 1
.
.
.
```

```
GOTO top_loop
out_loop:
.
.
.
```

Review Exercise

The following is a puzzle that uses GOTO and GOSUB statements, constructed in the fashion of old BASIC. This program will run in the VB/DOS environment without alteration. Using your mind and not the computer, follow the branching pattern of this routine as best you can. Here line numbers are used as labels for each line of the routine. This is the closest thing to a maze I can write in the context of this book and get away with it. The objective is to find the final value of variable c whenever an END statement is processed.

```
1 GOTO 5
2 GOSUB 4
3 GOTO 25
4 RETURN
5 GOSUB 10
6 a = 4
7 GOTO 15
8 a = 3
10 RETURN
15 GOSUB 8
20 GOTO 2
25 ON a GOTO 30, 40, 50, 60, 70
30 b = 4
35 GOTO 80
40 RETURN
50 b = 3
60 b = 5
65 GOTO 80
70 b = a
80 ON b GOSUB 100, 110, 120, 130, 140, 150
90 PRINT c
95 END
100 c = 3
```

```
105 RETURN
110 c = b
115 RETURN
120 c = 6
125 RETURN
130 RETURN
140 c = a
145 RETURN
150 c = c
160 RETURN
```

Part IV

Modularization

18

Methodologies of Program Operation

In this chapter, you'll learn about style as an issue in programming. The styles of operation in computer programs have changed dramatically since the 1970s, thanks in large part to graphic symbology. The construction of programs has changed as well, but for entirely different reasons. The Visual Basic for MS-DOS programming environment is designed to accept BASIC programs from decades of programming genres. Although it might be preferable that a VB/DOS application conceived and built today includes as many modern graphical controls as possible, the occasion may arise when you are hired, compelled, or inspired to translate an old BASIC program into a VB/DOS project. You'll need to know what you'll be dealing with.

Anatomy of a Metamorphosis

The primary difference between a program written in the original BASIC and one written in a modern dialect such as VB/DOS is that the older program is more conversational, whereas the newer one is more symbological. For instance, a program written in the

1964 edition of BASIC might ask, `"HOW WIDE IS THE WOODEN BEAM?"` or `"WHAT IS THE INTEREST RATE PER ANNUM?"` to obtain values for a formula. In a conversational mode, a BASIC program could be executed step-by-step, in a totally predictable manner. From your (the programmer's) point of view, the only unknown element in such a program would be the answers to the preceding questions. You could argue that it was simpler to program in the era of conversational programs because the programmer didn't have to consider very deeply what the user intended to do with the program, except perhaps to predict how wide the wooden beam could be.

As an example, let's look at two programs that operate in the style of two different eras, but have nearly identical purposes and core source codes. These programs calculate the zone of a sphere—or the measure of the area of a strip along the surface of a sphere. The sphere is divided by two parallel planes. Where those planes meet with the surface of the sphere, they form the boundaries of the zone. The area of the zone is calculated by these two programs. The formula is described mathematically as

```
z = 2 rh
```

where is the symbol for the constant pi, `r` is the radius of the sphere, and `h` is the distance separating the two planes. Imagine zoning off and measuring the area of the Earth's crust between 20 and 30 degrees north latitude, and you'll get a picture of this formula in your mind.

A *conversational mode* program asks questions of the user using interrogative sentences.

If BASIC had been invented before the era of the typewriter terminal, possibly its medium of communication with the computer and with the user could have been the telegraph wire. At first, the only medium of communication between user and program was the keyboard—which may seem like quite a lot of buttons, until you realize that the BASIC program had to send messages to the user and interpret her response from the keyboard like a question-and-answer session. Today, in retrospect, many programmers call this style of programming the *conversational mode*.

The conversational BASIC program uses no methods by the modern VB/DOS definition but rather the ANSI standard BASIC "commands" adopted in the mid 1970s. For this example, here is the old-style BASIC program in a form that will run within VB/DOS:

```
10 REM +++ FORMULA FOR ZONE OF A SPHERE +++
20 CLS
30 INPUT "ENTER THE RADIUS OF THE SPHERE"; R
40 INPUT "ENTER THE DISTANCE BETWEEN BISECTING PLANES"; H
50 Z = (2 * 3.1415927#) * R * H
60 PRINT
70 PRINT "THE ZONE AREA IS"; Z
80 END
```

It's easy to spot in the preceding example which instructions perform the role of conversing with the user: they're marked with the term INPUT. When it actually became technologically feasible for the user to respond to the BASIC program while it was running (would you believe BASIC is older than the capability for users to respond to programs?), the INPUT statement was devised as a means to acquire some characters from the user. The statement became as important to the language as the tin can on a string was to telephony.

INPUT **Statement**

Syntax:

```
INPUT [;]["prompt"][{; ¦ ,}]variable1[, variable2
  . . . variablen]
```

The INPUT statement is the primary method of acquiring textual or numerical data from the user while the VB/DOS program is running. Its purpose is to translate alphanumeric characters into data that will be stored in one or more variables listed toward the end of the statement.

INPUT assumes a sort of dialog is taking place between the program and its user while VB/DOS' graphical form mode of operation is inactive. In its standard syntax, the statement asks a question of the user, entered into the statement between quotation marks as *prompt*. This text will appear on-screen at the current position of the screen cursor when the program requires the listed input data. The variables that will act as containers for this data are listed at the end of the statement, separated from one another by commas. Generally, `INPUT` is used to acquire just one item of data.

The types of variables listed correspond in sequence to the types of data being acquired. If the acquired data is to be numeric and evaluated later in the program using mathematical expressions, the listed input variable should be numeric. If the acquired data is to be textual or alphanumeric, such as a name or serial number, the listed input variable should be a string variable demarked with a `$` character, for example, *`variable1$`*.

If *`prompt`* is included in the `INPUT` statement and if a comma falls between the closing quotation mark and the first input variable in the list, the interpreter will automatically send a question mark to the screen following *`prompt`* when input is requested of the user during runtime. If a semicolon is used instead to separate *`prompt`* from the first input variable, no comma is inserted at the time of request. If a semicolon precedes *`prompt`* in the `INPUT` statement when user input is requested, the textual cursor will appear on the same line as the text in *`prompt`*. Text typed in from the keyboard will then appear at the cursor location. If the semicolon is omitted, the cursor will appear on the line just below *`prompt`*.

If more than one variable is listed for input, the user is expected to use a comma during runtime as a *delimiter* or divider for the program to know when one datum ends and the next begins. Because commas and quotation marks are so often used as delimiters, they are not accepted as valid input characters for alphanumeric strings when using the `INPUT` statement.

During runtime, the `INPUT` statement will display any text within *`prompt`* on-screen and, if designated, display a question mark. The running program will then be placed in suspension, with no instructions being executed at all until the user makes a response from the keyboard and presses Enter. Once the user presses Enter, the program will continue execution in sequence and may at a later time assess and analyze the user's response.

Figure 18.1 shows the input screen from the Type I edition of the SphereZone program, at the end of its run. Notice there are no frills, no graphical controls—just textual prompts and user response to the right of the question marks.

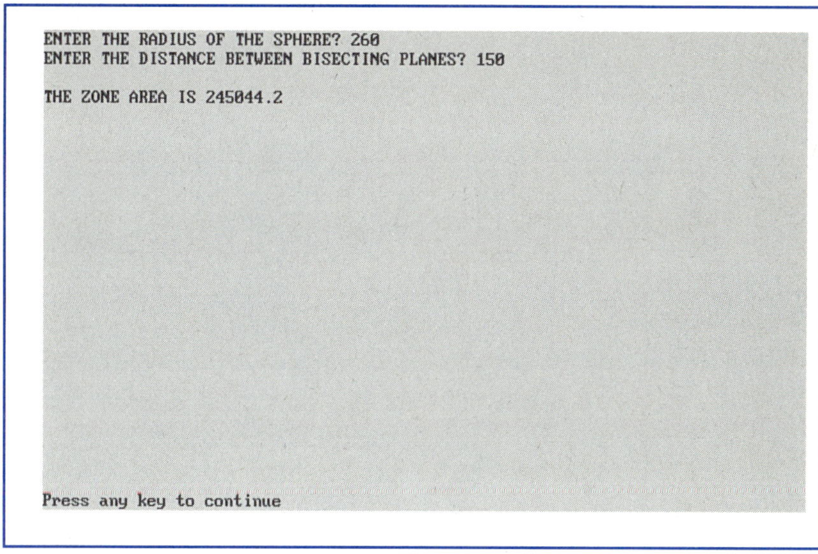

Figure 18.1. SphereZone in conversational mode.

The results of the SphereZone equation are displayed on-screen in the preceding example using one of the oldest statements in the BASIC language: `PRINT`.

PRINT **Statement**

Standard syntax:

```
PRINT [{;¦,}expression1{;¦,} expression2{;¦,}
   . . . expressionn{;¦,}]
```

where any *expression* listed within the statement may be either a mathematical expression that can be logically reduced to a real numeral value, or an alphanumeric string or joining of such strings using the concatenation operator `+`.

The `PRINT` statement is used primarily to place text on-screen at the current location of the screen cursor. The list of items to be printed to the screen appears immediately to the right of the `PRINT` statement. Any text that is to appear on-screen as it does within the statement must appear within quotation marks. Values or variables, by contrast, do not appear within quotation marks—the absence of quotation marks identifies the *`expression`* as having value and not alphanumeric content.

At any time before or after an *`expression`* in the list, a semicolon is interpreted as a directive to the interpreter to leave the screen cursor where it is. A comma is interpreted as a directive to move the screen cursor 13 characters to the right and, if the screen's rightmost border is reached, one line down if necessary. If no delimiter (bordering punctuation) appears after the end of the last printed item in the expression list, the cursor will automatically be moved to the leftmost position of the next line down.

If the `PRINT` statement appears on a line by itself, with absolutely no expressions or delimiters following it, the instruction is interpreted as a directive merely to move the cursor to the leftmost position of the next line down.

> **NOTE:** The `PRINT` keyword has many different syntaxes in VB/DOS, all of which are covered in succeeding chapters.

The Zone Crosses the Time Border

The modern computer application takes place within a form or window. Rather than making the user watch the screen for input prompts as if she were waiting for news over the teletype from a ship at sea, the user is presented with a display that reveals—not conceals—the program's entire purpose.

A modern graphical program does not converse with the user, but instead offers options.

Calculating the zone area of a sphere is not that groundbreaking in and of itself. Looking at the form as it first appears on-screen however, you'd certainly be able to decipher its purpose and, more than likely, its operation (see Figure 18.2).

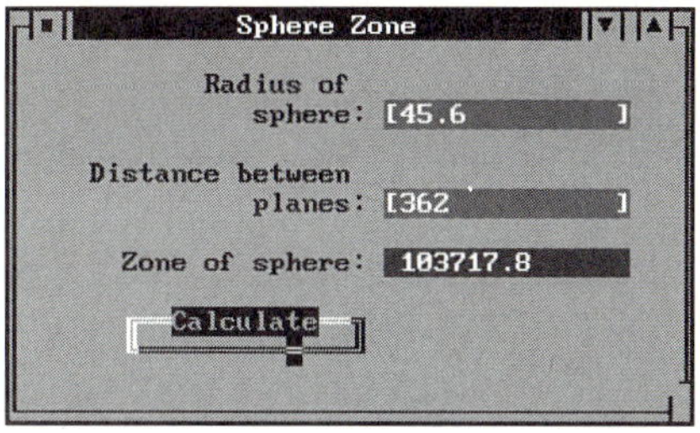

Figure 18.2. SphereZone, having emerged from the black hole.

Here are the major graphical controls and property settings for this form:

SphereZone Calculator

Project name: SPHRZON2.MAK
Constituent file: SPHRZONE.FRM

Object type	*Property*	*Setting*
Form	`.Left`	`21`
	`.Top`	`4`
	`.Width`	`42`
	`.Height`	`14`
	`.Caption`	`Sphere Zone`
	`.BackColor`	`15 - Bright White`
Text box	`.Left`	`22`
	`.Top`	`2`
	`.CtlName`	`Radius`
	`.Text`	(blank)
	`.BackColor`	`2 - Green`
	`.ForeColor`	`15 - Bright White`

continues

Object type	*Property*	*Setting*
Text box	.Left	22
	.Top	5
	.CtlName	PlaneDist
	.Text	(blank)
	.BackColor	2 - Green
	.ForeColor	15 - Bright White
Label	.Left	22
	.Top	7
	.CtlName	ZoneSphere
	.Text	(blank)
	.BackColor	4 - Red
	.ForeColor	15 - Bright White
Label	.Left	2
	.Top	4
	.Caption	Radius of sphere:
	.Alignment	1 - Right Justify
	.BackColor	15 - Bright White
Label	.Left	3
	.Top	7
	.Caption	Distance between planes:
	.Alignment	1 - Right Justify
	.BackColor	15 - Bright White
Label	.Left	6
	.Top	9
	.Caption	Zone of sphere:
	.Alignment	1 - Right Justify
	.BackColor	15 - Bright White
Button	.CtlName	ZoneCalc
	.Caption	Calculate

Now here's the only procedure in the modern version's entire source code:

```
SUB ZoneCalc_Click ()
' Formula for Zone of a Sphere
    r = VAL(Radius.Text)
    h = VAL(PlaneDist.Text)
    z = (2 * 3.1415927#) * r * h
    ZoneSphere.Text = STR$(z)
END SUB
```

You do not need to place a declaration for this routine at the modular level because this is an *event procedure,* and VB/DOS keeps track of such procedures without the need for `DECLARE SUB` statements. Translated into pseudocode, the preceding procedure would read as follows:

Procedure for calculating the area of a sphere zone:
Retrieve the value of r from a text box Radius.
Retrieve the value of h from a text box PlaneDist.
Calculate the sphere zone using the classic formula.
Output the results in a text box ZoneSphere.
End of procedure.

> **NOTE:** When entering a numeral value into the VB/DOS Code Editor that qualifies as a double-precision floating-point value, VB/DOS will automatically insert the pound sign (#) following the numeral.

Knowing what you know about properties, you should be able to identify `.Text` as a property by looking for the period that separates the property from its graphic object. `Radius`, `PlaneDist`, and `ZoneSphere` are three text boxes in the form. The textual contents of these boxes are addressed by adding `.Text` to their name.

Without going into too much detail (I do that later), look at what this program actually does. If you compared the mathematical formula for the area of a sphere zone to either of the two programs, you probably were able to locate the BASIC form of the formula. Notice that it doesn't appear much different from the algebraic form of the formula—which is partly why the theory of high-level programming is called *procedural algebra.* In both programs, letters represent values; as in algebra, these letters are *variables.* In VB/DOS, you can use entire words as variables, as long as these words aren't recognized by VB/DOS as instructional terms.

In SPHRZON1.BAS, the old BASIC program, the values for the formula are put into variables that are declared following the `INPUT` statements. In SPHRZON2.MAK, the VB/DOS application, text is extracted from the two input text boxes in the form and translated into values that are used in the formula. The result of the formula is translated back into text and placed in the output text box of the form. Remember that this procedure is not executed until the button named `ZoneCalc` is clicked.

The sphere zone formula itself is the one part of both programs that has kept its syntax over time, partly because procedural algebra is resistant to change. More obviously, there are generally no line numbers in VB/DOS programs, and lowercase is now prevalent. However, the methodology of user interaction with the BASIC program has changed drastically. As a result of this change, VB/DOS is a very different language from ANSI Standard BASIC, BASICA, or GW-BASIC. Note also that the pseudocode element provided applies equally to both examples.

As to the question of how the programs are executed, the rules there have changed as well. In SPHRZON1.BAS, the old-style BASIC program, you see how the `INPUT` statement places a line of text on-screen and then places the program in a state of suspension awaiting some response from the user. `INPUT` acts as a checkpoint of sorts, stopping the natural flow until the user shows the program some data. The conversational mode program knows what it's waiting for: it wants the user to press Enter so that it can place the data in a variable and get on with its business.

SPHRZON2.MAK, the more modern VB/DOS project, uses a similar suspension system, to borrow a phrase, though the schematics here are quite different. The newer application displays the whole input form, with labels designating where the input data is to go and a clearly-marked button on-screen that starts the calculation process. Although this mode of operation is supposed to be easier for the user, if you think about it, the user actually has to do more to operate the new program than she did for the old program. For instance, she'll probably need to use the mouse once or twice, or the Tab key, to move the cursor back and forth between fields. Instead of just pressing Enter and watching the program fly, she'll need to take the mouse and click `Calculate` to make the body of the program run.

Programmers also say a graphical application is easier to comprehend for the first-time computer user, but is it really? Imagine you've never used a computer before, and you run across two computers running these two programs simultaneously. Never mind which one's the prettiest. Which one would you understand—the one that has these rectangles and arrows all over it or the one that politely asks you to `ENTER THE RADIUS OF THE SPHERE?`

If you think you have an answer to that and if you think you've surprised yourself, consider having to use Excel or Harvard Graphics if either were a conversational mode program. Would you be able to follow the program as it asked you to do one thing after the other, without any hope of escape or alteration of the agenda? Now that you've at least asked yourself these questions, you probably understand something about program architecture.

Is There an Objective Difference?

The newer application in the example, SPHRZON2.MAK, is in many ways like its early-generation counterpart. It, too, prompts the user for information and suspends itself while it awaits input from the user. One major difference is that everything the program requires for input is displayed right up front, allowing the user to choose her own order of input. If there were five or six input lines instead of just two, the user would not necessarily have to enter data for the topmost line, then the next line down, and so on.

The other major difference is that although the new program waits in suspension for user input like the old program, it does not know by default just what it is waiting for. An explicit statement—the event procedure title itself—must state for the program just what it is waiting for. The term `ZoneCalc_Click` tells the program to wait for the user to click the button whose `.CtlName` is `ZoneCalc` before executing the statements within the procedure.

This type of syntax—applying an action to an object within a single term—is commonly called *object-oriented syntax.* Microsoft has introduced object-oriented syntax to its BASIC dialects, both VB/ Windows and VB/DOS. Using this syntax, a graphic object, such as a text box or a button, has its own "noun," and processes related to that object, such as printing or resizing, have their own "verbs." An earlier edition of BASIC might express the measurement of whether a mouse button was pressed within an instruction as follows: `IF MOUSE(0)=1 THEN PRINT AT 15,15;"You pressed the mouse button."` In VB/DOS syntax, the value of a pressed mouse button is implied, not expressed directly, as in the following example:

```
SUB Form_Click ()
    Form1.PRINT "You pressed the mouse button."
END SUB
```

An *event* is a graphical action that triggers a response from the program.

Here, `_Click` is a term for an *event,* or a graphical gesture or action made by the user that may trigger a programmed response on the part of the VB/DOS application.

Even if you're a novice programmer, you can tell from the preceding comparison that VB/DOS bears a loose resemblance to its progenitors. If you're a veteran of older BASICs, you probably also noted how the simple process of printing in the event of a mouse-button click has been elevated in stature from a mere clause to a subprogram module.

Summary

In a conversational mode program, the `INPUT` statement is used to effectuate a dialog with the user. `INPUT` displays a textual prompt on-screen, which generally asks a question of the user. In awaiting a response, `INPUT` places the running program in suspension. The user responds to an `INPUT` statement by typing in data—which is echoed to the screen—and pressing Enter. The program may then respond by showing result data using the `PRINT` statement.

In a graphical mode program, a window or form is used to display nearly all the user's major input fields, as well as the area where the user would make choices. This form is displayed and then the program is placed in suspension, awaiting an event specified by the programmer. This specification is made using object-oriented syntax, which is a more modern way of identifying an action and the recipient of that action using a single term rather than the sentence-form syntax of old BASIC.

Review Questions

Answers to Review Questions appear in Appendix B.

1. If a program includes the instruction

   ```
   TotalOutput.Text = VAL(Manpower.Text) * VAL(Years.Text)
   ```

   what mode of program is it most likely to be?

2. When a conversational mode program is placed in suspension by the `INPUT` statement, what instruction is pointed to by the program counter that tells the interpreter the next instruction to execute?

3. When a graphical mode program is placed in suspension after a form is displayed, where is the program counter?

19

The Module Hierarchy

In this chapter, you examine the framework of a Visual Basic for MS-DOS application in detail. Because the source code of an application is divided into modules with no obvious sequence of arrangement, it is difficult to read the source code to determine the order of execution for the procedures. Understanding the hierarchical relationship between modules and procedures of an application helps you better determine—or better yet, decipher—the order of execution of those modules.

Keeping Context with the Times

Microsoft Visual Basic for Windows is one of the first implementations of BASIC to limit the use of the GOTO and GOSUB instructions to the local procedure in which they appear. In more common editions of BASIC, *procedures* are defined as routines separate from the "main body" of the program, which generally contains the primary sequence of instruction execution. In Visual Basic for Windows, there is no "main body" of the program—just a group of procedures that call one another. VB/DOS is a bit more conventional, allowing for module-level code as well as old-style BASIC instruction syntax.

The structure of old BASIC is actually based upon machine language. BASIC was in many ways a restructuring of the same type of instructions that move individual bits and sometimes bytes along the massive, though isolated, continent of a computer's memory. Born of the low level of language, the `GOTO` and `GOSUB` statements are direct descendents of the "jumps" of assembly languages, which through the '50s to this day have generally been abbreviated as "JMP." Branching in this form—a simple jump from one instruction to another—constitutes the root of the decision-making process in programming.

Follow the logic a moment: If you were to follow a set of instructions written for you on paper, your natural tendency most likely would be to start at step 1 and proceed down the list in sequence. If you follow the steps one after the other to the letter, you may be following what could be considered a program—perhaps "recording" would be the better term—though it would not be a *logical process.* At the point the instructions display the word "If," logic enters the picture. You are asked to do this or that, and this division constitutes the first *branch.*

The first, and for a short time the only, branch instruction in the original BASIC was a conditional statement, `IF` *`expression`* `GOTO` *`line_number`*. Thus, the first instance of branching in BASIC was by way of avoiding the natural course of instructions, not setting it. A set of instructions would be executed, but if the result of those instructions proved an expression to be true, then the program should go do something else. In the development of the language, when `GOTO` became an instruction in and of itself, the branch instruction developed into something of a lower boundary, a way of saying "End of this section." After the end of a related set of instructions, the `GOTO` instruction would be a way of bowing out and moving back to another set.

Early BASIC instruction lines were numbered, and those numbers were generally rendered arbitrarily. Many of the BASIC programs running on DEC computers in the late '60s and early '70s had numbers like `00100`, `00110`, `00120`, but the first BASIC programs for microcomputers were generally numbered `10`, `20`, `30`, etc. When a programmer chose to insert a line in between two others, it was most likely 15 or 25, and then yet another inserted line was 18 or 28. Soon programmers ran out of insertion space. Microsoft helped a bit by allowing programmers to mix multiple instructions on one line, separating them with colons (:). Still, programmers derived the ability to integrate reusable instructions into their BASIC source code.

They did this (and I was among the guilty parties) by numbering segments of code that might have purposes in multiple programs with excessively high numbers. Programmers generally had the right to number instructions up to 65535. When I had a 36-line reusable segment, I'd number the instructions 65500, 65501, and so on. A new segment would start with 56713 and so on; the idea was to not duplicate my own numbers. Porting several code fragments into one interrelated program would be as simple as merging blocks of text together. . . or so I hoped.

The problem I faced continually was the one of uniformly global contexts. Variable names could be no more than two characters in length, so choosing odd names for variables was far more difficult than choosing free "lots" for line numbers in the territory of source code. For variables with far-reaching worldly purposes like radii or subtotals, I might standardize on RD or ST. But for variables I used for keeping track of how many times the joystick was toggled left, I needed to make sure my names wouldn't conflict. Otherwise, a variable that should have had a value from 0 to 9 might end up equaling 73.675.

The modern, modular BASIC made popular by Microsoft eliminates such decisions as these from the programming process. Modules and procedures can be programmed in advance and added to the source code as a textual appendage, or included using the $INCLUDE metacommand. The only space restrictions are those of your computer's conventional memory. As far as variable choices are concerned, you can use entire words—or perhaps some alphanumeric string that looks like a license plate—and even if the name of a variable you choose for a specific reason within a procedure conflicts with another entirely different variable within another procedure or at the modular level, VB/DOS knows to distinguish the two.

For example, variable x in one procedure refers to the number of white corpuscles in a cubic centimeter of blood, and in another procedure variable x refers to the number of Brazilians who claim to smoke more than two packs of cigarettes per day. If execution were to branch unconditionally from the middle of one procedure to the middle of the other, how does the VB/DOS interpreter decide, when xs collide, which x is more important? It can't, frankly, nor should it be forced to. You could decide, therefore, to allow x to be used only once within a program like in old BASIC so that these conflicts would not occur. That would, however, place restrictions on you as the programmer, rather than on the computer where they belong. So GOTO and GOSUB are now restricted to making only local jumps.

The Origin of Modules

The first BASIC programs were not divided into modules, procedures, or anything other than pages. They consisted of many pages of numbered instructions. A BASIC programmer of the 1970s didn't consider what area or region of the program a variable belonged to, because when a variable was declared—generally informally—the rest of the program had full access to that variable. Compared to the structure of modern VB/DOS, each old BASIC program consisted of one huge procedure.

Modular programming languages such as C existed long before BASIC became modular. The original idea behind BASIC was that it would be for beginners. When you became good enough at programming to be concerned about variable conflict reduction, you didn't need BASIC any more. Yet in certain cases, it appeared C programmers were having fewer problems than BASIC programmers; moreover, it is widely agreed that you should spend more time concentrating on the completion of the task at hand and less time on the maintenance of the program itself.

BASIC source code became much easier to manage when line numbers became optional features. The first real modular subdivision made to BASIC source code—the point at which the cell began to split—came with the introduction of *subprograms.* From the point of view of BASIC programmers of the day, a subprogram was an advanced type of subroutine that existed, in a sense, in its own little world. None of the existing variable values and dimensions within the main body of the source code applied to a *subprogram, except* for those few variables listed within a set of parentheses. Microsoft chose to mark subprograms within BASIC source code with the statement SUB. Although Microsoft doesn't use the term *subprogram* today with respect to VB/DOS, the declarative statement retains the original name Microsoft gave it.

SUB **Statement**

Syntax:

```
[STATIC] SUB procedure_name ([[BYVAL] argument1[()][AS type],
  [BYVAL] argument2[()][AS type], . . . ][BYVAL]
  argumentn[()][AS type]. . . ])
    instruction_block1
    [EXIT SUB]
    [instruction_block2]
END SUB
```

SUB is the primary procedural declarative statement in the VB/DOS vocabulary. The statement is used to enclose a procedure of a given name *procedure_name*. Execution can branch to this SUB statement from any point in the program if you invoke this procedure name within the source code or use the CALL statement.

A SUB procedure receives values from the procedure that called it, as *arguments* or *parameters* (the terms are interchangeable here). When a procedure is called from outside, those values that pertain to the procedure are listed within parentheses, separated by commas. These values are passed to the procedure. When a procedure is declared inside, those values are received in the order in which they were passed, and are assigned to variables that have names that might not necessarily be the same as those used for the procedure call. Contents of string variables can be passed in the same manner as values of numeric variables.

If the variable type of an argument is to change, or at least be ensured with specific reference, you can state the term AS *type* beside that argument. The contents of an entire array can be passed to a procedure as an argument, as long as the variable name of the array is identified with empty parentheses, `()`.

Under normal circumstances, any change made to the values of the arguments listed is reflected in the variables used as arguments in the procedure call. This reflection can be overridden for a specific argument by placing the term BYVAL before that argument. Doing so allows the variable used in the procedure call to retain its value, even if the value of the variable used to receive the argument has changed within the procedure.

Execution of the instructions within a SUB procedure occurs in sequence. A SUB procedure is terminated whenever an EXIT SUB or END SUB is reached during this sequence.

Under normal circumstances, the values of the variables with scopes that are local to the procedure, or that have not been declared as modular or global outside the procedure, are nullified whenever the procedure is exited. Use of the term STATIC before the SUB term changes the context of the procedure from standard local to static, allowing the interpreter to maintain the values and contents of variables used by the procedure after it is exited.

Microsoft is believed to be the originator of *user-defined functions* within BASIC source code. Originally, the definition of such a function could be expressed on only one line using the statement DEF FN (which stands for *define function*). Later, function definitions were promoted to formal clauses and are now considered procedures in their own right. In fact, in VB/DOS, any instruction that is not a part of a SUB procedure and is not a global or modular declaration is part of a FUNCTION procedure.

FUNCTION **Statement**

Syntax:

```
[STATIC] FUNCTION procedure_name ([[BYVAL] argument1[()]
  [AS type], [BYVAL] argument2[()][AS type], . . . ]
  [BYVAL] argumentn[()][AS type])
    instruction_block1
```

```
    procedure_name = expression1
    [EXIT FUNCTION]
    [instruction_block2]
    [procedure_name = expression2]
END FUNCTION
```

The FUNCTION statement acts as the header for those procedures that receive arguments in the same manner as a SUB procedure, but that return a single value or string contents to the procedure that called them in the manner of an equation. The FUNCTION statement itself appears to have precisely the same syntax as the SUB statement. One important difference between the syntaxes of the FUNCTION and SUB procedures is that the *procedure_name* of a FUNCTION procedure is treated like a variable within the procedure. Toward the termination of the FUNCTION procedure, a validly interpretable expression is assigned to that *procedure_name* with an equation. The value of this expression is considered the solution or result of the function as declared.

The syntax of arguments expressed within the FUNCTION statement is the same as the syntax of arguments within the SUB statement. Under normal circumstances, the values of the variables that have scopes that are local to the procedure, or that have not been declared as modular or global outside the procedure, are nullified whenever the procedure is exited. Use of the term STATIC before the FUNCTION term changes the context of the procedure from standard local to static, allowing the interpreter to maintain the values and contents of variables used by the procedure after it is exited.

A SUB procedure has no specific responsibility to provide any values or results to the rest of the program. By contrast, a FUNCTION procedure is charged with the responsibility of providing one value or alphanumeric string as the result of the function. Within the FUNCTION procedure, between the declaration and the END FUNCTION terminator, the name of the function itself—without parentheses—is shown. The function name is treated like a variable. The result of the function is assigned to this apparent variable—in fact, the assignment can be made at several different points in the procedure, but it must be made at least once. This way, the function name might represent that variable value outside of the function procedure.

For instance, because `twist` is not a reserved VB/DOS keyword, if one procedure contains the instruction `a = twist(c, d)`, the interpreter checks to see if `twist` is an array variable or a call to a function procedure. If a function declaration `FUNCTION twist(x, y)` exists someplace in the program, the function procedure `twist` executes. Like the `SUB` procedure, variables `x` and `y` are treated as inputs. Unlike the `SUB` procedure, the `FUNCTION` procedure has one output; someplace within the procedure, there must be a statement of assignment in the form `twist = `*`formula`*. Notice that `twist` has no parentheses in this assignment. The assignment is made as if `twist` were a standard variable because, like a variable, the term `twist` represents a value outside of the `FUNCTION` procedure.

Where Does It All Begin? Where Does It End?

The *startup file* is the first one executed in a project.

Under the default condition of the VB/DOS interpreter, no general (non-event) `SUB` or `FUNCTION` procedure in any module executes at all unless an instruction within the main module places a specific call to that procedure. This happens because the interpreter executes instructions belonging to the *startup file*—the module the interpreter executes. By default, this is the first module entered into the project.

Example

A commonly accepted modular structure is to have a startup procedure within one of your project's general modules, called `SUB Main ()`. Like its counterpart `main()` in the C programming language, `SUB Main ()` is generally used to specify the order of execution of the other major general procedures in the project. Often this order of execution is expressed as a cycle within an unconditional `DO-LOOP` clause. Unlike its cousin in the Visual Basic for Windows environment, however, `SUB Main ()` cannot be set to execute itself by default; a `CALL main` statement must be placed at the module level of the main module. Here's an example of a `SUB Main ()` procedure within the main module solely intended in this instance to specify the order of execution of other procedures, in this or other modules:

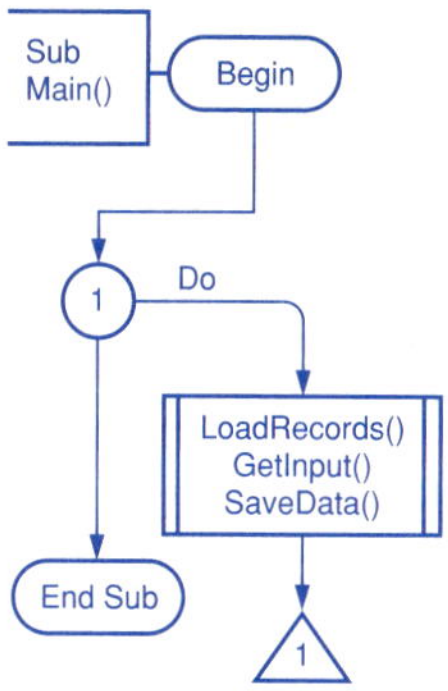


```
SUB Main ()
    DO
        LoadRecords
        GetInput
        SaveData
    LOOP
END SUB
```

Here calls to three arbitrarily named procedures exist within this or some other module. They are each called and executed in sequence continuously until program execution is stopped.

A project might contain more than one module, and there is no limit to how many procedures may exist within a module. So during runtime, from the interpreter's point of view, all the general procedures including `SUB Main ()` exist in one conglomerated pool.

Once added to a project, another module may be decreed the startup module. To make another module the startup file, perform the following steps:

1. From the Code Editor, select Set Start-up **F**ile from the **R**un menu. A dialog box will appear, as depicted in Figure 19.1.

2. Within this box is a list of the filenames of all general modules (extension .BAS) and all form modules (extension .FRM) currently enrolled within the current project. Highlighted within this list is the current startup module. To choose another module, click that module's filename and then click OK.

Once a form module has been made the startup file, the VB/DOS application will become entirely event-driven because no nondeclarative instructions are allowed at the module level of a form. No procedures will be executed at all unless a graphical event occurs having a `SUB` procedure associated with it. If no event procedures can be triggered by any graphical event, the application does nothing at all and will rest in limbo forever, or at least until the user presses Ctrl-Break.

Current Startup Module

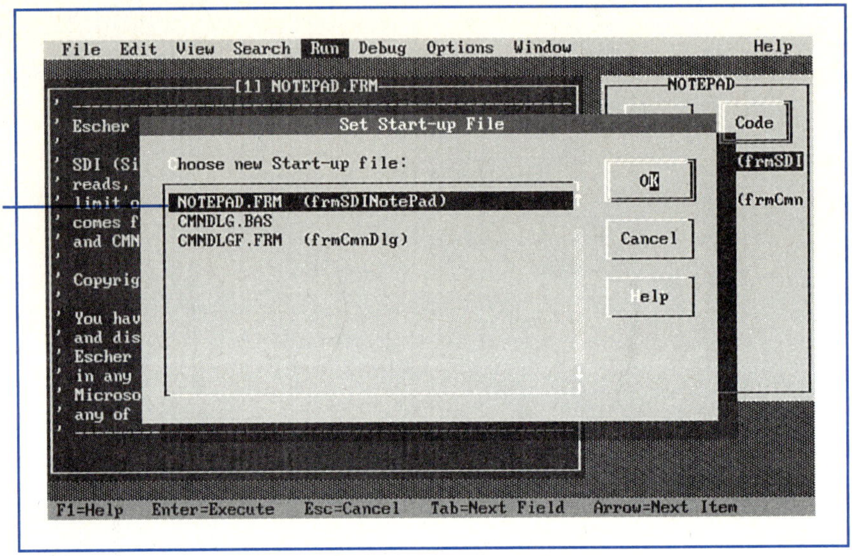

Figure 19.1. The startup file dialog box.

The Form of Forms

Each form module for a project is divided into three sections: the declarations section, the event procedures section, and the general procedure section—listed here in order of their consideration by the VB/DOS interpreter. Following the execution of the declarations section, the interpreter looks next to the event procedures section for the presence of a procedure called `Form_Load ()`. Here `_Load` is an event; specifically, it is the event of loading the form into the workspace in the first place. If this procedure exists, it is executed next. After `Form_Load ()` is complete, if there are any other event-driven procedures within the form module, VB/DOS suspends execution and waits for an event to occur that activates an event procedure.

If no procedure `Form_Load ()` exists for the first form module in the project and if any other event procedure exists within that module, VB/DOS suspends execution and waits for an event to happen that will execute one of those procedures. If no event procedures exist for this first form in the project, regardless of whether any procedures by any name exist in the general procedures section of the form module, no procedure is executed and the interpreter will be waiting for nothing to happen. This is why you can run a VB/DOS application that has no lines of source code in it and still receive a form named `Form1` on-screen while the interpreter waits for an event to occur.

When the properties belonging to a graphic object in one form are addressed from a procedure outside of that form, the procedure placing the address must specify the `.FormName` of the form containing the control, using the following syntax:

```
FormName.ControlName[(ArrayIndex)].Property
```

One way to override this default syntax is by way of the `$FORM` metacommand—the only one in the VB/DOS vocabulary not yet covered.

$FORM — Metacommand

Syntax:

```
{REM ¦ '} $FORM formname
```

The `$FORM` metacommand, placed within a form or general module, makes all the properties of the form whose `.FormName` property is specified by *`formname`* accessible by that module. Outside of the form's module, it is no longer necessary to specify the `.FormName` property of the form before specifying a graphic object's `.CtlName` belonging to that form. It is vitally necessary that the `.CtlName` properties of the specified form do not conflict with any other `.CtlName` for any object in any other form in the project.

Example

Suppose you add another form to the Expressor program that cooperates with the main form, whose `.FormName` is `Expressor`. At the module level of the new form, you would add this metacommand:

```
'$FORM Expressor
```

The procedures that exist within the general procedures section of a form module are executed only when called by name; otherwise, the interpreter never notices them. Likewise, every general module procedure executes only when called by name.

Whenever a form module subsequent to the startup form is loaded into the VB/DOS application's workspace using the `Load` statement or the `.Show` method, it is immediately executed if a procedure `Form_Load ()` exists for that form. If any other event procedures exist for that module, when the window for that module is active on-screen, the VB/DOS interpreter awaits an event that triggers the execution of one of those procedures.

Summary

The need for modular divisions within BASIC programs developed from the conflicts programmers faced when adding routines together. These conflicts concerned distinguishing line numbers from each other and making sure variable names weren't duplicated. VB/DOS procedures eliminate both possible areas of conflict by making line numbers optional—though an obsolete option—and having you state specifically which variables are to be shared between procedures.

With the exception of variable and functional declarations sections, all other executable instructions within a VB/DOS project exist within procedures of some sort. The two types of procedure declarations in VB/DOS are `SUB` and `FUNCTION`. The difference between `SUB` and `FUNCTION` is that `FUNCTION` returns a specific value within a variable name that doubles as the name of the `FUNCTION` procedure. Both `SUB` and `FUNCTION` procedures allow for input values between the parentheses of their declaration. But unlike the `SUB` procedure, a `FUNCTION` procedure passes a value back to the body of the program from which it was called. The values to be passed between procedures are presented as arguments within the procedure declaration and within the procedure call.

When a form module is made the startup file for a VB/DOS application, no nondeclarative module-level code may exist within that startup file. The application, therefore, must await some event for the program to work at all. Because, by default, a startup form displays itself—that is, is "loaded into the workspace"—then `Form_Load` becomes a valid startup event. The event procedure `SUB Form_Load ()` thus becomes the prime candidate for the startup procedure for that form.

Review Questions

Answers to Review Questions appear in Appendix B.

1. What part of a VB/DOS project always executes first without exception, whether or not it contains any code?
2. Assume a VB/DOS project has no general (non-form) module assigned to it, only a form module. There is no `SUB Form_Load ()` procedure within this module. Upon selecting **S**tart from the **R**un menu, what happens?
3. What instruction from `Form1` executes the first procedure of `Form2`?

20

Parameter Passing

In this chapter, you are offered insight into the logical mechanisms that allow values to be passed and shared between procedures in a Visual Basic for MS-DOS application. You'll understand to a greater extent why there are distinctions between different scopes of variables, and why the variables of a VB/DOS application are not simply shared among all the procedures and instructions of the program.

I Pass

To this point, when you've placed calls to SUB procedures using instructions within other procedures, you've stated the name of the procedure being called in an instruction or phrase by itself, along with any parameters the procedure may take, in a list delimited by commas. VB/DOS provides an optional second method for calling SUB procedures, with an explicit statement: the CALL statement.

[CALL] **Statement**

Syntax 1:

```
CALL procedure_name ([argument1, argument2. . . ])
```

Syntax 2:

```
procedure_name [argument1, argument2. . .]
```

When the CALL instruction is processed or when the name of a defined procedure is invoked within source code, a branch is made to the named SUB procedure. Any values to be passed to the procedure as arguments are listed beside the *procedure_name* in precisely the order in which they are to be received by the opening statement of the SUB procedure.

> **CAUTION:** If the term CALL is specified, the argument list is enclosed in parentheses. If CALL is omitted, the argument list is not enclosed in parentheses.

Example

Procedure calls using the CALL statement require parentheses.

Assume you have a SUB procedure called tri_area that figures the area of a right triangle, given the lengths of two of its sides. Here are two statements that would result in exactly the same branch to the procedure:

```
tri_area side1, side2
CALL tri_area (side1, side2)
```

The procedure that solves for the area of the right triangle might appear as follows:

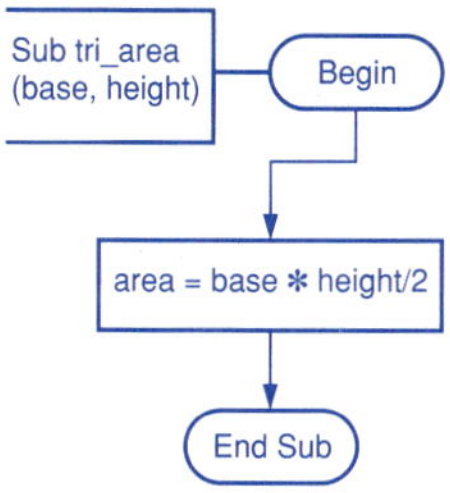


```
SUB tri_area (base, height)
   area = base * height / 2
END SUB
```

Arguably, this procedure might be expressed better using FUNCTION rather than SUB. As a result, the procedure call can be placed in the midst of a formula rather than placed as a statement by itself. Here's how the FUNCTION call and the revised procedure might appear:

```
Under_incline = tri_area (b, h)
.
.
.
FUNCTION tri_area (base, height)
   tri_area = base * height / 2
END FUNCTION
```

Another reason the procedure would perform better as a FUNCTION than as a SUB is that in the FUNCTION syntax, a separate variable area need not be declared for modular scope outside the procedure. This would be necessary with the SUB syntax because the scope of the calculations within a SUB procedure is confined to that local procedure. The result of the calculation would have no other way to get out of the confines of the procedure except by having been declared with a scope above local.

To illustrate, for SUB tri_area () to pass variable area back to the calling body, the instruction DIM SHARED area would have to be placed in the declarations section of the module containing both the call and SUB tri_area (). However, for FUNCTION tri_area (), you are free to place the procedure within a general module completely separate from any procedure that may call it. Upon executing the instruction a = tri_area (b, h), execution proceeds from wherever the call was placed to the general module. Yet there doesn't need to be any DIM SHARED declaration for a variable tri_area.

In Chapter 11, "Scope and Context," I listed the five variable scopes. To refresh your memory, Table 20.1 shows them again, along with the statements that declare variables for each scope.

Table 20.1. The five variable scopes.

Scope	*Statement*	*Definition*
local	`DIM`	Pertaining only to the procedure in which the variable is first invoked or declared, and having a value that is cleared when the procedure is exited.
static	`STATIC`	Pertaining only to the procedure in which the variable is first declared, although its value is maintained after the procedure is exited in case of possible reentry.
modular	`DIM SHARED`	Pertaining to all procedures in a module.
modular	`SHARED`	Pertaining to the module-level code and a particular procedure in a module.
cross-modular	`COMMON`	Pertaining to the modular-level code of all modules in the project.
global	`COMMON SHARED`	Pertaining to the entire source code.

Notice that at the beginning of both of the preceding example procedures, the variable names chosen for the procedures are different from the variable names that passed those values to the procedures. This is true because the variables themselves are not passed between procedures, just their values. Global variables don't have to be passed as parameters because every procedure is entitled to know its values or contents. On the other hand, local variables are kept local partly in an attempt to maintain their identity. You can perform the same `SUB` procedure or `FUNCTION` on several sets of variables, so the procedure must be able to accept its input from several sources. Because the variables in all the sources will be kept separate from each other, the variables in the procedure that solves for those input variables should be kept separate as well. This is why there are scope distinctions between variables.

The Natural Order of Things

In the right triangle formula, the parameter-passing order didn't really matter because the two parameters were multiplied together anyway. For most other procedures, however, the order in which the parameters are passed is crucial.

Example

Take for example this procedure call and its formula, which calculates the area of a right-circular cylinder. This procedure call and formula were taken from the Expressor application.

```
f1:
solution = surf_area_rccyl(p(0), p(1))
GOTO display_result

FUNCTION surf_area_rccyl (r, h)
surf_area_rccyl = (2 * PI) * r * h
END FUNCTION
```

Keep in mind that routine `f1:` and `FUNCTION surf_area_rccyl ()` appear in (or as) two different procedures. Notice that the input parameters for the function are stored in an array variable `p()`, whereas on the receiving end their values are assigned simply to unit variables `r` (radius) and `h` (height). Geometrically speaking, these values pertain to two distinctly different aspects of the cylinder, so their order within the parentheses must be maintained. The relation between the order of parameters in the passing and receiving lists determines the purpose of those parameters.

Example

From another area of the Expressor is a call to a `FUNCTION` procedure that needs more parameters. This is the Doppler shift formula, which determines the frequency of a light or sound wave emanated from a moving source, given the observed shifted frequency of that wave and the velocities of both the source of the wave and its observer:

```
f5:
solution = dopp_shift(p(0), p(1), p(2), p(3))
display_result:
readout.caption = STR$(solution)

FUNCTION dopp_shift (vo, vs, fo, c)
dopp_shift = ((c + vo) / (c - vs)) * fo
END FUNCTION
```

Again, `vo` is the velocity of the observer of a wave, `vs` is the velocity of the source of the wave, `fo` is the observed frequency of the wave, and `c` is the velocity of the wave (*c* is generally representative of the speed of light in physics equations, although the user of the program may want to substitute the speed of sound here). Again, the values are passed to the function with array variables but are received by unit variables. You could use any four valid numeric variables to pass values to `FUNCTION dopp_shift ()`, but the result of the equation would be the same. Here again, the order of the four variables within the parameter-passing sequences determines their purpose and relation to each other—not their names. This order can be arbitrarily defined when the procedure is written. Once this order is defined, however, it must be maintained within every call to that procedure.

Here is the standard syntax for calls to a `FUNCTION` procedure:

```
variable = procedure_name (parameter1, [parameter2...])
```

The function term formed by *`procedure_name()`* can also be used within a formula or expression and still be able to call the `FUNCTION` procedure. This is true because the called procedure defines for the VB/DOS interpreter how the function term logically reduces to a real value.

Example

When passing parameters between equations, the precision of those parameters must match. Thus, a single-precision floating-point variable must pass a value to another single-precision value in the receiving procedure. Suppose, however, for the sake of a receiving `FUNCTION` procedure, you need the formula to work on a rounded integer although the original variable doing the passing might be fractional. Say variable `c` is the variable you're rounding. The `FUNCTION` procedure can be written as follows:

```
FUNCTION wild_card (x, n, c)
c = INT(c)
.
.
.
END FUNCTION
```

Variable `c` is rounded inside the `FUNCTION` procedure. If the instruction that called it is `r = wild_card(u, t, v)`, then not only will `c` be rounded, but `v` as well. If you want the procedure to leave the passed variable alone, you need to state that up front at the procedure declaration, using the qualifier term `BYVAL` as follows:

```
FUNCTION wild_card (x, n, BYVAL c)
```

The term `BYVAL` stands for "only the value of" in this case. Including it means the rounding of `c` will not in any way affect the value of `v` in the calling procedure.

Summary

A branch to a `SUB` procedure is made through the use of a statement that may or may not contain the term `CALL`. A branch to a `FUNCTION` procedure, on the other hand, is made by implication—by stating the procedure name as an element of a mathematical expression or equation.

When passing parameters between procedures, the purpose of those parameters within the procedure is determined not by the name, type, or scope of the parameter, but by the parameters' chosen order within the parameter list. The order of the list in the instruction that calls the procedure and the order of the list in the declaration of the procedure must match for the procedure to operate. When parameters are passed successfully in this fashion, changes made to the variable that received the parameter value are reflected in the variable that passed the parameter value to the procedure. This reflection can be overridden in advance by use of the term BYVAL before the variable that has a calling counterpart that is to be left alone.

Review Questions

Answers to Review Questions appear in Appendix B.

1. In this chapter, you saw two different types of procedures—SUB and FUNCTION—perform the same type of arithmetic operation on the same parameters and yield the same results, except in different ways. Why is the instruction that calls the SUB procedure for this arithmetic operation considered a *statement,* whereas the instruction that calls the FUNCTION procedure for the same arithmetic operation is considered a *function*?

2. Syntactically speaking, why does a CALL statement enclose its arguments within parentheses, whereas the same statement made without the use of CALL omits those parentheses?

Part V

Arithmetic Functions

21

Function Classification

In this chapter, you'll examine what a Visual Basic for MS-DOS function is and does. Before you start examining these functions in detail in subsequent chapters of this section, you'll see how their return values can be classified as variable types.

The Function of the Matter

As you've learned thus far in this book, all a computer really does is perform logical operations. Literally, it compares two Boolean values and obtains the Boolean result. Because such operations mimic the appearance and behavior of mathematical operations at the base 2 level, logical comparisons and derivatives performed on one another repetitively and continually actually cause the computer to perform the same function as mathematics in the real world. Every mathematical function can somehow be described as a combination of logical comparisons, as discovered and proven by mathematicians such as George Boole and John von Neumann.

A *function* is an arithmetic operation performed on a value, variable, or expression.

When I say function in the context of the preceding paragraph, I refer to the role of mathematics in the modern world, and not the role of terms or instructions in VB/DOS. As defined in Chapter 3, "Grammar and Linguistics," a VB/DOS function is a more fundamental, less esoteric thing. A *function* is an arithmetic operation performed on a value, variable, or expression, which has a result that is returned in a single variable.

An *expression* in this case is not a figure of speech. An expression is any of the following:

- An arithmetic comparison between two values, having a result that is expressed logically as a binary state
- One or more values or variables arithmetically joined by functions or functional operators
- An assignment of value to a variable through another value, variable, or another expression

An *expression* is a mathematical comparison or combination of values.

An expression is a mathematical combination of values (or contents of strings, but not both) and functions. Fundamental mathematical functions are represented in VB/DOS by *operators* such as `+` and `/`. Functions such as the sine of an angle measurement or the ASCII code value of a character, however, are represented by abbreviated terms, each of which carries a set of parentheses. Within this set is the list of values or alphanumeric strings (or both) that the VB/DOS interpreter uses to derive a result.

A VB/DOS function is addressed by way of a reserved term. Once addressed, it performs a mathematical or logical operation on a set of values or textual contents. A VB/DOS function is said to yield a result, which is stored within a variable that utilizes the function. In all VB/DOS instructions that include intrinsic functions, the function is stated within the right side of an equation. This equation acts as an *expression of assignment,* in that the solution of the equation is a result that is placed within a single variable. This variable is the only term on the left side of the equation. This expression takes on the following form:

```
variable = function()
```

Example

As an example, here's one of the simplest function assignments:

```
a# = SQR(2)
```

You assign the value of the square root of 2 to variable `a#`. Here the intrinsic VB/DOS function is `SQR()`, which calculates the square root of whatever value or expression rests within its parentheses.

Some VB/DOS functions are not mathematical; in fact, a great many of them concern the manipulation of text. They operate in the same manner because textual assignments can be formulated like equations. A text function can be distinguished easily from a value function, in that a text function always contains the `$` character before its parentheses. As an example:

```
c$ = CHR$(65)
```

Here the character having ASCII code 65 is returned in the string variable `c$`. The character that `c$` now contains, by the way, is *A*.

Example

Often, a function contains more than one parameter, and these parameters are separated by commas as delimiters, as in the following example:

```
n$ - RIGHT$("D. F. Scott", 5)
```

Here the `RIGHT$()` function extracts the rightmost five characters from my name and assigns them to variable `n$`. When strings are stated explicitly within a function as in `"D. F. Scott"`, you as the programmer must resist the temptation to use correct English punctuation, which places the comma within the quotation marks. If the comma falls within the quotation marks, the interpreter assumes that comma to be the rightmost character in the string. When searching for a comma, the interpreter will not find one—it will instead find a `5` in the preceding example—and an error will be generated.

I Redeclare!

You now have been refamiliarized with all the fundamental terms necessary to discuss VB/DOS functions. Before going on with Part V, "Arithmetic Functions," I will introduce you to a series of statements that you may want to use from time to time to make variable type distinction a little easier when you're creating your formulas: `DEFCUR`, `DEFDBL`, `DEFINT`, `DEFLNG`, `DEFSNG`, `DEFSTR`.

DEFCUR, DEFDBL, DEFINT, DEFLNG, DEFSNG, DEFSTR

Statements

Syntax:

```
DEFCUR range[, range[, range. . . ]]
DEFDBL range[, range[, range. . . ]]
DEFINT range[, range[, range. . . ]]
DEFLNG range[, range[, range. . . ]]
DEFSNG range[, range[, range. . . ]]
DEFSTR range[, range[, range. . . ]]
```

These `DEF`*`type`* statements do not declare variables. Instead, they designate a range of the alphabet (as in `A-Z`) as reserved for a particular variable type, abbreviated by the letters following `DEF`:

`CUR`	Currency
`DBL`	Double-precision floating-point
`INT`	Standard integer
`LNG`	Long integer
`SNG`	Single-precision floating-point
`STR`	Alphanumeric string

After you use a `DEF`*`type`* statement within a form's or module's declarations area, variables within that module declared informally or declared without establishing types and having a first letter that falls within the range designated by the statement will automatically be given the data type specified by the three-letter abbreviation *`type`*. Normally, informally declared variables are designated as single-precision floating-point variables. A `DEFtype` statement can be used to override this distinction for variables that fall within certain ranges of the alphabet.

> **CAUTION:** Remember that unless declared otherwise (by formal statement or `Deftype` statement), a variable defaults to single-precision floating-point type.

Example

Many programmers, in the interest of memory conservation, override the single-precision default variable type with the following statement, placed within the declarations area of a VB/DOS application:

```
DEFINT a-z
```

Now, every variable is given a default data type of `INTEGER`, as if it were declared `AS INTEGER`. To give a variable a single-precision data type now, it can be declared `AS SINGLE` to override the integer distinction.

Some programmers like to reserve a letter or two for strings only, with such a statement as this:

```
DEFSTR z
```

From then on, they could write equations of assignment like `z = "Argon gas"` and the interpreter would not generate an error. When a default data type is established for a range of variables using `DEFtype`, the special character such as `#` or `$` is no longer necessary. This is acceptable for many programmers in the case of value variables. But because `$` is often used as the sole distinction in text between a string and value variable, few programmers historically have used `DEFSTR` to avoid using the distinguishing character. History, however, should not prevent you from taking your own course of action.

Summary

A function in VB/DOS is a mathematical operation performed on a set of values or alphanumeric strings, the result of which is returned within or assigned to a single variable. This variable is the sole element of the left side of the equation. The function exists somewhere within the right side of the equation, perhaps as part of a mathematical expression. A VB/DOS intrinsic function always has a set of parentheses for enclosing input parameters. The `DEF`*`type`* statement can be used to set the default data type for a variable before it is declared.

Review Questions

Answers to Review Questions appear in Appendix B.

1. What is the conceptual difference between a function of arithmetic and a function of VB/DOS?
2. Would the instruction `DEFINT A-Z` reserve single letters for use in integer variables?
3. Why are parentheses used in this book—even empty ones—to distinguish VB/DOS functions?

22

Conversion

In this chapter, you are introduced to the intrinsic Visual Basic for MS-DOS functions that take a single parameter of one type or form and convert it to a value or string of another type or form. These are generally the simplest of BASIC functions.

"Integize"

At times, you may need a value within a floating-point variable to be rounded to the nearest whole number, or perhaps you need to remove its fractional value altogether. Two functions for that purpose are `INT()` and `FIX()`.

`INT()` **Function**

Syntax:

```
solution% = INT(expression)
```

The `INT()` function rounds the logically simplified value of *`expression`* downward to the nearest integer or whole number. The result of this rounding is returned in the variable *`solution%`*.

FIX() **Function**

Syntax:

`solution% = FIX(expression)`

The `FIX()` function removes any fractional value from the logically simplified value of *`expression`*, leaving an integer or whole number value. This value is returned in the variable *`solution%`*.

Example

Here is a "conversation" with the VB/DOS Immediate window (command-line interpreter), which should help to distinguish the difference (although there is little) between the `INT()` and `FIX()` functions. The responses are shown in **`bold monospace`**.

```
a=4.9999
?INT(a)
 4
?FIX(a)
 4
a=-4.9999
?INT(a)
-5
?FIX(a)
-4
```

For a positive value of variable `a`, the `INT()` and `FIX()` functions return the same value. For a negative value of `a`, the results of the two functions differ by one because `Int()` rounds the value downward to the nearest whole number (a downward direction increases a negative value). In contrast, `Fix()` simply removes the fractional value without performing any true arithmetic on the variable.

Example

A common use for the `INT()` function is to make values more manageable and tangible. Suppose, for instance, you have a loop clause that is executed as many times as there are miles between two points. The distance between those two points is found algebraically, and it is almost certain to contain a fractional value. A loop clause cannot be executed 8.26 times or a time and a half; there can be only a whole number of iterations. This whole number can be derived by rounding the distance using the `INT()` function, as follows:

```
distance# = SQR(((x2 - x1) ^ 2) + ((y2 - y1) ^ 2))
d% = INT(distance#)
FOR clomp = 1 TO d%
    .
    .
    .
NEXT clomp
```

The loop clause is executed (`INT(distance#)`) times, without any fraction of a loop to worry about. Actually, VB/DOS loop clauses ignore fractional values if the `STEP` value is assumed to be 1. This way, however, variable `d%` can be addressed within the clause.

String Conversions

Earlier in this book, you wrote an application that could, among other things, convert a base 10 value to base 16. A VB/DOS intrinsic function can do that for you, but if I told you that in the beginning, you probably would not have learned as much about logic, would you? In any event, here are the base conversion string functions for VB/DOS: `HEX$` and `OCT$`.

HEX$() **Function**

Syntax:

`solution$ = HEX$(num_expression)`

The `HEX$()` function solves for the value of *num_expression*, rounds that number down to the nearest integer, and finds the hexadecimal (base 16) value of the number. This number is returned as a string, especially because it can contain the digits A through F (10 through 15).

OCT$() **Function**

Syntax:

`solution$ = OCT$(num_expression)`

The `OCT$()` function works the same way as `HEX$()` does, but its solution is an octal (base 8) number. Although it contains only digits 0 through 7, the solution is returned within a string variable *solution$*.

Example

A conversation with the CLI shows the preceding functions in action:

```
num=1495
?hex$(num)
5D7
?oct$(num)
2727
```

As you discovered in an earlier chapter, VB/DOS (as well as DOS and the BIOS itself) recognizes alphanumeric characters as numeric patterns. The patterns form a code that is called *ASCII,* after the name of the standards document that defines it.

ASC() **Function**

Syntax:

```
solution% = ASC("char$")
```

where *char$* is a single character.

The ASC() function obtains the ASCII (actually the ANSI) code value for the character designated as *char$*. This value is returned within the variable *solution%*.

CHR$() **Function**

Syntax:

```
solution$ = CHR$(expression)
```

where *expression* can be logically simplified to a legitimate ASCII code value.

The CHR$() function first accepts the whole-number value of *expression* and then looks up the ASCII (ANSI) code equivalent character for that value. This character is returned as the single-character contents of *solution$*.

Example

3 2 1

Here's an interesting situation in which you might find yourself as a programmer: Suppose you have a program that maintains a very large database of clients' names. A scroll bar is used in your program's main form to represent the position of the currently displayed record alphabetically, with respect to the entire clients database. You determine, however, that it would be a time-saver for the program if you split the database into 26 files organized alphabetically. Each file would be apportioned a particular letter of the alphabet, and only those records containing surnames beginning with that letter would be stored there. You want this fact to be "transparent" to the user, however, so you want the scroll bar to be able to tell the program which data file to look under for the current record.

Say the scroll bar is called `Scroller` and the text box that contains the letter being pointed to is `Display`. The value of property `Scroller.Value` is that value represented by the scroll box—what Macintosh users call the "thumb." In the ASCII code, the capital letter *A* is represented as number 65, and the other capital letters through to *Z* are represented up to number 90. When designing the form, the `.Min` property for `Scroller` is set to 65 and the `.Max` property to 90. Now `Scroller.Value` only registers a valid capital letter. Here's the procedure for determining which letter is being "dialed" when the user operates the scroll bar:

```
SUB Scroller_Change ()
Display.Caption = CHR$(Scroller.Value)
.
.
.
END SUB
```

The preceding procedure is waiting for a `_Change` in the position of the scroll box in `Scroller`. When that happens, the contents of the text box `Display` change to show the letter represented by the scroll box position. This letter is determined using the `CHR$()` function to convert `Scroller.Value`—which can only be a whole number between 65 and 90, thanks to the `.Min` and `.Max` settings made in Form Designer.

Often, you need to convert a numeric value to string contents, and vice versa. The `VAL()` and `STR$()` functions are for those purposes.

VAL() **Function**

Syntax:

```
solution = VAL(string$)
```

where *string$* can be an expression that concatenates several strings. The first set of nonspace characters in the string, however, must be a set of digits, or any characters that the VB/DOS interpreter would normally use to distinguish fractional numbers. Decimal points are recognized as such characters.

The `VAL()` function converts the first set of digits with number-delimiting characters in *string$* to a value that is placed within the variable *solution*. The first alphabetic character encountered within a string cancels the conversion process. A totally alphabetic character is therefore converted to 0. The contents of *string$* are unaffected by this conversion.

STR$() **Function**

Syntax:

```
solution$ = STR$(value)
```

The `STR$()` function converts the digits contained within *value* into an alphanumeric string, which is placed within the variable *solution$*. The value of the variable *value* is unaffected by this conversion.

Example

As you've learned, certain object properties are recognized as strings and others are recognized as values, without any distinguishing characters such as `$` to help you out. With that in mind, a result value of an equation is often placed within a text box on a form. Text boxes can have only alphanumeric contents; they do not interpret values directly. The following conversion comes from the two-dimensional distance converter program from Chapter 6, "Formulas":

```
SUB Go_Click ()
x1 = VAL(Box_x1.Text)
x2 = VAL(Box_x2.Text)
y1 = VAL(Box_y1.Text)
y2 = VAL(Box_y2.Text)
d# = SQR(((x2 - x1) ^ 2) + ((y2 - y1) ^ 2))
Distance.Text = STR$(d#)
END SUB
```

The derived distance value has to be converted into an alphanumeric string using `STR$()` before that solution can be displayed within the text box `Distance`.

Finally, here are five functions that convert values from one type to another: `CCUR()`, `CDBL()`, `CINT()`, `CLNG()`, and `CSNG()`.

`CCUR()`, `CDBL()`, `CINT()`, `CLNG()`, `CSNG()` — Functions

Syntax:

```
solution = Ctype(expression)
```

where *type* is the abbreviation for the variable type being converted to, as introduced in Chapter 21, "Function Classification."

The `Ctype()` functions solve for the logically reduced value of *expression* and then convert that expression to the specified variable type, even if that type requires more bytes than are necessary to represent the value. The result must be assigned to a variable having a type that is equivalent to the type being converted to.

Summary

Values can be rounded or truncated to whole-number values using the `INT()` and `FIX()` functions. Base 10 numbers can be converted to base 16 and base 8 using the functions `HEX$()` and `OCT$()`, respectively. The ASCII code value for a character can be obtained using `ASC()`; likewise, a character can be obtained from its ASCII code value using `CHR$()`. String contents are converted to a numeric value using `VAL()`, and a value is converted into a string using `STR$()`. Values can have their variable types converted and reassigned to a variable of a new type, using the `C`*`type`*`()` functions.

Review Questions

Answers to Review Questions appear in Appendix B.

Using the functions introduced in this chapter, and without the aid of the computer, estimate the solutions to the following expressions:

1. `INT(3.1415927)`
2. `ASC("A")`
3. `CHR$(ASC("z"))`
4. `INT(ASC("A"))`
5. `VAL("1600 Pennsylvania Avenue")`

23

Practical Math

In this chapter, you are introduced to the intrinsic Visual Basic for MS-DOS functions that concern algebraic, trigonometric, and logarithmic calculations.

Algebraic Functions

Two functions that involve the sign of the numeric value (whether the value is positive or negative) are `ABS()` and `SGN()`.

`ABS()` — **Function**

Syntax:

```
solution = ABS(expression)
```

The `ABS()` function returns the absolute value of the result of *expression*, within the variable *solution*. This is equivalent to the value of the original expression, unsigned.

SGN() **Function**

Syntax:

```
solution% = SGN(expression)
```

The `SGN()` function returns a value that represents the sign of the logically reduced value of *`expression`*, within the variable *`solution%`*. This representative value can be any of the following:

–1	if *`expression`* is negative
0	if *`expression = 0`*
1	if *`expression`* is positive

Example

For this example, you'll need to think a bit figuratively because it would take forever to explain the specifics. The concepts of `ABS()` and `SGN()` are so simple that, at first, it might not seem you need such functions. After all, if you know `a = -42`, do you need `SGN(a) = -1` to tell you that you have a negative number on your hands?

As a VB/DOS programmer, you'll learn that these functions become far more valuable in complex situations. Say you're writing a charting program that displays the progress of trading an issue of stock on the New York Stock Exchange. For each day of trading, a vertical bar is plotted along an x/y graph showing the range between the issue's high and low trading value for the day. The bar may be wide or narrow, but that width in and of itself doesn't show the viewer the general *trend*, which is whether the overall trading value is lower or higher than that during the previous trading session.

Say the closing value for each day is held within the array `closing()`, and that the day being plotted is traced within the loop variable `day`. Naturally, "today's" bar would be bar number `day`, and yesterday's would be number `day - 1`. The difference in the values over a two-day period is determined by the following expression:

```
trend = closing(day) - closing(day - 1)
```

Suppose you want a green bar to represent a gaining day and a red bar to represent a losing day. You can set the color of the bar with the following clause:

```
SELECT CASE SGN(trend)
    CASE -1
        colr = 4   'Red
    CASE 1
        colr = 2   'Green
    CASE 0
        colr = 0   'Black
END SELECT
```

In the preceding clause, `SGN(trend)` can yield only one of three values, all of which are covered here. The value rendered matches in sign only the sign of the value of `trend`.

If each trading "point" on the chart were represented by a pixel on the graph, the length of the bar between the high and low value on the day would be found using the following expression:

```
range = ABS(high(day) - low(day))
```

Here `high(day)` and `low(day)` are arrays that store the high and low trading values.

It's Hip to Be SQR

In this section you'll learn about the more basic mathematical intrinsic functions, starting with the square root function term.

SQR() **Function**

Syntax:

```
solution = SQR(expression)
```

The `SQR()` function returns the square root of the logically reduced value of *`expression`*, within the variable *`solution`*.

Example

By now you're familiar with the two-dimensional distance-finding formula:

```
d# = SQR(((x2 - x1) ^ 2) + ((y2 - y1) ^ 2))
```

VB/DOS gives you four functions that relate to trigonometry: `SIN()`, `COS()`, `TAN()`, and `ATN()`.

`SIN()`, `COS()`, `TAN()`, `ATN()` — Functions

Syntax:

```
solution = SIN(expression)
solution = COS(expression)
solution = TAN(expression)
solution = ATN(expression)
```

These four functions return the sine, cosine, tangent, and arctangent, respectively, of the logically reduced value of *`expression`*. This value is returned in the variable *`solution`* as a unit of *radians*, which are divisions of a circular arc.

Example

Because you have a tendency to think in terms of degrees, it is necessary to convert degrees to radians—what VB/DOS uses to determine sines and cosines—before you can evaluate the trigonometric expression. A conversation with the VB/DOS CLI shows how you can do this:

```
pi=3.1415927
deg = 90
?SIN(deg*(pi/180))
1
```

Finally, here are the functions regarding logarithms: `LOG()` and `EXP()`.

LOG(), EXP() **Functions**

Syntax:

```
solution = LOG(expression)
solution = EXP(expression)
```

The `LOG()` function returns the natural logarithm of the logically reduced value of *`expression`*, within the variable *`solution`*. Likewise, the function `EXP()` returns the base of natural logarithm *e* raised to the power of the logically reduced value of *`expression`*, within the variable *`solution`*.

Example

You can determine the base 10 logarithm for a value (in other words, answer the question, "10 raised to what power equals what value?"). You do so by dividing the natural logarithm of 10 by the natural logarithm of the value in question. Use the following function declaration:

```
DEF FNLog10(value) = LOG(value) / LOG(10)
```

Summary

The absolute value of an expression is obtained with `ABS()`; the sign of that expression can be obtained with `SGN()`. The square root of an expression is obtained with `SQR()`. VB/DOS's trigonometric functions are `SIN()`, `COS()`, `TAN()`, and `ATN()`. The natural logarithm of an expression is found with `LOG()`, and the number to which natural logarithmic base *e* is raised to equal an expression's value is obtained with `EXP()`.

Review Questions

Answers to Review Questions appear in Appendix B.

If `x = 6` and `y = 9`, solve for the following:

1. `ABS(x - y)`
2. `SGN(x - y)`
3. `SGN(ABS(x - y)`

24

String Functions

In this chapter, you study how Visual Basic for MS-DOS terms, fashioned to resemble arithmetic functions, actually operate on the contents of an alphanumeric string or string variable. For instance, you use VB/DOS string functions to alter or adjust the contents of strings so they can be displayed better or stored within a record, or so that you can extract certain fragments of information from that record.

String of Pearls

The *memory map* regulates the storage of object code, of intermediate VB/DOS p-code, and of variable values and contents.

When a function operates on a value stored within a variable, the contents of that variable are represented in a reserved region of the computer's memory. The location of this region is maintained by VB/DOS, or by the object code that is stored along with a compiled VB/DOS application, within a sort of *memory map.* Tinkering with such maps using intrinsic BASIC functions and statements like PEEK and POKE is, for the experienced programmer, the logical equivalent of bungee jumping. In some cases, the fact that the program can crash is what keeps programmers poking along.

When a function operates on the alphanumeric contents of a string variable, those contents are represented as a reserved region of the computer's memory. As you've seen in several previous chapters, each character of a string is represented as a pattern of bits.

The code for this pattern is called ASCII (the American Standard Code for Information Interchange, which is followed by much of the world outside of America). ASCII is a more logical pattern than, for instance, Morse Code. It is more logical because the equivalent code number for any given character can easily be determined arithmetically using binary logic rather than arbitrary guesswork.

Each character of an alphanumeric string is stored within one byte. Each byte of a string is generally stored in memory beside the other, in sequence. The region of memory containing the string has left and right "bounds," which are to some degree manipulable by the VB/DOS interpreter. You may remember from earlier study how variable values with different types (integer, double-precision floating-point, and so on) are stored within regions of memory with differing bounds. In other words, a double-precision value can be stored within eight bytes, whereas an integer can be stored within two. To convert a double-precision value to an integer, from the point of view of the interpreter, is a process of moving the bounds and repositioning the value within those bounds, after shaving away those bytes containing the fractional portion of the value. Likewise, shaving away the trailing spaces from a string such as `"Sheffield[space][space][space][space][space]"` is accomplished by the interpreter's moving the bounds for the stored element of data. The mechanisms for storing values and storing textual contents do not actually differ much from each other.

What is different in the way a string is contained from the way a value is contained is that you have more control over the byte containment process with respect to strings. When you informally declare a variable as equalling a value, as in `pi = 3.1415927`, you create a four-byte containment region. You can make it an eight-byte region by converting the value to double-precision using `CDBL()`, but there would not be much point in doing so unless you were to add a more detailed fraction to the value. When you informally declare a string variable as containing specific contents, as in `ship$ = "Sheffield"`, you create a nine-byte containment region. To make it into a 14-byte region, you can write an equation such as `ship$ = ship$ + "[space][space][space][space][space]"`. Likewise, you can change the upper bounds of the string by adding text to the beginning, as in `ship$ = "HMS[space]" + ship$`. (Note that the term *[space]* here substitutes for one character.)

Now you have an 18-byte region, although at first the trailing spaces may not appear to be of much use. However, suppose you're storing data to disk in the form of records containing vital information about British Naval vessels of the Falklands War. A record in a random-access file is defined to be a precise number of characters long. Somewhere within each record is a specific 18-character region containing the name of a vessel. If the name of the vessel contains fewer characters than the name of the region, the trailing spaces are necessary to separate the vessel's datum (item of data) from the next item in the record. This way the name of the ship's captain doesn't bleed into the name of his vessel.

The type of control you as programmer have over the string containment process can at first be likened to the type of control a person has over the contents of the IRS Form 1040 each April. However, when you realize there is logic behind the mechanism, you can more easily supply the logic for that mechanism. To explain: You determine that the storage mechanism for string variables involves code. A coded value from 0 to 255 is stored within each byte of a string. Suppose you were to treat this string as a series of values by encoding vital information in sequence as characters and storing that data as a string rather than as an integer or, more wasteful yet, as a single-precision variable.

TIP: To save memory, store some numbers as strings. If three low value numbers are used to describe the state of some operation within the program, you can give the values for each state a character code. The characters can then be concatenated (joined together) and stored as a single string—as in `status$ = fuel$ + coolant$ + battery$`. What might have required six (or, informally declared, 12) bytes to represent now takes only three.

You would, however, need to program the mechanism for storing the code as a procedure. If you use this mechanism for encoding an entire array of thousands of items, however, the memory you save may begin to be measured in kilobytes.

Perhaps the most important function relating to controlling a string variable in this manner is the `LEN()` function.

LEN() **Function**

Syntax:

```
value% = LEN(string_exp$)
```

where *string_exp$* is any expression joining one or more strings of alphanumeric text.

The LEN() function returns the number of characters currently being stored within the expressed string, in the numeric variable *value%*.

Example

Here's the LEN() function at work, as demonstrated through a conversation with the VB/DOS CLI:

```
ship$="Sheffield"
?LEN(ship$)
 9
```

The function simply counts the number of characters in the string.

Because LEN() is a function like any other intrinsic VB/DOS function, its result can be assigned to a variable:

```
ship$="Sheffield"
ln=LEN(ship$)
?ln
 9
```

Example

Suppose a string array variable nam$() contains a list of surnames. The string space allocated for each datum in the array is only as long as the name contained within the string. For instance, the name *Enrik* is stored within a five-character string, whereas

To *pad* a string is to fill it at the end with spaces or null characters to make it fit a given storage space.

Magnusson is stored within a nine-character string. A record stored to disk contains a 25-character field for surnames called `n$()`, regardless of how long each surname is. When the length of each surname is less than 25, the right side of the string is *padded* with space characters. The following routine supplies the padding:

```
FOR nam% = 1 TO UBOUND(name$, 1)
    ln% = LEN(nam$(nam%))
    pad% = 25 - ln%
    n$(nam%) = nam$(nam%) + SPACE$(pad%)
NEXT nam%
```

Here's the preceding procedure translated into pseudocode:

Start counting from 1 to the number of names in the array.
Assign the length of the name currently being counted to this variable.
Subtract this length from 25.
Place this many spaces at the end of the name before storing it.
Count the next name.

The loop clause uses the variable `nam%` to keep count as iterations proceed from 1 to the number of items in the array `nam$()`, as determined by the function `UBOUND()`. The length of each name in the array is found by the `LEN()` function on the second line. This length is subtracted from 25—the length of each field to be stored to disk—to derive the number of spaces to be added to the end of the `nam$(nam%)` before it is added to `n$(nam%)`. The `SPACE$()` function adds a specific number of spaces to the end of `nam$(nam%)`.

SPACE$() **Function**

Syntax:

```
string$ = SPACE$(number%)
```

The `SPACE$()` function returns a series of *`number%`* space characters, within string variable *`string$`*.

The `LEN()` function can be best put to use when invoked in a procedure that contains the other major string functions in the VB/DOS vocabulary: `LEFT$()` and `RIGHT$()`.

LEFT$(), RIGHT$() **Functions**

Syntax:

```
substring$ = LEFT$(string$, number%)
substring$ = RIGHT$(string$, number%)
```

The `LEFT$()` function extracts the first *number%* characters in sequence from the larger string *string$* and assigns those characters as contents of the smaller string variable *substring$*. Likewise, the `RIGHT$()` function extracts the last *number%* characters of a string in sequence from the larger string *string$* and assigns those characters as contents of the smaller string variable *substring$*. In both functions, if *number%* is larger than the length of *string$*, the entirety of *string$* is returned in *substring$* without any characters added to either side of the string.

Example

Here you can see the `RIGHT$()` function at work with the aid of the VB/DOS CLI:

```
ship$="Sheffield"
?RIGHT$(ship$,5)
field
```

Here the `RIGHT$()` function counts the first five characters from the right of `ship$` toward the left and extracts those characters. The returned extracted characters are displayed from left to right and not backwards, as in *dleif*.

It's important to note that the `.Text` property of a text box and the `.Caption` property of a label or other graphic object that uses labels can be substituted for *string_exp$* in any of these functions.

The VB/DOS interpreter treats the stated properties of graphic objects as if they were string variables, for the sake of these functions.

Example

The procedure introduced previously did not take into account cases in which a person's surname is longer than 25 characters. Certainly, the 25-character name is a rare case; but if the surname exceeds 25 characters, you have no choice but to trim the longer name down to the first 25 characters. Here's how to determine and execute the trimming:

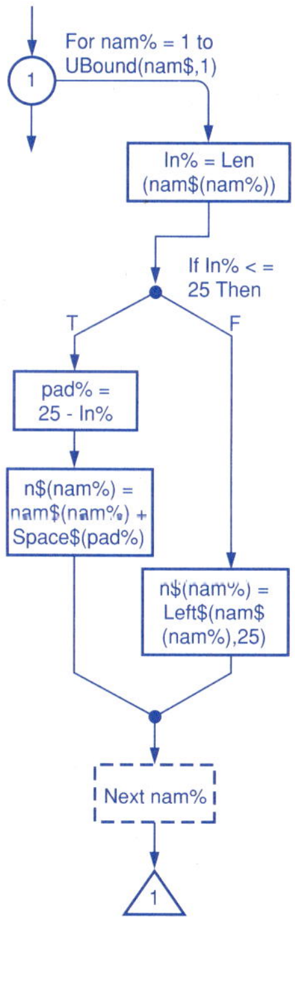


```
FOR nam% = 1 TO UBOUND(nam$, 1)
    ln% = LEN(nam$(nam%))
    IF ln% <= 25 THEN
        pad% = 25 - ln%
        n$(nam%) = nam$(nam%) + SPACE$(pad%)
    ELSE
        n$(nam%) = LEFT$(nam$(nam%), 25)
    END IF
NEXT nam%
```

An `IF-THEN-ELSE` clause divides the naming operations into a true side and a false side. The true side is executed when the length of `nam$(nam%)` is less than or equal to 25; the false side is executed when the surname is too long to fit in the record. In such a case, the function `LEFT$()` is used to extract the leftmost 25 characters from `nam$(nam%)` and place them within `n$(nam%)`. Note that I haven't been using the word *name* as a variable in these procedures because `Name` is a reserved keyword in VB/DOS.

When people's names are stored to disk as a table using the preceding procedure, the padding of spaces attached to the names that are shorter than 25 letters allows each name to fit neatly into the slot or field created for each name. The procedure that retrieves these names knows where to look to retrieve a particular name in the sequence because each stored field has a fixed beginning and ending byte location, regardless of the size of the data stored within the field. When the data is retrieved, however, you need to strip the trailing spaces from each name so that you won't have to mail envelopes with names that appear like these:

```
Lester              C.   Thurow
Robert              B.   Reich
Milton                   Friedman
```

Thankfully, you have access to VB/DOS functions that automatically remove whatever spaces you padded each name with. They are `LTRIM$()` and `RTRIM$()`.

`LTRIM$(), RTRIM$()` **Functions**

Syntax:

```
string$ = LTRIM$(string_exp$)
string$ = RTRIM$(string_exp$)
```

where *`string_exp$`* is any logical expression containing one or more concatenated strings or string variables.

The `LTRIM$()` function removes all spaces from the left side of the expressed string. Likewise, the `RTRIM$()` function removes all spaces from the right side of the expressed string.

Example

After retrieving the padded names you stored to disk earlier, you can use `RTRIM$()` to remove any trailing spaces from each name, as follows:

```
FOR nam% = 1 TO UBOUND(n$, 1)
    nam$(nam%) = RTRIM$(n$(nam%))
NEXT nam%
```

Notice that you don't have to use any arithmetic here to remove the spaces from the end of the name. The VB/DOS interpreter knows, when given the directive by `RTRIM$()`, to search for any trailing spaces that may exist and purge them.

LSET and RSET are used to justify text within strings that contain spaces as padding so the padding can be bunched up on one side of the strings or the other.

LSET, RSET — **Statements**

Syntax:

```
LSET field$ = entry$
RSET field$ = entry$
```

The LSET and RSET statements assign the textual contents already assigned to *entry$* to a string full of spaces: *field$*. The length of *field$* is not changed; instead, spaces within *field$* are replaced by the contents of *entry$*. The LSET statement enters *entry$* within *field$* starting at the leftmost character of *field$*, thus creating a left-justified field. Likewise, the RSET statement enters *entry$* within *field$* starting at the rightmost character of *field$*, creating a right-justified field. If there are more characters in *entry$* than there are in *field$*, only the leftmost characters of *entry$* appear in *field$* for both statements. The length of *field$* remains the same.

String of Strings

Earlier in this chapter, I introduced the function SPACE$() as a function for placing a certain number of spaces into a string variable, generally as padding. A related function, derived from earlier in BASIC's history, is STRING$().

STRING$() — **Function**

Syntax 1:

```
word$ = STRING$(number%, "char$")
```

Syntax 2:

```
word$ = STRING$(number%, ascii_char%)
```

The `STRING$()` function issues a designated *number%* of repeated characters as the string variable *word$*. Under Syntax 1, the single character to be repeated is expressed as *char$*, between quotation marks. Under Syntax 2, the single character to be repeated is expressed as the ASCII code equivalent of the character that is expressed as *ascii_char%*.

Example

Assume you're designing a printout for a price sheet for your retail store. Your price sheet will show retail prices for items you sell, line by line. After the name of each item, you'd like a series of asterisks linking the item to its price. You don't know in advance how long the item name will be, nor how many characters will constitute the price. The following procedure determines how many asterisks you would need to use between the item name and its price for a line that's 66 characters long.

```
FOR nam% = 1 TO UBOUND(item$, 1)
    li% = LEN(item$(nam%))
    prce$(nam%) = "$" + STR$(price(nam%))
    lp% = LEN(prce$(nam%))
    numast = 66 - li% - lp%
    PriceList.PRINT item$(nam%); STRING$(numast, "*");
      prce$(nam%)
NEXT nam%
```

Here's pseudocode for the preceding procedure:

Count from the first to the last item
in the array.
Acquire the length of the current item
in characters.
Make the price string equal to "$" joined
with the alphanumeric form of the price
of the current item.

Acquire the length of this new price string.
The number of asterisks between these two strings will be 66 minus the length of both strings.
Print to the price list the current item's name, the number of asterisks required, and the current price.
Count the next item.

The lengths of the item name string and price string are assigned to variables `li%` and `lp%`, respectively. Variable `prce$` is created by concatenating a dollar sign with the string-converted form of the price value. VB/DOS requires the names of string variables to be different from the names of value variables, so the *i* was removed from *price* in `prce$`. Naturally, the string must be created before its length is obtained. I used variable *`numast`* to determine the number of asterisks necessary to fill the space between the item name and the price so that both appear flush left and right on the price list. The `.PRINT` method then prints three items in succession, the second being a string of asterisks formed by the function `STRING$(numast, "*")`.

`STRING$()` is one example of what in old BASIC was called a *command function,* which was the term for a function that performs the role of a command. The interpreter is told to produce a row of characters of a specified type. Two similar functions that qualify as command functions by the old definition are `LCASE$()` and `UCASE$()`.

`LCASE$(), UCASE$()` **Functions**

Syntax:

```
string$ = LCASE$(string_exp$)
string$ = UCASE$(string_exp$)
```

The `LCASE$()` function converts all alphabetic characters appearing within the expressed string or string concatenation *`string_exp$`* to lowercase letters. Likewise, the `UCASE$()` function converts all alphabetic characters appearing within the expressed string or string concatenation *`string_exp$`* to uppercase letters.

Example

A conversation with the VB/DOS CLI demonstrates the use of both preceding case conversion functions:

```
ship$="Sheffield"
ship$=UCASE$(ship$)
?ship$
SHEFFIELD
ship$=LCASE$(ship$)
?ship$
sheffield
```

In the Midst of Strings

Up to now, you've been working with functions that concentrate on either the left or right side of the string, or the whole string. There will be instances in your programming career when you need to know whether the user entered a particular string of characters someplace in the middle of a large text box. The `INSTR()` function determines not only if that text was entered, but where it appears.

INSTR() **Function**

Syntax:

`position& = INSTR([first_char%], string_exp1$, string_exp2$)`

The `INSTR()` function initiates a search for the string or string concatenation expressed by *string_exp2$*, within the larger *string_exp1$*. The length of *string_exp2$* must be less than 65,536 characters. If the search turns up a match, the number of the character in the larger string where the first character of the smaller string appears is returned as long integer variable *position&*. The first character of the larger string is considered character number 1. If the smaller string does not appear exactly within the larger string or if *string_exp2$* is larger than *string_exp1$*, the function returns a null value (0). If the long integer *first_char%* is expressed, the search begins with that character position of the larger string. The value of *first_char%* can be no larger than 65,535.

Example

As an example of the INSTR() function, assume you have an application called App with a search-and-replace text function. When you select that function from the menu, a dialog box form pops up requesting the text to look for in the body of a document called Document and the text to replace it with. This dialog box has a .FormName of Replacer; its procedure, which starts the search-and-replace operation, is as follows:

```
SUB Start_Click ()
srch$ = SearchText.Text
rplc$ = ReplaceText.Text
IF LEN(srch$) = 0 OR LEN(rplc$) = 0 THEN
    Replacer.HIDE
    EXIT SUB
END IF
trgt$ = App.Document.Text
pos = INSTR(trgt$, srch$)
IF pos = 0 THEN
    MSGBOX "Text not found.", 0, ""
    EXIT SUB
END IF
App.Document.SelStart = pos - 1
App.Document.SelLength = LEN(srch$)
App.Document.SelText = rplc$
Replacer.HIDE
END SUB
```

Here's pseudocode for the preceding procedure:

Procedure awaiting a click on the Start button:
Acquire the text to search for from a text box.
Acquire the text it is to be replaced with from the other text box.

If the length of either specimen of text is 0, then
This must be a "pocket cancel," so take this dialog box off the screen and
Exit this procedure.
End of condition.
Take the text from the document.
Find the place where the search text begins within the target text.
If the search text is not there, then
Notify the user.
Get out of this procedure.
End of condition.
Otherwise, start to indicate the beginning of the search text in the document.
Extend the selector for the length of the search text.
Replace the selected text with the replacement string.
Remove this dialog box from the screen.
End of procedure.

First, this procedure assigns the text being searched for to the variable `srch$`. If the user did not type anything into this box (`IF LEN(srch$) = 0`), there's no point in searching for nothing; the dialog box is hidden, and the procedure is exited.

For the sake of this example, the entire document is assigned to variable `trgt$`. Now the crucial `INSTR()` function is invoked, searching for the first instance of `srch$` within `trgt$`. The search begins with character number 1 and proceeds one character at a time. Variable `pos` should contain the location of the first character where `srch$` is located within `trgt$`. If `pos = 0`, evidently the search string doesn't exist within the target, and a message box is displayed to that effect.

When the procedure finds a match for `srch$` within `trgt$`, the found text is automatically selected as a property `.SelText` of the text box, and it is replaced by making that property equal to the replacement string `rplc$`. The text selection properties are covered in depth in Chapter 36, "Textual Properties."

The preceding example demonstrates how search-and-replace functions work when you know precisely what text you're searching for. Assume you need a procedure that searches for an element of text based on its *construction,* not its contents. Say, for instance, you're looking for a ZIP code—not a specific one, just any ZIP code. You know a ZIP code is at least five digits appearing next to one another. You can't use `INSTR()` to search for unknown text, so you'll probably need to employ the help of the `MID$()` function.

`MID$()` **Function**

Syntax:

*substring$* = MID$(*string$*, *start_pos&*, *number%*)

The `MID$()` function extracts a *number%* of characters from a string in sequence from the larger string *string$*, starting at character position *start_pos&* counting from the left of *string$*. The extracted characters are then assigned to the smaller string variable *substring$*.

Example

Here's a procedure that looks for anything resembling a ZIP code:

```
SUB Zip_Click ()
total = LEN(Document.Text)
trgt$ = Document.Text
FOR pos = 1 TO total - 4
    IF MID$(trgt$, pos, 1) > CHR$(48) AND MID$(trgt$, pos, 1)
    ➥ < CHR$(57) THEN
        zipfind = zipfind + 1
        IF zipfind = 5 THEN
            Document.SelStart = pos - 5
            Document.SelLength = 5
            zp$ = Document.SelText
            MSGBOX "Possible ZIP code " + zp$ +
              " found at position " + STR$(pos - 5), 0, ""
        END IF
    ELSE
        zipfind = 0
```

```
    END IF
NEXT pos
END SUB
```

Pseudocode for the preceding procedure is as follows:

```
Procedure awaiting a click on the Zip button:
Find the length of the entire document.
Call the text of this document the target string.
Count from the first to the fourth from the last
  character in the document.
    If the character at this position is a digit, then
        Add one to the potentiality that this is a
          ZIP code.
        If this potentiality equals five digits, then
            Indicate the text at this point.
            Indicate five characters from this point.
            Place the indicated text in a string
              variable.
            Tell the user this can be a ZIP code and
              where it was found.
        End of condition.
    Otherwise,
        Strike any hope of this being a ZIP code.
    End of condition.
Count the next character.
End of procedure.
```

This procedure belongs to the main form, not to a dialog box. First, the length of the text typed into `Document` is obtained and assigned to variable `total`. The text itself is assigned to `trgt$`. The loop clause keeps a count of characters called `pos`, starting with the first character and ending with the fifth from the end—because ZIP codes are five characters long. Within the loop clause is a conditional clause using the `MID$()` function, which tests to see if the specified single character `MID$(trgt$, pos, 1)` has an ASCII value between 48 and 57—which would make that character a digit. If it is indeed a digit, one is added to an independent counter variable `zipfind`.

When `zipfind = 5`, the procedure has found five digits in a row. The digits are then extracted from behind the current count position `pos - 5` and displayed in an appropriate message box. If the procedure did not find enough digits in sequence, `zipfind` is reset to 0.

In VB/DOS, the term `MID$` can also be used as a statement, which in effect reverses the order of the transaction in the `MID$()` function.

MID$ **Statement**

Syntax:

```
MID$(string$, start_pos&[, number&]) = substring$
```

The `MID$` statement replaces the text currently assigned to *`string$`*, starting at cursor position *`start_pos&`* counting from the left, with the text contained within *`substring$`*. If *`number&`* is expressed, that number of characters are removed from *`string$`* and replaced with the first *`number&`* characters from the left of *`substring$`*.

> **NOTE:** The `MID$` statement takes parameters within parentheses just like the `MID$()` function although the operation of both terms is quite different. Notice how the statement *changes* the state of a string of characters, whereas the function *reports* the state of a string without changing it. Still, I identify the `MID$` statement without parentheses in the textual descriptions for the sake of consistency.

Summary

A string variable is stored in memory with each byte representing a character of the string. Unlike the storage techniques given a numeral value, string contents in memory are given left and right bounds that can be manipulated by changing the contents of the string. The length of a string in memory is returned with the `LEN()` function.

A sequence of spaces is created using the command function `SPACE$()`. Similarly, a sequence of any single character is created using `STRING$()`. Leading and trailing spaces can be trimmed from a string using the `LTRIM$()` and `RTRIM$()` functions, respectively. A smaller string can be entered into a larger string full of spaces. The larger string's contents can be justified using the `LSET` and `RSET` statements. Any string's alphabetic characters can be converted to upper- or lowercase using `UCASE$()` and `LCASE$()`, respectively.

The leftmost and rightmost portions of any string can be extracted and assigned to another string variable, using `LEFT$()` and `RIGHT$()`, respectively. A number of characters from the middle of any string can be extracted and assigned to another string variable using the `MID$()` function. A number of characters within the middle of any string can be replaced by a sequence of characters from another string using the `MID$` statement. The character position of the first instance of a smaller string within a larger string can be obtained by using the `INSTR()` function.

Review Questions

Answers to Review Questions appear in Appendix B.

Assume in the course of programming, `srch$` is assigned the following string contents. Without using the computer as an aid, determine the result of the following functions:

```
When in the course of human events
```

1. `LEFT$(srch$, 4)`
2. `RIGHT$(srch$, 7)`
3. `MID$(srch$, 4, 1)`
4. `MID$(srch$, 9, 4)`

Suppose in the course of the same program you invoke the following instruction:

```
MID$(srch$, 6) = "in, of, and around"
```

5. What are the current contents of `srch$`?

25

Defined Types and Functions

In this chapter, you experiment with creating your own variable types and declaring variables using those types. You then use your customized types to pass composite variables to and from procedures. Later, you'll explore the original, sometimes simpler method of adding customized mathematical functions to the Visual Basic for MS-DOS vocabulary.

The Composition of Variables

Microsoft uses the term *user-defined variables* to describe variable types that are defined by you as the programmer. Initially, this distinction does not make a great deal of sense, because I've already defined the user as the person who operates the programs that have variables that are defined, if not altogether created, by the programmer. I could use the term *programmer-defined variables*, but what I am really talking about are variables that contain other variables.

A *composite variable* is a programmer-defined combination of numerals and strings that is treated as a single variable.

A *composite variable* in VB/DOS is a container for multiple numeral, string, or other composite variables, addressed together as one unit using a single arbitrarily defined term and invoked within an instruction using object-oriented syntax.

In a composite photograph, multiple images of one object viewed from different angles appear on the same page. In a composite drawing sketched by a police artist, portions of generic faces are combined to produce a likeness of a suspect. Similarly, a composite variable in VB/DOS is made up of other variables. In the same way that a composite photo is really more than one photo and a composite drawing is composed of pieces of more than one face, a composite variable is made up of more than one variable. It is not really a variable, however; it is merely addressable as if it were a variable.

The mechanism of a composite variable in VB/DOS is somewhat related to the way properties relate to graphic objects on a VB/DOS form. Suppose, for instance, you use four variables throughout an application to refer to aspects of one real-world item, such as a transaction in your personal checkbook. Using VB/DOS's composite variable mechanism, you can declare these aspect variables to be *properties* of checkbook transactions. In doing so, you render transactions to be, to some extent, virtual objects in the context of your application. Thus, it seems natural to use object-oriented syntax to refer to your checkbook properties, as in `Transaction.Number`, `Transaction.Recipient`, or `Transaction.Debit`.

Referring to properties in this manner does not, however, mean that `Transaction.` becomes an object by the formal definition of the term used in computing. If it did, you would be able to use the programming language to construct methods such as `Transaction.Record` or `Transaction.Cancel`, and call such methods as directives to your application as if they were keywords in the language vocabulary. VB/DOS does not contain facilities for programmer-defined methods; therefore, composite variables cannot be true objects—at least not in the current release.

The declarative statement used to create composite variables is the `TYPE-END TYPE` statement.

TYPE-END TYPE

Statement

Syntax:

```
TYPE typename
    variable1 AS existing_type
   [variable2 AS existing_type]
    .
    .
    .
   [variablen AS existing_type]
END TYPE
```

The TYPE-END TYPE clause is used within the module-level code of the startup module of an application to declare programmer-defined composite variable types for that application. It can also be used in .BI files attached to the same module-level code by way of the $INCLUDE metacommand. The *typename* for the composite variable is arbitrarily defined by you as the programmer, although it must not be a reserved keyword, a declared variable name, or a term used in the program for any other purpose.

Each variable that comprises the composite variable is listed within the clause. Listings of variables do not count as declaratives; these variables must be declared elsewhere in the program. The invocation of each variable is only meant as a reservation for its place within the composite variable being declared. The type of variable being listed must be specified; this type can be any numeral value or string variable type, or any previously declared composite type but not an array variable.

Example

Suppose in your application there is a routine that draws a rectangle someplace on the background screen, given that rectangle's origin point coordinates, width, and height. You can pass the rectangle-drawing routine a single parameter containing all four variable values, which have been declared to be of user-defined category `Rectangle`. Here's how the `Type` declarative clause for rectangles might appear:

```
TYPE Rectangle
    x AS INTEGER
    y AS INTEGER
    w AS INTEGER
    h AS INTEGER
END TYPE
```

The purpose of `TYPE Rectangle` is to describe the upper-left corner of a rectangle and the rectangle's length and width. Later in the course of the program, you may write the instruction `DIM SHARED BigBox AS Rectangle`. From then on, the variable `BigBox` can be passed as a parameter between procedures. The variables designated to be part of this type declaration can be changed at will; the variable `BigBox` changes in turn.

Example

Using NAMEFRM2.FRM as a guide, here is a user-defined type declaration that specifies an entire record by itself:

```
TYPE Record
    LastName AS STRING * 30
    FirstName AS STRING * 20
    MidInit AS STRING * 3
    Address AS STRING * 50
    City AS STRING * 20
    State AS STRING * 5
    Zip AS STRING * 10
END TYPE
```

In the preceding clause, the `*` character does not stand for multiplication but as a delimiter between the `STRING` type identifier and the number of characters each element contains. Each composite variable must have a fixed byte length in memory for the interpreter to manage it. The interpreter always knows the number of bytes in an ordinary numeral variable, and an ordinary string variable has a marked beginning and end. This way, a `surname$` can equal either "Yu" or "Witherspoon" without the shorter name requiring several spaces of padding at the end.

A *field* is a fixed portion of memory or of a display, reserved for a specified element of data.

The string element of a composite variable must have a fixed number of characters, however, because with a virtually unlimited number of declared components, the interpreter must know where the variable contents start and stop in memory. Imagine each byte or character of a composite variable as a symbol painted on a white picket fence. A single-precision value is always written over four pickets (bytes), but the contents of an ordinary string variable may take up as many as 255 pickets and as few as zero. The `*` extension helps establish fenceposts between planned sections of the composite fence. In more formal computing terminology, each fence segment is called a *field.*

> **NOTE:** String and numeric variables can be mixed within type declaration clauses.

The `DEF FN`-itive Function

Perhaps every great innovation in the history of high-level language programming was devised in the interest of reducing redundancy. The macro in "macro assembler" is a set of instructions that is called with one instruction so that repetitive functions need not be written repetitively.

Serious programming in the first edition of BASIC must have been a real pill. For one thing, few people knew there would ever be any serious programming in BASIC. When programmers began writing long BASIC dissertations with the same scientific formula repeated several times in the source code, without the aid of copy and paste, the exercise soon grew tiresome. The first mechanism for facilitating repetitive functions, before the advent of the `FUNCTION` procedure, was the `DEF FN` statement. At first it was limited to one instruction line. To maintain compatibility with older versions of BASIC, the statement is provided in VB/DOS.

DEF FN **Statement**

Syntax 1:

```
DEF FNname ([argument1, argument2,...argumentn])
  = expression
```

where *expression* is any combination of variables or values, using mathematical operators or intrinsic functions, that may logically be reduced to a numeral value.

The DEF FN statement allows the specified FN*name* to substitute in the source code for the included *expression* wherever it occurs. Its purpose is to evaluate the mathematical *expression* using the listed arguments as parameters. For substitution to take place, DEF FN must be executed like a standard instruction before any instance of FN*name*() occurs within the source code; preferably, the statement should appear at the front of the startup module. In compliance with early conventions, the letters FN must appear before the function *name* whenever the function is later invoked in the text. The resulting programmer-defined function name may be treated as though it were an intrinsic VB/DOS function. DEF FN may be used to define the function named FN*name* only once during the course of a program's source code.

The call to the FN function appears within a standard expression, as in the following:

```
variable = FNname([argument1, argument2,
   ...argumentn])
```

Parameters are optional within an FN function call, but parentheses are not. A parameterless FN call would be rather pointless, however, because at best it could only yield the same value whenever it is invoked.

The values within the parameters listed in the FN call are passed to the DEF FN instruction, whose listed *argument* variables assume those values in sequence. These argument variables are then used, in turn, within the included *expression*. In this syntax, the solution to the function FN*name*(), in all cases, is the same mathematical combination of values, regardless of circumstances or operating conditions; there can be no IF or SELECT statements to conditionally alter the evaluation. DEF FN is generally reserved for defining fixed financial or scientific formulas, like the present value of an annuity or the surface area of a cylinder.

Example

Earlier in the book, when you constructed the prototype Expressor program, you included a series of FUNCTION procedures constructed in the manner of the right-circular cylinder surface area function as follows:

```
FUNCTION surf_area_rccyl (r, h)
surf_area_rccyl = (2 * PI) * r * h
END FUNCTION
```

You could have chosen instead to use a series of DEF FN statements at the front of the startup module, constructed as follows:

```
DEF FNsurf_area_rccyl (r, h) = (2 * PI) * r * h
```

The advantage to this method is that the definition is shorter, and the structure of the program can be reduced by several modules. The disadvantage of this method is that the letters FN must appear before any invocation of the function name. Also, the current construction of the program enables you to write complex FUNCTION modules with conditionalized solutions. Suppose one of the parameters drastically changes the way the formula is evaluated; there's no way a condition can be expressed using Syntax 1 of the DEF FN function. However, Syntax 2, which follows, is more versatile.

DEF FN — Statement

Syntax 2:

```
DEF FNfunction_name ([[BYVAL] argument1[()]
  [AS type], [BYVAL] argument2[()][AS type], . . . ]
  [BYVAL] argumentn[()][AS type])
    [STATIC variable_list]
```

```
    instruction_block1
    FNfunction_name = expression1
    [EXIT DEF]
    [instruction_block2]
    [FNfunction_name = expression2]
END DEF
```

Syntax 2 of the DEF FN takes much the same form as that of the FUNCTION procedure definition statement, but it does not define the boundaries of a module. Instead, the function acts as the boundary of a *clause* that can appear within module-level code or within a SUB or FUNCTION module. Regardless of the position of the DEF FN function clause, the variables used within the clause are automatically given cross-modular scope, whether or not they were declared with any other scope earlier. Variables invoked internally within the clause can be declared local to the clause using a STATIC local declaration immediately following the DEF FN statement. This is the only instance of clause-level variable declaration within a VB/DOS module.

For the most part, Syntax 2 of the DEF FN statement is functionally identical to the FUNCTION statement, although DEF FN does not distinguish function procedures from the rest of the program. Perhaps what is most unique about DEF FN is how much more difficult it is to manage and use than its newer FUNCTION counterpart.

Why include DEF FN in the course of this discussion? As you learn to program in BASIC, you will most likely—more to the point, you *should*—take apart older BASIC programs, add new features to them, and modernize the way in which users communicate with them. DEF FN is a remnant of older versions of Microsoft QuickBasic, so you will no doubt run across it in the course of translation. One good way to modernize an old QuickBasic program is to systematically trash DEF FN clauses wherever you find them. Syntax 1 of the DEF FN statement, however, can have some continued usefulness even in newer VB/DOS programs.

Summary

A composite variable is a container for several other non-array variables. You as the programmer establish the term for this variable, as long as it does not conflict with a reserved VB/DOS keyword or another variable, graphic object, or line-labeling term currently in use within the source code. When a composite variable type is declared, component variables may be addressed as properties of the composite variable, as if the composite were an object. The `TYPE-END TYPE` clause is used to declare composite variables. The variables listed within the clause are not declared by the clause; they are declared elsewhere.

Programmer-defined functions are arbitrarily named terms that may be added to the VB/DOS vocabulary for the sake of the current VB/DOS application, using the `DEF FN` statement. On one line by itself, `DEF FN` defines a mathematical formula to be substituted in the text by the function `FN`*`name`*`()`. An alternative syntax expands `DEF FN` into a clause that has much of the construction of the `FUNCTION` statement, although `DEF FN` does not define the boundaries of a procedure as does `FUNCTION`.

Review Questions

Answers to Review Questions appear in Appendix B.

1. Can a composite variable include both string and value variables?

2. Composite variables use object-oriented syntax for addressing individual elements. If at one point the value of one element of a composite variable is set to the value of a regular variable, and the value of that regular variable changes later in the program, does the value within the composite variable change as well?

3. If `i` is an undeclared variable, and after executing `DEF FN` variable `i` is declared `STATIC`, then after executing `END DEF`, what is variable `i` equal to?

4. Because a composite variable is not a variable, why is it called "composite variable"?

26

The Random-Number Generator

In this chapter, you experiment with one of the more intriguing features of this or any other high-level programming language, the piece that appears to act for the most part on its own: the interpreter's generator for "random" numbers. As a Visual Basic for MS-DOS programmer, you use randomization to set up conditions for experiments, as well as create the random element for tests, simulations, and games.

Whether 'tis by Chance or by Circumstance...

Having thoroughly expounded upon the more logical processes of computing thus far in this book, you might think that there could be no process within a computer that could possibly take the random element into account. You might think so, and this *is* so. In fact, there is no true random-number generator within any computer or any interpreter or compiler. Rather than skip to the next chapter, however, you should note that there is a logical function within VB/DOS that appears to generate random numbers with no specific input or parameters passed to it. The `RND()` function is one of the oldest functions in the BASIC language, and it seems to have been unscathed by the more purposeful path of progress.

RND() **Function**

Syntax:

```
number! = RND[(process!)]
```

where *process!* is any single-precision floating-point number, the sign of which, when *process!* is expressed, is crucial to the generation process.

The `RND()` function returns what appears to be a random single-precision floating-point number between 0 and 1. The value of *process!* affects the random-number generation process. A particular "random" number is generated for each *process!* value passed to the function if `process! < 0`. A particular sequence of random numbers may exist within an application for each number generation, in which case the same sequence is generated each time the application is executed. The next number in this sequence can be generated if `process! > 0` or if *process!* is omitted altogether. The previous random number is regenerated if `process! = 0`.

The random number generation process in VB/DOS is actually dependent on the current value yielded by the `TIMER()` function. The result is a sequence of numbers that appears to be random when pulled out of the proverbial hat. After running applications that use random numbers again and again, however, you might notice that the same sequence of randomization appears each time. This would get a little frustrating if you were trying to maintain a constant level of difficulty for a blackjack game.

This repeated-sequence problem is easily solved through the invocation of the `RANDOMIZE` statement.

RANDOMIZE **Statement**

Syntax:

`RANDOMIZE[(seed%)]`

The RANDOMIZE statement *reseeds* the random-number generator for an application. In other words, it changes some of the constants in the random generation algorithm so that a different sequence of random numbers can be generated, thus eliminating the possibility of number prediction. If *seed%* is expressed, a particular sequence of random numbers referred to by *seed%* is initiated. If *seed%* is omitted, a "random" seed is initiated, the choice of which seed value is based on the current state of the random-number generator itself.

Example

You can see that the generator really does appear to pick numbers out of a hat, as demonstrated by this conversation with the VB/DOS CLI:

```
?RND(1)
 .7055475
?RND(1)
 .533424
?RND(I)
 .5795186
?RND(1)
 .2895625
?RND(1)
 .301948
```

Each time the same function is invoked, and each time a different response is generated. It is possible, however, that a program that invoked the random-number generator five times would, throughout several executions, generate the same sequence of "random" numbers each time, unless the `RANDOMIZE` statement appears somewhere toward the beginning of the VB/DOS application. Without typing `RANDOMIZE` first, try invoking the VB/DOS Immediate and Output windows and typing `?RND(1)` into the Immediate window five times. Unless Microsoft "tweaked" its random-number generator since the time of this writing, you should see the exact same five numbers as those in the preceding code lines. Next, try restarting the VB/DOS interpreter, typing `RANDOMIZE` into the Immediate window, and then typing `?RND(1)` five times. None of the responses in the Output window should equal those listed in the preceding code lines.

Example

The following function returns a random integer value between 0 and 15:

```
rnum = INT(RND * 15)
```

The value returned by `RND()` (or `RND` without parentheses, if you prefer) is always between 0 and 1. Thus, if you multiply the value by 15, the result will always be between 0 and 15. Making this result into an integer allows the interpreter to pick a number between 0 and 15.

Example

A similar function can be used to pick a capital letter between *A* and *Z*:

```
letr = INT(RND * 26) + 65
letr$ = CHR$(letr)
```

The ASCII code value for character *A* is 65. The 26 uppercase letters in the alphabet fall in the ASCII code from 65 to 90, in sequence. After picking a number from 0 to 25, the result is added to 65 to obtain an uppercase letter from the ASCII code, which is assigned to string variable `letr$`.

Example

It's inevitable that, at some time in the career of the game programmer, you will use the random-number generator to shuffle cards. If you assume the standard deck contains 52 cards (54 if you count jokers), it would be easy to pick a single card out of the deck with the function `INT(RND * 52) + 1` (not counting card number 0). The shuffling process, however, from the point of view of the computer, picks 52 random cards from this deck successively. You can't say `FOR card = 1 TO 52` and have the randomizing process merely repeat itself because it's possible that the interpreter could pick the same card more than once. The shuffled deck can have only one instance of each card. Each time that card is picked for the new deck, some indicator must remain to prevent the card from being picked again.

```
RANDOMIZE
FOR plac = 1 TO 52
choose:
    extract = INT(RND(1) * 52) + 1
    IF slot(extract) = 1 THEN GOTO choose
    card(plac) = extract
    slot(extract) = 1
NEXT plac
```

Here is the preceding procedure translated into pseudocode:

Reseed the random-number generator.
Start counting card places from 1 to 52.
   Pick a card between 1 and 52.
   If this number has been chosen before, then go back
    and pick another card.
   Otherwise, assign this card number to the deck.
   Record this card as having been chosen once.
Count the next card.

You assume that each card number is representative of a particular card; for instance, card number 1 could be the ace of spades.

Summary

Random-number generation is accomplished in VB/DOS through the use of the `RND()` function. A set sequence of random numbers exists virtually for each application although that sequence can be replaced with another sequence using the `RANDOMIZE` statement. Each random number generated by the VB/DOS interpreter has a value between 0 and 1. This value can be multiplied and made into an integer, resulting in the appearance of the computer picking a whole number from a specified range.

Review Questions

Answers to Review Questions appear in Appendix B.

1. In the expression `RND(1) * 72`, the function randomizes a number between 0 and what?

2. Why are the parentheses in the `RND()` function optional?

3. Can the `RANDOMIZE` seed for the random-number generator be a random number?

Part VI

Form Design

27

The Form

In this chapter, you examine the role of the form as a graphic object. The term "graphic" in this instance is used more loosely because graphic forms in Visual Basic for MS-DOS are not displayed using what is normally called the "graphics" screen of DOS. A graphic object is more graphically graspable, if you will, than objects that are literally drawn to the graphics screen, such as a grid dot. Although forms are produced using the IBM Extended Character Set of your computer's BIOS, they do hold the key to making your application more readily comprehensible by your users.

Later, you'll see the properties that relate to the appearance of a form window in the VB/DOS workspace. You also see examples of these properties—as you do for the other properties covered in Part VI, "Form Design"—being set with the VB/DOS Form Designer properties bar, as well as with source code.

Form Versus Substance

A *form* is a region of the screen where graphic objects are contained.

For the sake of VB/DOS, a *form* is a region of the screen where textually-based graphic objects, controls, and textual items may be contained. You might want to include graphic forms in your VB/DOS applications because the form maintenance system handles much of the graphical interaction on your behalf. You might *not* want to include graphic forms in your VB/DOS applications because the form maintenance system takes much of the graphics production system away from you.

The *workspace* is the area of the screen where forms and tools reside during runtime.

The form maintenance system is, for the most part, a sophisticated way to handle text on-screen. When the form system is running, the graphics system is inactive. You can't plot lines, circles, or bitmaps within a VB/DOS form or anywhere outside of it as long as there's a form inhabiting your application's workspace. The *workspace* is the area of the screen where forms and VB/DOS tools reside—although they may not necessarily appear there—during an application's runtime.

This makes it perhaps all the more confusing when I use the term "graphic object" to refer to an item such as a button or list box that can appear within a form. Notice, however, I do not say "*graphics* object." In the 1970s, the designers of the IBM Extended Character Set had enough foresight to know that computer users would need border characters, or extensions to the ASCII code that produce symbols that can be joined together at the end to form boxes. The "forms" they assumed you'd make were more on the order of IRS tax forms or invoices. Certainly, you could make an invoice out of a VB/DOS form, but few real-world forms come equipped with menu bars and option buttons.

All the graphic components of a VB/DOS forms application have not only filenames, but also control names so they can be addressed by the source code. As discussed in Chapter 19, "The Module Hierarchy," when a VB/DOS application containing a form module starts running, the interpreter loads the first form—by default called `Form1` unless otherwise named—into the workspace. This is the only instance where the interpreter loads a form into the workspace by itself. When you construct a VB/DOS form with Form Designer, you can assign it a new form name with a property setting. The property for a graphic object is addressed at all times in the source code using the following syntax:

```
Form.Property
```

The following is a property whose contents you will be setting with every VB/DOS application you write.

Form.FormName Property

`.FormName` is a textual property that contains the name of the antecedent form as it will appear in the source code. This is not the filename of the form module. `.FormName` must consist of only one grouping of characters without any spaces. This property cannot be set at runtime with an equation; it can be set only at design time with the VB/DOS properties bar.

The *antecedent* is the graphic object referred to by a property.

The following new term is used in this book to refer to the graphic object that is the "owner" of the mentioned property: The *antecedent* is the graphic object referred to by a property. It generally appears before the period that separates that property from the graphic object in the property's full name.

This term is borrowed from English grammar; remember how a pronoun (such as *it*) refers back to its antecedent?

Regardless of what name a form is given at design time, when the project containing that form is running, the form itself can be loaded into memory using the `LOAD` statement.

LOAD **Statement**

Syntax:

```
LOAD objectname
```

The `LOAD` statement addresses a graphic object belonging to the currently running application by name, loads it into memory as well as into the workspace without displaying it, and holds it in suspension until an instruction is executed that forces that object to be shown. Any instructions belonging to that form's `SUB Form_Load ()` procedure will then be executed.

Example

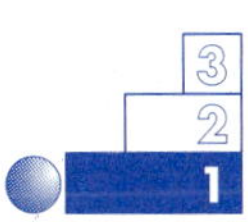

If a form named `Panel` belongs to your application, here is the instruction that will load it into the workspace:

```
LOAD Panel
```

Note that the form hasn't been displayed yet. A form can "exist," in a sense, as part of the current workspace without having to be seen. When a form module is loaded, if that module contains a procedure named `SUB Form_Load ()`, that procedure is executed at once. The `LOAD` statement becomes, in effect, a branch to that procedure.

To make the loaded (or unloaded) form formally visible, use the `.SHOW` method.

.SHOW **Method**

Syntax:

`[`*formname*`.]SHOW [`*style*`]`

The `.SHOW` method displays a loaded form. If the form hasn't been loaded into the workspace yet, it will be loaded automatically. If the *formname* is omitted, the graphic form sharing the current module with the currently executing procedure will be shown. The optional *style* value, when set to `1` (`0` is the default), makes the displayed form *modal*—no other window can accept input from the user until this form is somehow exited. If the antecedent form is not yet loaded into memory using the `LOAD` statement, then the `.SHOW` method causes the `SUB Form_Load ()` procedure for its antecedent form, if there is one, to be executed.

The two instructions introduced thus far in this chapter have counterpart instructions that are their own undoing. They are `.HIDE` and `UNLOAD`.

.HIDE **Method**

Syntax:

`[`*formname*`.]HIDE`

The .HIDE method takes a form that is currently being shown and removes it from the screen until further notice. It virtually occupies the same coordinates on-screen. Controls on the hidden form can still be referred to within the source code. Operation of the form by the program is not suspended; however, operation of the form by the user is suspended.

UNLOAD **Statement**

Syntax:

```
UNLOAD objectname
```

The UNLOAD statement removes the loaded form or graphic object specified from the workspace, as well as from memory. The object continues to exist as a form within the project and as a stored file on disk if it has been stored. This statement is necessary for a compiled VB/DOS application because it does not have the services of the VB/DOS interpreter to "shut down" each form automatically once the compiled program is formally exited.

What Is This Thing Called Love?

One of the primary intentions of the creators of windowed operating environments was for new users to be able to deduce the meaning and function of at least some of the on-screen controls without having to refer to the instruction manual. Perhaps if the creators' intentions were fully realized, those in the teaching and instruction business would be out of a job. Nonetheless, there are those who have learned to operate the window "gadgets" and drop-down menus of the Macintosh System and Microsoft Windows without reading anything whatsoever beforehand. These people have become proficient computer users, to some extent, without help. Yet many aren't certain what the individual controls and gadgets are officially called, whether by Apple or Microsoft (the two generally differ).

Some of these users—with good reason—might ask, "What does it matter what these things are called as long as I know how to use them properly?" If you went to a foreign country and didn't speak the language, you would still know how to use the telephone; likewise, if your native environment is GEM, X/Window, or the Macintosh Finder and you're visiting the Windows environment, is it really necessary to know the name of the combo box, the control box, and the slider bar?

As a programmer in VB/DOS, you need to know what Microsoft calls the gadgets and controls of the individual windows because you will address them by name in the source code. There is no universal convention for the names of visual controls in a windowed environment. For instance, what Microsoft calls a *scroll box*—the sliding gray square between the two arrows of a scroll bar—is what the Macintosh calls a *thumb*. (Microsoft isn't nearly as liberal with its choice of metaphors as is Apple. Perhaps this is for the best because at least you won't have to set properties like `Thumb.Position`.)

Would Someone Open a Window?

Figure 27.1 points out the various elements of a window with which you're already familiar and shows Microsoft's names for those elements. At the upper-left corner is the window's *control box*, which when double-clicked closes the window. When clicked once, the control box offers options for manipulating and positioning the window.

At the upper-right corner of this particular window, from left to right, are the *minimize* (down arrow) and *maximize* (up arrow) buttons for that window. Keep in mind that these two buttons, as well as these two terms, are not opposite to each other in this context. To minimize a window is to suspend the application for that window and to place its box symbol toward the lower-left corner of the forms screen, or the *desktop*. You resume execution of the application when you double-click this symbol. Figure 27.2 shows a minimized form window.

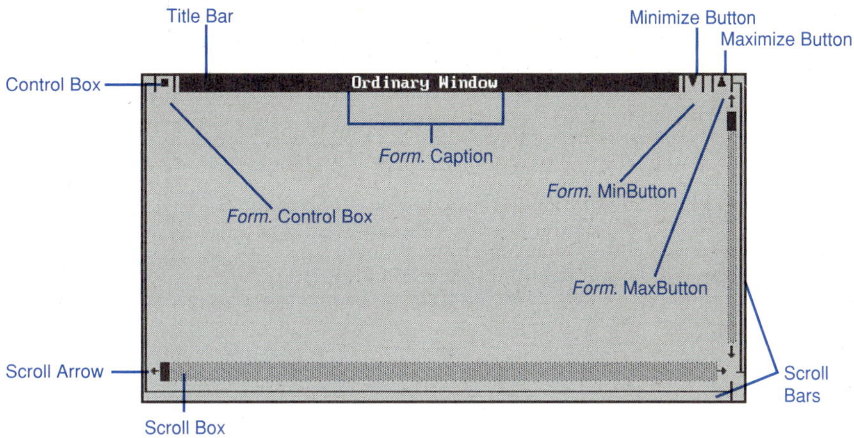

Figure 27.1. The components of a window.

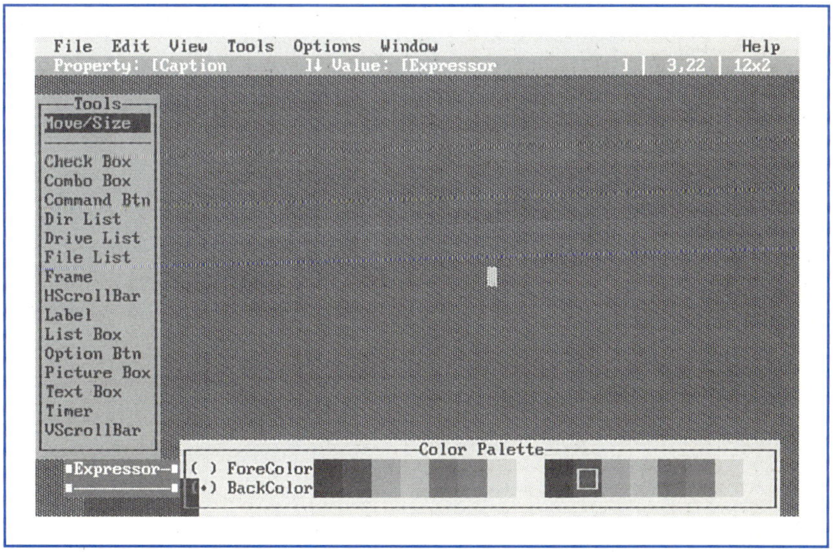

Figure 27.2. A form, minimized to a fraction of its former self.

By contrast, to maximize a window is to give that window full reign of the screen. This process does not change the execution state of the application. When the window is maximized, the maximize button is replaced with the *restore* button, which is marked with the up arrow on top of the down arrow. Microsoft developed this minimization/maximization concept for use with Windows, as what it calls the *Multiple Document Interface* (*MDI*). VB/DOS borrows the basic substance of the MDI code so multiple forms are manageable by the working application without your having to plot the application's position, movement, or minimization.

You are already familiar with such commonly used graphic controls as the title bar—with which you can move the window as well as maximize and restore the window by double-clicking it. The sliding indicator between the two arrows on the scroll bar is the *scroll box.* The arrows are called *scroll arrows.* In many applications, clicking the area between the scroll box and a scroll arrow scrolls the contents of the window in the direction of that arrow one *page,* or approximately one window-length of text or contents. Microsoft has not named the area between the scroll box and scroll arrow. For the sake of this discussion, I call this area the *paging area.*

The Fine Art of Property Setting

Throughout the rest of the book—especially throughout Part VI—I relate the various properties belonging to VB/DOS graphic objects, along with their possible settings. In many cases, properties for a graphic object are set not within the body of the source code, but by you during programming, using the VB/DOS properties bar. This particular process is called *setting properties at design time,* meaning the application is not running and perhaps source code is not yet entered into the application. You can use certain instructions to set or change the properties of a graphic object while the application is running—while instructions are being executed. This process is called *setting properties at runtime.*

When introducing each property term, I show you how the instruction that sets this property is phrased. Not all properties of a

VB/DOS graphic object can necessarily be set at design time, nor can all properties of that object necessarily be set at runtime. Therefore, you'll only be seeing example instructions for those properties whose settings are supported at design time. With that in mind, here is the first of the properties that deal with window appearance and contents.

Form.ControlBox Property

The .ControlBox property is set to a true or false value, reflecting whether the window's control appears in the form for this window. By default, *Form*.ControlBox is set to true (–1). The following VB/DOS instruction resets this property:

```
Form1.ControlBox = 0
```

where Form1 can be replaced by the name of the form being referred to. This property can also be reset or set at design time, although this setting takes effect only when the application is run.

The properties for showing the maximize and minimize buttons are set in a similar manner.

Form.MaxButton Property

The .MaxButton property is set to a true or false value, reflecting whether the window's maximize button appears in the form for this window. By default, *Form*.MaxButton is set to true (–1).

Form.MinButton Property

The .MinButton property is set to a true or false value, reflecting whether the window's minimize button appears in the form for this window. By default, *Form*.MinButton is set to true (–1).

The following two VB/DOS instructions will reset the preceding properties:

```
Form1.MaxButton = 0
Form1.MinButton = 0
```

where `Form1` can be replaced by the name of the form being referred to. These properties can be set or reset at design time, although these settings take effect only when the application is run.

Following is the property used to make distinctions between window types in VB/DOS.

Control.BorderStyle or *Form*.BorderStyle Property

The `.BorderStyle` property represents the style of IBM graphic characters used by a VB/DOS form window. The border styles recognized for controls and forms are defined in Table 27.1.

Table 27.1. Border styles recognized for controls and forms.

Style	*Definition*
Form border styles	
0	No border (totally confined to its present position)
1	Fixed single border (manipulable through use of window gadgets, although not resizable at runtime)
2	Resizable single border
3	Fixed double border (not resizable, although movable and closable using the control box)
4	Resizable double border
5	Fixed solid border
6	Resizable solid border
Control border styles	
0	No border
1	Fixed single (solid line)

Example

Suppose on your main application form you have a button marked `Help`. You might need a dialog box to inquire about what the user needs help with. Using Form Designer, you've previously created an all-purpose dialog box having contents and purpose that can be defined at the time the user clicks a button in the main form. You have already given the dialog box the `.FormName` of `Dialog` and set its `.BorderStyle` to type 3 because you cannot set this property at runtime. Here is how the code for the `Help` button might look:

```
SUB Help_Click ()
LOAD Dialog
Dialog.HelpLine.Caption = "Enter a Help Subject:"
Dialog.Command1.Caption = "Index"
Dialog.Command2.Caption = "Find"
Dialog.Command3.Caption = "Close"
Dialog.SHOW
END SUB
```

The event this procedure is answering is a single click on the `Help` button. The dialog box is designed to be blank so that the program can feed text into it for whatever purpose necessary and thus have a reusable dialog box. Notice that the text property-setting instructions fall between the instructions `LOAD Dialog` and `Dialog.SHOW`. When `Dialog` is loaded into memory (or whatever passes for memory at the time), the properties for all the controls are addressable by the program, although the form is not yet visible. When the textual properties are set, the dialog box can then be shown, and it appears to have a specific purpose rather than a general one.

Notice also how `Dialog` is referred to by its `.FormName` because this procedure belongs to a form outside of this one. When you refer to a graphic element of another form from within a form, each object is addressed by its "full name," using the syntax *`Form.Object.Property`*. This syntax is also used whenever a procedure within a module outside of the stated form addresses a graphic object within that form.

Now suppose you have another button on your main form that starts a process that searches for a certain instance of text in a document. Here's how the code for that button might appear:

```
SUB Search_Click ()
LOAD Dialog
Dialog.HelpLine.Caption = "Search for what text?"
Dialog.Command1.Caption = "Index"
Dialog.Command2.Caption = "Search"
Dialog.Command3.Caption = "Cancel"
Dialog.SHOW
END SUB
```

This example demonstrates another advantage to using generic forms and dialogs: the availability of transportable code. The preceding procedure is not that much different from the one before. For the most part, you need to program the mechanics of the box display procedure only once. You could then use **C**opy and **P**aste from the **E**dit menu to move the content of the procedure `SUB Help_Click ()` inside `SUB Search_Click ()`. Then you could edit the text and captions accordingly.

CAUTION: Before these procedures can be executed again, the Dialog form must first be unloaded using `UNLOAD Dialog`. The most convenient place for such an instruction to appear would be during an event procedure such as `SUB Cancel_Click ()`, which would be executed when the user exits the help or text search procedures with a button click. This way, when the instruction `LOAD Dialog` is executed again, a conflict does not occur.

State Determination

Naturally, you might not want your application to plot anything urgent to a form that is currently minimized. Therefore, to determine what state the form's window is in at the moment, VB/DOS offers the following property.

Form.WindowState **Property**

The current setting of the `.WindowState` property is an integer that represents the operating state of the antecedent form as one of the following conditions:

0	Framed or bordered
1	Minimized; reduced to a representative icon
2	Maximized; unbordered, and given reign over the entire screen

Example

You can use the `.WindowState` property to manually set the operating state of a window from within a form or general module. Rarely would it be necessary to use this property to obtain information about the current form (the form in which this procedure resides). Because a form cannot await user events when it is in a minimized state, it is unnecessary for an event procedure to determine for itself whether its form is unminimized. However, suppose a routine that writes data to a certain text box appears outside the form module for that text box. A conditional clause could be written as follows:

```
IF MainForm.WindowState <> 1 THEN
    MainForm.Text1.Text = "Activate"
END IF
```

This way, if `MainForm.` is minimized, this routine will not execute.

Summary

A form as a graphic object—when its design is completed and it is given its `.FormName`—is executed by the VB/DOS interpreter by first loading the form into the workspace using the `LOAD` statement and then displaying the form with the `.SHOW` method.

During the creation of a VB/DOS application, many of the properties of a form and its constituent controls are set at design time. If the value or content of these property settings is altered by the program, these properties are set at runtime. Certain properties belonging to a form represent whether its window contains minimizing (reduction to an icon) and maximizing (expansion to full screen) buttons, as well as whether the form contains a control box in its upper-left corner. Whether these property settings are available for a particular form depends on the window type designated for that form.

A window's border style can be set using its `.BorderStyle` property. Oftentimes, the user will be able to discern which form window is the main form and which is subservient, by looking at the boldness of the windows' borders. The operating state of a window is represented by the `.WindowState` property. You can use this property to set the operating state of a form manually, although its usefulness in determining the current state through inference is generally restricted to procedures outside the context of a form.

Review Questions

Answers to Review Questions appear in Appendix B.

1. Do you need to load a form into memory first before invoking the `.SHOW` method?

2. When a form is taken out of memory using the `UNLOAD` statement, does it retain its place as part of the project?

3. Syntactically speaking, why are `LOAD` and `UNLOAD` *statements* with regard to bringing forms into the workspace, and `.SHOW` and `.HIDE` formal *methods* in object-oriented syntax?

28

Managing List Boxes

As I introduce you to the controls that comprise the standard repertoire of Visual Basic for MS-DOS, I start by discussing the properties, methods, and events that are specific to list boxes. You see how items are added to a list box and how the operation of a list box differs from that of a combo box. Next, you examine VB/DOS' special provisions for directory-oriented list boxes.

Gaining Control

A *control* is a graphic object used for data acquisition and display.

The fact that computer applications are by nature different from one another, and that the choices you make when using such applications are therefore differentiated, should not mean that the act of making choices or selections is different from application to application. There should be a certain level of familiarity a user has with the controls within a graphic application, even if he is using it for the first time. Where there are differences in the way controls work, there should be a valid engineering reason for that difference. A *control* is a graphic object placed on a form specifically for the acquisition and display of data in a manner with which the user may easily become familiar.

A list should be identifiable as a list; similarly, states or conditions should be easily set with buttons. One objective of programming should be determining how many nonstandard selections or choices can be represented in the program through familiar, standardized controls and to what extent operations should be graphically represented in unique, nonfamiliar ways if such ways are more efficient.

List Boxes and Combo Boxes

What distinguishes the use of a drop-down list box from that of a drop-down menu is that the menu generally presents *command* selections, whereas the list box presents choices of items, settings, or conditions. The chosen item within a list is displayed within the single uppermost text line of the list box that is permanently visible. A *combo box* is a version of the text box control that includes some extra device for displaying or making choices that may allow the user to type his choice within the text line, especially in cases where the choice is not available in the list.

When a standard list box is placed onto a form at design time, by default the VB/DOS interpreter gives it the name `List`*n*, where *n* is the accession number of the list box; similarly, the default name given a combo box is `Combo`*n*. There is only one item in the VB/DOS toolbox for drawing both list boxes and combo boxes; the two items are actually distinguished with a property setting.

Combo.Style Property

The `.Style` property is set to an integer that denotes the appearance of a list on the form. Its possible settings are as follows:

`0` A drop-down combo box with a down arrow button, having a list that is displayed only when that button is clicked. Its choice field is editable with the cursor.

`1` A standard combo box without a down arrow button, having a list that is always displayed. Its choice field can be edited with the cursor.

2 A drop-down list box with a down arrow button, having a choice field that cannot be edited.

A list box begins its life on the form with no items in it. It is up to the source code to feed items into the list one by one.

.ADDITEM **Method**

.REMOVEITEM

Syntax:

```
listname.ADDITEM text$ [, index%]
listname.REMOVEITEM index%
```

The `.ADDITEM` method places the textual contents of `text$` into the list or combo box that has the control name `listname`. By default, the text is placed at the end of the list. Optionally, the place of the new item in the list can be specified by number within `index%`. Items in a list are counted or indexed starting with 0; the value of `index%` must be no greater than the number of items in the list minus 1. You cannot add a string of items to a list from a text file.

The `.REMOVEITEM` method eliminates the item addressed by `index%` from the specified list or combo box.

Example

Assume that as a test you place a standard list box on a form. You want to have one button add an item to this list and another remove that item from it. Here is the code for both button-click procedures:

```
SUB Command1_Click ()
List1.ADDITEM "Test", 0
END SUB
```

```
SUB Command2_Click ()
List1.REMOVEITEM 0
END SUB
```

CAUTION: If your program has a cluster of `.ADDITEM` instructions in a sequence and none of them specify a list index, the VB/DOS interpreter knows by default to add one item to the list after the other starting with item 0. If, however, you choose to specify index numbers directly with the `.ADDITEM` method, be sure you don't make any holes in the list, as you would if you attempt to add item 4 to the end of a two-item list. An error is generated upon such attempts.

When there are not more items assigned to a standard list box than can be displayed, the list box appears as a rectangle. At the moment the list box overflows, the VB/DOS interpreter automatically adds a scroll bar to the right of the box. A combo box at rest on the form appears as a single line of text with a down arrow button beside it. The list that drops below this line follows the same rules of display as the standard list box.

Example

In the Expressor program used periodically throughout this book as an example application, a combo box appears with which the user selects a formula to be solved. Here is how the formula names are added to this list:

```
SUB Form_Load ()
CalcList.ADDITEM "Surface Area of RC Cylinder"
CalcList.ADDITEM "Volume of RC Cylinder"
CalcList.ADDITEM "Zone Area of Sphere"
CalcList.ADDITEM "Force of Earth/Body Attraction"
CalcList.ADDITEM "Doppler Shift Transmitted Freq."
.
.
.
END SUB
```

You will most likely want to place `.ADDITEM` instructions in the `SUB Form_Load ()` procedure because *seeding* the list is considered stage-setting for the form, and `SUB Form_Load ()` is the stage-setting procedure that is automatically executed when the form is entered into memory.

Example

Thus far in the Expressor, I've developed five formulas for this application. If you had 105 instead, the repetitive invocations of `CalcList.ADDITEM` might become tiresome. Conceivably, in the future you could place the text descriptions for each formula within a string array and add each string to the list in sequence, as follows:

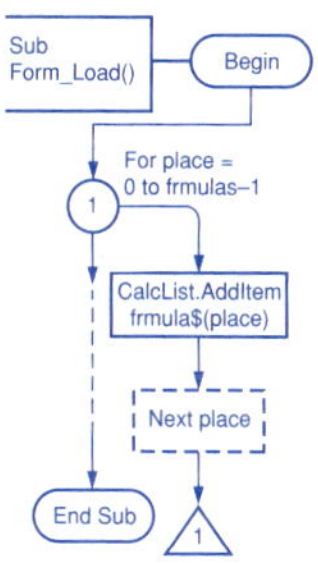


```
SUB Form_Load ()
FOR place = 0 TO frmulas - 1
    CalcList.ADDITEM frmula$(place)
NEXT place
.
.
.
END SUB
```

When an item is added to a list, it is considered a property of that list, and therefore its contents and their aspects are addressed with property terms.

Object.List Property

The `.List` property is accessed in the manner of a control array; the contents of a list item at a particular index are addressed as `.List(`*index*`)`. The property can be treated in the same manner as an array variable. Thus, if a place in the list has been apportioned using `.ADDITEM`, the text contents of the list at an index can be assigned to a string variable as follows:

```
string$ = [object.]List(index)
```

For example:

```
ret$ = CalcList.List(5)
```

Likewise, the text contents of a list at an index can be changed by reversing the order of the equation:

```
[object.]List(index) = string$
```

Object.ListCount Property

The `.ListCount` property is always set to the number of items currently inhabiting the antecedent list or combo box; thus, a list box with five items has a `.ListCount` of 5. The value of `.ListCount - 1` is therefore the index of the last item in the list. You as the programmer cannot set this property.

Object.ListIndex Property

The `.ListIndex` property contains the index of the previously chosen item in the list. A choice can also be forced using this property, by assigning an index value to it. If no item is chosen, `.ListIndex` is set to –1 (not to be confused with the Boolean value for True in this context).

Example

In the Expressor, I used the `.ListIndex` property to determine which formula was chosen:

```
SUB ApplyFormula_Click ()
FOR in = 0 TO 4
p(in) = VAL(param(in).text)
NEXT in
ndx = CalcList.ListIndex + 1
IF ndx = -1 THEN GOTO The_end
ON ndx GOTO f1, f2, f3, f4, f5
```

```
.
.
.
END SUB
```

Here the value of `CalcList.ListIndex + 1` is assigned to variable `ndx`. I added 1 so that the first formula addressed would be item 1 rather than item 0.

VB/DOS allows for items in a list box or combo box to be automatically sorted in alphabetical order, with digits falling before letters.

List.Sorted or *Combo*.Sorted Property

The `.Sorted` property denotes whether automatic sorting for a list box or combo box is set to true (–1) or false (0). This property can be set only at design time. When the `.Sorted` property for a list is set to true, the sort takes place *before* the list box is shown; sorting does not continue throughout the duration of the program. Therefore, if an `.ADDITEM` method is invoked that includes a specific index number, the item will appear in the list at the designated place, although this may mean that the list becomes unsorted. The value of the `.Sorted` property, however, is not affected by any addition made to the list at any place, regardless of whether the list actually does become unsorted.

Example

Here's a sample application with the sole purpose of testing your ability to manage lists. In the following test application, your form is a drop-down, noneditable combo box having a `.Sorted` property that is preset to true at design time. Clicking a button adds an item to the list for this combo box, but the item will be out of order. As stated previously, this does not change the `.Sorted` property for this box, so you need a routine to tell you whether the list is actually in order.

Figure 28.1 shows this test procedure in its running state.

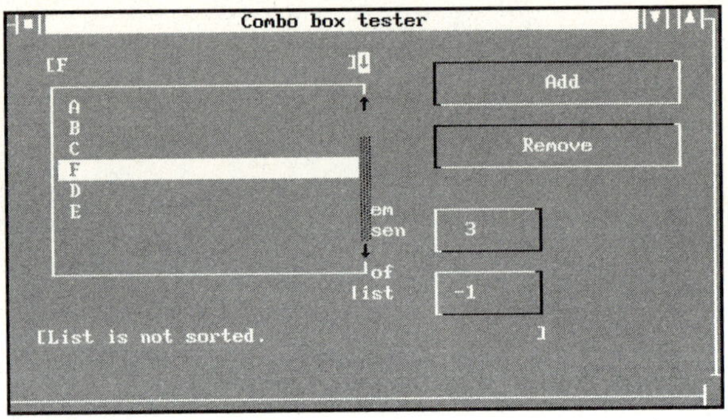

Figure 28.1. The combo box test procedure.

List Test Application

Project Name: LISTTEST.MAK
Constituent File: LISTTEST.FRM

Object Type	*Property*	*Setting*
Form	`.Width`	`43`
	`.Height`	`18`
	`.Caption`	`List box tester`
Combo box	`.Style`	`2 - Dropdown List`
	`.Sorted`	`True`
Button	`.Caption`	`Add`
Button	`.Caption`	`Remove`
Text box	`.CtlName`	`Chosen`
	`.Text`	(blank)
Text box	`.CtlName`	`SortState`
	`.Text`	(blank)
Text box	`.CtlName`	`Message`
	`.Text`	(blank)

Object Type	*Property*	*Setting*
Label	.Caption	List item chosen
	.Alignment	1 - Right Justify
Label	.Caption	Sort state of list
	.Alignment	1 - Right Justify

```
SUB Form_Load ()
Combo1.ADDITEM "E"
Combo1.ADDITEM "C"
Combo1.ADDITEM "A"
Combo1.ADDITEM "B"
Combo1.ADDITEM "D"
END SUB
SUB Command1_Click ()
Combo1.ADDITEM "F", 3
SortState.Text = STR$(Combo1.Sorted)
END SUB
SUB Command2_Click ()
Combo1.REMOVEITEM 3
SortState.Text = STR$(Combo1.Sorted)
END SUB
SUB Combo1_Click ()
Chosen.Text = STR$(Combo1.ListIndex)
SortState.Text = STR$(Combo1.Sorted)
END SUB
SUB Combo1_DropDown ()
FOR count = 1 TO Combo1.ListCount - 1
    this_char$ = LEFT$(Combo1.List(count), 1)
    last_char$ = LEFT$(Combo1.List(count - 1), 1)
    IF ASC(this_char$) < ASC(last_char$) THEN
        Message.Text = "List is not sorted."
        EXIT SUB
    END IF
NEXT count
Message.Text = ""
END SUB
```

In the procedure `SUB Form_Load ()`, five items are loaded into the list, obviously not in alphabetical order. When the procedure starts and `Form1` appears, clicking on the combo box's down arrow results in a display of a sorted list: `A ¦ B ¦ C ¦ D ¦ E`. The procedure `SUB Command1_Click ()` adds one item manually to this list, and certainly out of order, resulting in the following list: `A ¦ B ¦ C ¦ F ¦ D ¦ E`. `SUB Command2_Click ()`, in turn, removes item number 3 (the fourth item) from the list. Both buttons place the textual form of the value of combo box property `.Sorted` in the text box `SortState`.

Procedure `SUB Combo1_Click ()` is executed whenever the user clicks the area of the list. In other words, the event itself does not pay attention to the specific list item chosen although that item may be determined through the procedure. In this procedure, the `.ListIndex` of the chosen item is placed into the text box `Chosen.` and the value of VB/DOS's `.Sorted` property is placed within `SortState`. When `F` is added to the list out of order, the contents of `SortState` remain `-1`; the interpreter still thinks the list is sorted. As Figure 28.1 shows, the interpreter continues to contend the list is sorted, even when `F` is the fourth element rather than the sixth. You need to be able to tell when this list is in order and when it's not.

Here is procedure `SUB Combo1_Click ()` written as pseudocode:

Procedure for when the user clicks a list item in the combo box:
Place the alphanumeric form of the index of the chosen item in the appropriate text box.
Place the alphanumeric form of the state of the .Sorted property in its appropriate text box.
End of procedure.

This is the purpose of procedure `SUB Combo1_DropDown ()`. The event `_DropDown` occurs whenever the down arrow button of the combo box is clicked. This procedure is executed at that time and renders a message to text box `Message.` if the contents of the list are not in order. The procedure starts a loop counting from index number 1 (the *second* item in the list) to the value of the `.ListCount` for this list—the number of items in it—minus 1, having a result that is the final index number for the list.

Pseudocode for the procedure `SUB Combo1_DropDown ()` is as follows:

Procedure for when combo box 1 drops its list:
Start counting from the index number of the second item
to that of the next-to-last item in the combo box.
Extract the first character of this list item.
Now extract the first character of the list item
just preceding it.
If this character falls beneath the order of the
last character in alphabetic sequence, then
Tell the user this list is not sorted.
Get out of this procedure.
End of condition.
Count the next item.
Clear the text box.
End of procedure.

Variable `count` is keeping count of the index number that the loop is currently processing. The first text character of this item is compared to the first character of the *preceding* list item to determine whether it falls in sequence before the previous item, after that item, or is equivalent to that item. The function `Asc()` is used to derive the ASCII (actually the ANSI) code number for the extracted characters. The code numbers are then compared to each other. If the next number in sequence is less than the one preceding it, the letter of the next item in sequence must fall before the preceding one. The list must therefore be out of order. If so, a message to that effect is delivered to text box `Message.`, and the procedure is immediately exited because its purpose is served. If the loop completes itself totally, the list must therefore be in order. So the text contents of `Message.` are set to blank. The result of all this is that `Message.` blanks itself when the list is sorted.

The preceding procedure used a new event, `_DropDown`, which is introduced in the following section.

`Combo_DropDown` Property

The `_DropDown` event is recognized whenever the user clicks the down arrow of the antecedent combo box. This event is reserved exclusively for such controls.

Taking on a Load

Three of the items found within the VB/DOS toolbox are dedicated to one relatively infrequent—though very important—programming purpose: the production of a file selector box. Such a window (most likely type 3) would be used to choose a file to load into memory or to designate the directory location and filename of a file being saved to disk.

As you've seen already, three special list box graphic devices are available from the VB/DOS toolbar. The following properties pertain specifically to these devices.

`Drive``.Drive` Property

The *`Drive`*`.Drive` property (this is not a typographical error) is set to the text of the selected item in the antecedent drive list box, the name of which need not necessarily be *`Drive`*. The format of this text is as follows:

```
drive:\ [volume_name]
```

The preceding line is *not* the syntax of an instruction but is instead the format of the textual setting of the `.Drive` property. The full volume name attributed to the drive device at the time it is formatted appears between square brackets following the device identifier.

`Dir``.Path` Property

The `.Path` property is set to the text of the selected item in the antecedent directory list box. The format of this text is as follows:

```
drive:\[subdirectory[\subdirectory. . . ]\]
```

The text of the `.Path` property reflects the subdirectory path where a file resides or where a search is being conducted for a file. The text does not contain the filename for a file.

File.FileName Property

The .FileName property is set to the text of the selected item in the antecedent file list box. The format of this text is as follows:

```
filename.ext
```

The text reflects only the name of the file itself with its three-letter extension, regardless of the location of that file.

File.Pattern Property

The .Pattern property is set to the search pattern, which each file for the antecedent file list box is matched against, to determine whether that file should appear in the list. Such a pattern can and usually does contain wildcard characters such as * and ? to stand for any number of characters or a single character, respectively.

Natural Selection

The final example for this chapter uses all three categories of directory-oriented list boxes to construct a rudimentary yet all-purpose file selector box. It is used as a form module that can be added to any VB/DOS project that requires a file selector. The reusable form appears as shown in Figure 28.2.

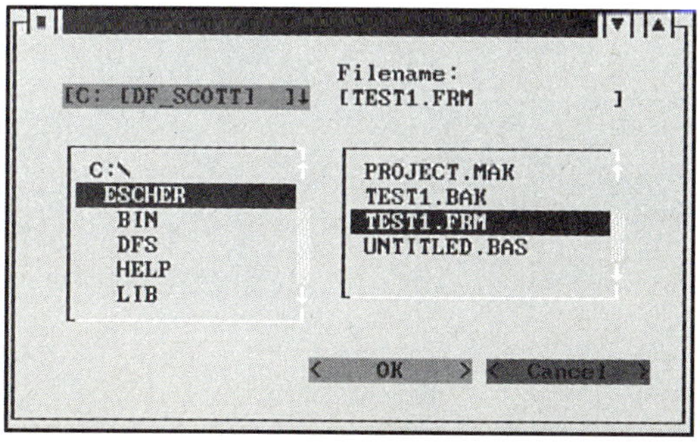

Figure 28.2. The sample file selector box.

Here is the listing for the generic file selector form:

File Selector Box

Project Name: SELECTOR.MAK
Constituent Files: SELECTOR.FRM

Object Type	*Property*	*Setting*
Form	`.Width`	`50`
	`.Height`	`17`
	`.FormName`	`Selector`
	`.Caption`	(blank)
	`.BorderStyle`	`3`
Drive	`.Left`	`3`
	`.Top`	`2`
	`.Width`	`18`
	`.Height`	`1`
Dir List	`.Left`	`3`
	`.Top`	`4`
	`.Width`	`18`
	`.Height`	`8`
File list	`.Left`	`23`
	`.Top`	`4`
	`.Width`	`21`
	`.Height`	`7`
Text box	`.CtlName`	`Filename`
	`.Text`	(blank)
Label	`.CtlName`	`Prompt`
	`.Caption`	`Filename:`
Button	`.CtlName`	`OK`
	`.Caption`	`OK`
Button	`.CtlName`	`Cancel`
	`.Caption`	`Cancel`

For the Selector to work cooperatively with other projects, you need to add the following lines to the front of the startup module of the cooperating application:

```
COMMON SHARED TargetFile$, Pattern$, prmpt$
COMMON SHARED cancl AS INTEGER
```

The rest of the Selector's source code reads as follows:

```
SUB Form_Load ()
IF Pattern$ = "" THEN
    File1.Pattern = "*.*"
ELSE
    File1.Pattern = Pattern$
END IF
Filename.Text = File1.Pattern
cancl = 0
IF prmpt$ = "" THEN
    Prompt.Caption = "Filename:"
ELSE
    Prompt.Caption = prmpt$
END IF
END SUB
```

The initial search pattern is sent to the Selector by the global (cross-modular) string `Pattern$`. The first conditional clause checks to see if `Pattern$` has any contents at all; if not, the search pattern is set to `"*.*"` (all files). The text box called `Filename.` displays this pattern once the Selector box is opened. Global variable `cancl` is a flag denoting whether the `Cancel` button is clicked so that the program that called the file selector knows if it is not supposed to look for a filename returned by the form. Because this is a global variable, you must reset it manually when the form opens.

```
SUB Drive1_Change ()
Dir1.Path = Drive1.Drive
CHDRIVE Drive1.Drive
END SUB
SUB Dir1_Change ()
File1.Path = Dir1.Path
```

```
File1_Click
END SUB
```

The _Change event occurs in the preceding cases whenever the current contents of the choice lines in the drive and directory list boxes, respectively, are altered, whether by mouse or keyboard. Procedure Drive1_Change () is invoked whenever the current choice in the drive list is changed; subsequently, it has the directory list alter itself to reflect the new drive being scanned and tells DOS to change scanned drives as well.

```
SUB File1_Click ()
Filename.Text = File1.Filename
END SUB
SUB File1_DblClick ()
OK_Click
END SUB
```

When a file in the file list is clicked once, its name is entered into the Filename. text field. The user may then click OK to choose the file. If it is double-clicked, that means the file is chosen, and OK need not be clicked. You only want to write the choice procedure once, though, so you have procedure File1_DblClick () branch to the following procedure:

```
SUB OK_Click ()
pth$ = Dir1.Path
IF File1.Filename = "" THEN
    fil$ = Filename.Text
ELSE
    fil$ = File1.Filename
END IF
IF RIGHT$(pth$, 1) = "\" THEN
    Filename.Text = pth$ + fil$
ELSE
    Filename.Text = pth$ + "\" + fil$
END IF
TargetFile$ = Filename.Text
UNLOAD Selector
END SUB
```

The format of the .Path property can be confusing. If the current path being scanned is the root directory, the backslash appears at the end of the path, as in C:\. However, if the path is a subdirectory, the final backslash is omitted. Therefore, the conditional clause is added to assess whether there's a backslash at the end of the path so that the procedure may assemble the full filename in the proper format. The filename is returned to the form that called the Selector, within the global variable TargetFile$.

```
SUB Cancel_Click ()
cancl = 1
TargetFile$ = ""
UNLOAD Selector
END SUB
```

This procedure is executed in case the user clicks Cancel. The cancl flag (you can't write out *cancel* because it is a reserved word in VB/DOS) is set to 1, and the filename return variable TargetFile$ is set to a null string.

To operate this selector: The current list of accessible logical drives is available from the drive combo box, which is operated like a normal combo box. To scan a different subdirectory, double-click that subdirectory in the directory list box. To close the subdirectory being scanned, click any other directory in the list. To choose a file, either click its name in the file list and click OK, or double-click its name.

It's Time for a Change

An important event appears in a few of the preceding procedures: _Change.

*Object*_Change Event

The _Change event occurs whenever the contents of the antecedent graphic object are changed for any reason, whether by the program or by the user.

Some offshoots of the `_Change` event are reserved for directory list boxes and file list boxes. They are covered in the next few sections.

Dir`_PathChange` Event

The `_PathChange` event occurs whenever the path currently being scanned to obtain the contents of the antecedent directory list box is changed for any reason, whether by the program or by the user.

File`_PatternChange` Event

The `_PatternChange` event occurs whenever the pattern currently being applied against the current path to obtain matching files for the antecedent file list box is changed for any reason, whether by the program or by the user.

Summary

VB/DOS maintains provisions for list boxes as well as combo boxes, which are like list boxes except that they use extra graphic devices such as down arrow buttons and often use editable text areas. The style of a combo box is set using the `.Style` property reserved for combo boxes.

Items are added to and removed from a list or combo box using the `.ADDITEM` and `.REMOVEITEM` methods, respectively. When added to a list, the contents of a list item can be addressed using the property `.List`, generally in the manner of a control array. The property `.ListCount` registers the number of items currently inhabiting a list. The property `.ListIndex` returns the index or accession number of the previously chosen item from the list. Items in a list can be sorted in alphabetical and numerical order before they are displayed by presetting the `.Sorted` property for that list to –1 (true).

VB/DOS reserves three special types of list boxes for use in file selectors: drive or device lists, directory or path lists, and file lists. The VB/DOS interpreter fills these lists automatically with the current directory information gathered from DOS.

Review Questions

Answers to Review Questions appear in Appendix B.

1. Assume it is 1959, and you have compiled a list of the United States within any kind of standard list box. You have 48 items in this list, and suddenly you receive word that two more items are to be added to the list. The `.Sorted` property for your list box is set to –1, and the list box is currently visible on-screen. When you use `.AddItem` to add Alaska and Hawaii to your list box, *without* expressing any index number, what are the indices for your two new states?

2. Assume it is 1998, and you have compiled a list of the United States within any kind of standard list box. Columbia (formerly the District of Columbia) and Puerto Rico are comfortable in their new positions as states of the union, and the President has signed the executive order now officially making Guam a state as well. Sewing a 53-star flag with geometric symmetry is difficult enough; your job is to add Guam to your official list box of states. Assuming the `.Sorted` property for your list is set to –1 and the list box is not yet loaded into memory, what will the index be for the list entry for Guam?

Review Exercise

Borrowing some source code from the procedures used in this chapter, write a procedure that informs the user whether his list is sorted whenever a button is clicked.

29

Options and Scroll Bars

In this chapter, the subjects are split down the middle. The first half of the chapter deals with the use of options and check boxes within a form, whereas the second half deals with the implementation of independent scroll bars. In the Options section, you learn more about control arrays and how a set of related controls can be directed using one source code procedure. In the Scroll Bars section, you see how scroll bars are best used to designate value shifts, ranges, and regions of an object being viewed.

Grouping Controls Within a Form

Setting an option dot beside a set of options in a form can be compared to choosing an item from a list. An options set generally offers the user a smaller degree of choice than a list box offers. Furthermore, the list of options in a set is always fixed.

Multiple *check boxes* may be checked at one time.

What distinguishes a set of options from a set of check boxes is that multiple check boxes can be set or checked, whereas only one option dot in a set can be checked at a time.

The Visual Basic for MS-DOS interpreter considers all the option dots in a set to be related elements. If no subdivisions of the form exist and if one option dot is set, another option dot elsewhere on the form is reset. Check boxes are not so interrelated because several boxes in a form can be checked at one time, regardless of subdivisions. A check box is generally used to set the binary state of some aspect or function of the program.

Option buttons can only be set one at a time.

Figure 29.1 shows an accessory form for an application, with three option dots on the left and three check boxes on the right. Here you can see how their functions are distinguished; you can save a file in only one format, so only one option should be set for the `Save as:` group. Any or all of the boxes in the group on the right side can be set.

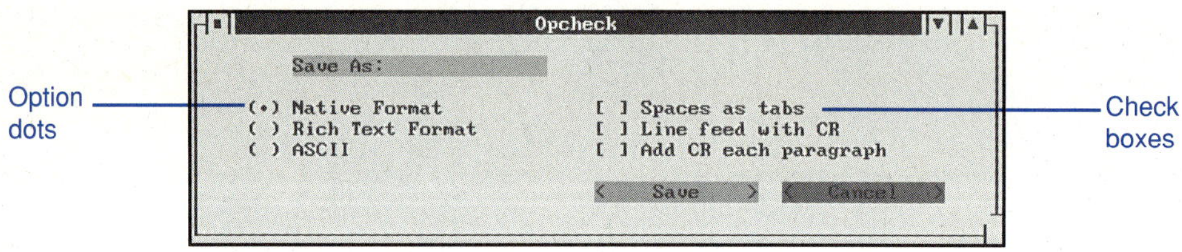

Figure 29.1. Option dots and check boxes compared.

A *frame* is used to separate groups of options from other parts of a form.

You can subdivide a form with a *frame,* wherein groups of options that are to be divided from other options in the form can be placed. A *frame* is a subdivision of a form that divides groupings of elements, such as options, from groups in other frames and groups elsewhere on the form.

Adding a frame to a form is, in a sense, similar to putting a box within a box and having the "child" box be subordinate to the "parent" box. From the point of view of the programmers of VB/DOS, this isn't *similar to* placing a child within a parent; it *is* placing a child within a parent. For the controls placed within a frame to appear to belong together, they must fit entirely within that frame.

For a control to belong to a frame, or rather to be the "child" of that frame, it must be placed within that frame directly from the toolbox. A control cannot be drawn onto the main portion of a form, be dragged later into the area of a frame, and then belong to that frame. When a control belongs to a frame and the frame is moved, the control moves with it. When a control does not belong to a frame and the frame is moved, the control stays behind. Figure 29.2 shows the option dots from the preceding form re-created as part of a frame.

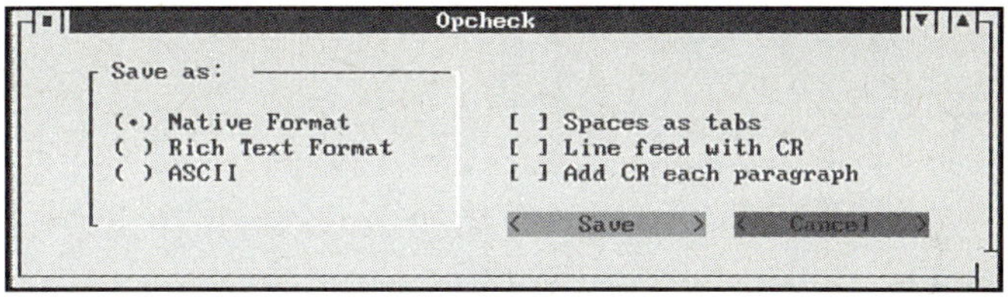

Figure 29.2. To frame or not to frame.

Now you can add another set of option dots to the form or another frame without those options being interrelated to those within this frame.

`.Value` is the property used to determine whether an option dot is set or a check box is checked.

`Object``.Value` Property

The `.Value` property has different purposes with respect to the following types of antecedent objects: `Check`, `Command`, `Option`, and `Scroll`. In the case in which `.Value` refers to option dots, the setting of that property is true or false, reflecting whether the option is set or reset, respectively. In the case of check boxes, `.Value` is set to 0, 1, or 2—not true or false—reflecting whether the antecedent box is reset, set, or dimmed (made unavailable), respectively. In cases of buttons, `.Value` is set to true or false depending on whether the button is being pressed. In cases of scroll bars, `.Value` returns the relative position of the scroll box along the coordinate scale set for the antecedent scroll bar.

Keep in mind how the scroll bar uses `.Value` because you test this property with scroll bars later in this chapter.

Example

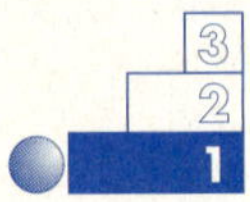

Suppose you have a string variable in the preceding form that is set to a space when the check box marked Spaces as tabs is set. Here's a routine that assigns the proper value to the string variable:

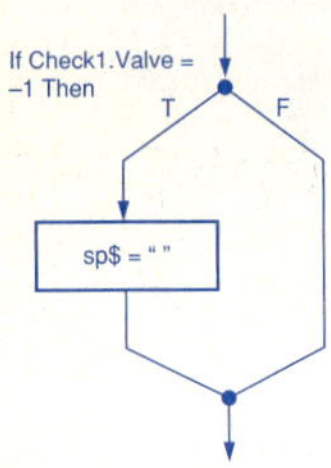


```
IF Check1.Value = -1 THEN
    sp$ = " "
END IF
```

If the box is not checked, `sp$` is left alone.

Example

Suppose the program determines which option dot from the preceding frame is set. Execution branches to any of three procedures as a result of setting the option dot and clicking the `Save` button. Here is a procedure that might determine how branching takes place:

```
SUB Save_Click ()
SELECT CASE -1
    CASE Option1.Value
        Standard_Save
    CASE Option2.Value
        RTF_Save
    CASE Option3.Value
        ASCII_Save
END SELECT
.
.
.
END SUB
```

Here's the preceding example written in pseudocode:

Procedure for clicking the Save option dot:
In case any of the following options are set:
For the first option,
Execute the procedure for standard saving.

For the second option,
Execute the procedure for RTF conversion.
For the third option,
Execute the procedure for ASCII conversion.
End of cases.
.
.
.
End of procedure.

The `SELECT CASE` clause compares all three `.Value` properties to logical truth (–1) for equality. Only one of these values is set to –1 because these are, after all, values for option dots. There can be, therefore, only one procedure branch.

Grouping Controls Within the Source Code

A *control array* is a set of similar, related controls that are referenced as a group.

Presently, the VB/DOS interpreter sees each option dot and check box in the preceding form as a separate, individual control. Each dot and each box, therefore, has its own event procedures associated with it. In cases of options that are closely related to each other, it might be more convenient if the code for an options group could be reduced to one procedure. You can accomplish this by assigning each control in the set of option dots or check boxes, as part of a unified group. The members of this group share the same control name, whereas each individual member is addressed by way of a subscript, in the manner of an array variable. Such a group is called a *control array.* A control array is a set of similar, related controls in a form that are referenced together as a group and that have an operation that is jointly defined by a single procedure in the source code.

In a control array, the graphic objects are grouped together and given a collective name, such as `Option1()`. The parentheses are included to distinguish that the control name refers to an array. A control array should consist of a group of graphic objects having nearly identical appearances and somewhat related purposes.

To design a control array, perform the following steps:

1. In Form Designer, plot a control to the form that acts as a model for all the controls in the array. You can edit the textual contents of each control independently later.
2. Indicate the control and select **C**opy from the **E**dit menu.
3. To add the second control to the array, select **P**aste from the **E**dit menu. A dialog box appears.
4. This dialog box asks if you want to create a control array (you'd think it would have guessed by now). Respond to the dialog box by clicking OK. The control array is now officially in existence.
5. The second element in the array appears elsewhere in the form and is surrounded at its corners by indicator nodes. Drag this control to its proper position on the form. Its contents are identical to those of the copied control; at this time you may choose to edit the `.Text` or `.Caption` property for this control.
6. To add more elements to the array, select **P**aste from the **E**dit menu and repeat the preceding step.

Example

You can apply the control array procedure to the previous `SELECT CASE` clause so that the procedure branch can be made at the moment any of the option dots are set rather than waiting for the `Save` button to be pressed. Here's the revised procedure:

```
SUB Option_Click (Index AS INTEGER)
SELECT CASE Index
    CASE 0
        Standard_Save
    CASE 1
        RTF_Save
    CASE 2
```

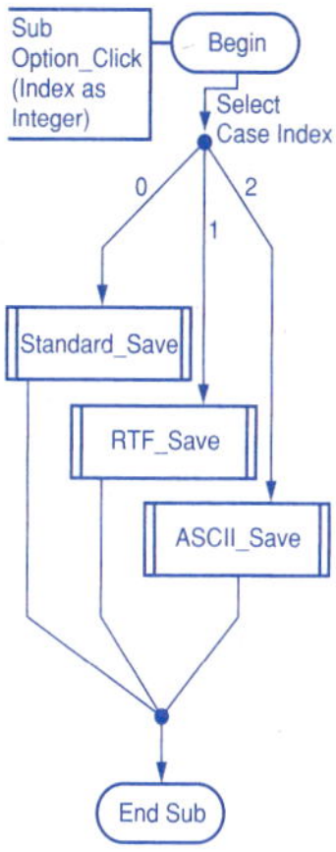


```
        ASCII_Save
END SELECT
END SUB
```

The event procedure is responded to as if all three controls in the array together constitute one big control called `Option`. When the VB/DOS interpreter creates a framework for the event procedure, it automatically places `Index AS INTEGER` between the parentheses as both a declaration and a passed parameter. The index of the set option dot is returned within the variable `Index`. The `SELECT CASE` clause now compares `Index` to the three possible values (0, 1, and 2) for equality. Because the option set must be clicked for this procedure to execute, one of the branches must be made.

Scroll Bars

It's time to switch subjects and talk about scroll bars. In VB/DOS, the relative position of the scroll box between the two arrows is represented by a coordinate value stored within the property `Scroll.Value`. Figure 29.3 depicts how the coordinate system of a horizontal scroll bar works.

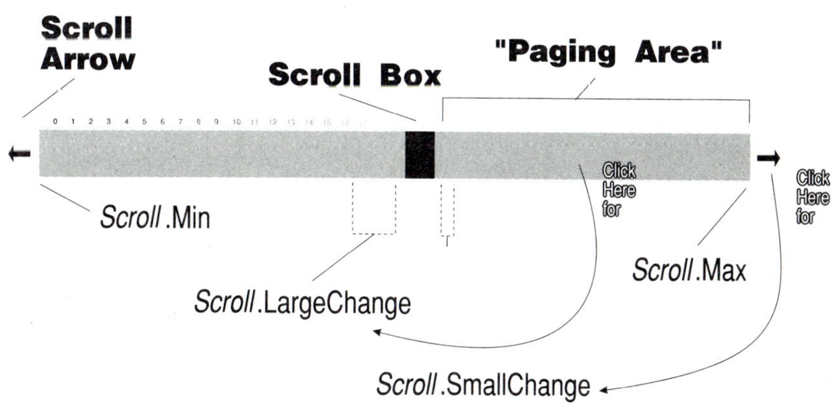

Figure 29.3. The breakdown of a scroll bar.

The coordinate system of a scroll bar exists without regard to the scroll bar's current size. Consider each scroll bar as a number line extending from one integer (generally 0) to another. The minimum and maximum values along this line exist at the left and right, or top and bottom, points on this line. The number values at these points are assigned to properties `.Min` and `.Max`. There are `Scroll.Max - Scroll.Min` coordinate points along this line. Again, the pixel length of a scroll bar has nothing to do with its coordinate system.

Following are the property terms that can be attributed exclusively to a scroll bar.

`Scroll.Max` and `Scroll.Min` Properties

The `.Max` and `.Min` properties of a scroll bar are set to the maximum and minimum coordinate values of the scroll box along the bar. These properties can be set to any integer between –32,768 and 32,767, inclusive, as long as `.Max` remains greater than `.Min`. When set, the length of the scroll bar is divided into `.Max - .Min` intervals. Moving the scroll box along the bar sets `Scroll.Value` equal to the interval where the box currently rests.

`Scroll.SmallChange` and `Scroll.LargeChange` Properties

The value of `.SmallChange` represents the number of intervals the scroll box traverses along the bar when one of the arrow buttons is clicked in the direction of that arrow. The value of `.LargeChange`, similarly, represents the number of intervals the scroll box traverses along the bar when the user clicks between the scroll box and one of the arrow buttons in the direction of that arrow. This zone of the scroll bar is often called the *paging area*.

Now that you know some things not only about arrays but how items within a range are represented on-screen, you can make some amendments to the `NameForm` application introduced back in Chapter 8, "Strings." The revised application can store lists of names within arrays, and it uses a scroll bar as a device for selecting individual names from the array range. The revised `NameForm` form appears as shown in Figure 29.4.

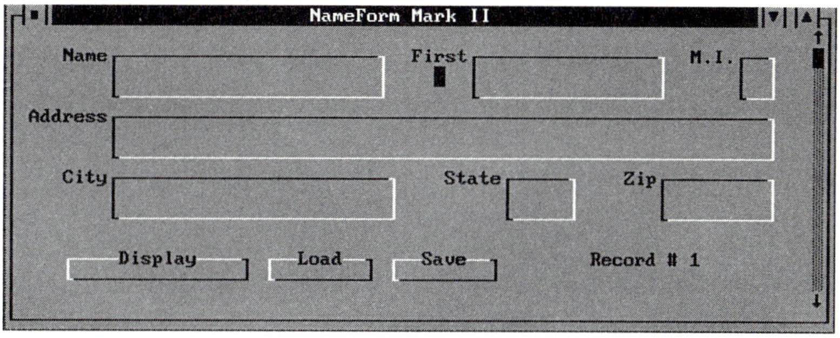

Figure 29.4. NameForm Mark II.

The following table shows the controls added to the Mark I edition of the form.

Name-Only Record Entry, System Mark II

Project name: NAMEFRM2.MAK
Constituent files: NAMEFRM2.FRM, SELECTOR.FRM

Object Type	*Property*	*Setting*
Form	.Width	74
	.Hcight	16
VScroll bar	.Left	71
	.Top	0
	.CtlName	RecordShown
	.Min	1
	.Max	1000
	.SmallChange	1
	.LargeChange	10
Button	.Left	4
	.Top	11
	.CtlName	Display
	.Caption	Display

Object Type	*Property*	*Setting*
Button	.Left	22
	.Top	11
	.CtlName	TableLoad
	.Caption	Load
Button	.Left	33
	.Top	11
	.CtlName	TableSave
	.Caption	Save
Label	.Left	55
	.Top	11
	.CtlName	Register
	.Caption	Record #

At the right side of the form, you add a scroll bar. The `.SmallChange` property is set to `1` (the default anyway), which means the program proceeds to the next record in the list (`RecordNo + 1`) if you click the down arrow or to the previous record (`RecordNo - 1`) if you click the up arrow. The `.LargeChange` property is set to `10`, which makes 10 the value of one page of records. The records now pages down by 10. Here are the amended procedures for the revised application: General declarations section:

```
'$FORM Selector
DECLARE SUB RecordShown_Change ()
DECLARE SUB AssessFilename ()
OPTION BASE 1
DIM SHARED LstName$(1000), FrstName$(1000), MdInit$(1000),
[ic:ccc]Adress$(1000), Cty$(1000), Stat$(1000), Zp$(1000)
DIM SHARED RecordNo AS INTEGER
```

The first statement, `OPTION BASE 1`, resets the system for the sake of this program so that the first address of an array is 1 and not 0. Notice the string array variable names chosen are each one letter removed from their text box equivalents on the form because variable names and object names may not match. On the last line, `RecordNo` is dimensioned as a unit integer to be `SHARED` throughout all procedures in the module, not as an array variable.

```
SUB RecordShown_Change ()
RecordNo = RecordShown.Value
IF RecordNo < 1 THEN
    RecordNo = 1
END IF
Reg$ = "Record #" + STR$(RecordNo)
Register.Caption = Reg$
LastName.Text = LstName$(RecordNo)
FirstName.Text = FrstName$(RecordNo)
MidInit.Text = MdInit$(RecordNo)
Address.Text = Adress$(RecordNo)
City.Text = Cty$(RecordNo)
State.Text = Stat$(RecordNo)
Zip.Text = Zp$(RecordNo)
END SUB
```

The key variable here is `RecordNo`; it ties all the elements of a record together. If you consider the data generated by this program to be a database, `RecordNo` would be the sole relation in this base. The key instruction here is `RecordNo = RecordShown.Value`. This is where the sole index to all eight string array variables below this instruction is set to the interval value of the scroll box along the bar.

The event `_Change` signifies a movement of the scroll bar called `RecordShown`, which is added to the form. This slider changes the visible record number, which is registered now as part of `Reg$` in a new label in the lower-right corner.

Here's the general concept of the preceding procedure, written as pseudocode:

Procedure for when the scroll bar value changes:
Change the current record number to reflect the scroll bar value.
If the registered scroll bar value is less than 1, then
Make the record number 1.
End of condition.
For the register, place the record number beside the words "Record #."
Place this register in its proper position.

Change the textual contents of all the text boxes in the form to reflect the current values of each of their representative arrays for the current record number.

.

.

.

End of procedure.

Here's the new `Form_Load ()` procedure for the application:

```
SUB Form_Load ()
RecordShown.Value = 1
RecordShown_Change
END SUB
```

You may remember that in every VB/DOS program the procedure `SUB Form_Load ()` executes automatically once the form is invoked. The control name for the scroll bar in this application is `RecordShown`. Its initial `.Value` is set to `1` because record number 1 (not number 0) is the first to be displayed.

```
SUB Address_Change ()
Adress$(RecordNo) = Address.Text
END SUB
SUB City_Change ()
Cty$(RecordNo) = City.Text
END SUB
SUB FirstName_Change ()
FrstName$(RecordNo) = FirstName.Text
END SUB
SUB LastName_Change ()
LstName$(RecordNo) = LastName.Text
END SUB
SUB MidInit_Change ()
MdInit$(RecordNo) = MidInit.Text
END SUB
SUB State_Change ()
Stat$(RecordNo) = State.Text
END SUB
```

```
SUB Zip_Change ()
Zp$(RecordNo) = Zip.Text
END SUB
```

With these brief procedures, whenever new text is typed into any of the text boxes on the form, the contents of the string array variable for the current record number change automatically.

The way this program works now, you can set the scroll bar to any record number you choose and type a person's record for that number. You may then scroll to any other record number. When scrolling back to a filled record number, the record reappears.

Generally, a scroll bar is placed on the form as an independent control. Optionally, a scroll bar can be invoked as a part of a text box control, for cases in which the text within the box overflows the area of the box. The following invocation, `.ScrollBars`, is made only at design time.

Text.ScrollBars Property

The `.ScrollBars` property is set to a two-bit binary value (not an editorial comment). Bit 0 on the right (the least significant bit) is set to 1 if the horizontal scroll bar for the antecedent text box is to be displayed. Likewise, bit 1 on the left (the most significant bit) is set to 1 if the vertical scroll bar for the text box is to be displayed. In decimal, the value of `.ScrollBars` can be set to any of the following:

0	No scroll bars (default)
1	Horizontal bar
2	Vertical bar
3	Both scroll bars

Summary

For each group of option dots that appears in a form, only one dot can be set at one time, thereby designating a single selection from a list. By contrast, many check boxes in a group can be set within a form at one time. Groups can be divided into subgroups by placing elements of those subgroups within a *frame*, which is a rectangular subdivision of a form. Each item in a list or group box has a `.Value` property attributed to it, which designates whether that control is currently set.

A *control array* is a formal grouping of controls addressed within the source code like an array variable, with a single name and a subscript index within parentheses. This is a different type of grouping from a graphic or frame grouping, in which related elements are drawn into a frame and are thus considered as resting on that frame.

A scroll bar is divided into equally spaced intervals numbered between its `.Min` and `.Max` property values. These intervals exist logically, regardless of the actual pixel length of the scroll bar in a form. Text boxes can have scroll bars apportioned to them using the `.ScrollBars` property, but these bars are not scroll bar controls by the formal definition.

Review Questions

Answers to Review Questions appear in Appendix B.

1. Can a frame control be part of a control array?
2. If you drag a control into a frame, does it become part of a control array?
3. Can a control array exist partly within, and partly outside of, a frame?
4. Can you set the minimum value of a scroll bar belonging to a text box to another value?

30

Dialog Boxes

In this chapter, you examine the creation and display of dialog boxes, which are brief windows the program uses to communicate with the user. Dialog box windows are not forms by the Visual Basic for MS-DOS definition, so they are not designed beforehand. Instead, the contents of a dialog box are defined within the source code and are displayed using VB/DOS instructions.

Reaching into the Message Box

Dialog boxes are generally displayed for two purposes: to determine the user's response to a yes or no question, or to warn or notify the user of some occurrence within the program. The instruction used to display message boxes in VB/DOS is MSGBOX.

MSGBOX **Function or Statement**

Function syntax:

```
response% = MSGBOX (message$[, code%[, title$]])
```

Statement syntax:

```
MSGBOX message$[, code%[, title$]]
```

The `MSGBOX` instruction, however it is phrased, displays onscreen a dialog box containing the message that is presented as the argument *message$*. The value of the integer *code%* denotes specifically what contents besides the *message$* are to appear in the dialog box. The value of *code%* is evaluated binarily, with each bit in the binary value representing an element or style designation of the dialog box. This is a collective value, equal to the sum of any number (or no number) from each section shown in Table 30.1.

Table 30.1. Message box contents codes.

Addend	*Associated Feature*
Button inclusion	
0	Display `OK` button.
1	Display `OK`, `Cancel` buttons.
2	Display `Abort`, `Retry`, and `Ignore` buttons.
3	Display `Yes`, `No`, and `Cancel` buttons.
4	Display `Yes`, `No` buttons.
5	Display `Retry`, `Cancel` buttons.
Default button programming	
256	Make second button the default.
512	Make third button the default.

If *title$* is expressed, the contents of the title bar are set to *title$*; otherwise, the title bar remains blank by default.

If `MSGBOX` is written as a function, the dialog box can return a value to the variable expressed as *response%*, designating which button the user pressed as a response to the dialog. This value can be any of the following:

Return value	*Button pressed*
1	`OK`
2	`Cancel`
3	`Abort`
4	`Retry`
5	`Ignore`
6	`Yes`
7	`No`

Example

The following instruction displays a simple dialog box:

```
MSGBOX "Project saved successfully."
```

The dialog box resulting from this statement appears in Figure 30.1.

Figure 30.1. The simplest of dialog boxes.

Example

Here's a more complex dialog box, which elicits a response from the user:

```
message$ = "Proceeding will mean the contents of the
  current form will be cleared. Proceed anyway?"
response = MSGBOX(message$, 260, "Big Huge Test")
```

In this instance, the message is long enough that, to keep the instructions shorter, it first is assigned to string variable `message$`. This is the first argument of the function (note the syntax). The value `260` is equal to 4 (display `Yes`, `No` buttons) plus 256 (make second button the default). You could have expressed the second argument as `256 + 4` if you didn't want to strain your brain. The resulting dialog box appears as shown in Figure 30.2.

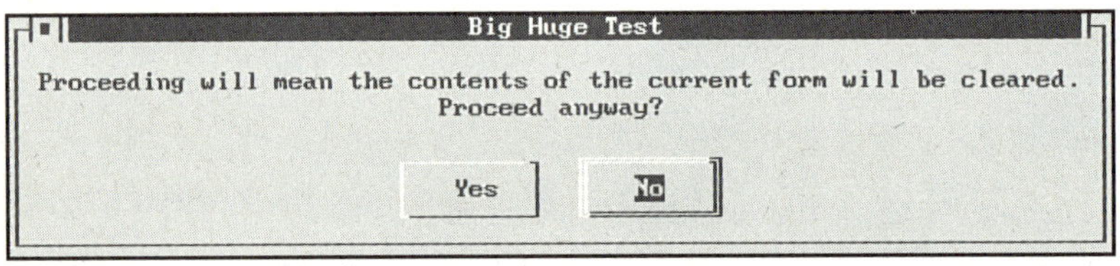

Figure 30.2. A slightly more complex dialog box.

Notice how the extra highlighting appears around the `No` button as a result of adding 256 to the second argument of the function. If the user clicks this button or presses Enter, the value `7` is returned to the variable `response`.

A *modal* window suspends the operability of every other window while it is operating and until it is exited.

Dialog boxes in VB/DOS—just as they are in the rest of the Windows environment—suspend every other window on-screen until they have their response. Such a window is called *modal.*

By contrast, a *modeless* window allows other windows on-screen to be operated while it is active. These are two terms that don't seem to define themselves in the context of Windows, so try to memorize them.

The Input Box

One type of dialog box that receives *textual* input from the user is the *input box,* which is supported in VB/DOS with a function.

INPUTBOX$() **Function**

Syntax:

```
response$ = INPUTBOX$ (message$[, title$[, default$
  [, xcoord%, ycoord%]]])
```

The INPUTBOX$() function uses the message within *message$* as a prompt for a textual response to be entered by the user on a text line appearing within the dialog box. The contents of this line are limited to a maximum of 31 characters and can be seeded in advance by expressing *default$*. The title of the input box window can optionally be expressed as *title$*.

Normally, the input box appears in the center of the screen. To place it anywhere else on-screen, the origin character of the window can be expressed as coordinates *xcoord%*, *ycoord%*. An input box always contains two buttons: OK and Cancel. If the user clicks Cancel, the contents of *response$* will be a null string. If the user clicks OK, the contents of the text line are returned as *response$*.

Example

The following function places on-screen an input box that requests a password from the user:

```
message$ = "Enter a password:"
response$ = INPUTBOX$(message$, "", "TRIPWIRE")
```

The second parameter in the function nullifies the title of the dialog box. The third parameter, "TRIPWIRE", places a default password in the text line. The resulting input box appears as shown in Figure 30.3.

Notice that there is quite a bit of white space between the message text and the text line. The size of an input box is fixed, so this space is allotted for longer messages. Carriage return and line feed characters can be required within the message string for multiple lines.

Figure 30.3. The password input box.

Summary

A dialog box is not a form by the standard VB/DOS definition; it is a temporary window provided as a resource of the Windows environment. The contents of this box are rendered to the `MSGBOX` instruction, along with a sum value having binary or bitwise contents that reveal what type of response buttons inhabit the dialog box.

An input box is a type of dialog box that elicits a textual response from the user. VB/DOS's input boxes have a fixed size and always have `OK` and `Cancel` buttons.

Review Questions

Answers to Review Questions appear in Appendix B.

1. To elicit a textual response from the user, should you use a message box or an input box?

2. Using the `MSGBOX` and `INPUTBOX$` terms, does the program display modal or modeless windows?

3. Why should a file selector box, such as `SELECTOR.FRM`, necessarily be a modal dialog box?

31

Control Manipulation and Organization

In this chapter, you study the methods, events, and properties that relate to addressing, organizing, and manipulating graphic objects in general, in contrast to the control-exclusive instructions you've studied in the previous four chapters. Some of the instructions explained in this chapter have already been introduced to you through previous examples. This chapter formally establishes their purpose and function. You also see how to index, tag, and focus on controls in a form.

A Control by Any Other Name

As you've seen in several examples, a control on a form is addressed within the source code of a program by its control name. There are two other subsidiary properties Visual Basic for MS-DOS provides for referring to a control, which are described in the following sections.

Control.CtlName Property

The .CtlName property for a control is set to an arbitrary name at design time. This property becomes the name that is stated to the left of the period when the graphic object is addressed within the source code of the program, using object-oriented syntax.

Control.Index Property

The .Index property is used to refer to elements of a control array, especially because all elements within an array share the same .CtlName property. The control is referred to by its designated array name. Following that, the index of a control within an array is stated as a subscript value within parentheses. Indices for controls within an array are designated in sequence at design time. Their sequence can also be reorganized at design time.

Control.Tag Property

The .Tag property for a control is set at design time to an arbitrary name other than its control name or index. By default, the .Tag for a control is a null string.

The .Tag property may not seem to be very useful in the context of VB/DOS. The control already has one name, and you may wonder why it needs a pseudonym. The reason for a second name is as follows: There will be times when you'd like to have a routine that compares one control to another, just as if that control were a variable of a specified data type. VB/DOS does recognize the data type CONTROL for graphic objects inhabiting a form, so you can compare controls by using mathematical expressions. However, object-oriented syntax does not allow you to refer to objects subjectively. In other words, the control name of an object cannot be used as the subject of a comparison. To borrow a term from football, this is an *illegal procedure.*

The solution to this situation—albeit one that sounds more political than logical—is to create a second name for a control, when necessary, to act as its subjective name.

Looking at Things Subjectively

The purpose for the `.Tag` property is not at all self-explanatory, so I'll use a model. Assume the VB/DOS application you're writing is a type of database manager, where the names for each data file appear in boxes strewn about a form that acts as a sort of freestyle desktop, like the directory window of the Macintosh Finder. To incorporate several data files into one query—to establish a relation—the user is asked to pick up the data filenames that will relate to one another, as they appear on-screen, and drag them into a collective box—to be specific, a text box with a list of all the related files.

An event procedure is programmed to detect whenever a symbol is dropped into the text box. However, the way the interpreter works, the event is based around the box that the symbol is being dropped into, not the symbol that is being moved. With that in mind, the objective is to have your event procedure determine which filename entered the box. The box is the object of your event procedure, but the filename symbol is the subject.

For this test, I used Form Designer to make a huge form. In the lower-left quadrant of this form, I placed a frame control with a `.CtlName` of `Datalist`. On the right, I made eight label yellow single-line label controls, all in a control array. I gave the first label a `.Tag` of `Datafile`, a `.CtlName` of `Datafile`, and a `.Caption` of `Datafile 1`. I then copied and pasted the label seven times, changing the numeral on the `.Caption` each time to `Datafile 2`, `3`, and so on. I left the `.DragMode` of each label (a property you'll learn much more about later) at its default value of `0 - Manual`. With that out of the way, here's the event procedure for dragging a control from out of the form into the frame:

```
SUB Datalist_DragDrop (Source AS CONTROL, x AS SINGLE,
  y AS SINGLE)
SHARED listx AS INTEGER, listy AS INTEGER
IF Source.Tag = "Datafile" THEN
    Source.Left = Datalist.Left + listx
    Source.Top = Datalist.Top + listy
    Source.BackColor = 11
    IF listy >= 12 THEN
```

```
        listy = 2
        listx = listx + 22
    ELSE
        listy = listy + 2
    END IF
END IF
Source.DRAG 0
END SUB
```

The `_DragDrop` event occurs whenever a graphic object or control with drag capability is dragged and dropped on top of the antecedent object. The key element of this procedure is on the very first line, at the declaration `Source AS CONTROL`. Up to now, you've declared variables `AS INTEGER` or `AS DOUBLE`, but in this instance, `AS CONTROL` refers to a *structural* form of declaration, not to a numeric form. The toy being dragged into the box is a control, and here it may actually be declared as such using the term `AS CONTROL`. When this happens, all the property data associated with the control—size, position, and contents—are passed along with it.

With that in mind, here's the preceding procedure as pseudocode:

Procedure for dragging a control atop the data file list:
Bring the next x/y coordinates in from the module level.
If the tag given the dragged control is `"Datafile"`*, then*
  The left coordinate of the next item in the ordered list is set relative to the upper-left corner of the list itself.
  The upper coordinate of the next item in the ordered list is set relative to the upper-left corner of the list itself.
  Make the dragged control bright cyan.
  If you've reached the end of the list, then
    Make the next slot the beginning of the next column.
    Set the left position of the next column.
  Otherwise,
    Make the next slot two spaces down.
  End of condition.
End of condition.
Cancel the current drag.
End of procedure.

The term `Source` for the control data structure being dragged is the default name given it in this procedure by the VB/DOS interpreter; you can change it to some other arbitrary name. In the previous procedure, all the properties that belong to the source control are copied and "absorbed," in a sense, by the term `Source`. Thus, if `Datafile(1).Tag = "Datafile"`, then because all the `Datafile` controls in the array have a `.Tag` of `Datafile`, `Source.Tag = "Datafile"`. You'll play with this test application more in upcoming chapters.

Like Parent, Like Object

The term `Parent.` in the VB/DOS vocabulary behaves like a property for the sake of `Source.` or other terms that may substitute for `Source.` Yet it also behaves like an object from the point of view of whatever other objects may be attributed to it within the same instruction. Following is a closer look at this two-way term.

`Parent.` **Object acting as Property**

Syntax:

`Source``.Parent`

The `Parent.` object is used to refer to the parent form of a control whose constituent properties have already been passed to a procedure. This property passing takes place by way of declaring the data structure at the beginning of the procedure, in the form *`Source`* `AS CONTROL`. Once a control is passed to the procedure as if it were data, the control that is passed can be referred to by way of the indirect reference *`Source`*`.`, regardless of the type of control that is passed. *`Source`*`.` can then be used to refer to all the properties apportioned to the passed control. The properties of the form containing this control are therefore addressable from within the procedure as properties of `Parent.`

Example

Suppose, in the preceding test application, the `Dataform` window runs out of datafile-representative labels to drag. You want the program to emphasize this fact by "turning off" the window background, perhaps by turning it dark gray. Here's an instruction that effectuates this color change, placed within the `SUB Datalist_DragDrop` event procedure:

```
Source.Parent.BackColor = 8
```

To send a directive back to the form to which the `Source.` control originally belonged, that form can be addressed within the procedure as `Parent.`, whatever the `.FormName` of the form may be.

Example

Next, suppose your `Dataform` has a text box inside it, and you'd like to send a message to it when the form is "turned off." Here's how that instruction might appear:

```
Source.Parent.Message.Text = "Out of datafiles."
```

In this instance, `Message.` is an arbitrary name for a text box belonging to the parent form. You don't need to know the `.FormName` of the form, yet you do need to know the `.CtlName` of the object within that form to address it directly. Thus, the conglomerate reference `Source.Parent.Message.Text` refers to the text within a text box that is definitely called `Message`, residing in whatever the parent form is of whatever control is dragged into the box.

The use of `Parent.` is important especially in instances where you plan to use *multiple* forms cooperatively to effectuate the same graphic operation. When one form or graphic object is the recipient of some operation, especially a drag-and-drop operation, and any of the other forms can be the source, using the `Source AS CONTROL` declaration and the `Parent.` object will be invaluable.

Pulling Tabs

In most everyday DOS programs, the user can type text into a field, press Enter, and then enter text into the next field. In Microsoft's graphical applications including its Windows apps, pressing Enter generally substitutes for clicking the default button, which in many forms is the `OK` button. If the user presses Enter thinking the cursor will move to the next field, the application might respond by assuming the entry of text for this form is complete. As a result, the form is stored as a formal record with a bunch of null fields.

In the first `NameForm` application listing (Mark I), if you entered the text boxes into the form in the order they were presented, you should be able to enter text into one field at runtime, press Tab, and proceed in sequence to the next logical field. In other words, you won't jump from the *last name* field to the *ZIP code* field. The VB/DOS interpreter maintains a *tab index* for each control, among other reasons, so that there is a logical sequence to the fields in a form.

Control.TabIndex Property

The `.TabIndex` property is set to the numerical place in the tabbing sequence of the antecedent control. By default, the tabbing sequence of controls in a form is established as its order of creation at design time; this sequence can be reorganized at design time or runtime. Labels are assigned `.TabIndex` properties by default, although pressing Tab does not cause an indicator box to appear around the label as if it were an operable control. Labels and nonoperable controls are skipped in the tabbing sequence, regardless of their `.TabIndex` property settings.

Control.TabStop Property

The `.TabStop` property is a true or false flag designating whether the antecedent control can be indicated by pressing Tab during runtime. By default, `.TabStop` is set to true (–1). A control can be a tab stop like a bench can be a bus stop. To designate that the tab route does not stop at the antecedent control—in a sense, to remove the bench from the bus stop—set its value to false (0).

Figure 31.1 shows the form for the `NameForm` application Mark II, along with the `.TabIndex` settings for each text field typed within their respective fields. All objects in VB/DOS have a `.TabIndex` property, even if it is not used, as in the case of labels and command buttons. The `.TabIndex` settings that are "missing" from Figure 31.1 are assigned to the other controls on the form.

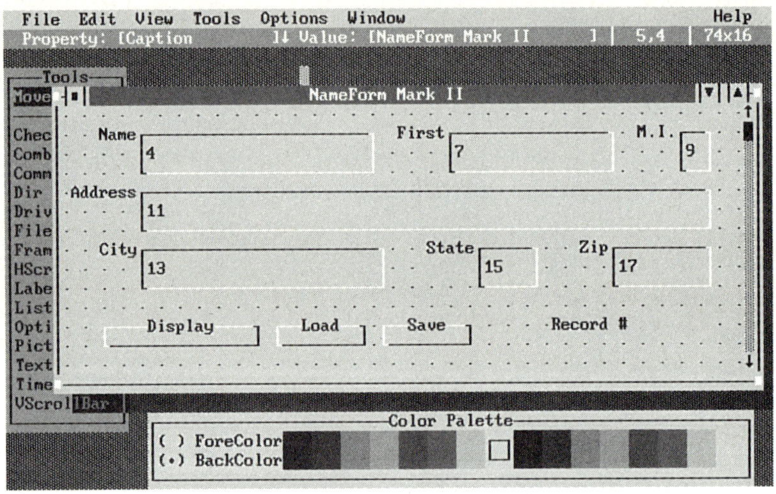

Figure 31.1. Your local tab stop route.

Suppose you want to add a field called `Company Name` between the middle initial field and the address field. You can easily make the form larger: Move the address, city, state, and ZIP code fields down and insert the company name field. The trouble is, the tab index for this new field will be 19, which falls above the tab index for the ZIP code field of 12. Having established the fact that the `.TabIndex` for the middle initial field is 2, you can logically reset the `.TabIndex` for the new company name field to 3. The indices for all successive controls are automatically moved down one. The control that previously had the index of 3 is now bumped to 4. Figure 31.2 shows the amendments made to the form, along with their `.TabIndex` results.

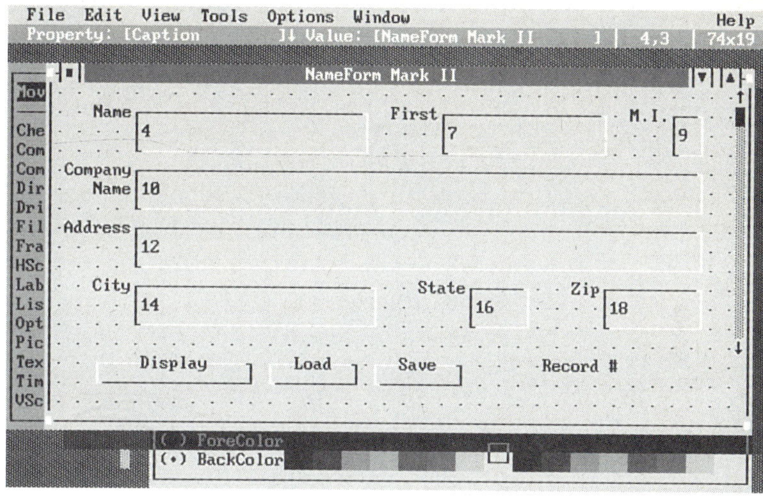

Figure 31.2. A change in plan.

Monitoring Activity

A control *has the focus* when it is active and awaiting user input.

In any window that has multiple fields and controls, Microsoft has the user who doesn't use a mouse press the Tab key repeatedly until the control she wants to operate is somehow indicated on-screen. If the control is a text box, the cursor appears within that box. If the control is a visual device, a *focus indicator* box appears around its caption. In VB/DOS, a control that *has the focus* is the control currently indicated by a hazy rectangle, designating that the control is active or awaiting input from the user. By default, the control within a form that has the focus first is the first input-accepting control in the `.TabStop` sequence.

Acquiring the focus in VB/DOS is an event comparable to intercepting a football pass. Capturing the focus makes a control, in effect, the "ball carrier." Naturally, VB/DOS considers this an event in and of itself.

*Control*_GotFocus and *Control*_LostFocus Events

The `_GotFocus` event occurs whenever the antecedent control acquires the focus, as a result of the user indicating that control with the mouse or the Tab key, or by direct setting of the focus by the program. Acquiring the focus makes this particular control the active control for now. Consequently, the `_LostFocus` event occurs whenever the antecedent control loses the focus, assuming that it ever had the focus.

If necessary, the program can set the focus of a control manually, thus forcing on it the role of active control.

Control.SetFocus — **Method**

Syntax:

```
Control.SetFocus
```

The `.SetFocus` method manually appoints the antecedent control to be the active control, thus giving it the focus.

Example

Suppose your application has several buttons in one form, and a procedure in this or some other form wants to see which button is actually pressed. The supplementary identification of this button could actually be read into a string variable, as the following example instruction demonstrates:

```
nam$ = Screen.ActiveControl.Tag
```

Here `ActiveControl.` refers reflexively to whatever control currently has the focus. Any button that has just been pressed automatically has the focus. For the sake of `.Tag`, `ActiveControl.` is the object. To be a reflexive reference, however, `.ActiveControl` must be the *property* of something. Therefore, like `.Parent` in an earlier example,

`.ActiveControl` is an object acting as a property. The VB/DOS interpreter has assigned it as the exclusive property of everything, in a sense. Everything, in this sense, is referred to by the object `Screen.`, which is the necessary object for `.ActiveControl` to fulfill its role as property. There can be only one active control on-screen at any one time.

Following are the object terms used to acquire data about the active screen graphic object.

`ActiveControl.` — Object acting as Property

The `ActiveControl.` object, when used in conjunction with the universal reference `Screen.`, refers to whatever control currently is active or has the focus, on any form.

`ActiveForm.` — Object acting as Property

The `ActiveForm.` object, when used in conjunction with `Screen.`, refers to the currently active form. These terms are used as objects for the properties normally associated with the graphic objects they refer to and take the place of within instructions. From the point of view of `Screen.`, however, both `ActiveControl.` and `ActiveForm.` are treated as properties of the overall `Screen.` object.

`Screen.` — Object

The `Screen.` object refers to the universal (screen-encompassing) coordinate system. It is used whenever a property of the whole screen, such as `.ActiveControl`, is invoked.

The *clipboard* holds text that is being transferred between graphic objects.

Here's a quick introduction to the VB/DOS clipboard, which you'll be using from time to time to copy text from one graphic object to another. Suppose your application has a button in it marked `Copy`, whose purpose is to place text from a particular text box onto the VB/DOS clipboard. The *clipboard* is a region of memory where text is held for transfer between two graphic objects or other system elements.

`Clipboard.` **Object**

The `Clipboard.` object acts as the antecedent object for all clipboard-specific methods within a procedure.

Example

Here's the procedure for clicking on the `Copy` button, which transfers text to the VB/DOS clipboard:

```
SUB Copy_Click ()
Clipboard.SETTEXT EntryBox.Text
END SUB
```

The preceding procedure was invoked with the occurrence of a type of event with which you are familiar. Here is a review.

Object_Click and *Object_DblClick* Events

The `_Click` event occurs when the user clicks the antecedent object using the mouse. Likewise, the `_DblClick` event occurs when the user double-clicks the antecedent object.

The subject of the VB/DOS clipboard is covered in greater detail in Part IX, "Data Management."

Summary

A control appearing on a form can be assigned a `.Tag` property, which acts as its alias. Controls can be passed in the same manner as normal data (as parameters to procedures), as long as the control name is declared within the parentheses of the procedure's opening `SUB` statement as having data type `CONTROL`. The form that contains the control passed as a parameter to the procedure can be addressed reflexively using the object/property hybrid term `Parent`.

All the controls on a form are given a `.TabIndex` property, which establishes the route the focus indicator bar takes when the user of the application repetitively presses the Tab key. The Tab key route follows the sequence established by the order of `.TabIndex` properties. This sequence is established by default at design time as the order of the controls' creation. When the user presses Enter while the focus indicator is over a control, he is operating that control as if he were using the mouse button. The control being operated on and being indicated is considered the active control and, therefore, *has the focus.* The form that contains the active control, likewise, is the *active control.* A control can be rendered exempt from receiving the focus by setting the `.TabStop` property for that control to false (0).

The `.ActiveControl` and `.ActiveForm` can be addressed indirectly by using those terms. All properties and settings apply to these indirect references just as they would to their direct-reference antecedent objects. `.ActiveControl` and `.ActiveForm` relate back to the universal object `Screen`.

Review Questions

Answers to Review Questions appear in Appendix B.

Using object-oriented syntax, write references for the following properties:

1. The contents of a text box called `Surname`.
2. The tab index for an option dot called `Group(1)`.
3. The alias for a picture called `BobTheBear`.
4. A reflexive reference to the textual contents of the active control.

5. A reflexive reference to a text box called `Status` passed as a parameter to a procedure.
6. A reflexive reference to a text box called `Status` appearing within the active form.
7. A reflexive reference to a text box called `Status` appearing in the same form as that which contains the control that was passed to the current procedure.

32

Control Appearance

In this chapter you examine—or rather, in light of how far you've come, review—the properties and methods relating to the appearance, style, and positioning of graphic objects.

Front and Center

When I present a complete listing of a Visual Basic for MS-DOS application, for each graphic object in the listing I provide settings for the properties that describe where the object is and how big it is. Here are the definitions of those properties for your review.

Form.Left and *Control*.Left Properties

The .Left property of a form is set to the distance in characters between the origin point of the form and the leftmost edge of the screen. The origin point is the first user-addressable character in the upper-left corner of the form. If the form has borders, the origin appears around this point. The `.Left` property of a control is set to the distance in characters between the origin point of the control and the leftmost point on the form.

Form.Top and *Control*.Top Properties

The `.Top` property of a form is set to the distance in characters between the origin point of the form and the uppermost edge of the screen. The `.Top` property of a control is set to the distance in characters between the origin point of the control and the uppermost point on the form.

Form.Width and *Control*.Width Properties

The `.Width` property of a graphic object is set to the distance in characters between the two vertical sides of that object.

Form.Height and *Control*.Height Properties

The `.Height` property of a graphic object is set to the distance in characters between the two horizontal sides of that object.

When a control contains text, it's sometimes difficult for a new programmer to distinguish which controls have a `.Caption` property and which have a `.Text` property. A control can have only one or the other. Following are the distinguishing factors between the two properties.

Object.Caption Property

The `.Caption` property, with respect to a control, is set to the textual contents of the antecedent control having a type that is one of those listed previously. With respect to a form, the property refers to the textual contents of its title bar. This property can be set again at any time.

Forms, check boxes, command buttons, frames, labels, menus, and option buttons all have `.Caption` properties.

Object.Text Property

The `.Text` property is set to the textual contents of the antecedent control, which can be a text box, list box, combo box, or directory list box. With respect to list and combo boxes, the `.Text` property is set to the currently chosen item in the list.

When a control is first created and placed on the form, it starts its life as black on white because the `.ForeColor` property of new controls is set to black by default, and the `.BackColor` property is set to white by default.

Control.BackColor and *Control*.ForeColor Properties

The `.BackColor` property reflects the current background color of its antecedent object. The `.ForeColor` property represents the plotting color of text and graphical elements—such as borders—of its antecedent object. Both properties are expressed as integers ranging from 0 to 15, representing the standard IBM CGA color palette registers.

Within Form Designer is a color palette with which you can set the initial `.ForeColor` and `.BackColor` properties of a form or other object, as depicted in Figure 32.1.

To set color properties for an object:

- Indicate the graphic object to be recolored. If this object is a form, click on any area within the form that is not inhabited by a control. If this object is a control, click that control so that it is surrounded by indicator nodes.
- To set the `.ForeColor` property for this object, set the option dot in the palette marked `ForeColor`. Next, choose a color from the palette by clicking on that color. The color change is immediately reflected in the Form Designer workspace.

- To set the `.BackColor` property for this object, set the option dot in the palette marked `BackColor`. Next, choose a color from the palette by clicking on that color. The color change is immediately reflected in the Form Designer workspace.

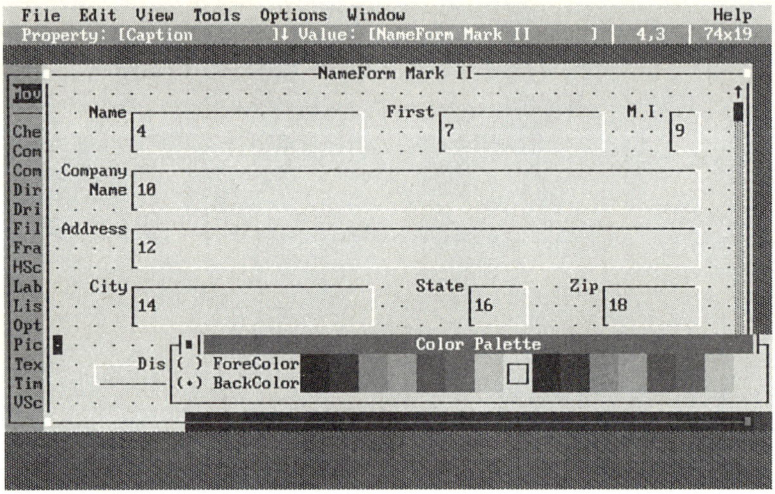

Figure 32.1. Visual Basic for MS-DOS' idea of an artist's studio.

The Visual Basic for MS-DOS Control Panel

VB/DOS is modeled after Visual Basic for Windows, which relies upon the Windows environment to set certain characteristics of appearance for it, using the Windows Control Panel. DOS—the operating environment for VB/DOS, for all intents and purposes—has no control panel, so VB/DOS had to provide it with one. The VB/DOS Control Panel is shipped with every copy of VB/DOS, and it is a VB/DOS application in and of itself. Its running form appears in Figure 32.2. You'll find it as a VB/DOS application named CONTROLP.MAK in your source code directory.

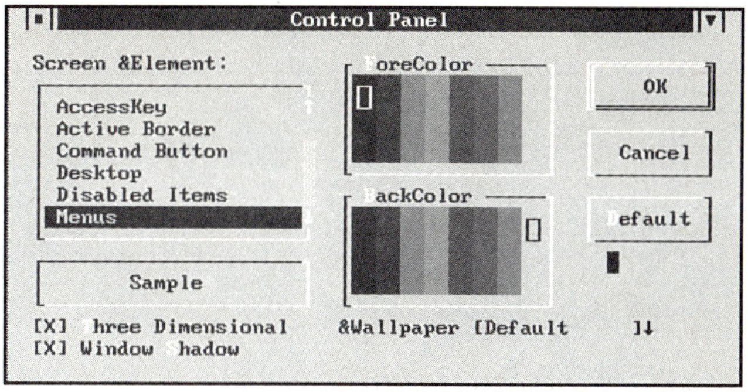

Figure 32.2. The Panel at work.

Because not all VB/DOS applications can rely upon the VB/DOS Control Panel application to set particular operating characteristics for it, VB/DOS has made `.ControlPanel` a property, which is attributed to the `Screen.` object introduced in Chapter 31, "Control Manipulation and Organization." The property is introduced in the following section.

`.ControlPanel` **Property**

Syntax:

```
Screen.ControlPanel(characteristic%) = setting%
```

The `.ControlPanel` property is used to refer to certain appearance characteristics of the VB/DOS workspace whenever forms are made active. The property is unused when forms are inactive. The value of `characteristic%` can refer to any of the characteristics listed in Table 32.1.

Table 32.1. `.ControlPanel` **characteristics.**

Characteristic	*Pertains to*
0	The color given a letter in a text label that shows which key, when pressed along with Alt, activates the labeled control
1	The background color of the border of the active form
2	The foreground color of the border of the active form
3	The color produced by the "shadow" of the active window falling on the desktop
4	The default color given command buttons
5	The background color of the workspace desktop
6	The foreground color of the workspace desktop
7	The number given the desktop's default "wallpaper" background pattern
8	The color given a disabled item in a drop-down menu
9	The background color of the menu and menu bar
10	The foreground color of the menu and menu bar
11	The background color of the active selection in the menu and menu bar
12	The foreground color of the active selection in the menu and menu bar
13	The background color of scroll bars
14	The foreground color of scroll bars
15	A true/false value denoting whether a three-dimensional effect is to apply to graphic objects. (That is, whether a play of light and color will make buttons look raised and text boxes look indented.)

Characteristic	*Pertains to*
16	The background color of the form's title bar
17	The foreground color of the form's title bar

Summary

The `.Left` and `.Top` properties of a form denote the distance of that form's origin point from the leftmost and uppermost points, respectively, of the screen. The `.Left` and `.Top` properties of a control likewise denote the distance of that control's origin point from the leftmost and uppermost points, respectively, of the form in which the control resides.

When addressing text with a property, the term `.Text` is reserved for use in addressing the contents of text boxes, as well as list and combo boxes. The textual contents of all other types of controls, as well as the title bar of a form, are addressed by the term `.Caption`.

The `.ForeColor` of a graphic object is the foreground color used for its text as well as for most of its graphical content. The `.BackColor` of an object is the background color used for the area of that object not inhabited by text or graphics. You might find it more convenient to set color properties at design time using the color palette. The `.ControlPanel` property is used to set desktop appearance characteristics during the runtime of the program.

Review Questions

Answers to Review Questions appear in Appendix B.

1. What is the default setting for `Screen.ControlPanel(4)`?
2. In a picture box in which 50 white characters, representing stars, are placed geometrically on a blue field, what is the `.BackColor` setting for the picture box?
3. Editable text is addressed using what property term?

33

Menus

In this chapter, you learn the procedure for adding a menu bar to a form, as well as how the menu hierarchy is maintained. You see individual menu items acting in place of graphic controls. Next, you examine the properties that relate to menu items. You'll also explore arranging other Visual Basic for MS-DOS controls to act as a menuing system that can substitute for the menu bar.

Le Menu

The menu bar is the only VB/DOS graphic control not available from the toolbox.

The menu bar is the one type of control that is not available through the VB/DOS toolbox because the contents of a menu bar are not actually graphic objects. In fact, they are the only controls belonging to a form that are not graphic objects. They are addressable to some extent within the source code, however, using object-oriented syntax. On a VB/DOS menu bar, each menu selection is treated like a graphic control placed on the form. Selecting an item from a VB/DOS menu is treated the same way—with the same event name—as clicking a command button on a form.

Now, witness the creation of a menu bar for the application NameForm Mark III. You'll be making this latest revision of the test application look as depicted in Figure 33.1.

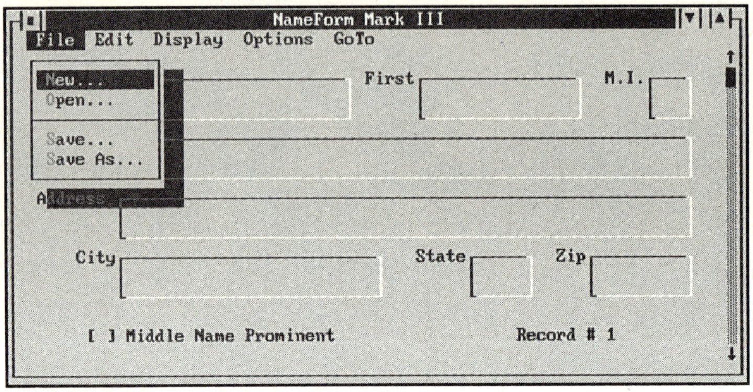

Figure 33.1. Would you care to see the menu?

In the previous chapter, I added an extra line to this form; subsequently, some of its procedures were altered to read as shown in the following.

Declarations:

```
'$FORM Selector
DECLARE SUB RecordShown_Change ()
DECLARE SUB AssessFilename ()
OPTION BASE 1
DIM SHARED LstName$(1000), FrstName$(1000), MdInit$(1000),
➥ CompanyNam$(1000), Adress$(1000), Cty$(1000),
➥ Stat$(1000), Zp$(1000)
DIM SHARED RecordNo AS INTEGER
COMMON SHARED TargetFile$, Pattern$, prmpt$
COMMON SHARED cancl AS INTEGER
```

It's easy to tell here which variables belong to all the procedures in just the NAMEFRM3 module (DIM SHARED) and which variables pertain to this module as well as the SELECTOR module (COMMON SHARED).

Procedures:

```
SUB CompanyName_Change ()
CompanyNam$(RecordNo) = CompanyName.Text
END SUB
```

Now array variable `CompanyNam$()` is a regular part of the database table and receives its contents from the text box `CompanyName`.

```
SUB Display_Click ()
RecordNo = RecordShown.Value
FullName$ = FirstName.Text + " " + MidInit.Text + " "
  + LastName.Text
WorkPlace$ = CompanyName.Text
StreetAddress$ = Address.Text
Residence$ = City.Text + ", " + State.Text + "  "
  + Zip.Text
Next_Line$ = CHR$(13) + CHR$(10)
Envelope$ = FullName$ + Next_Line$ + WorkPlace$
  + Next_Line$ + StreetAddress$ + NextLine$
  + Residence$
MSGBOX Envelope$
END SUB
```

Here you see `CompanyName` also taking its rightful place in `SUB Display_Click ()`. Subsequently, I added one line to `SUB RecordShown_Change ()` to make `CompanyName` part of the formal record:

```
CompanyName.Text = CompanyNam$(RecordNo)
```

Menus are created through the use of a separate window called the Menu Design window. To create a menu bar for a form, perform the following steps:

1. From the Form Designer, select **M**enu Design Window from the **W**indow menu. The form being designed is overwritten with the window as depicted in Figure 33.2.

2. The Menu Design window contains a large text box that acts as a type of outliner. The selections to appear within the menu at all levels appear here, displayed as a menu selection hierarchy. To add a menu category to this window, type the name of the category as it will appear on-screen into the text line marked `Caption:`. To assign a key to be paired with the Alt key as an alternate keystroke to this menu item, precede with an ampersand (`&`) the letter within the item caption that will act as the Alt pair key. For instance, the entry `&File` assigns Alt-F as the alternate keystroke to bring up the **F**ile menu.

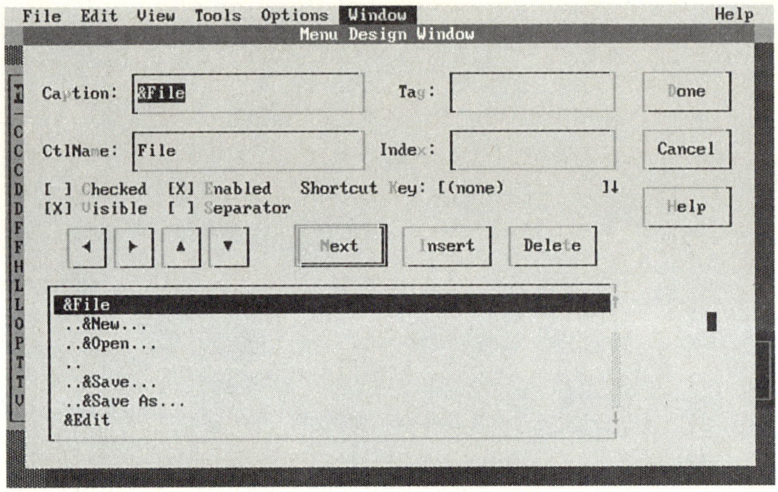

Figure 33.2. The Menu Design window at work.

3. Type the control name to be assigned to this menu selection item in the line marked `CtlName:`. You have now set the two main properties of a menu selection item. A menu item has `.Caption` and `.CtlName` properties just as a command button does. The `.CtlName` you just entered acts as the reference for this menu item within the source code.

4. To assign a Shift or Ctrl key combination as an alternate keystroke for this menu item, choose that keystroke from the combo box marked `Shortcut Key:`.

5. To set or reset any of the three true or false properties associated with this menu item, check or uncheck the box next to `Checked`, `Enabled`, or `Visible`.

6. To make the current menu item a separator line that separates selection groupings, check the box marked `Selector`. The current menu item appears in the list as two dots (..) set off by themselves.

7. To enter the menu item in the list, click the `Next` button.

8. To designate a menu item already on the list as subordinate to the category above it—as **O**pen is subordinate to **F**ile—click the right arrow button in the window. This shifts the caption of this category four dots to the right, designating that item as belonging to a drop-down menu for the category above it. There can be up to five levels of submenus in a Visual Basic for DOS menu bar system.
9. To delete an item from the list, indicate that item and click the `Delete` button.
10. To add space to the list for another item, indicate the item that currently occupies the space and click the `Insert` button.
11. To shuffle the order of a menu item in the list, first indicate that item. Next, click the up arrow or down arrow button to move that item up or down through the list.
12. To promote an item on the list to categorical rank, indicate the item to receive the promotion and click the left arrow button.
13. To abort menu bar creation, click the `Cancel` button.
14. When the menu bar is at an operable state and ready for testing, click `Done`.

Example

To experience the thrill of creating menu bars, go into the existing NameForm Mark II form and delete the buttons along the bottom. You may want to resize the form so that there's not so much blank space at the bottom. Next, using the procedure outlined previously, enter the following menu into the Menu Design window.

Captions	*Control Names*
`&File`	`File`
`..&New...`	`FileNew`
`..&Open...`	`FileOpen`

Captions	*Control Names*
`..`	`separator1`
`..&Save...`	`FileSave`
`..&SaveAs...`	`FileSaveAs`
`&Edit`	`Edit`
`..&Cut`	`EditCut`
`..Cop&y`	`EditCopy`
`..&Paste`	`EditPaste`
`&Display`	`Display`
`&Options`	`Options`
`&GoTo`	`GetRecordNo`

Previously, a button on this form had a `.Caption` of Display and a `.CtlName` of Display. Now there is a menu item with the same name. Now that the button is gone, the procedure `SUB Display_Click ()` originally attributed to that button automatically applies to the menu selection. `Display` is treated in this context as a graphic object although it is not.

In the following sections are the three terms used in the source code for properties listed in the Menu Design window. These terms designate the operative state of a control—and in this case, a menu selection is a control.

Control.Enabled Property

The `.Enabled` property is set to a true/false value, designating whether the antecedent control is responsive to user events. By default, this property is set to true. To turn off a control but leave it within a form or grayed within a menu, you can set this property to false.

Control.Visible Property

The .Visible property is set to a true or false value that designates whether the antecedent control can be seen, to be responsive to user events. An invisible control is nonresponsive. By default, this property is set to true. To make this control disappear or to eliminate a selection from a menu temporarily, you can set this property to false.

Menu.Checked Property

.Checked is the only property that is specific to menu items as controls. The .Checked property is set to a true or false value, designating whether a check mark appears beside the selection in a menu. This property does not change the effect of the menu or of any objects to which its event procedures may refer. It merely sets or resets a check mark beside the selection. Use this property to designate whether an option is set to on or off.

More Foreign-Looking Menus

Here's an unusual type of control: Suppose you have an application whose main form does not have a menu bar for one reason or another. For instance, the form is supposed to represent the astronomical location of the stars on a given day of the year. A constantly displayed menu bar would be an interference. One creative way to overcome this burden is to make it so the menu can appear whenever the user drags the mouse pointer over a certain region of the screen.

Instead of making the entire menu appear—and potentially startling the user—you could instead display a *symbol* for the menu whenever the pointer is dragged over the region. Clicking the symbol then brings up the entire menu. This test requires three forms: one that represents the main form, another that acts as the menu symbol, and a third that is the primary menu itself, replacing the menu bar. You may have read that a form is the primary repository for multiple elements of data. What that definition does not convey is that a form is also any self-contained graphic object of any size, such as a one-by-ten slip with the word "Control" on it. Figure 33.3 shows the test control application with all three forms active.

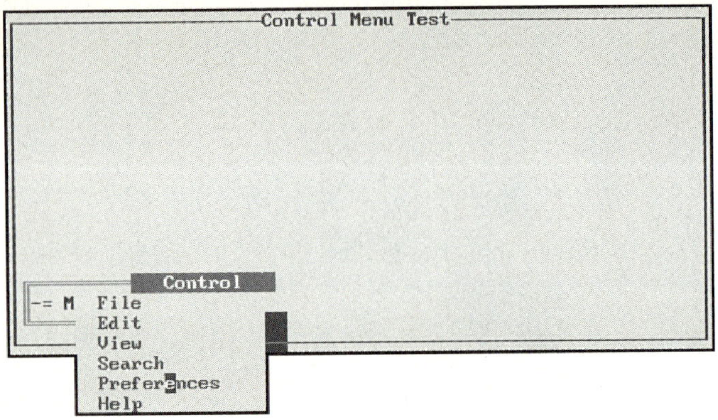

Figure 33.3. The menu non-bar.

The sizes and colors of objects here are arbitrary; the source code still works properly if you make the "MENU" region large or small. The following table lists the more important property settings.

Alternative Menu Test System

Project name: CTRLMENU.MAK
Constituent files: CTRLTEST.FRM, CTRLSLIP.FRM, CTRLMENU.FRM

CTRLTEST.FRM
Startup Form

Object Type	*Property*	*Setting*
Form	`.FormName`	`ContrlTest`
Label	`.BorderStyle`	`2 - Double Line`
	`.CtlName`	`MenuShow`
	`.Caption`	`-=MENU=-`

CTRLSLIP.FRM
Startup Form

Object type	*Property*	*Setting*
Form	.Width	13
	.Height	1
	.FormName	Contrl
	.BorderStyle	0
Label	.Left	0
	.Top	0
	.Width	13
	.Height	1
	.Caption	Control
	.Alignment	2 - Centered

CTRLMENU.FRM
Startup Form

Object type	*Property*	*Setting*
Form	.Width	27
	.Height	6
	.FormName	ContrlMenu
	.BorderStyle	0
Control array		
Label	.Left	0
	.Top	0
	.Width	27
	.Height	1
	.CtlName	MenuItem

A menu item set up as a control array can simplify the code the menu executes by creating one event for a series of items. Menu control arrays work in much the same way as graphic control arrays: the individual items are sorted by the `Index` parameter. The menu control array uses the same `CtlName` on successive items, with the `Index` value being incremented accordingly.

The control array's `.Index` numbers are 0 through 5, respectively, and their captions were chosen arbitrarily for the sake of this test. Should you choose later to incorporate this code into another application, you can change these `.Caption` properties.

`CTRLTEST.FRM` is the startup module for this application, so it is up to its `SUB Form_Load ()` procedure to bring the other two form modules into play.

CTRLTEST.FRM

```
SUB Form_Load ()
LOAD ContrlMenu
LOAD MenuSlip
END SUB
SUB MenuShow_MouseMove (Button AS INTEGER, Shift AS INTEGER,
➥ X AS SINGLE, Y AS SINGLE)
MenuSlip.Left = ContrlTest.Left + MenuShow.Left + X + 3
MenuSlip.Top = ContrlTest.Top + MenuShow.Top + Y + 2
MenuSlip.SHOW
END SUB
```

The previous procedure executes whenever the mouse pointer travels into the area of object `MenuShow`. The objective here is to make the red box marked `Control` show itself whenever the pointer enters the `-=MENU=-` area. The procedure first sets the coordinates of the red `MenuSlip` to the current location of the mouse pointer relative to the rest of the screen plus a slight offset. The VB/DOS interpreter registers `X` and `Y` as relative to the menu box, not to the screen coordinate system. But if you ask the interpreter to plot something to character (X, Y), it will evaluate `X` and `Y` in this instance as relative to the screen, and the slip will end up way in left field. The offsets make the slip show up just to the right of the mouse pointer location when the `.SHOW` method is invoked.

CTRLSLIP.FRM

```
SUB Contrl_Click ()
ContrlMenu.Left = ContrlTest.Left + ContrlTest.MenuShow.Left
➥ + 6
ContrlMenu.Top = ContrlTest.Top + ContrlTest.MenuShow.Top
➥ + y + 2
```

```
ContrlTest.MenuShow.Enabled = 0
ContrlMenu.SHOW
END SUB
```

The preceding procedure is next in the execution sequence. If the user wants to pull down the `Control` menu, she'll move the pointer over into the area of the red `MenuSlip` and click the index button once. The menu appears in yet another form, whose coordinates are placed using the same mechanics as in `SUB MenuShow_MouseMove ()` earlier. So that a mouse move doesn't cause `SUB MenuShow_MouseMove ()` to be executed once again, throwing the entire sequence off, the `.Enabled` property of the area `MenuShow` is set to false (0).

CTRLMENU.FRM

```
SUB MenuItem_Click (Index AS INTEGER)
ContrlMenu.HIDE
MenuSlip.HIDE
ContrlTest.MenuShow.Enabled = -1
END SUB
```

Once the menu category is clicked, both the menu and its adjacent slip are made to disappear. The active state of the area `MenuShow` is set back to true (–1), and the sequence can start all over again. The ellipsis marks where the selection-deciphering routines go when you integrate this menu system into your own application.

CTRLTEST.FRM

```
SUB Form_MouseMove (Button AS INTEGER, Shift AS INTEGER,
➥ X AS SINGLE, Y AS SINGLE)
MenuSlip.HIDE
END SUB
```

This final procedure is executed whenever the mouse pointer moves outside the menu area. In effect, it keeps the `Control` menu slip hidden. The procedure has to be executed continually because there's really no way to tell a VB/DOS procedure, "When you don't see the mouse pointer, do this." You can only expect a mouse pointer event "when you do see the pointer." You really have no choice here but to tell the interpreter, "If you see the pointer, hide the object."

Strangely enough, there is a way to tell the interpreter, "If you don't see the object, do something to the pointer." You'll study pointers in Chapter 34, "Dragging."

The Mystery of the Implicit Branch

I presented this alternative menu application for two reasons: First, by seeing a bit of what it takes to jerry-rig a menu system manually, you might gain some appreciation of what the VB/DOS menu bar system does for you automatically. Second, and perhaps most important, is that this is the first application you've built that contains three form modules. Notice there are no explicit branch instructions in any of the five procedures listed, yet control passes easily between them. This exemplifies the primary difference between VB/DOS and every other BASIC for DOS produced heretofore: The order of procedural execution is not stated within the source code. Because a VB/DOS source code listing doesn't list SUB or FUNCTION procedures in the order of their execution, it becomes imperative that you carefully study the event declarations and perhaps map out on paper the order of each event. This is not easy by any means. In fact, if I were to present the listing of CTRLMENU.MAK without any English-language descriptions or accompanying photographs whatsoever, it's unlikely that even an expert VB/DOS programmer would be able to make order out of the chaos immediately. Structured programming in VB/DOS is, therefore, very much in the eye of the developer.

Summary

The menu bar is not a graphic object nor are any of its constituent selections. Nonetheless, the menu bar is given object-oriented syntax within the source code of VB/DOS applications. Menus are created with the aid of the VB/DOS Menu Design window.

Review Questions

Answers to Review Questions appear in Appendix B.

1. From a design point of view, why is a menu bar not included in the standard VB/DOS toolbox?

2. What does the ellipsis (...) in the `.Caption` of a menu command generally signify?

3. When an event procedure applies to a button and that button is removed from the form to be replaced with a menu command having the same `.CtlName` as the removed button, where does the event procedure "go" while the replacement takes place?

34

Dragging

A *drag* operation copies an image from the control.

In this chapter you learn how Visual Basic for MS-DOS interprets and executes events that involve *dragging.* You might have used a computer with which you could delete files by dragging them to a "trash can" icon. This drag is accomplished by clicking on the item to be deleted and holding down the index button of the mouse, dragging the pointer to the trash can while still keeping the index button held down, and finally releasing the button. The way VB/DOS interprets such events, certain controls on a form classified as *targets* act as the receivers of images of other controls. The receiving of these images is interpreted as a *drag* event. You learn how to program such events in this chapter.

Dragging Everything Out into the Open

When designing a form, you move a control on the form being designed by dragging the control to its new position. When the application containing that form is run later, it is said that the user can drag a control on top of another—like a file icon being dragged on top of a trash icon. Generally, such figures of speech require generations to develop. With respect to software, however, a generation is often scaled down to about a month.

When an application is running, *to drag a control* (in the way Microsoft uses the term) is to click and hold down the index button over a control, and then carry either a duplicate image of that control's border or a *drag icon* assigned to that control. A drag icon follows the mouse pointer as it is dragged across the screen. The object on which the dragged image "lands" is considered the *target* object. The object where the image originated is considered the *source*.

Examine this act in more detail. VB/DOS controls in a form running in an application are, by nature, fixed in their place. The drag operation does not move the control itself from one place to another. Normally, if the user were to click and hold the mouse pointer over a control, nothing would happen. If the user were to release the button without moving the mouse, however, she could generate a `_Click` event. For the drag operation to be enabled for a control, its *drag mode* is set to `1`. Now when the user clicks and holds the mouse pointer over the control, a solid black single-lined border appears around that control, which follows the pointer as long as the index button is depressed.

As far as VB/DOS is concerned, all that has taken place thus far is just special effects without meaning. The drag event that actually initiates the execution of some code takes place at some point while the dragged image is over the target control; more to the point, the drag event takes place from the point of view of the target. If a control image is dragged on top of a control that isn't expecting this image to drop by, the entire operation is ignored. In other words, if dragging event procedures haven't been programmed for the target control, that control won't accept company.

The two drag events in the VB/DOS vocabulary are introduced in the following sections.

*Control*_DragDrop Event

The `_DragDrop` event for a control is recognized when the image from another control is dragged on top of it and the mouse button is released. The procedure for this event takes three parameters: the `Source` object where the dragged icon originated declared as having type `CONTROL`, and the `X` and `Y` coordinates of the mouse pointer at the time of the drop.

*Control*_DragOver Event

The _DragOver event takes place for a control when the image from another control is dragged on top of it, regardless of whether the mouse button is released. The procedure for this event takes four parameters: the Source object where the dragging icon originated declared as having type CONTROL, the current X and Y coordinates of the mouse pointer, and an integer that registers the state of progress of the drag operation. This integer is given any of the following values by the interpreter:

0	The pointer is entering the area of the target control.
1	The pointer is exiting the area of the target control.
2	The pointer is found to be within the area of the target control.

There are two ways to initiate a drag operation in VB/DOS. In the manual mode, the .DRAG method can be used to allow dragging of a specific control, as well as to terminate the drag. Before the .DRAG method is initiated, however, the control is fixed to the form and is not moved at runtime. In the optional automatic mode, the .DRAG method is not necessary. The VB/DOS interpreter takes charge of the entire drag process. The .DragMode property determines which mode is in use for a particular control.

Control.DragMode Property

The .DragMode property for a control is set to 1 to make that control automatically draggable at runtime. By default, this property is set to 0, which means dragging can be enabled with source code, either one time only with the .DRAG method, or through the remainder of the program with the instruction *Control*.DragMode = 1 until disabled with *Control*.DragMode = 0. Note that this property is a *flag* and not a Boolean true or false register, so .DragMode cannot be set to –1.

When a control's .DragMode property is set to 0 (manual), the following method can be used to initiate a drag.

.DRAG **Method**

Syntax:

```
Control.DRAG integer%
```

The `.DRAG` method is used to manually start or stop the dragging process for a control, whether the `.DragMode` for that control has been set. This is especially helpful if the control's `.DragMode` is set to 0 (manual) and, by default, cannot be dragged. The value of *integer%* can be any of the following:

0	Cancel dragging of the specified control.
1	Initiate dragging of the specified control when the `.Drag` method appears within an event procedure for the antecedent control.
2	End dragging of the control and signal a `_DragDrop` event for that control.

Wild Object Rustling

In Chapter 31, "Control Manipulation and Organization," I introduced a portion of a test application that showed symbols representing data files being dragged into a sort of collective corral. The symbols were organized into a list once in the corral but left where they were dropped when dragged out of the corral onto the main form. The application in its active state is depicted in Figure 34.1.

The sizes of the objects in this form are not an important issue; the important property settings are provided in the following.

List Item Drag Test System

Project name: DATAFORM.MAK
Constituent file: DATAFORM.FRM

Object type	*Property*	*Setting*
Form	`.FormName`	`Dataform`
Frame	`.CtlName`	`Datalist`
	`.Caption`	`Database 1`
Control array		
Label	`.CtlName`	`Datafile`
	`.Caption`	`Datafile` *`index+1`*
	`.Tag`	`Datafile`
	`.DragMode`	`0 - Manual`
	`.BackColor`	`14 - Yellow`

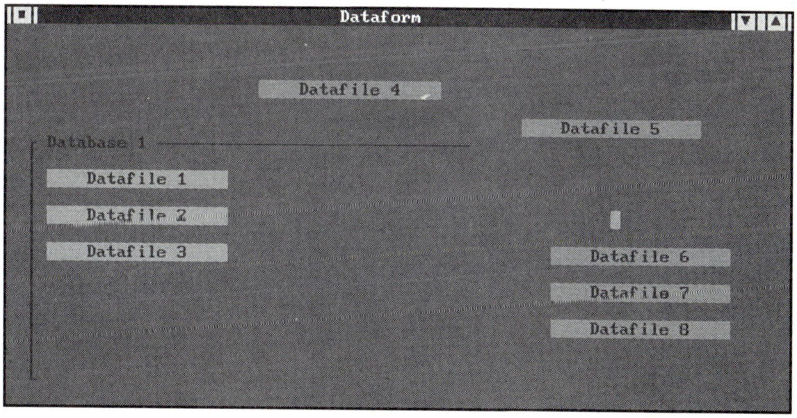

Figure 34.1. Shootout at the Data Corral.

For this example, you create eight `Datafile` labels (an arbitrary number) for the control array—enough to play with. In a larger application, you could paste filenames into the `.Caption` properties of these labels. The point of this application is to model a graphical method for ordering the joining of like data elements together into a group.

General declarations:

```
DIM listx AS INTEGER, listy AS INTEGER
DIM grabpoint AS INTEGER
```

These three variables are of prime importance to this module. Variables `listx` and `listy` hold the next open slot on the `Datalist` frame. Remember, once a symbol is dragged into the frame, it is immediately placed in a "slot" held open for it; the origin character of that slot is at (`listx`, `listy`). Notice also the variable scopes—this time you're trying declarations at the modular level and having procedures borrow those variables that are needed using the `SHARED` redeclaration.

Procedures:

```
SUB Form_Load ()
SHARED listx AS INTEGER, listy AS INTEGER
listx = 2
listy = 2
END SUB
```

At the time the module starts, the initial slot coordinates are set to (2, 2), which is just below the upper-left corner. This gives the frame a bit of a margin.

```
SUB Datafile_MouseDown (Index AS INTEGER, Button
➥ AS INTEGER, Shift AS INTEGER, X AS SINGLE,
➥ Y AS SINGLE)
SHARED grabpoint AS INTEGER
grabpoint = x
Datafile(Index).DRAG 1
END SUB
```

The purpose of this procedure is to make variable `grabpoint` keep track of precisely the point at which the `Datafile` symbol was grabbed. This `grabpoint` becomes an offset when placing the symbol back at the form so that when the user releases the index button during the drag operation, the symbol doesn't slip mysteriously to the right, and it remains at rest where it was laid. The user can arbitrarily pick up a `Datafile` symbol at a point a few characters to the right of its origin point. Variable `grabpoint` keeps track of just how many characters that is. When the symbol is put back atop the form, the VB/DOS interpreter can place the origin point of the symbol that many characters to the *left* of the mouse pointer location.

It's important to note here that you leave the `.DragMode` properties of all the elements of the `Datafile()` control array at 0 (manual) so that the `_MouseDown` event is recognized. If you had set the `.DragMode` properties of the control array elements to 1 (automatic), the VB/DOS interpreter would start the drag process *before* it could recognize the `_MouseDown` event or any other button-related event such as `_Click`.

Next comes the event procedure for dragging graphic objects atop the `Datalist` frame:

```
SUB Datalist_DragDrop (Source AS CONTROL, x AS SINGLE,
➥ y AS SINGLE)
SHARED listx AS INTEGER, listy AS INTEGER
IF Source.Tag = "Datafile" THEN
    Source.MOVE Datalist.Left + listx, Datalist.Top
    ➥ + listy
    Source.BackColor = 11
    IF listy >= 12 THEN
        listy = 2
        listx = listx + 22
    ELSE
        listy = listy + 2
    END IF
END IF
Source.DRAG 0
END SUB
```

The `.MOVE` method, which is described in the following section, makes moving graphic objects and controls possible.

.MOVE — Method

Syntax:

`Control.MOVE left%[, top%[, width%[, height%]]]`

The .MOVE method moves the designated control on a form to the coordinate location on that form specified as the term's parameters. Only the *left%* parameter must be specified to move the control horizontally to the new character position *left%*. If *top%* is specified, the control is moved vertically as well. If *width%* or *height%* is specified, the control is resized once it is moved.

In effect, the .MOVE method performs the work of two instructions. The .MOVE instruction that appears in the preceding procedure, for instance, replaces the following two equations:

```
Source.Left = Datalist.Left + listx
Source.Top = Datalist.Top + listy
```

The Datalist frame, besides receiving the _DragDrop event, does precisely nothing within this form; a text box or a picture box (especially a picture box) could do an equally fair job of nothing. I chose a frame for the Datalist "corral" rather than a text box or a picture box—which look similar—primarily because controls are replotted with the .MOVE method on top of the frame, whereas the same controls would be replotted beneath a text or picture box, out of sight to the user.

The procedure for dropping objects onto the form (outside the frame) is modeled after the frame's _DragDrop procedure:

```
SUB Form_DragDrop (Source AS CONTROL, x AS SINGLE,
➥ y AS SINGLE)
SHARED listx AS INTEGER, listy AS INTEGER, grabpoint
➥ AS INTEGER
IF Source.Tag = "Datafile" THEN
    Source.MOVE x - Dataform.Left - grabpoint - 1,
    ➥ y - Dataform.Top - 1
    Source.BackColor = 14
    IF listy <= 2 THEN
        listy = 14
        listx = listx - 26
    ELSE
        listy = listy - 2
```

```
    END IF
END IF
Source.DRAG 0
END SUB
```

Here's the preceding procedure written as pseudocode:

Procedure for dragging a control atop the form:
Bring the next x/y coordinates in from the module level, along with the point at which the control was grabbed.
If the tag given the dragged control is `"Datafile"`, *then*
  Move the control to the current mouse pointer location, minus the number of characters between the pointer and the control's origin point.
  Make the dragged control bright yellow.
  If you've reached the beginning of the list, then
    Make the next slot the end of the previous column.
    Set the left position of the previous column.
  Otherwise,
    Make the next slot two spaces up.
  End of condition.
End of condition.
Cancel the current drag.
End of procedure.

Summary

In graphical operations involving dragging, to drag a control is not the same operation as to move that control. During dragging, an image copied from the control follows the mouse pointer although the control maintains its position. By contrast, moving a control relocates it to a new position. This image can be of either the border of the control being dragged or an icon referenced by the `.DragIcon` property. The control being dragged is considered the source. The destination object where the image is to land is considered the target.

Controls on a form cannot be dragged, by default. You can set their `.DragMode` property to `1` to initiate automatic dragging. Otherwise, you can make any control draggable within an event procedure for that control, using the .DRAG method. While a control is draggable, events for clicking or double-clicking that control are not recognized. Event procedures for dragging controls provide coordinate information that can be helpful in programming operations that actually move the control from one position on the form to another, using the .MOVE method.

Review Questions

Answers to Review Questions appear in Appendix B.

1. What is the crucial difference between a *drag* operation and a *move* operation?
2. Is the event procedure awaiting the _DragDrop event always considered the target of the drop?
3. Are the coordinates stated within a .MOVE operation expressed relative to the screen, the current form, or the control to which the event procedure belongs?

35

Conventional Output

In this chapter, you are introduced to the statements, functions, and properties that concern text production in Visual Basic for MS-DOS. Throughout its history, the designers of Microsoft BASIC have bit-by-bit compiled a type of character descriptor code, that describes—for the sake of the interpreter—the way in which an element of data being printed should appear. You study the code in this chapter, and some examples are presented utilizing the code in `PRINT USING` instructions, as well as in `PRINT` instructions involving the `FORMAT$()` function.

In Search of Finer .PRINT

I presented this analogy in a previous book on Visual Basic for Windows, and I think it's also fitting in the context of VB/DOS. Observing the BASIC programming language from the perspective of a computing historian is similar to a designer or engineer observing how a particular model of car has changed shape and function over the decades—for instance, the Ford Thunderbird or the Pontiac LeMans. When a car is altered drastically from a two-seater sports coupe (the '57 Thunderbird) to a long, six-passenger, four-door sedan (the '65 Thunderbird), the people behind the reengineering of the product say such changes are necessary to suit people's needs in a progressing society. The same is said when a particular model is altered from a long, six-passenger, four-door sedan (the '79 LeMans) to a two-seater sports coupe (the '89 LeMans).

Those of you who have witnessed the redesign of literally everything merchandisable know the need for change is most prevalent in the minds of engineers. The '57 Thunderbird was a perfectly good car. The time came, however, to design another car or else lay off a perfectly good team of engineers. In computing, the need for change is far more frequent than in the automotive industry, perhaps because the rapid growth of computing as an industry fostered within its participants a more advanced level of impatience. A central processing unit can be blazingly fast until the advances in technology make it look chillingly slow by comparison. Still, some degree of permanence—call it heritage—remains in the design and engineering of a computing device, even when its performance is raised by another exponential factor in its redesign. The Intel 486DX2 CPU utilizes much of the same logic in its design as its distant ancestral progenitor, the Intel 4004—which was used in the mid-70s to control traffic lights.

I drive a 1983 Datsun 280ZX. In and of itself, that has little to do with VB/DOS, except for the following: In tracing the design history of the Z, I find the '83 model a comfortable blend of the newer engineering prevalent in the late '80s models and the heritage of the "Ladybird" Z in the early '70s models. I like taking notice of what design elements remain intact over the years and what elements are replaced in the interest of progress or better architecture. BASIC has been my programming language like the Z has been my car. In VB/DOS, some of the subtleties in the architecture of its BASIC predecessors remain, but not without having been shrouded within the newer and brighter latticework of logical design progress.

From the depths, however, a ray or two of original inspiration does peer out into the modern world, a refracted emanation filtered through layer upon layer of reengineering and revision. One such ray of refurbishment is the `.PRINT` method.

.PRINT — Method

Syntax:

```
[Object.]PRINT [expression1{;¦,} expression2{;¦,}
   . . . expressionn[{;¦,}]
```

where each *expression* consists of any valid, logically interpretable mathematical or string expression. A mathematical expression, in this case, is composed of one or more values or variables combined arithmetically using operator symbols such as `+` or function terms such as `INT()`. A string expression is composed of one or more elements of text, whether they are alphanumeric phrases, string variables, or string functions such as `RIGHT$()`. Multiple-element string expressions can be concatenated using the `+` operator. Text that is to be printed literally must appear within double quotation marks, as in `"Hello"`. Double quotation marks themselves can be printed using the function `CHR$(34)`, the function itself appearing outside any quotation marks. Likewise, you can express other special characters not appearing on the keyboard by using the `CHR$()` function.

The `.PRINT` method is used to direct textual data to the screen when forms and graphic objects are active. `.PRINT` displays the logically reduced form of each expression in its expression list. If *Object.* is specified, the recipient of the printed text is either the stated graphic object, such as `Form1`, or an output device, such as `Printer`. If the recipient *Object.* belongs to a form other than the one containing the `.PRINT` method, the form name is specified before the object name, with both names separated from each other by a period.

If the `PRINT` instruction appears without any antecedent within a form module, printing is directed to the currently active form. If the `PRINT` instruction appears without any antecedent within a general module (.BAS extension), printing is directed to the background screen. If forms are active, printing might be obscured.

The semicolon and comma as delimiters have specific uses with respect to the `.PRINT` method and `PRINT` statement. Each expression in the list is separated from the others by one of these delimiters. If two expressions are separated from each other by a semicolon, the text of both expressions is printed next to each other (side-by-side). If two expressions are separated from each other by a comma, the interpreter inserts a tabulation character at the end of the first expression before printing the start of the second. A tabulation in this instance is equivalent to 14 spaces.

The VB/DOS interpreter recognizes a virtual cursor for the graphic objects that receive text using the `.PRINT` method. This cursor's coordinate position is registered within properties of the graphic object, called `.CURRENTX` and `.CURRENTY`. Whenever a `.PRINT` method has completed execution, it by default leaves the virtual cursor at the beginning (the left side) of the line immediately following the one just printed. If the `.PRINT` method is closed with a semicolon, the cursor position is set at the immediate end of the text just printed, without the interpreter executing a carriage return to the next line. If the `.PRINT` method is closed with a comma, the cursor is tabulated to the next 14-column stop and remains there without the interpreter executing a line feed to the next line.

If the `.PRINT` method or `PRINT` statement appears on a line by itself, a carriage return with a line feed is generated. In other words, the "print head" is set to the far left by the carriage return and one line down by the line feed—like what happens when you press the Return key on an electric typewriter. The virtual cursor's position is set at the beginning of the next line below the previously printed one.

`PRINT` seems like a simple enough instruction until you try to explain it to somebody. Part of the reason the instruction is so complex today is that functionality has been added to it over time since 1964. Remember, when BASIC was first compiled on a college mainframe, the `PRINT` command was the language's only instruction for direct visual output. `PRINT` did all the display work for BASIC, back before the advent of point-addressable graphics. On many systems, the only display device for the computer was the printer.

Imagine an old Digital Equipment DECwriter. This was, for the most part, an oversized typewriter on stilts; it did include a full typewriter keyboard. For many terminal systems, the DECwriter was the input/output device. For this reason, the `PRINT` command in BASIC and the WRITE command in FORTRAN developed a typewriter-like mode of operation, keeping track of such things as carriage position, tab stops, and line feeds. A carriage return was—and still is—a character in the ASCII code.

Example

Text appearing within graphic objects used as controls is set using the `.Caption` property.

VB/DOS maintains three categories of objects, which are distinguished from each other by their capability to receive text. The first category is a graphic object to be used specifically as a control. Text is assigned to such control devices by setting their `.Caption` properties as equivalent to that text, as in the following instruction:

```
Command1.Caption = "Cancel"
```

The user cannot edit on-screen the text that is assigned as a `.Caption`.

Example

Text appearing within text boxes is set using the `.Text` property.

The second category of text-receiving object is the text box, which is generally used as an explicitly marked area or field for the entry or display of text. Text is assigned to this category by setting its `.Text` property equivalent to that text. Conversely, text can be acquired from a text box by assigning its `.Text` property to a string variable, as in the following instruction:

```
name$ = Surname.Text
```

The primary difference between the operation of a text box and a captioned control is that the text box is a *receptacle* for user-entered text, thus making text exchange within the source code a two-way process. Text is acquired from a text box as easily as it can be assigned to it, by merely reversing the order of items in the equation. The type of object that can take advantage of the `.PRINT` method—the third type of text-receiving object—can best be thought of as a terminal, like the old DECwriter. In essence, each time you create a new form or picture box, you're creating for all intents and purposes a new terminal.

The various delimiters used in the PRINT instruction can be considered directives to this virtual terminal to move the "printhead" in some way. The following example shows a statement that could be used in the event of a benchmark program "erroring out":

```
Scorecard.PRINT "Your final score is";scor,
  "Highest score :";hiscor;"."
```

The semicolons here have the interpreter print the value of the stated variables beside the text. Because these are values, the interpreter knows to add spaces between the text and values, so it isn't necessary here to include an extra space within the quotation marks. The comma after each literal expression (text appearing within quotation marks) has the interpreter "press Tab"—tabulate to the next tab stop on the line.

Another way to space elements of text from each other is through the use of functions. Two functions for this purpose appear in the following sections.

TAB() **Function**

Syntax:

`TAB(column%)`

The `TAB()` function is used to move the text cursor to the specified *column%*. The width of a column is equivalent to the width of a character.

SPC() **Function**

Syntax:

`SPC(spaces%)`

The `SPC()` function is used to move the text cursor a specified number of *spaces%* to the right. A space is equivalent in width to any other character.

> **NOTE:** Although `TAB()` and `SPC()` are officially considered functions, they bend the laws of BASIC syntax for functions in an instruction. For instance, you cannot say `"a% = TAB(5)"` because `TAB()` is not a function that returns a value to a numeral variable. You also cannot state `"a$ = TAB(5)"` because `TAB()` does not actually substitute for string contents in an expression. Instead, both `TAB()` and `SPC()` act as directives, telling the interpreter to move the cursor to a specified column or a certain number of spaces to the right, respectively. The two functions can appear in a `PRINT` instruction as substitutes for characters.

Example

The difference between the `TAB()` function and the `SPC()` function becomes evident when you substitute one for the other. Here are two instructions containing text to be printed within the same text box. Figure 35.1 shows the results of the following instructions:

```
Form1.PRINT "Schorr"; TAB(45); "Daniel"
Form1.PRINT "Schorr"; SPC(45); "Daniel"
```

In Figure 35.1, the `TAB()` function is moving the cursor to location 45 on the screen—which is always at the same point, no matter what you print. Meanwhile, the `SPC()` function is counting one, two, three... up to 45 spaces to the right of the last character printed—which in this case was the final *r*.

One more terminal-control command from the old days making its appearance as an VB/DOS method is `.CLS`.

.CLS — **Method**
CLS — **Statement**

Syntax:

```
[Object.]CLS
```

The `CLS` instruction clears the specified graphic object of any printed or plotted contents, textual or graphic. If forms are active on-screen and *Object.* is not specified, the textual contents of the form within which the `CLS` instruction appears are cleared. Graphic objects within that form remain where they are, however, and retain their contents. If forms are not active or if a graphic screen is active, `CLS` will clear the entire screen of its contents.

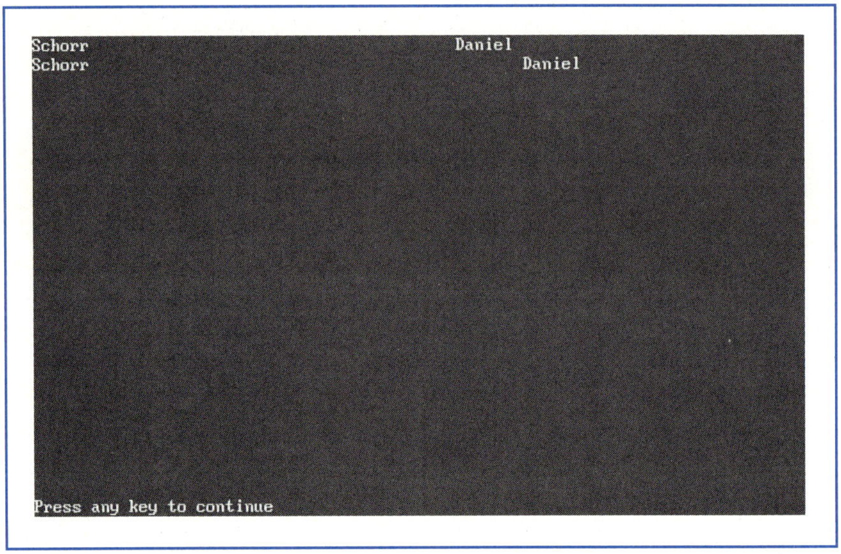

Figure 35.1. Daniel Schorr. You've seen him tabulated. Now see him spaced out.

Example

Nothing can be simpler than clearing the contents of a picture box:

```
Picture1.CLS
```

Gobbledygook Made Logical

As mentioned earlier in this chapter, Microsoft has developed a text descriptor language for describing the appearance, display, or printing format of an element of text. Naturally, for almost every Microsoft language and application that uses the descriptor system, Microsoft has managed to make subtle variations. For the most part, the VB/DOS language borrows its descriptor system from earlier versions of QuickBasic. Two VB/DOS instructions utilize this descriptor system: `FORMAT$()` and `PRINT USING`.

`FORMAT$()` **Function**

Syntax:

```
string$ = FORMAT$(expression[, descriptor$])
```

The `FORMAT$()` function converts the logically reduced value of the stated *`expression`* to an alphanumeric string, in the same manner as the `STR$()` function. In this instruction, *`descriptor$`* is a sequence of characters placed between quotation marks or a string variable that contains this sequence. The individual characters in the sequence are directives to the interpreter specifying how the individual characters comprising the specified *`expression`* will appear. If *`descriptor$`* is not specified, the `FORMAT$()` function stops here. Otherwise, it applies an appearance format—described using Microsoft's number format descriptor code—as the format for this value. If *`descriptor$`* is to be written out, it must appear within quotation marks. If it is not to be written out, the descriptor can be assigned to a string variable in advance, using an equation.

PRINT USING **Statement**
.PRINT USING **Method**

Syntax:

```
[Object.]PRINT USING descriptor$; [expression1{;¦,}
 expression2{;¦,} . . . expressionn[{;¦,}]
```

where *descriptor$* is a validly interpretable sequence of characters or a string variable representing such a sequence. Each character of *descriptor$* directs the interpreter as to the manner in which the individual characters comprising the logically reduced value of the stated expressions appear.

The PRINT USING instruction displays the logically reduced values of each numeral expression in the list, in the format specified by *descriptor$*. The method and statement syntaxes of the instruction follow those of the PRINT instruction primarily although each expression stated must have a numeral value or must be logically reducible to a numeral value.

Examples

Several characters act as number formatters in Microsoft's code. Instead of listing them all like some programmer's manual-rewriting service, I show you examples of some of these format descriptors in action, using the VB/DOS CLI as a guide.

```
number=12.95
text$=format$(number, "0000.00")
print text$
0012.95
```

Each zero within the descriptor saves an absolute place in the text string for a digit, whether a value exists for the place of that digit. The preceding descriptor definitely displays a four-digit whole-number, two-digit fractional-number value. The period in the descriptor reserves the place for the decimal point.

```
text$=format$(number, "####.##")
print text$
12.95
```

The use of the pound sign (#) within a descriptor holds a place for a digit in the converted text, unless no value exists for that digit.

```
text$=format$(number, "$####.##")
print text$
$12.95
```

A dollar sign within the descriptor places a dollar sign within the text at that place.

```
text$=format$(number, "*******$#######.##")
print text$
*******$12.95
```

You can use asterisks and other symbolic characters as leading or trailing characters within a descriptor.

```
text$=format$(number, "###%")
print text$
1295%
text$=format$(number,"###.##%")
print text$
1295.%
```

The percentage sign used in a descriptor places a percentage sign within the converted text. However, the value before the percentage sign is then multiplied by 100.

```
number=1563534
text$=format$(number, "###,###,###,###")
?text$
1,563,534
```

You can use commas as delimiters for every thousandth place in a base 10 value.

```
number=157
text$=format$(number, "-####")
?text$
#157
```

The underscore character is used here to identify a lead-in character—in this case a pound sign, which is also used to hold a digit place. The underscore signifies that the character to follow it is to be treated as a character to be printed. Dates and times can be combined on the same line using this underscore, even though the punctuation for some formats of dates and times is often used as part of the descriptor language.

Example

```
number=-15.5
?format$(number, "##.##;(##.##)")
(15.5)
```

The semicolon is used here to separate the format for negative values from the format for positive values. Here you're telling the interpreter to display negative values within parentheses.

Example

```
fmt$="##.##;(##.##);"+CHR$(34)+"Zero"+CHR$(34)
?fmt$
##.##;(##.##);"Zero"
number=0
?format$(number,fmt$)
Zero
```

This final example is perhaps a bit confusing. The format descriptor language conceived by Microsoft allows you to display any textual string within the descriptor, as long as that text is enclosed in quotation marks. However, quotation marks cannot be assigned as part of a string using the normal equation because in VB/DOS an equation used to assign text requires that text to be placed in quotation marks. Therefore, you can only use the function `CHR$(34)` to assign a quotation mark as part of a string. In the preceding example, the concatenation is assigned to `fmt$`.

The second semicolon in the descriptor is used for specifying the appearance format for a zero value. In this case, the descriptor string `fmt$` contains the text string "Zero." Now the `FORMAT$()` function spells out `Zero` whenever the value is zero. Otherwise, the value appears in accountants' format.

Summary

The `PRINT` instruction manifests itself in VB/DOS not only as a statement but as a method, which dispatches text to a specific graphic object or output device. The `.PRINT` method can print multiple items in sequence, separated by delimiters having functions that were derived from the earliest use of the `PRINT` command in old BASIC for TTY terminals.

VB/DOS maintains three categories of text-receiving graphic objects. The first is the command control object, which receives its text by assignment to the property `.Caption`. The second is the interactive text box, which receives its text by assignment to the property `.Text`. The third is the virtual terminal, which is the conventional primary output area for textual processes and interaction. This area receives its text from the `.PRINT` method. Virtual terminal display areas are handled as if they were display typewriter pages with carriage returns and tab stops.

Microsoft uses a format descriptor code for describing the textual appearance of numbers and values. A measure of this code is supported by VB/DOS through the `FORMAT$()` function.

Review Questions

Answers to Review Questions appear in Appendix B.

What `FORMAT$()` descriptor could be used to display the following text, given the values listed:

1. `value = .15, text$ = "15%"`
2. `value = 365.5, text$ = "****365.50"`

3. *value* = Now, *text$* = "5 PM"

4. *value* = 0, *text$* = "Unchanged"

5. *value* = Now, *text$* = "by 8:00 PM tonight at the earliest."

Part VII

The Screen

36

Textual Properties

In this chapter, you briefly examine the properties of text that belong to graphic objects. You then further investigate the notion of the *virtual cursor* that accompanies all objects that the Visual Basic for MS-DOS interpreter sees as *virtual terminals.* Finally, you experiment with two methods for judging how much space the text to be printed will consume within a graphic object.

The Ten-Minute Text Editor

Now that you're more than halfway through this book, chances are that you've played with running text boxes on-screen once or twice. Perhaps you've noticed how efficiently the cursor operates within active text boxes. You can reposition the cursor using the mouse pointer, indicate large segments of text and delete them with the Delete key, and generally do much of the fiddling with text that you might find yourself doing with a word processor. Yet your VB/DOS source code contains no instructions for making the cursor indicate text segments nor any event procedures awaiting a tap of the Delete key.

No computer programs are magic, and absolutely nothing happens in a computer without properly phrased instructions beforehand—nothing besides a power spike. Your compiled VB/DOS applications containing text boxes definitely do contain instructions to the CPU as to how to manipulate text. To the computer, those instructions appear no different than the compiled form of the instructions you actually write yourself.

With earlier editions of Microsoft BASIC, programmers found ways to integrate code packages, such as ready-to-roll text boxes, into their compiled programs. The source code for these packages might have been in C or even assembly language. If they were written in a proper format, they could be included—using the `$INCLUDE` metacommand—as libraries at the front of the source code, or linked to the program at compile time using the Microsoft Link utility (a copy of which is shipped with VB/DOS). Enterprising developers made some of these libraries available for sale on the open market, so BASIC programmers who weren't too proficient in C or assembly could make ten-minute text editors on the fly. The BASIC programmer would have to make explicit instructions to the compiler to include these libraries, but as long as she knew how to phrase these instructions, she could concentrate her programming efforts more on her personal embellishments to the text editor, such as search and replace, or underlining and boldfacing.

When you drag a text box element onto a form under construction using Form Designer, you're actually instructing the VB/DOS Compiler (in advance) to include a library along with your compiled code that makes this editable text box work. You don't have to concoct any peculiar phraseology or edit any cryptic "make file"; you simply make an implicit instruction to the VB/DOS system. The trend in application development is currently making more and more commands implicit, making the program configure all the crude and unusual-looking details on the part of the user or programmer. This leaves that person with only a simple click-and-drag operation, a menu selection, or some other simple event that starts the detail configuration process automatically.

In this chapter, you see a couple of user commands added to a simple text box form, which starts this form on its way to becoming a real, usable application. Figure 36.1 shows the graphical platform you'll be using for now.

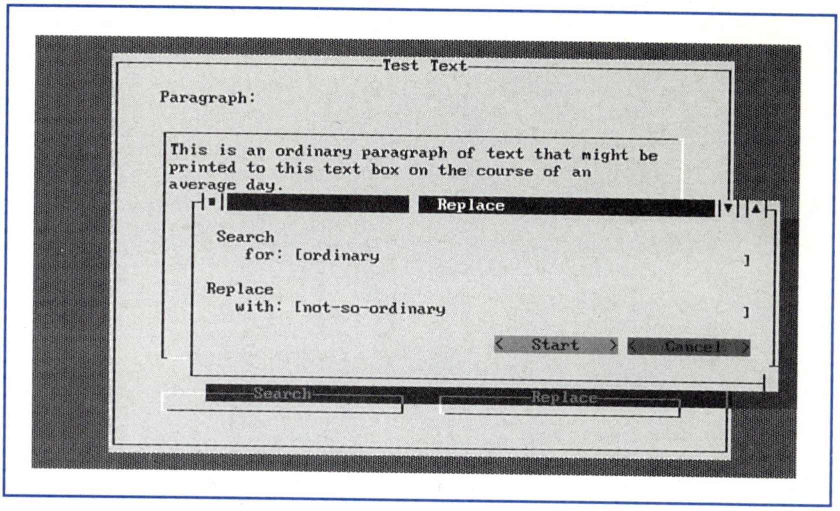

Figure 36.1. Just add buttons. No need to microwave.

Text Editor Framework

Project name: TESTTEST.MAK
Constituent files: TESTTEXT.FRM, SEARCHER.FRM, SRCHRPLC.FRM

TESTTEXT.FRM

Object Type	*Property*	*Setting*
Form	`.Width`	`65`
	`.Height`	`23`
	`.FormName`	`TestText`
Text box	`.Left`	`4`
	`.Top`	`3`
	`.Width`	`55`
	`.Height`	`14`
	`.CtlName`	`BigTextBox`
	`.Text`	(blank)
	`.BackColor`	`15 - Bright White`

continues

Object Type	*Property*	*Setting*
Button	.Left	4
	.Top	18
	.Width	26
	.Height	2
	.CtlName	Search
	.Caption	Search
Button	.Left	33
	.Top	18
	.Width	26
	.Height	2
	.CtlName	Replace
	.Caption	Replace
Label	.Left	4
	.Top	1
	.Width	10
	.Height	1
	.Caption	Paragraph:
	.Alignment	0 - Left
SEARCHER.FRM		
Form	.Width	62
	.Height	8
	.FormName	Searcher
Text box	.Left	10
	.Top	2
	.Width	48
	.Height	1
	.CtlName	SearchText
	.Text	(blank)
Button	.Left	31
	.Top	4
	.Width	13
	.Height	1
	.CtlName	Start
	.Caption	Start
	.BackColor	10 - Bright Green
	.Default	True

Object Type	*Property*	*Setting*
Button	.Left	45
	.Top	4
	.Width	13
	.Height	1
	.CtlName	Cancel
	.Caption	Cancel
	.BackColor	12 - Bright Red
	.Cancel	True
Label	.Left	1
	.Top	1
	.Width	8
	.Height	2
	.Caption	Search for:
	.Alignment	1 - Right Justified
SRCHRPLC.FRM		
Form	.Width	62
	.Height	11
	.FormName	Replacer
Text box	.Left	10
	.Top	2
	.Width	48
	.Height	1
	.CtlName	SearchText
	.Text	(blank)
	.BackColor	15 - Bright White
Text box	.Left	10
	.Top	5
	.Width	48
	.Height	1
	.CtlName	ReplaceText
	.Text	(blank)
	.BackColor	15 - Bright White
Button	.Left	31
	.Top	4
	.Width	13

continues

Object Type	*Property*	*Setting*
	.Height	1
	.CtlName	Start
	.Caption	Start
	.BackColor	10 - Bright Green
	.Default	True
Button	.Left	45
	.Top	4
	.Width	13
	.Height	1
	.CtlName	Cancel
	.Caption	Cancel
	.BackColor	12 - Bright Red
	.Cancel	True
Label	.Left	1
	.Top	1
	.Width	8
	.Height	2
	.Caption	Search for:
	.Alignment	1 - Right Justified
Label	.Left	1
	.Top	4
	.Width	8
	.Height	2
	.Caption	Replace with:
	.Alignment	1 - Right Justified

TESTTEXT.FRM
Startup Form

```
SUB Form_Load ()
LOAD Searcher
LOAD Replacer
END SUB
```

As is becoming customary, the `SUB Form_Load ()` procedure of the startup form loads the other forms to be used in the application by their `.CtlName`.

```
SUB Search_Click ()
Searcher.SHOW
END SUB

SUB Replace_Click ()
Replacer.SHOW
END SUB
```

These procedures are the only two other procedures in the entire form. They activate their respective subservient forms once the buttons are clicked.

SEARCHER.FRM

```
SUB Cancel_Click ()
Searcher.HIDE
END SUB
```

On the flip side, clicking `Cancel` takes this form off the screen.

```
SUB Start_Click ()
srch$ = SearchText.Text
IF LEN(srch$) = 0 THEN
    Searcher.HIDE
    EXIT SUB
END IF
trgt$ = TestText.BigTextBox.Text
pst = INSTR(trgt$, srch$)
IF pst = 0 THEN
    MSGBOX "Text not found.", 0, ""
    EXIT SUB
END IF
TestText.BigTextBox.SelStart = pst - 1
TestText.BigTextBox.SelLength = LEN(srch$)
found$ = TestText.BigTextBox.SelText
Searcher.HIDE
```

```
MSGBOX "Search string '" + found$ + "' found at position"
   + STR$(pst) + "."
END SUB
```

To better determine what's going on, here's the previous procedure written as pseudocode:

Procedure for clicking on the Start button:
Place the contents of the text to search for into a string variable.
If there's really nothing in this string, then
On second thought, get rid of this form and exit this procedure.
End of condition.
Place the contents of the text to search through into another string variable called the "target."
Find the position of the search text in the target text and make that a variable in and of itself.
If the attempt to find the search text in the target text turns up nothing, then
Tell the user the text isn't there and exit the procedure.
End of condition.
Otherwise, place the selector at the beginning of the text that is found,
Have the selector indicate the next number of characters to the right as in the search text string.
Place the indicated text in a string variable.
Take the search form off the screen.
Tell the user this text is found and where.
End of procedure.

The VB/DOS interpreter maintains an internal location of a cursor for a text box object at all times. In the previous procedure, the location of this cursor can be addressed with respect to the index of the specific character that currently resides to its right. You can set the cursor's location by assigning an index to it, and then use it to select and extract a region of text with property settings.

Combo.SelStart and *Text*.SelStart Properties

The .SelStart property is set to a value that designates where the cursor appears within the text in a text box. This is where extraction from this body of text begins. Each character of text within the box has its own index number, starting with character 1 at the beginning of the text. Setting the value of .SelStart places the cursor to the right of the indexed character; setting it to 0 places it at the beginning of the text. The cursor position is also referred to as the *insertion point.*

Combo.SelLength and *Text*.SelLength Properties

The .SelLength property is set to the number of characters being extracted to the right of the cursor position .SelStart. This text "selection" is normally invisible to the user at runtime.

Object.SelText and *Text*.SelText Properties

The .SelText property is set to the contents of the text being extracted from the text box. This text does not appear indicated on-screen as if the user marked this text with the mouse; the extraction process is invisible to the user. Setting the .SelStart and .SelLength properties of a text box automatically sets the .SelText property to the characters starting at position .SelStart and extending for .SelLength characters.

The text indication process using .SelStart and .SelEnd is not displayed on the screen.

Now take a look at how the previous procedure is modified to make room for replacing the text that is found with text from someplace else.

SRCHRPLC.FRM

```
SUB Start_Click ()
srch$ = SearchText.Text
rplc$ = ReplaceText.Text
IF LEN(srch$) = 0 OR LEN(rplc$) = 0 THEN
    Replacer.HIDE
    EXIT SUB
END IF
trgt$ = TestText.BigTextBox.Text
pst = INSTR(trgt$, srch$)
IF pst = 0 THEN
    MSGBOX "Text not found.", 0, ""
    EXIT SUB
END IF
TestText.BigTextBox.SelStart = pst - 1
TestText.BigTextBox.SelLength = LEN(srch$)
TestText.BigTextBox.SelText = rplc$
Replacer.HIDE
END SUB
```

You only needed to add two lines to modify the procedure: First, you placed the text to insert into the box in variable `rplc$`, second, rather than have a message box tell the user where the text is, an expression places the contents of `rplc$` into the text directly. After the values of `.SelStart` and `.SelLength` have been set, the contents of the `.SelText` property automatically are set to the indicated text in the text box. Resetting the `.SelText` property by way of a simple expression of assignment `TestText.BigTextBox.SelText = rplc$` acts automatically in the reverse, not only to set the property but the contents of the text box as well.

```
SUB Cancel_Click ()
Replacer.HIDE
END SUB
```

By now, you probably don't need pseudocode to comprehend the type of the preceding procedure.

Throughout the property listings in this chapter, as well as throughout this book, you've probably seen references to the `.Alignment` property, which is described in the following section.

Label.Alignment Property

The `.Alignment` property for a label is set to an integer that describes how the text within that label is aligned. The property can be set to any of the following values:

0	Left justification (default)
1	Right justification
2	Centered

Can We Get a Picture?

You have probably wondered what the purpose is of the VB/DOS picture box control, knowing that while the VB/DOS forms screen is active, the system cannot display graphics. Frankly, the concept of the VB/DOS picture box is confusing from my angle as well, yet perhaps I can shed some light—dim though it might be—on the subject.

VB/DOS acquires its forms and windows concepts from Visual Basic for Windows. In VBWin, a picture box is a graphic element that can display both text and graphics. You can have a method called `.LOADPICTURE` bring a picture into a picture box and then use that picture as a backdrop for text to be brought into the picture box using the `.PRINT` method.

For VB/DOS applications to be, for the most part, compatible with VBWin applications being translated using the Form Translator program included in the VB/DOS package, the Form Designer had to maintain some semblance of VBWin's picture box control, regardless of whether it could display a picture. (At the time of this writing, some Microsoft documentation states you can, in essence, draw a picture within a VB/DOS picture box by printing characters that form a collective image.)

The VB/DOS picture box provides a certain level of control over the text being placed within it that a standard text box does not provide. Text in a text box is considered by the VB/DOS interpreter to be written out in one long string, just broken up in places and wrapped around. Text in a VB/DOS picture box has height and width. If you want to display a table or a list of data entries in columns, therefore, you can use the `TAB()` function within a `.PRINT` method to make the proper spacing between columns. You also can have the interpreter move the cursor within the picture box both vertically and horizontally, using statements borrowed from earlier versions of Microsoft BASIC.

Suppose you want to make sure the text you print to a picture box fits within that box. If you were using a text box, you could simply find the number of characters it could hold by multiplying its `.Width` by its `.Height`. If the `LEN()` (length) of the text goes beyond the total, perhaps the text string could be truncated.

The same formula works for a picture box; however, VB/DOS provides two methods for discerning the width and height of text to be printed to a picture box, form, or to the printer before it is printed there.

Object.TEXTHEIGHT and *Object*.TEXTWIDTH — Methods

Syntax:

```
value% = [Object.]TEXTHEIGHT(string$)
value% = [Object.]TEXTWIDTH(string$)
```

The `.TEXTHEIGHT` and `.TEXTWIDTH` methods are invoked to some extent like functions, although they are expressed using object-oriented syntax. These methods return the predicted height and width in characters, respectively, of the text expressed in *`string$`* as it might appear within the specified *`Object.`* when it is printed there using the `.PRINT` method. These values are returned within the integer *`value%`* as if the methods were functions. These methods work only with virtual terminal objects such as a picture box or form, or the printer device. If *`Object.`* is not specified, the form containing the currently executing procedure is assumed.

In much the same way the interpreter maintains a `.SelStart` property containing the cursor position for a text box, two properties are maintained for a form or picture box containing the current cursor coordinates: `CurrentX` and `CurrentY`.

Object.CurrentX, *Printer*.CurrentX, *Object*.CurrentY, and *Printer*.CurrentY Properties

The `.CurrentX` and `.CurrentY` properties for a virtual terminal graphic object are set by the current coordinates of the cursor for that object. By default, these coordinates are expressed graphically as characters, unless the `.ScaleMode` property for the object is set otherwise. The settings for these properties are relative to the current coordinate scale for the graphic object or device.

Each time a `.PRINT` method is invoked, the `.CurrentX` property for the object receiving the text is increased by a certain number of characters (or whatever units are in use at the time). At the end of the `.PRINT` instruction, assuming no trailing delimiters appear at the end, the cursor moves to the next line, thus increasing the `.CurrentY` property of the object. By default, the `.CurrentX` property is then reset to 0.

You'll be using these new methods and properties in the chapters that follow.

Summary

The position of the cursor among text appearing within a text box can be set using the `.SelStart` property. If text is to be extracted from this cursor position forward, the number of characters to be extracted can be expressed as the `.SelLength` property. The extracted text thus becomes the `.SelText` property.

The predicted character width and height of text to be printed within a form or picture box, or to the printer, can be obtained using the `.TEXTWIDTH` and `.TEXTHEIGHT` methods, respectively. These methods are expressed within an equation almost in the manner of functions although with object-oriented syntax. The current cursor coordinates within a virtual terminal object are accessible through the `.CurrentX` and `.CurrentY` properties.

Review Questions

Answers to Review Questions appear in Appendix B.

1. Why are there no `.CurrentX` or `.CurrentY` properties for a standard text box?
2. Suppose you set the `.SelStart` property to any positive number and then set the `.SelLength` property to any positive number. What would describe the current contents of the `.SelText` property?

37

Bitmapped Plotting

In this chapter, you learn how to draw graphic images directly on the non-*form*-al DOS screen using the Visual Basic for MS-DOS plotting mechanism. You'll study the concepts of pens and palettes, and see some of the more rudimentary methods for windowing using a DOS graphics screen. You'll also study the origins and development of the screen coordinate system.

PreSCREENing

I've made much of the fact (perhaps too much) that VB/DOS's "graphical" controls reside in the DOS character-mode screen only. To this point, you've been using the "form screen"—what VB/DOS calls `SCREEN 0`—primarily because it's easier to get results with forms than it is with a blank screen.

VB/DOS's bitmapped graphics system requires that the application not be showing any forms on-screen. This doesn't mean a program that uses bitmaps can't use forms as well, just as long as both systems aren't addressed at the same time. The `SCREEN` statement from the depths of Microsoft BASIC's etymology helps maintain the permanent barrier between the two systems.

SCREEN **Statement**

Syntax:

```
SCREEN mode%[, comp_color%][, active_page%]
 [, visible_page%]
```

The SCREEN statement is used to switch graphics modes and resolutions from one system of translation to another. It also may be used to designate which *page* or region of memory will act as the receiver for graphics instructions. The graphics resolutions supported by VB/DOS are listed in Table 37.1.

Table 37.1. Accepted SCREEN address modes.

SCREEN mode	*Graphics array type*	*Text grid*	*Pixel resolution*	*Registers/ palette*
0	Textual	80x25 (VGA)		64/16
1	CGA	40x25	320x200	4/16
2	CGA	80x25	640x200	2/2
2	EGA	80x25	640x200	2/16
3	Hercules	80x25	720x348	2/16 grays
4	AT&T/Olivetti	80x25	640x400	16/16 grays
7	EGA	40x25	320x200	16/16
8	EGA	80x25	640x200	16/16
9	EGA	80x25	640x350	16/64
10	VGA Mono	80x25	640x350	4/9 grays
11	VGA	80x30	640x480	2/262,144
12	VGA	80x30	640x480	16/262,144
13	VGA (MCGA)	40x25	320x200	256/262,144

The listings in the table represent the standard operating resolution and array for the supported screen modes.

The specification `comp_color%` is reserved for `SCREEN 0` text mode, or for `SCREEN 1` systems that use CGA adaptors and composite, rather than RGB, monitors. EGA and VGA arrays use RGB monitors. A `comp_color%` setting of 0 on most such systems disables color output; some CGA hardware may behave differently. For all other graphics arrays, the setting should be left blank. A comma set by itself following the `mode%` setting forces the interpreter to ignore this setting when necessary, as in `SCREEN 3, , 0, 1`.

The `active_page%` and `visible_page%` settings, when stated, direct future graphics instructions to particular regions of memory or *pages* containing graphics data. Only one such region, called the *visible page*, represents the current contents of the screen. Various *active pages* may represent graphical contents that are currently invisible until made visible using the `SCREEN` statement. Each page in memory is given an integral number. The number of pages available in a system depends upon the graphics array being used by the computer and the amount of system or video memory available to it. Setting the `active_page%` directs all future graphics statements to the stated page in memory. Setting the `visible_page%` directs the interpreter to make the stated page visible. If graphical data was previously sent to the stated page, that data is immediately displayed without your having to wait for slow draws or pattern fills. Setting the `active_page%` and the `visible_page%` to the same page causes graphics instructions to be sent directly to the screen, which is where they are sent by default.

Example

Here is a "screen test" program I devised that takes you (if you have a standard VGA system) on a tour of the various color screen modes:

```
DATA 1,16,2,2,7,16,8,16,9,64,10,9,11,256,12,256,13,256
DO
    READ mode, maxcolors
    SCREEN mode
    LOCATE 25, 1
```

```
    PRINT "Graphics mode"; mode
    FOR linecolor = 0 TO 320
       LINE (0, linecolor)-(320, linecolor), linecolor
         MOD maxcolors
    NEXT linecolor
stpr:
IF INKEY$ = "" THEN GOTO stpr
LOOP UNTIL mode = 13
```

Here's the preceding routine written as pseudocode:

Here's a list of screen modes and the number of color registers per mode, rendered as pairs.
Beginning of loop:
  Read a pair of modes and register maximums from the above list.
  Set the screen resolution to the mode just read.
  Place the text cursor on the 25th row, one column to the right of the left edge.
  Print the current graphics mode.
  Start counting from 0 to 320 and call it the current line color.
    Draw a horizontal line from x pixel 0 to x pixel 320 and give that line the current line color. If the color count is higher than the maximum read, then "wrap it around" to the lowest register using modulo arithmetic.
  Count the next color.
Mark this line "stpr."
If the user has not pressed a key, then reexecute the above line.
Continue executing this loop until the mode number read is 13.

The preceding routine is precisely that, a *routine*. Notice the lack of procedural boundaries that generally accompany an example of this size. The instructions that handle bitmapped graphics are expressed using conventional BASIC syntax, not object-oriented syntax. The flavor of the language changes, almost the way an author uses oft-archaic words the more romantic he tends to be feeling at the time. Notice also the old-style routine exit that makes an informal loop with the INKEY$ statement between two instructions until the user presses a key, releasing the program from the loop. You'll learn more about such old-though-not-forgotten techniques later, but this point is important now: Conventional BASIC instructions are not event-driven, so once the conventional process is set forth, once an instruction is executed, the interpreter without hesitation finds the next instruction and executes it. There's no END SUB that places the system in limbo, awaiting the next event.

Graphics Arrays

Back to the subject of graphics arrays: If you've studied plane geometry, you've probably been introduced to the Cartesian coordinate system of René Descartes. In the system, each point in "space" is represented by a pair of coordinates. All points in a bitmap are addressed in a similar manner. Figure 37.1 demonstrates the general scheme of the theoretical BASIC coordinate system.

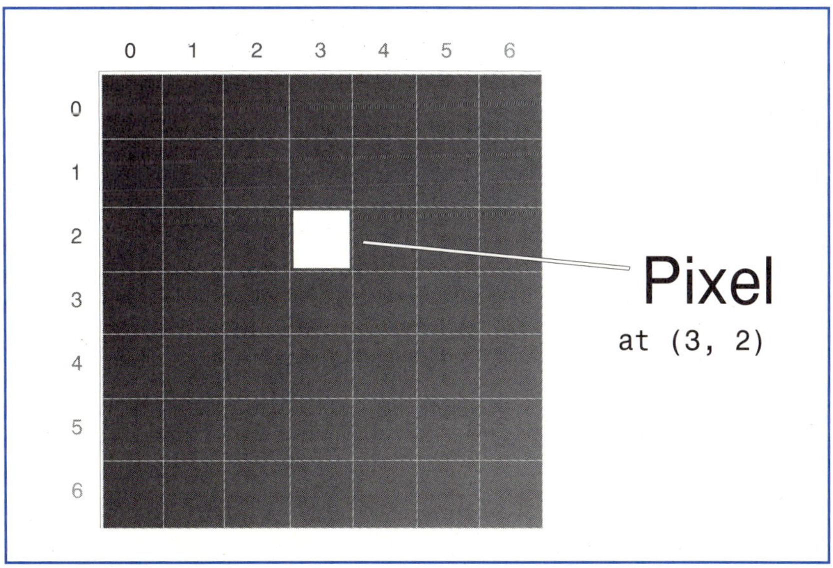

Figure 37.1. Descartes meets Microsoft.

In all graphical computers, each unit in the coordinate system is represented in memory by a certain number of bits. Usually, the combination of bits for a pixel represents, using binary coding, the color of the pixel at that point. This is true for most VGA graphics systems. Memory within these systems is specially apportioned for the VGA card itself so that the motherboard's main memory can be used for other purposes. In VB/DOS, as with every graphical computer devised to date, when you plot a point of a particular color to a specified location, you change the bitwise pattern of the portion of memory that corresponds to that point. The new pattern then represents the new color of that point.

The Video Graphics Array (VGA) is not really a piece of hardware but a theory, a method for interpreting data in memory. If you studied the SCREEN modes in Table 37.1, you may have noticed the mathematical proportions between the screen resolution of a mode and the number of color registers for that mode. A 320x200 screen may have 256 color registers available to it, but double the resolution to 640x400 (multiply both axes by 2) and the number of registers available is reduced by a factor of 16. Reason: Remember Chapter 10, "Number Systems," which covered the binary numeral system. The number 256 is equal to 28. It takes eight bits, therefore, to represent in binary a number that can range to 255. In a 256-color graphics array, therefore, eight bits are required to represent one pixel in memory.

Now increase the resolution; multiply the number of pixels being represented horizontally by 2 (a two-bit number) and the number of pixels being represented vertically by 2 (a two-bit number). If the *page* that represents the screen in memory is to maintain its identity, it must maintain its *size*. If you increase the number of pixels being represented by a factor of four, the number of color registers available must be reduced by a four-bit number. Four bits taken away from 28 leaves 24, or 16 registers per pixel.

Table 37.2, for the sake of reference, describes the first 16 colors in any system of representation from EGA to VGA.

Table 37.2. QuickBASIC and RGB color conversion chart.

Color value	*QB Color*	*RGB functional representation*
0	Black	`RGB(0, 0, 0)`
1	Blue	`RGB(0, 0, 191)`
2	Green	`RGB(0, 191, 0)`
3	Dark Cyan	`RGB(0, 191, 191)`
4	Red	`RGB(191, 0, 0)`
5	Magenta	`RGB(191, 0, 191)`
6	Dark Yellow	`RGB(191, 191, 0)`
7	Page White	`RGB(191, 191, 191)`
8	Gray	`RGB(64, 64, 64)`
9	Bright Blue	`RGB(0, 0, 255)`
10	Bright Green	`RGB(0, 255, 0)`
11	Bright Cyan	`RGB(0, 255, 255)`
12	Bright Red	`RGB(255, 0, 0)`
13	Bright Magenta	`RGB(255, 0, 255)`
14	Bright Yellow	`RGB(255, 255, 0)`
15	Bright White	`RGB(255, 255, 255)`

In most computer systems, plotting or *setting* a point to a certain color changes the bitwise value of the location in memory that corresponds directly to the specified point. This setting in memory is what changes the color of the pixel on-screen.

PSET **Statement**

Syntax:

```
PSET [STEP](pixelx!, pixely!)[, color%]
```

The PSET statement sets the color value of a coordinate point on-screen represented by the coordinates (*pixelx!*, *pixely!*). If *color%* is specified, PSET sets the color value of the point to any of the standard color registers supported by the current SCREEN resolution mode. If *color%* is not specified, PSET sets the point's color value to the last value specified by the COLOR statement.

If STEP is included in the method, the coordinates expressed by (*pixelx!*, *pixely!*) are considered by the VB/DOS interpreter to be relative to the last point plotted, or to (0, 0) if no point has been plotted previously. The last point plotted within a graphic object can be obtained using the POINT() function.

Example

Here's a routine that plots a dotted diagonal line to the screen:

```
FOR plt = 0 TO 50 STEP 5
    PSET (plt, plt)
NEXT plt
```

There are 11 dots in this line because the interpreter counts from 0 to 50 by fives, starting with 0. The value of variable plt represents both the x- and y-axis values for the PSET statement. For each iteration of the loop clause, the plot point is spaced as many pixels down as to the right. Pixels may not necessarily be square, depending upon which SCREEN resolution you're using and furthermore upon the specifications of your graphics hardware and running drivers. In other words, a block of pixels plt wide and plt high may not necessarily appear geometrically equilateral.

Example

Suppose the diagonal dotted line is to extend from some unknown point where plotting has taken place previously. You could use the STEP extension to have the virtual pen jump to a location relative to the previous plot coordinates, as follows:

```
FOR dot = 1 TO 11
    PSET STEP (5, 5)
NEXT dot
```

This routine produces a dotted line identical in form to the one generated by the routine preceding it although its plot position starts at the point returnable as (POINT(0), POINT(1)). In other words, it starts at the last point that received a plot, or at (0, 0) if no plotting has taken place. With each iteration, the PSET method steps the "virtual pen" five spaces to the right and five spaces down. You can express 5 both times as a constant because each STEP takes place relative to the last point plotted to the screen. The method uses POINT(0) and POINT(1) (although not explicitly) as offsets for the relative coordinate system.

There is, thankfully, a more direct method for drawing a line, using the LINE statement.

LINE — Statement

Syntax:

```
LINE [[STEP](startx!, starty!)]-[STEP](endx!, endy!)
  [, color%][, B][F]
```

The LINE statement sets the color value of a linear series of all addressable pixels represented in memory extending from the coordinates (*startx!*, *starty!*) to (*endx!*, *endy!*). The two coordinate pairs are always separated by a hyphen. The color value for each pixel in the series is set regardless of whether it is visible at present.

If the first coordinate pair is omitted, the interpreter assumes the line to extend from the last plotted point to the coordinates specified by the second pair, which cannot be omitted. The hyphen remains in the method instruction, nonetheless. The last point plotted within a graphic object can be obtained using the `POINT()` function. If no points have been plotted for that object, initial coordinates of `(0, 0)` are assumed.

If `STEP` is included before the first pair of coordinates, those coordinates are assumed to be relative to the last point plotted before the instruction is executed, as represented by `POINT(0)` and `POINT(1)`. If `STEP` is included before the second pair of coordinates, those coordinates are assumed to be relative to the first pair of coordinates.

If *`color%`* is specified, the `LINE` statement sets the color values of the pixels in the series to any of the color registers supported by the current `SCREEN` resolution. If *`color%`* is not specified, the `LINE` statement sets the series' color value to the value last specified by the `COLOR` statement.

If `B` is included toward the end of the `LINE` statement, the instruction draws not just a line but a *box* with opposite corners that are expressed as the two pairs of coordinates. The box extends from point (*`startx!`*, *`starty!`*) to (*`endx!`*, *`starty!`*) to (*`endx!`*, *`endy!`*) to (*`startx!`*, *`endy!`*) and back to (*`startx!`*, *`starty!`*). Only coordinate sets 1 and 2 need to be specified. If `F` is included beside `B`, the box is filled with the color used to plot the box itself. By default, the filling color and pattern are transparent. If `B` or `BF` is included and *`color%`* is omitted, the comma used as a delimiter for *`color%`* remains, as in `,,BF`.

Example

In the screen test routine, you included this instruction:

```
LINE (0, linecolor)-(320, linecolor), linecolor
  MOD maxcolors
```

Because the y coordinates in both pairs are `linecolor`, the plotted `LINE` is perfectly horizontal.

You use the `LINE` statement whenever you want to draw a box; there is no "BOX" statement in VB/DOS although there are `BOX` statements in other versions of BASIC. In a similarly odd fashion, to draw an arc or a curved line, you invoke the `CIRCLE` statement.

CIRCLE **Statement**

Syntax:

```
CIRCLE [STEP](centerx!, centery!), radius![, color_reg%]
    [, ang_start!, ang_end!][, aspect!]
```

The `CIRCLE` method plots a series of points in a curve, all of which geometrically converge around a center point specified as `(centerx!, centery!)`. By default, these points take the form of a circle; however, by specifying the latter three optional parameters, you can plot an arc or ellipse instead.

Unless `aspect!` is specified, each point in the series is plotted at a distance of `radius!` pixels from the center coordinates. If `color_reg%` is specified, the series is plotted using the specified color register.

If `ang_start!` and `ang_end!` are specified, plotting of the circle begins at a point that forms an angle `ang_start!` radians relative to the center point and extends to a point that forms an angle `ang_end` radians relative to the center point. The radian range specifiable for these parameters is (–2 * pi) – (2 * pi). If neither parameter is specified, the curve is plotted as a closed shape, as either a circle or an ellipse. By default, the fill style for an object is transparent.

The value of `aspect!`, when specified, represents the ratio of height to width for the series, for use in plotting noncircular arcs or ellipses. A 4:1 ratio of height to width is represented as an `aspect!` of 4, which forms a tall ellipse. Conversely, a 1:4 ratio is represented as an `aspect!` of .25, which forms a squat ellipse. In cases where `aspect!` is specified, the value of `radius!` becomes, geometrically speaking, half the length of the *major axis* of the ellipse—being the widest obtainable diameter of the ellipse.

If `STEP` is included with the `CIRCLE` statement, the coordinate pair following `STEP` is interpreted as being relative to the last point plotted, or to `(0, 0)` if no point has previously been plotted.

Example

Here's an easy circle, plotted in the center of a type 13 MCGA screen:

```
SCREEN 13
CIRCLE (160, 100), 120, 15
```

Example

Sometimes graphical images are generated for no practical reason at all; perhaps out of experimentation, they just seem to show up, and you and I like them. One such example appears in Figure 37.2.

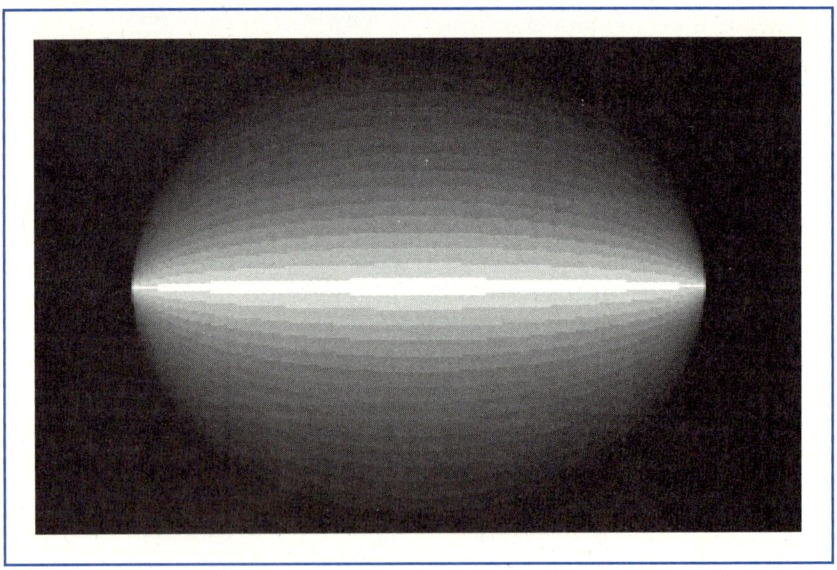

Figure 37.2. Who cares what it is; isn't it pretty?

Here's the routine used to generate the image in the figure:

```
SCREEN 13
FOR aspect = 0 TO .8 STEP .005
  CIRCLE (160, 100), 120, 47 - ((aspect * 19) + 16),
    , , aspect
```

```
NEXT aspect
stpr:
IF INKEY$ = "" THEN GOTO stpr
```

Variable aspect represents the height-to-width ratio of the ellipse being plotted. The first ellipse plotted in the sequence—the brightest one—is practically a horizontal line. As the elliptical loop continues, each ellipse shifts ever more toward darkness. The ellipse plotted at the end of the loop is, as close as possible, a perfect circle although the aspect ratio at loop's end is actually .8. A pixel is not perfectly square; it's actually a bit taller than it is wide in SCREEN 13, by a factor of about 20 percent. A true square pixel for this mode, therefore, has 80 percent the height logically as it has width—thus the .8.

The purpose for the color conversion formula 47 - ((aspect * 19) + 16) is to gradiate the color being plotted from color 47 backwards to color 32. In the MCGA 256 color palette's default settings, color settings 32-47 by default are a series of 16 gray shades from off-white to just-above black. Variable aspect can serve a dual purpose in this loop by multiplying its value by 19 to arrive at the level of gradience.

Living Color

Generally, when a specific color register is omitted from a drawing statement, the VB/DOS interpreter assumes you want to draw in the "default" color, whatever that may happen to be. You can use a few statements that may be issued beforehand to designate just what color that is.

PALETTE **Statement**

Syntax:

PALETTE *register%*, *color%*

The PALETTE statement sets the current color represented by the designated color *register%* to the stated *color%* value. The integral range of *color%* depends upon the capabilities and specifications of the computer's graphics hardware, as well as the currently active SCREEN mode.

COLOR **Statement**

Syntax 1: SCREEN mode 0

`COLOR [forecolor%][, backcolor%][, bordercolor%]`

Syntax 2: SCREEN mode 1

`COLOR [backcolor%][, palette%]`

Syntax 3: SCREEN modes 4, 12, 13

`COLOR forecolor%`

Syntax 4: SCREEN modes 7, 8, 9, 10

`COLOR [forecolor%][, backcolor%]`

The COLOR statement is used to designate the color register that will be used by the interpreter for displaying text. When *forecolor%* is stated, all text printed to the screen is displayed in the stated *forecolor%* register. When *backcolor%* is displayed, the default background color—which is ordinarily black—is changed to the stated *backcolor%* register. The color values for these registers may be set beforehand using the PALETTE statement.

The order of parameters in the COLOR statement depends upon the currently active SCREEN mode. Mode 0 allows the screen *bordercolor%* to be set. Mode 1, which is reserved for CGA four-color graphics, allows for the switching between the two standard CGA palettes, represented here as palette 0 and 1. For other screen modes, the limits of the color registers depend on the computer's graphics hardware and on the maximum number of colors supported by the current SCREEN mode.

Now that you're thoroughly confused, let me attempt to clarify all of this: The graphics hardware of EGA and VGA systems has enumerated all the colors it is capable of providing to your screen. This cornucopia of colors (on EGA systems, more like a cafeteria) is called the *palette*. Your graphics system can only display so many of the colors from this palette at one time—perhaps only 16, maybe as many as 256. Because of this limitation, your hardware maintains a list of color *registers* whose values reflect the color selections from the greater palette. The hardware has chosen from this palette in advance although you may override this choice by using the PALETTE statement to set one of the color registers to a different palette color.

The COLOR statement, by contrast, only affects certain elements of the screen graphics process. For all graphics arrays, a separate set of registers is used to denote which color register acts as the default text color and which color register acts as the default background color. Once the internal color registers have their colors selected as you want, you may then use the COLOR statement to assign one of those registers as the color for printing text. On EGA and VGA systems, COLOR refers to the register that is used for all text printing instructions *to follow*; for older graphics arrays where only one color may be used for text at a time, COLOR is used to assign the register for future as well as existing text.

Example

```
SCREEN 13
DIM colorno AS LONG
FOR rad = 100 TO 2 STEP -1
    CIRCLE (150, 100), rad, rad
    PAINT (150, 100), rad
NEXT rad
FOR colorno = 0 TO 65535 STEP 10
    FOR pal = 1 TO 255
        PALETTE pal, colorno
    NEXT pal
NEXT colorno
```

Here's pseudocode for the preceding routine:

```
Go to 320x200x256 resolution.
Make a long integer for the color palette counter.
Start counting backward from 100 to 2, by 1.
   Place a circle at mid-screen, whose radius is
     the current count value and whose color is
     also the current count value.
   Fill the circle just painted with the same color.
Count the next lowest radius value.
With all circles plotted, start counting upward from
  0 to 65,535 by 10, as a color number.
   For each count loop in progress, count from 1 to 255.
      Set the currently counted palette to the
        current color number.
   Count the next register.
Count the next color.
```

In this example, variable `rad` serves a dual purpose, counting both the circle radius and the color register used to plot the circle. You also invoked one statement thus far uncovered: `PAINT`.

PAINT — **Statement**

Syntax:

```
PAINT [STEP] (interiorx, interiory)[, {color_reg% ¦
  fill_pattern$}][, bordercolor%][, overlap_pattern$]
```

The `PAINT` statement is used to fill an enclosed area of adjacent pixels, giving them the color stored in the specified register *`color_reg%`*. If no *`bordercolor%`* is specified, these pixels consist of any group of adjacent pixels whose current color register value is equal to the value of that of point (*`interiorx`*, *`interiory`*). The paint operation is like a fountain fill, beginning at point (*`interiorx`*, *`interiory`*) and proceeding to spill color into the area until a border is reached, whether it be a pixel of another color or the screen border.

If *`color_reg%`* is specified, the color that fills the area is taken from that color register. If *`bordercolor%`* is specified, the paint process fills over all pixels whose values are *not* the specified *bordercolor%*, up until that color register is reached. Thus, a filled polygon containing other text and graphics may be filled up to the polygon's *bordercolor%*.

A *fill_pattern$* may be specified that consists of up to 64 characters, each of which represents eight bits of a bitwise pattern. This pattern may be overlaid like strips of wallpaper (for very tiny rooms) forming a repetitive pattern. A checkered pattern, for instance, can be formed by the expression `CHR$(204) + CHR$(51)`, which places the binary bit pattern 11001100 over the pattern 00110011. When specified, *overlap_pattern$* is a single-character string representing a pattern that the paint process fills over when encountered.

One way you can improve the efficiency of the previous routine is by placing the entire array of palette registers into an array variable and using a single statement to set the register values all at once.

PALETTE USING **Statement**

Syntax:

`PALETTE USING array[(start_index%)]`

The `PALETTE USING` statement sets an entire group of palette registers in sequence to the contents of the designated *array* variable. If no *start_index%* is specified, the first element of the array is assumed to apply to palette index number 0; however, if one is specified, the first element of that array applies to that index number. Thus, a *start_index%* of 1 allows the default background color (generally 0) to be left as is.

Example

Here's the modified version of the "corona generator" routine:

```
SCREEN 13
DIM colorno AS LONG
```

```
DIM parray(255) AS LONG
FOR rad = 100 TO 2 STEP -1
    CIRCLE (150, 100), rad, rad
    PAINT (150, 100), rad, rad
NEXT rad
FOR colorno = 0 TO 65535
    FOR pal = 1 TO 255
        parray(pal) = colorno + pal
    NEXT pal
    PALETTE USING parray(1)
NEXT colorno
```

The way the routine works now, the long integer array `parray()` holds a list of color values, which are assigned to it by the expression `parray(pal) = colorno + pal`. Variable pal is part of a nested loop. In VGA graphics, a color whose value is one more than another, when placed next to that other value, is just barely brighter than that value. The effect, therefore, is of a subtle gradient rather than a glaring stripe. The `PALETTE USING` statement starts seeding the palette array, starting with register number 1 and leaving the background color (black) alone.

Summary

The VB/DOS coordinate system is based on a grid of pixels. The system by which they are organized is considered a graphics array, based on a system of Cartesian geometric coordinates. The number of plottable points within each coordinate system helps determine the number of bytes in memory that will constitute the graphics array. Each region of memory reserved for such an array is called a page. The resolution and graphics translation array necessary for the current application can be chosen using the `SCREEN` statement.

The `PSET` statement is used to plot a point to a form, a picture box, or the printer. The `LINE` statement is used to plot a line or series of points; however, it can also be used to plot filled and unfilled boxes. You can draw a circle, ellipse, or unclosed arc using the `CIRCLE` statement. If starting and ending angles are specified using this method, an arc is plotted. The `PAINT` statement is used to fill a closed area, such as a `CIRCLE`, with a uniform color or pattern.

Most graphics hardware built today maintains a large list of color values called the palette. Only a certain number of these colors can be shown on-screen at any time. The color values for the registers that choose colors from this palette can be set using the `PALETTE` and `PALETTE USING` statements. You can set the default colors for text printing and some graphics operations using the `COLOR` statement.

Review Questions

Answers to Review Questions appear in Appendix B.

1. If the graphics screen has just been cleared using `CLS` and a `PAINT` statement is executed, what happens?
2. If the graphics screen has been cleared using `CLS` and a `CIRCLE` statement has just been executed, wherein *ang_start!* and *ang_end!* have been specified, then when a `PAINT` statement is executed without specifying a color, what happens?
3. Why are there so many syntaxes for the `COLOR` statement?

Review Exercise

Write a procedure that draws a circle gradually, as if it is being drawn with a compass and pen. Use the `CIRCLE` statement and specify the start and end angles of the arc being drawn. **Hint:** Use a loop clause that counts the current value of the end angle.

38

Manual Windowing

In this chapter, you study the origins and development of the screen coordinate system. You will see how such systems are manipulated, created, and even overlapped on each other. Later, you'll be introduced to the concept of "turtle graphics," a way of mimicking the movements of a plotter pen on-screen.

You Have to Draw the Line Someplace

Microcomputers of the late 1970s and early 1980s used their own fixed-screen coordinate systems so that programmers would know, in a sense, where to draw the line. The coordinate systems of the first microcomputer BASIC implementations used parameter pairs to address individual pixels or pixel blocks on-screen. The block at the upper-left corner of the screen was generally addressed as (0, 0). Because people dealt with relatively low-resolution television sets for output back then, the lower-right block was generally some value like (128, 64). Line-plotting statements such as the ones pioneered by AppleSoft BASIC utilized two pairs of these x- and y-axis coordinates as beginning and end points. More advanced BASICs utilized circle-plotting statements that used perhaps two pairs of coordinates representing the "corners" of the circle-plotting area, or one pair representing the center and a third value for the radius of the circle. BASIC interpreters were considered advanced if they could draw circles like this.

Actually, the concept of addressing points on-screen or cursor locations with parameter pairs was quite advanced for the mid-1970s because minicomputer and mainframe computer programmers generally weren't afforded such tools on their own systems. Arguably, the major advances in programming languages premiered on home computers such as the Apple II, the TRS-80, and the Atari 400/800 long before the big computer companies of today considered such innovations to have any purpose beyond the recreational.

One major reason parameter pairs were so innovative is as follows: At times, programmers wanted to plot data to just one rectangular region of the screen. On character-based minicomputers, plotting to the screen always began in the upper-left corner. The screen-plotting mechanism was as graphically complex as typing a picture of something on your portable typewriter; text and graphic blocks were "typed" to the screen. To get something to appear in the middle of the screen, like typing something in the middle of a piece of paper, the programmer had to carriage return down several lines and then tab to the right several spaces. These lines and spaces could be programmed in advance as y- and x-axis offset coordinates, respectively. The `PRINT` command could return the carriage the number of lines in the offset variable `OY`, and the `TAB()` function could space the cursor to the right for the number of spaces in the offset variable `OX`.

With home microcomputers, variables `OX` and `OY` (or variables with other names but the same purpose) could be addressed within parameter pairs as *geometric* offsets. While the environment of character-based minicomputers existed within a virtual IBM Selectric II typewriter, the environment of such pioneering graphic computers as Apple's and Atari's was Cartesian geometric space, which gave not only programmers but also mathematicians a great deal more freedom of expression. The technique they utilized was to have `OX` and `OY` serve as offset intervals from the *origin* point (0, 0). These offsets allowed for the creation of a *virtual origin* of a semi-independent plotting region of the screen. By plotting to a point such as `(75 + OX, 25 + OY)` in effect, a point `(75, 25)` virtually exists in the programmer's mind relative to this semi-independent region. The programmer could then comfortably ignore OX and OY, concentrating on the region as if it was a screen unto itself.

Perhaps you've guessed what I'm leading up to. Later interpreters, using BASIC as well as other languages, allowed for the declaration of these independent regions without the use of offset variables within the plotting statement. No one is sure who gets the credit for first naming these declarable regions *windows.*

Windows, therefore, were created as programmer conveniences and not as the ease-of-use devices that certain marketing divisions might have you believe. Face it, computers are really no easier to use today than they ever were. They are, in fact, far more complex devices than they were five years ago, although their complexity has merely become more understood by the public at large. Windows themselves have made computers more complex by introducing a new order of multiplicity to the computing environment. By having more than one of something within a computer in the first place, the computing environment is established.

The Second-Generation Window

In the original Microsoft BASIC manifestation of the "window," continued here in Visual Basic for MS-DOS, it is a portion of the entire graphics array, magnified to fill the screen or, as you shall see in the following sections, the current *viewport*. Here is how VB/DOS interprets the window.

WINDOW **Statement**

Syntax:

```
WINDOW [SCREEN] (x1%, y1%)-(x2%, y2%)
```

The WINDOW statement rescales the interpreter's logical and physical coordinate system. By default, a one-to-one correspondence exists between the image in memory and the image depicted on-screen. The upper-left corner coordinates are generally addressed as (0, 0). Following the execution of `WINDOW`, unless the term `SCREEN` is also specified along with the statement, the coordinate system is remapped so that coordinates (0, 0) refer to the lower-left corner of the screen. The `WINDOW` statement moves the view of the image in memory so that the origin coordinates (0, 0) become `(x1%, y1%)`. In the second pair of coordinates, the value of `x2%` represents the number of pixels extending from the upper-left corner coordinates of the conventional screen to the rightmost edge of the screen (leftmost if negative). The value of `y2%` represents the number of logical points extending from the logical lower-left corner of the conventional screen to the top of the physical screen.

The actual screen resolution does not change after you invoke `WINDOW` although the values of all four parameters can extend beyond the physical boundaries of the current resolution and can be negative numbers. If the first pair of coordinates is greater in value than the second pair of coordinates, the interpreter flips the association of the coordinate pairs so that the first pair refers to the lower-right corner. At all times, the ratio of width to height is retained at one-to-one. You should place the `WINDOW` statement before any graphics plotting instructions; otherwise, the interpreter will ignore it.

Example

By adding the following instruction to the corona generator example from Chapter 37, "Bitmapped Plotting," the view of the circle—which was originally centered on the screen—is magnified so that only the lower-left quadrant is showing:

```
WINDOW SCREEN (0, 100)-(160, 200)
```

The remainder of the circle is "plotted," only off the screen. Because the `SCREEN` term is included, `(0, 100)` becomes the upper-left corner (not the lower-left) and `(160, 200)` becomes the lower-right (not the upper-right).

A *viewport* is a rectangular subdivision of a graphics screen to which graphic output is restricted.

For the sake of charting, it might be convenient to apportion a smaller segment of the screen as the graphics *viewport*. In VB/DOS, a viewport is like the old-style window, using an internal offset that makes some other point on-screen the origin.

VIEW **Statement**

Syntax:

```
VIEW [SCREEN] (leftx%, topy%), (rightx%, bottomy%)
  [, backcolor%][, bordercolor&]
```

The VIEW statement designates a rectangular portion of the screen called the viewport as a restricted region for displaying bitmapped graphics. Text can continue to be displayed outside the borders of the viewport. The physical upper-left corner of this viewport is at the point `(leftx%, topy%)`, and the physical lower-right corner is at `(rightx%, bottomy%)` (If a WINDOW state is in effect, these coordinate pairs become the lower-left and the upper-right, respectively.)

If the term SCREEN is not stated along with VIEW, the coordinate pair at the physical location `(leftx%, topy%)` becomes addressable as the logical coordinates `(0, 0)`. If SCREEN is stated, the physical screen coordinates are retained. If *backcolor%* is stated, the background color within the viewport is set to the value retained in the stated register. This is the viewport equivalent of setting the full screen background color using the COLOR statement. If *bordercolor&* is stated along with VIEW, the color of the rectangle at the perimeter of the viewport is set to the palette color specified by the long integer, *not* to the color stored in the corresponding register.

I've mentioned the POINT() function a few times in the previous chapters. Because previous versions of Microsoft BASIC used the keyword POINT for different purposes, in VB/DOS the instruction manifests itself in two ways, as described in the following section.

POINT() **Function**

Syntax 1:

```
coordinate% = POINT(axis%)
```

Syntax 2:

```
color% = POINT(pixelx!, pixely!)
```

In Syntax 1, the `POINT` function returns within the integer *`coordinate%`* the last screen, viewport, or window coordinate to receive a plot from a graphics instruction. The value of *`axis%`* passed to this function designates which coordinate will be returned. Integer *`axis%`* can take any of the following values:

0	Current x coordinate of screen or viewport
1	Current y coordinate of screen of viewport
2	Current x coordinate of window
3	Current y coordinate of window

In Syntax 2, the `POINT` function returns the palette color value of the pixel at the specified coordinates, within the integer *`color%`*.

A related function aids in determining the ASCII code identity of the character plotted to a certain location in a graphics screen and is also another job for the overworked `SCREEN` keyword.

SCREEN() **Function**

Syntax:

```
data% = SCREEN(row%, column%[, colorflag%])
```

The `SCREEN()` function returns data concerning the character plotted to the graphics screen at cursor location (*`row%`*, *`column%`*), to the integer variable *`data%`*. If *`colorflag%`* is not stated, the function returns the ASCII character code of the character found at that location or a 0 if no character is found there (ASCII code 32 represents a space). If `colorflag%` is set to 1, the function returns the color register number of the foreground color used to plot the character found at the stated location.

Of Bitmaps and Reptiles

When the LOGO programming language was first developed in the early 1970s, one of its major selling points was that child programmers would be able to interact well with it, by giving it commands to which the system would instantly respond. As you might imagine, for a language geared for use by young people, LOGO didn't have many provisions for bar- and pie-charting. LOGO's idea of graphics more resembled crayon drawing—perhaps "crayon drawing" would have been the better name.

In LOGO's "turtle graphics" system, as it was instead called, the bitmapped graphics area of the screen contained a kind of virtual pen that was referred to as the "turtle." To start drawing, the programmer placed the turtle on the page and set him forth in a particular direction. To change the direction of the line, the programmer "twisted" the turtle. In the original documentation, which was also geared for children, a green turtle was seen moving about the page, leaving a colored trail behind him.

When LOGO was later remarketed toward business people in an attempt to sell more copies, the turtle character was removed from the documentation and replaced with a far less interesting "virtual pen." Perhaps the decision to ax the turtle was a bit hasty because today many computer users have become accustomed to dragging files into bulging trash can symbols using something called a mouse. In any event, the term "turtle graphics" is still used to refer to a system where commands are given to a virtual pen, which is told to move a certain direction for a certain distance a step-at-a-time. A remnant of this system remains in VB/DOS today, in the form of the DRAW statement.

DRAW **Statement**

Syntax:

```
DRAW command_string$
```

where `command_string$` is either a validly interpretable string of turtle drawing command characters or a reference to a string variable containing such characters.

The `DRAW` statement invokes the VB/DOS turtle graphics system for the graphics screen, or the currently active viewport or window. The statement's sole parameter is a string of characters whose sequence instructs the interpreter how to operate the system's virtual pen. Each command in this string takes the following syntax:

```
[PREFIX]CHARACTER(S)[parameter1][,parameter2]
```

With one exception, each drawing command is a single character that directs the `DRAW` interpreter to operate the pen in a particular manner. The command can have one parameter, or two parameters separated from each other by a comma but not by a space. Space characters separate draw commands within a command string. Either of two prefix commands can precede the command character, placing restrictions on the stated command.

Table 38.1 lists the accepted commands for use in a `DRAW` command string.

Table 38.1. DRAW command characters.

Command	*Definition*
Prefixes	
B	Move the pen one step in the direction it is currently pointing, without plotting any points along the way. (Can appear as a command by itself.)
N	Plot a point without moving the pen. (Can appear as a command by itself.)

Command	*Definition*
Movement	
D[*units%*]	Move the pen down the specified number of *units%*. If *units%* is not stated, one unit is the default.
E[*units%*]	Move the pen up and to the right the specified number of *units%*.
F[*units%*]	Move the pen down and to the right the specified number of *units%*.
G[*units%*]	Move the pen down and to the left the specified number of *units%*.
H[*units%*]	Move the pen up and to the left the specified number of *units%*.
L[*units%*]	Move the pen to the left the specified number of *units%*.
M[{+ | –}*x%*,*y%*	Move the pen to the designated coordinates *x%*,*y%*. If a + or - precedes the coordinates, movement is made relative to the current pen location, rather than the coordinate system of the plotting area.
R[*units%*]	Move the pen to the right the specified number of *units%*.
U[*units%*]	Move the pen up the specified number of *units%*.
Image manipulation	
A[*angle%*]	Point the pen at the designated angle. (All pen motions up, down, or to the left or right are relative to the current angular heading of the pen.)
TA[*angle%*]	Turn the pen the designated number of compass degrees (not radians) relative to its current heading.

continues

Table 38.1. Continued.

Command	*Definition*
S[*scale%*]	Set the pixel scale factor for a "unit" of movement, to a value between 1 and 255. The default value is 4.
C[*color%*]	Set the pen's plotting color to the designated *color%* register value.
P[*icolor%*], [*bcolor%*]	Set the plotting color for painting the interior of closed objects to the designated *icolor%* color register. Optionally, set the replotting color of borders of a closed object to the designated *bcolor%* color register.

Example

The quickest way you can test the DRAW statement is to write a routine that clears the screen, takes DRAW commands directly from the keyboard, and executes them on the fly. For the sake of brevity, I've excluded the scaling and interior painting commands and concentrated upon those commands that serve to move the pen (or "turtle") about the plotting area.

```
DIM cmd$(10)
DATA "B","N","D","E","F","G","H","L","R","U"
FOR no = 1 TO 10
    READ cmd$(no)
NEXT no
SCREEN 9
COLOR 15
stpr:
dr$ = INKEY$
IF dr$ = "" THEN GOTO stpr
FOR no = 1 TO 10
```

```
  IF dr$ = cmd$(no) THEN
    DRAW dr$
       EXIT FOR
    END IF
NEXT no
GOTO stpr
```

Here's pseudocode for the preceding routine:

Prepare a string array with ten units.
Here is a series of accepted DRAW *commands.*
Start counting from 1 to 10.
  Read the counted data element from the
   above list into the prepared array.
Next count.
Go to 640x350 resolution.
Use bright white as the plotting color.
Call this line the "stopper."
If the user hasn't pressed a key, then
 go back to the stopper line.
Start counting from 1 to 10.
  If the key pressed by the user
   is the same as the one being
   counted in the array, then
    Execute this as a DRAW *command.*
    Exit this loop.
  End of condition.
Count the next element.
Go back to the stopper line.

For this example to work, you must hold down the Shift key when entering a DRAW command. Any character that isn't a DRAW command is ignored; the rest is executed immediately. An example of the screen output you're likely to see from this test appears as shown in Figure 38.1.

Figure 38.1. The DRAW command test, or an organizational chart for your state legislature.

This example is perhaps the quickest way of making you familiar with the DRAW statement. You might consider using it for applications in which vectored drawing and image scaling are necessary elements—for example, floor planning or organizational charting.

Summary

The VB/DOS interpreter maintains a physical image of the currently active bitmapped graphics screen, as well as a logical image. A larger or smaller logical image can be remapped into the physical image using the WINDOW statement. When the screen becomes a window of this definition, the physical resolution of the screen does not change although logical coordinate points are addressed as if the resolution has changed. Graphics instructions can have their active realm limited to a rectangular viewport region of the screen, using the VIEW statement.

The color of the pixel nearest any specified pixel coordinates can be obtained using the POINT() function. You can obtain the ASCII code number or the color of the character plotted to the graphics screen at any specified location using the `SCREEN()` function.

The `DRAW` statement invokes a special interpreter for the execution of pen-drawing graphics commands. These commands are composed of small groups of characters, which can be placed together in a large string for `DRAW` to interpret and execute all at once.

Review Questions

Answers to Review Questions appear in Appendix B.

1. Does the `PSET` statement affect the values of properties `POINT(0)` and `POINT(1)`?
2. On executing the instruction `VIEW SCREEN (30, 0)-(320, 180)`, the point referred to by logical address `(30, 0)` can be found at what physical coordinates?
3. On executing the instruction `VIEW (30, 0)-(320, 180)`, the point referred to by logical address `(30, 0)` can be found at what physical coordinates?

39

The Printer

In this chapter, you begin to direct Visual Basic for MS-DOS output to the `Printer.` device. This device has a few properties and methods that are specific to the printer.

Hard Copy

Like a form or a picture box, the printer is considered by VB/DOS to be a *virtual terminal,* which receives text using the `PRINT` instruction in the manner of an old TTY or DECwriter terminal printer. To print to the printer from any procedure appearing within any module, you can use the `.PRINT` method to address the printer as demonstrated in the following line:

```
Printer.PRINT "This is an example line of text."
```

In keeping with earlier versions of BASIC, VB/DOS maintains the older `LPRINT` statement for sending text to the printer.

LPRINT **Statement**

Syntax:

```
LPRINT [USING descriptor$][{;¦,}expression1{;¦,}
  expression2{;¦,} . . . expressionn{;¦,}]
```

where any *expression* listed within the statement can be either a mathematical expression that can be logically reduced to a real numeral value, or an alphanumeric string or joining of such strings using the concatenation operator +.

The LPRINT statement is used to send text to the printer at the current location of the printer's own cursor, which is maintained by the VB/DOS interpreter. The list of items to be printed to the screen appears immediately to the right of the LPRINT statement. Any text that is to appear on the page as it does within the statement must appear within quotation marks. Values or variables, by contrast, do not appear within quotation marks—the absence of quotation marks identifies the *expression* as having value and not alphanumeric content.

At any time before or after an *expression* in the list, a semicolon is interpreted as a directive to the interpreter to leave the printer cursor where it is. A comma is interpreted as a directive to move the printer cursor 13 characters to the right and, if the printer's rightmost margin is reached, one line down if necessary. If no delimiter (bordering punctuation) appears after the end of the last printed item in the expression list, the cursor is automatically moved to the leftmost position of the next line down.

If the LPRINT statement appears on a line by itself, with absolutely no expressions or delimiters following it, the instruction is interpreted as a directive merely to move the cursor to the leftmost position of the next line down.

If USING *descriptor$* is included with the statement, each *expression* in the statement must evaluate to be a value and not string contents. The values are each reformatted as described by *descriptor$*. The format of *descriptor$* for the LPRINT USING statement is the same as for the PRINT USING statement and for the FORMAT$() function.

place the next character to print at the 67th column (not the 68th, because the first column is numbered 1, not 0). As the line stands, after the header line prints, `LPOS(0)` returns a value of 1 because the carriage return is executed due to the lack of a delimiter at the end of the instruction.

If you have a laser printer, the preceding routine would certainly print text to the page, but it wouldn't necessarily eject that page unless it's already flooded with text beyond its margins. The following method acts as the page ejection instruction.

Printer.NEWPAGE — **Method**

Syntax:

```
Printer.NEWPAGE
```

The `.NEWPAGE` method is invoked to eject the page currently being printed. For a dot-matrix printer, this method causes the platen to roll the page until the perforation reaches the tear bar if tractor-feed pages are properly set. For a laser printer, this method causes the actual print process to begin, placing data that has officially been "printed" onto the page and sending that page out of the printer.

To state that the end of a document has been reached, the `.ENDDOC` method is invoked.

Printer.ENDDOC — **Method**

Syntax:

```
Printer.ENDDOC
```

The `.ENDDOC` method is invoked to signal the completion of the document currently being printed and to send the ejection signal for the last page to the printer. Some laser printers take this as a signal to reset their internal parameters.

Summary

The printer, like the screen, form, or picture box, is considered by the VB/DOS interpreter to be a virtual terminal. Therefore, certain characteristics of the `Printer.` object are maintained independently. You can send text to the printer using the `Printer.PRINT` method or the more conventional `LPRINT` statement.

The `LPOS()` function returns the number of characters printed since the last carriage return was issued to the printer. The `.NEWPAGE` and `.ENDDOC` methods both serve to eject the current page from the printer and reset the `LPOS()` value.

Review Questions

Answers to Review Questions appear in Appendix B.

1. After printing the famous line from the movie *Network*, "I'm mad as hell and I'm not going to take it anymore!" what is the value of `LPOS(0)`?
2. If you place a semicolon to the right of the quotation mark closing the line, what would be the value of `LPOS(0)` then?
3. If you were to place a tab character in front of the line, what would be the value of `LPOS(0)` then?

Part VIII

Event Trapping

40

The Timer

In this chapter, you learn how the timer is used in Visual Basic for MS-DOS as a control on a form to regulate when certain events can take place and when procedures can be executed. Normally, instructions in a procedure are executed once. By embedding instructions in a loop clause or by expertly manipulating the various branches, instructions can be executed multiple times. Within VB/DOS, however, you can program instructions to be executed continually, periodically, or after a set interval. Unlike other languages, however, VB/DOS's continual execution mechanism is dependent on a specific graphic object: the timer object.

Where Did I Leave My Watch?

Just when you thought VB/DOS was esoteric enough, I introduce you to a graphic object that is not really an object. In any computing environment, the running application, the operating system, terminate-and-stay-resident programs, drivers, and interrupt files each vie for control of the system, and MS-DOS is not a multitasking system. It therefore does not apportion all the running processes in the system individual slices of time as does Microsoft Windows. Instead, each process has to find an interrupt vector for itself and search for the proper time to make itself known—hoping it doesn't step on someone else in the process. The whole procedure is not unlike trying to obtain fame and stardom through frequent appearances on public-access cable television.

Partly because BASIC is such a popular language for programming or modeling time-intensive games, a mechanism must be maintained for keeping exact time. When your computer system can be a 286/12 or a 486DX2/66 (about 782 times as fast), when you can have a 640K DOS 3 machine or a 16-megabyte 32-bit system with QEMM on line, or when you can be using an IBM PC or other computer, a versatile timing system that can run in any computer becomes necessary. Therefore, VB/DOS offers a versatile system for keeping chronological (real-world) time. First, you need to be able to access the computer system's own internal timer.

TIMER — **Internal Variable**

Syntax:

```
time& = TIMER
```

The `TIMER` internal variable is continually set by the interpreter to the number of seconds that have elapsed since midnight, according to the time being kept internally by the computer. This number is expressed as a single-precision, floating-point value.

Example

You can use `TIMER` in timing situations where fractions of a second are not critical. The following example shows how you can determine how many seconds elapsed during the execution of a routine:

```
StartTime = TIMER
.
.
.
EndTime = TIMER
```

```
Elapsed = EndTime - StartTime
e$ = "Total elapsed time: " + Elapsed
TimeDisplay.Text = e$
```

The ellipsis here substitutes for the routine being timed. Notice how both variables `StartTime` and `EndTime` are set to the value of the same internal variable `TIMER`. The two variables have different values, however, because the VB/DOS interpreter automatically updates `TIMER` to reflect the number of seconds that have elapsed since 12:00 a.m. With `StartTime` subtracted from `EndTime`, the result is a single-precision value denoting the number of seconds elapsed between the execution of the first assignment instruction and the execution of the second one.

Times and Dates as Text

The VB/DOS interpreter maintains two internal string variables for printing the current date and time: `DATE$` and `TIME$`.

DATE$

TIME$

Internal Variable

Syntax:

```
string$ = DATE$
string$ = TIME$
```

The internal variable `DATE$` is always 10 characters long and is continually maintained automatically so that its contents always reflect the current system date. This date is returned in the format *mm-dd-yyyy*. Likewise, `TIME$` always reflects the current system time. The time is returned in the format *hh:mm:ss*.

Example

You can change the contents of DATE$ and TIME$ by directly assigning them new strings that are interpretable as valid dates and times, respectively. As a result, the system date and time are manually reset. Here's how you can reset them from the Immediate window CLI:

```
date$="9/30/91"
time$="6:33:45"
```

Notice that you can use slash marks in the DATE$ assignment in place of dashes—VB/DOS accepts either. Also, the current year can be abbreviated to the final two digits.

If Only They Could Make It Tick

Besides the system time, VB/DOS offers a separate timer control that can be assigned to a particular form. A *timer* is assigned to a form by clicking the timer button in the VB/DOS toolbox. The timer is then placed on the form to be timed as if that timer were a textual label. In Form Designer, the Timer label appears on the form. At runtime, however, this image is not visible, so it really doesn't matter where the timer object is placed as long as it doesn't conflict with another graphic object. The user cannot operate the timer graphic object; it operates itself and generates an event by itself.

*Timer*_Timer Event

The _Timer event takes place for a form that contains a timer control, after each passing of a certain interval of time as specified within the *Timer*.Interval property.

CAUTION: The TIMER() function in VB/DOS refers to the time kept by the computer system clock, while the _Timer event refers to the time maintained by VB/DOS's simulated chronological timer. These are two different timing systems.

The .Interval property is the only property that is specific to a timer control.

Timer.Interval Property

The .Interval property for a timer is the amount of time in milliseconds (thousandths of a second) the form's timer is to count before invoking a _Timer event. The property value ranges from 0 to 65,535 milliseconds, where 60,000 milliseconds equal one minute. The .Interval property is often set to 1,000 so that events occur every second.

Example

The most obvious use for the timer control is to have a form display the current real-world time. Assume a timer has been placed into a form. The .Interval property of this timer is set to 1,000. Here is a procedure that displays the time as the caption of a label:

```
SUB Timer1_Timer ()
    TimeNow.Caption = Time$
END SUB
```

By itself or within another procedure, the line TimeNow.Caption = Time$ is executed once, displays the current time, and then becomes as useless as a stopped clock. With the preceding procedure, the _Timer event is generated regardless of what the user is doing at the time. The current time appears in the label TimeNow. once every second.

If you were more conservative with your time and wanted TimeNow to display the current time only every minute, you would reset the .Interval property to 60,000, set the .Enabled property of the timer to true (–1) so that it might work, and rewrite the preceding procedure as follows:

```
SUB Timer1_Timer ()
    TimeNow.Caption = RIGHT$(Time$, 5)
END SUB
```

Because the second hand is meaningless if the interval is set to minutes, you can use the `RIGHT$()` function to extract the first five characters of `Time$`, leaving off the seconds digits.

Example

The `.Interval` property counts up to only one minute, five seconds, but that doesn't mean you can't keep certain elements of time independently. Suppose you have an application that maintains in memory a document that is being composed. You want this document to be backed up to disk every five minutes—regardless of what the user is doing at the moment—as a background process. Assuming the `.Interval` property is set to 60,000 and the timer is `.Enabled`, here's how the branch to the back-up procedure might appear:

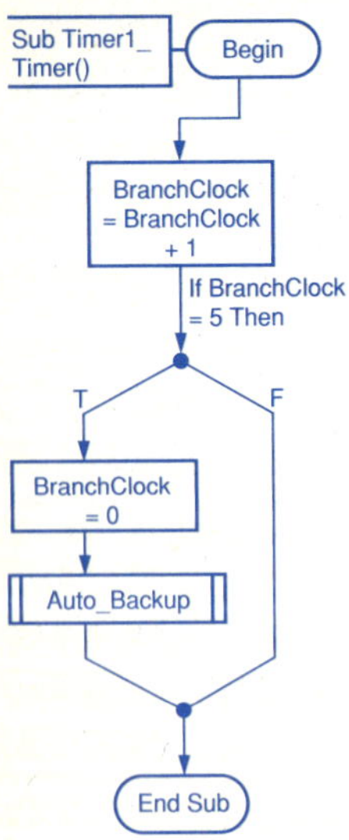


```
SUB Timer1_Timer ()
BranchClock = BranchClock + 1
IF BranchClock = 5 THEN
    BranchClock = 0
    Auto_Backup
END IF
END SUB
```

Here's pseudocode for the preceding procedure:

Procedure awaiting a timer signal:
Add one to the number of minutes being kept.
If there are five minutes in the tally, then
Reset the tally.
Execute the backup procedure.
End of condition.
End of procedure.

With the `.Interval` set to minutes, the event procedure for `_Timer` is executed every minute. Each minute, a count of 1 is added to an accumulator variable `BranchClock`. When the minutes are 5, the count is reset and the branch is made to the `Auto_Backup` procedure.

Summary

The computer system's internal timer can be accessed using the `Timer` internal variable, which returns the number of seconds that have passed since the computer last counted midnight. The VB/DOS interpreter can translate this information into realistic-looking data using the `Time$` and `Date$` internal variables.

Normally, the VB/DOS interpreter doesn't time the execution of a form within a project in real-world time. To engage such timing for a form, you drag a timer control into the form from the VB/DOS toolbox. This control is invisible at runtime. When the timer is engaged by setting its `.Enabled` property to true (–1), the timer generates an event after each `.Interval` of milliseconds. An event procedure called *`Timer_Timer`* can be assigned to this event.

Review Questions

Answers to Review Questions appear in Appendix B.

1. The maximum value of the `.Interval` property is roughly equivalent to how many minutes and seconds?
2. What terms, along with its delimiters (extra punctuation), are used to describe the following?

   A. The passing of the set VB/DOS interval

   B. The VB/DOS real-world chronometer

   C. The VB/DOS function that registers the passage of seconds since midnight

The Keyboard

In this chapter, you learn how Visual Basic for MS-DOS handles events related to pressing and releasing individual keys on the keyboard. To the left of your mouse (or to the right if you're left-handed) is a rather interesting device for processing user input that dates back to the 18th century. It's called a keyboard, and VB/DOS has not forgotten its existence. You see how the VB/DOS interpreter processes events related to the keyboard and individual keypresses. You then examine ways keystrokes can be assigned as substitutes for graphic control inputs.

The Thing with All the Letter Buttons on It

If you've ever played with Microsoft's Flight Simulator, you know that the keyboard can be programmed to be an elaborate control mechanism for simulations. If you're playing in Piper Cherokee mode and you throttle up, you hold down the plus key on your keyboard. Likewise, you use the minus key to throttle down. The longer you hold down the key, the more the throttle is moved one way or the other.

Historically, it has been difficult to program the keyboard for use as such a controller using standard BASIC. One of the older methods for handling instantaneous keyboard events which still works under VB/DOS is the `PEEK` command. `PEEK` is used to look into a register of memory to see if a certain key was being held down. The *scan code* of the held-down key often appeared in that memory address. This process is called *polling for keys* (generally, no cash prizes are awarded for guessing the right key). This literally is a search for the digital form of the electrical signal generated by a key touching a metal plate inside the keyboard unit.

The problem with polling in this way was that the execution of these polling routines was difficult to regulate. At first, before the advent of timers and statements such as `ON TIMER GOSUB`, the program had to branch to the key-polling subroutine whenever it could. There was no real way of regulating the specific time the polling took place. As a result, the programmer had no intervals. Once in a while the program would branch, using `GOSUB`, to the key-polling subroutine. To make sure the keyboard was polled often, programmers included numerous `GOSUB` commands in the code. If they were programming a flight simulator (A flight simulator in BASIC? Are you kidding?) or something like it, when the user let go of whatever key acted as the throttle-up button, the program would not "know" the throttle-up was released until after the next `GOSUB` to the key-polling subroutine. By that time, the throttle might have increased by another 10 percent, and if you're leaking fuel, another routine might generate an explosion.

Today, VB/DOS offers two different mechanisms for recognizing and "trapping" keypresses, one of which operates with graphics-oriented applications, and another using object-oriented syntax that is used for form-oriented applications. The graphics-oriented mechanism is based on the keyword `KEY`.

KEY **Statement**

Syntax 1:

```
KEY {key%, string$ ¦ LIST ¦ ON ¦ OFF}
```

where *`string$`* is either a string of characters delimited by quotation marks or a string variable representing such characters.

Syntax 1 of the KEY statement is used to assign any string of characters to a function key. When the program runs, pressing the function key causes the textual contents of *string$* to be printed, as if its characters were typed on the keyboard. The value of *key%* can be any of the following:

Key value	*Corresponding function keys*
1 - 10	F1 - F10
15 - 25	Programmer-specified keys
30 - 31	F11 - F12

Optionally, if LIST is specified, the interpreter generates to the screen a list of the function key textual assignments. KEY OFF turns off all event-trapping by way of the keyboard; KEY ON reinitiates event-trapping.

Key values of 15 through 25 are reserved for the addition of programmer-specified function keys, which are created by way of Syntax 2.

Syntax 2:

```
KEY(key%), keystroke$
```

Using Syntax 2, the KEY statement defines a certain sequence of keys that is normally describable as a keystroke—as a programmer-specified key. This keystroke is assigned the key value of *key%*, which in this syntax can range in value from 15 to 25. This key value can then be assigned a textual substitution string using Syntax 1 of the KEY statement. The contents of *keystroke$* are generally expressed using the CHR$() function. In this instance, keyboard scan codes can be substituted for the ASCII character codes for control and functional keys. Some of the accepted key scan codes are as follows:

Key scan code	*Key*
29	Ctrl
56	Alt
42	Left Shift
54	Right Shift

Key scan code	*Key*
28	Enter
14	Backspace
15	Tab
55	Print screen
70	Scroll lock
69	Num lock

CAUTION: Be careful not to confuse the function key values for `key%` with the key scan codes used in the `CHR$()` functions for `keystroke$`.

Example

Suppose you have a program in which typing the word "HELP" brings up the help screen. In many programs, the F1 function key calls up help, so you want an easy way for both "HELP" and F1 to give assistance to the user. The following procedure assigns the text to the appropriate key:

```
KEY 1, "HELP" + CHR$(13)
```

Here, `CHR$(13)` acts as a carriage return.

Example

Now suppose you also want Alt-? to act as a help screen provider. This sequence isn't normally considered a function key, but if the slot is open, you can assign this keystroke to programmer-specified key value 15 with the following instruction:

```
KEY(15) = CHR$(56) + "?"
```

The keystroke is recognized now although it doesn't do anything yet. To engage it, enact the following instruction:

```
KEY 15, "HELP" + CHR$(13)
```

Notice the syntactic distinctions between the two preceding instructions: The former is structured like an expression of assignment, whereas the second is structured like a call to a procedure.

Later in BASIC's history, the ON KEY GOSUB statement was developed, which forced a branch to a subroutine whenever a key was pressed. In VB/DOS, this statement is somewhat related to the other instructions involving the KEY keyword.

ON KEY GOSUB **Statement**

Syntax:

```
ON KEY(key%) GOSUB linelabel
```

The ON KEY GOSUB statement forces execution of the current routine or procedure to branch to the stated *linelabel* upon a press of the designated *key%*. The *linelabel* must reside on the same level of code as the branch instruction. The value of *key%* can be any of the following:

Key value	*Corresponding function keys*
0	All function keys currently defined
1 - 10	F1 - F10
11 - 14	Up, left, right, and down arrow keys
15 - 25	Programmer-specified keys
30 - 31	F11 - F12

Of Forms, Keys, and Polls

If this weren't a book on programming, you might assume that this discussion concerned the electoral balloting system. When forms are active in VB/DOS's SCREEN 0, the interpreter recognizes keypresses as events. The problem this creates for you as a programmer is that VB/DOS events "belong" to controls. If the purpose for the keyboard is to operate controls on a form, it's no problem to assign a keypress event to a control. If the keypress is meant to affect some unseen value in memory, however, your objective is to determine which control or which form module processes the event.

Following are the main events recognized for keypresses.

`Control_KeyDown` or `Control_KeyUp` Events

The `_KeyDown` event for a form or control is recognized whenever that graphic object has the focus and a key is pressed on the keyboard. The `_KeyDown` event continues to be recognized for that control as long as that key remains depressed. Two parameters are passed to the procedure for this event: the scan code for the depressed key (not to be confused for the ASCII code value of the character the key generally represents) and an integer having a bitwise pattern that represents the depression state of the shifting key. This integer can take any of the following values:

0	No shifting keys pressed
1	Either Shift key pressed
2	Either Ctrl key pressed
3	Ctrl + Shift pressed
4	Alt key pressed
5	Alt + Shift pressed
6	Alt + Ctrl pressed
7	Alt + Ctrl + Shift pressed

The `_KeyUp` event for a graphic object is recognized whenever that object has the focus and a key that had been depressed on the keyboard is released. Logically speaking, the event is recognized when the key scan code previously registered returns to 0. The procedure for the `_KeyUp` event is passed the same values by the VB/DOS interpreter as the `_KeyDown` event.

Example

Suppose you need a quick procedure to register what the scan code is for a key because the ASCII (ANSI) code for a character is not the same as the scan code for its corresponding key. All you need on the form is a simple text label and nothing else. Here's a procedure that returns the key scan code for any key pressed:

```
SUB Form_KeyDown (KeyCode AS INTEGER, Shift AS INTEGER)
Label1.Caption = STR$(KeyCode)
END SUB
```

Simply enough, the textual value of the key scan code is placed within `Label1`.

If you want the contents of the label to clear itself when the depressed key is released, you can add the following procedure:

```
SUB Form_KeyUp (KeyCode AS INTEGER, Shift AS INTEGER)
Label1.Caption = ""
END SUB
```

Example

Earlier in this chapter, I discussed a set of controls for "throttling" up and down using the keyboard. You can program such a control using the `_KeyDown` event and set up a scroll bar to represent the state of the control in the form. Figure 41.1 depicts this form in action.

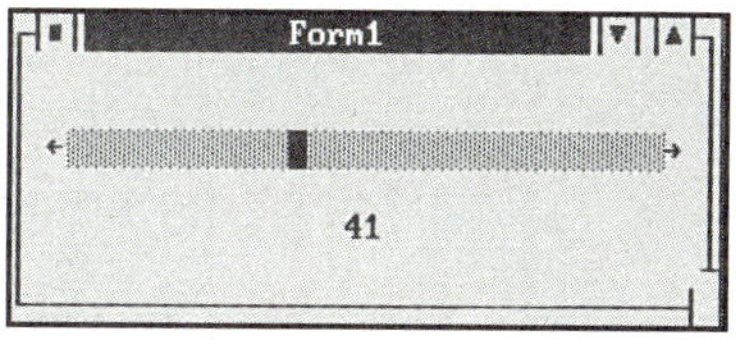

Figure 41.1. The scroll key form.

"Scroll Key" Throttle Control Tester

Project name: SCROLKEY.MAK
Constituent file: SCROLKEY.FRM

Object Type	*Property*	*Setting*
Form	.Width	38
	.Height	8
VScroll bar	.Max	100
	.LargeChange	10
Label	.Alignment	2 - Center

```
SUB HScroll1_KeyDown (KeyCode AS INTEGER,
  Shift AS INTEGER)
SELECT CASE KeyCode
    CASE 48
        IF HScroll1.Min <= HScroll1.Value -
          HScroll1.LargeChange THEN
            HScroll1.Value = HScroll1.Value -
              HScroll1.LargeChange
        END IF
    CASE 189
        IF HScroll1.Min <= HScroll1.Value -
          HScroll1.SmallChange THEN
            HScroll1.Value = HScroll1.Value -
              HScroll1.SmallChange
        END IF
    CASE 187
        IF HScroll1.Max >= HScroll1.Value +
          HScroll1.SmallChange THEN
            HScroll1.Value = HScroll1.Value +
              HScroll1.SmallChange
        END IF
    CASE 220
        IF HScroll1.Max >= HScroll1.Value +
          HScroll1.LargeChange THEN
            HScroll1.Value = HScroll1.Value +
              HScroll1.LargeChange
```

```
        END IF
END SELECT
Label1.Caption = STR$(HScroll1.Value)
END SUB
```

The preceding procedure is a relatively more complex SELECT CASE clause than you've utilized before. The clause compares the value of KeyCode to the key scan values of the 0, –, =, and \ keys, from top to bottom. The keys perform the following functions on the scroll box:

0	.LargeChange to the left
–	.SmallChange to the left
=	.SmallChange to the right
\	.LargeChange to the right

Each CASE in the clause first checks to see if there is enough room to move the scroll box in the direction designated by the pressed key, using a subordinate conditional IF-THEN clause. If there is enough room, the scroll box is moved by adding the value of HScroll1.SmallChange or .LargeChange to HScroll1.Value, which represents the current scroll box position. When the SELECT CASE clause is completed, that position is reflected in the label below the scroll bar.

You might find it easier to use ASCII code rather than key scan code to detect keypresses. In such cases, VB/DOS supplies a key event that recognizes ASCII (ANSI) code: _KeyPress.

*Control*_KeyPress Event

The _KeyPress event for a form or control is recognized whenever that graphic object has the focus and a key is pressed on the keyboard. The ASCII code value of the character having its corresponding key pressed is the sole parameter passed to the procedure for this event.

Example

If it's easier for you to think in ASCII, the `CASE` statements from the preceding procedure can be modified, respectively, as follows:

```
CASE ASC("0")
CASE ASC("-")
CASE ASC("=")
CASE ASC("\")
```

What immediately makes this procedure easier to implement is that you can substitute the `ASC()` function for the ASCII value of the character in quotation marks. This saves you a trip to the ASCII table in Appendix A of this book. The cost of simplifying this procedure is the fact that it now runs a bit slower than its key scan code progenitor.

Assigning Keystrokes to Buttons

When you operate a dialog box that contains the `OK` and `Cancel` buttons, pressing the Enter key generally substitutes for clicking `OK`, and pressing Esc substitutes for `Cancel`. Here, `Yes` and `No` buttons can be substituted for `OK` and `Cancel` because the two keys still perform much the same purpose. The VB/DOS interpreter cannot intuit which buttons in a form perform the yes/no functions, so the interpreter is informed which buttons can be assigned the Enter and Esc keystrokes with property settings.

Command.Default and *Command*.Cancel Properties

The `.Default` property for a button is set to true (–1) if the user is allowed to press Enter in place of clicking that button. Similarly, the `.Cancel` property of a button is set to true if the user is allowed to press Esc in place of clicking that button.

Summary

To allow the VB/DOS interpreter to recognize function keys, the `KEY` keyword is provided. One syntax of the `KEY` statement allows a textual string to be assigned as substitute typing for a function key. Another syntax allows you to specify a nontextual keystroke, such as Alt-A, as an alternate function key. You can then use the `ON KEY GOSUB` statement to force the interpreter to branch to a specific line upon a designated keypress.

VB/DOS recognizes events for keypresses that occur during the time a graphic object running in the VB/DOS application has the focus. While that object has the focus, the VB/DOS interpreter can await `_KeyDown`, `_KeyUp`, or `_KeyPress` events for that object. The latter event recognizes the ASCII (ANSI) code for the character corresponding to the key that was pressed, whereas the other two events recognize the key scan code for the particular key pressed, as returned to VB/DOS by your computer's BIOS.

Review Question

Answers to Review Questions appear in Appendix B.

The procedure `SUB HScroll1_KeyDown ()` presented in this chapter moved the scroll bar left or right based on the value of the key scan code passed to that event procedure by the VB/DOS interpreter itself. Based on what you know about VB/DOS, DOS, and key scan codes, speculate on the following: Suppose the user of this test program were to press at the same time two of the four keys being scanned. What is most likely to happen?

1. The VB/DOS interpreter will add the bitwise values of the two scan codes, resulting in a sum that equals none of the four codes being searched for in the `SELECT CASE` clause. None of the `CASE`-dependent instructions will be executed.

2. The BIOS will scan for each key code in numerical order so that one key is considered pressed before the other key is considered pressed, by virtue of that key's precedence in the code sequence.

3. The timing system of the computer will know one key was really pressed before the other one, rather than both being pressed at the same time. So, by virtue of the quickness of the computer's reflexes over the user's, one key will come out in front of the other.
4. The BIOS will apply priority to one key over the other, resulting in an implied hierarchy of key importance such that one key blanks out the other, making it more likely one key is considered "pressed" than another.

To find the answer to this question, I added a list box to the `ScrollKey` form called `KeyPresses`. At the end of procedure `SUB HScroll1_KeyDown ()`, I added this instruction:

```
KeyPresses.ADDITEM STR$(KeyCode)
```

Each time one of the scanned-for keys is pressed, its code is added to the list. By examining this list, you can determine the solution to the quandary I've presented.

42

Registering Errors

In this chapter, you are introduced to the error-trapping mechanism of Visual Basic for MS-DOS. Normally, when an error occurs during the processing of a program, the interpreter alerts the user to this fact with an alert box, and the process might shut down. However, you might want to include methods for taking corrective steps to solve manageable problems before the process shuts down. In such cases, VB/DOS offers you error traps, which send execution of the program to a specific routine. You will learn how to invoke these routines in this chapter. Later, you'll examine conditions in which even the most advanced error traps might not be of much help.

To Err Is Not Only Human

A *computing error* is the result of any process that fails to perform in the manner in which it is intended or designed.

One of the common definitions that most requires altering when translated into the realm of computing is that of the word *error*. An error in computing is not necessarily an error in your judgment or a syntax error. An error in computing is the result of any process that fails to perform in the manner in which it is intended or designed, and which, by its nature or in the interest of preventing disaster, prevents logical program execution from continuing.

Errors are a natural part of programming—in fact, they're necessary. Without errors, it's almost impossible for you to know what course of action to take when you develop a program. A flurry of errors might help you know when a particular course of action is unworkable. If I program an application from an idea in my head and the program compiles right the first time—without generating any errors—something is wrong. When I see errors being generated by my programs from the start, I know the programming process is actually unfolding rather smoothly.

In earlier editions of BASIC, programmers generally had to program error-trapping routines that waited for the user to make an error, such as responding to the numeric `INPUT` command `WHAT IS YOUR CURRENT AGE IN YEARS?` with the alphanumeric phrase `NONE OF YOUR BUSINESS`. The forms mechanism for VB/DOS was designed to minimize user-generated errors. For example, the function `VAL(Text1.Text)`, which extracts a numeral value from a text box, can ignore alphanumeric characters and search only for numbers. In a way, this is a major advance for computing. On the other hand, it now takes a deliberate process on your part to determine whether letters really were entered into a numeric field by accident.

Still, errors are generated for the most part by faults in the source code. As a programmer, you should let these faults occur. Covering them with an error trap that ignores the fault could lead to a processing catastrophe later in the program. Perhaps it is best for you to add error-trapping routines to the code of the program last, after the application's source code appears foolproof.

Baiting the Trap

Here's how an error-trapping routine works: A statement is placed within a procedure, setting branching to a particularly labeled line whenever an interpreter-recognized error occurs. When that happens now, processing is not stopped in the normal manner, but instead execution branches immediately to the statement following the error label in the procedure, regardless of what instruction caused the error. Following is the statement that baits the proverbial trap.

ON ERROR [GOTO ¦ RESUME] **Statement**

Syntax:

```
ON [LOCAL ]ERROR {GOTO label¦RESUME NEXT¦GOTO 0}
```

The ON ERROR branching statement sets an error trap that, when invoked for the first time within an application, forces execution of the current procedure to jump to a specified line label whenever any error occurs that would normally suspend or interrupt the normal process of execution. As long as the procedure continues to execute without trouble, branching to the label immediately takes place on the occurrence of an error.

The phrase ON ERROR GOTO 0 is used to terminate an error trap and allow the VB/DOS interpreter to again suspend execution in the case of a serious error. The phrase ON ERROR RESUME NEXT is included as a way of allowing you to tell the interpreter to ignore any errors that might come along and to resume execution with the next instruction following the one that caused the error.

If LOCAL is specified, the interpreter searches for the presence of *label* only within the current level of code or within the current procedure. Otherwise, the error-trapping routine can exist on the modular level, and ON ERROR GOTO calls within procedures are able to address it.

The RESUME statement takes the program out of the error-trapping routine and back into the main body of the program.

RESUME **Statement**

Syntax:

```
RESUME {[0] ¦ NEXT ¦ label}
```

The RESUME statement is reserved for the end of error-trapping routines within a procedure. Invoked on a line by itself or accompanied by a 0, the statement sends execution back to the statement that caused the error that sprung the trap. The formerly erroneous statement is then reexecuted to see if it generates the same error a second time.

The phrase `RESUME NEXT` sends execution back to the statement immediately following the one that caused the error. The phrase `RESUME` *`label`* sends execution back to the statement immediately following the specified *`label`*.

Example

An error trap might be necessary for such potential errors as trying to find a specific filename on disk and not finding it, as modeled by the following procedure fragment:

```
SUB FileFind (filepath$)
    ON ERROR GOTO NoFile
    Selector.SHOW 1
    OPEN targetfile$ FOR INPUT AS #1
    .
    .
    .
NoFile:
    IF ERR <> 53 THEN
        msg$ = ERROR$(ERR)
        MSGBOX (msg$, 16)
        STOP
    ELSE
        msg$ = "File " + targetfile$ + " not found."
        MSGBOX (msg$, 16)
        RESUME NEXT
    END IF
.
.
.
EXIT SUB
```

Here is pseudocode for the error-trapping routine, starting at the line marked by the label `NoFile:`

If the error is not a file-not-found error, then
   Tell the user what the error actually is.
   Place this error message in a message box.
   Stop the program.
Otherwise,
   Tell the user what file wasn't found.
   Tell the user this in a message box.
   Resume the program where it left off.
End of condition.

Suppose it is possible for the file selector box invoked by the instruction `Selector.SHOW 1` to return a nonexistent filename to the routine that invoked it. If such a travesty occurs, instead of stopping execution altogether, a branch is made to the line `NoFile`. At this time, the internal variable `ERR` is polled to see if the error number generated is error 53 (file not found). If the error is any number other than 53, an error message is generated to that effect, and execution is manually forced to `STOP`. If `ERR` is 53, the name of the file that isn't found is added to the message box before it is displayed. The `RESUME NEXT` reverse branch statement enables execution to continue, however, with the line following the one that caused the error.

> **NOTE:** Using the SELECTOR.FRM created earlier, it is impossible for the `Selector` form to generate a nonexistent filename unless the user typed it specifically. If the filename is selected from a directory list, that file must exist because its name appears in the directory. Conceivably, however, the file might be corrupt, resulting in one of many possible error values.

The preceding fragment introduced you to a number of error-related instructions, which are described in the following sections.

ERR **Internal Variable**

The internal variable ERR is set by the interpreter to the number code of the last error that occurred during processing of the program. If no error has occurred, ERR = 0. You can set this variable to any value for use in simulating error conditions when testing the applicability of error-trapping routines. Setting the value of ERR manually, however, does not result in the automatic generation of an error.

ERROR$() **Function**

Syntax:

```
string$ = ERROR$(ercode%)
```

where *ercode%* is an integer value corresponding to a valid error code. Internal variable ERR can be used as *ercode%*.

The ERROR$() function returns a text string describing the error code that is passed to the function, within the string variable *string$*.

Two more instructions round VB/DOS's error-related vocabulary: the ERROR statement and the ERL internal variable.

ERROR **Statement**

Syntax:

```
ERROR ercode%
```

where *ercode%* is an integer value corresponding to a valid error code. Internal variable ERR can be used as *ercode%*.

The ERROR statement forces the interpreter into believing that the error specified by *ercode%* has occurred. This statement is particularly useful when you test the applicability of error-trapping routines.

ERL **Internal Variable**

The internal variable ERL is set by the system to the number of the line that last generated the error, assuming you use the old BASIC method of numbering lines—which is supported by VB/DOS as an option. If an application doesn't have line numbers, this variable is useless.

"We Sing the Song of the Sewer..."

If you're an Art Carney fan, you're probably singing the preceding song now; however, this song is also the official anthem of professional debuggers. Errors are relatively nice because you can trap them, tame them, and release them using error-trapping routines. Bugs are not so nice. Generally, bugs cause things to go wrong with the program, although from the interpreter's point of view, everything is proceeding fine. Sometimes a mess is in the eye of the beholder, and a computer doesn't have eyes.

A *bug* is an error that cannot be detected by the interpreter.

A program bug, technically speaking, is not an error. A bug could lead to the generation of errors, but there's really no way the interpreter can track the presence of a bug. A *bug* in computing is the result of any process failing to perform in the manner it was intended or designed, that cannot be detected automatically by the interpreter or compiler. Thus, by its nature, a bug allows logical program execution to continue along a potentially disastrous course.

While testing Visual Basic for Windows for another book, I programmed an application in which I plotted a point to the screen using a mouse pointer that I programmed manually. A device I called the compass echoed the direction in which I moved the pointer. While I was developing this project, my program contained a few bugs that were difficult to find. For days, whenever I plotted a point, my compass control registered that point as being located 180 degrees in the other direction from where it actually was. From the computer's point of view, nothing was going wrong. It was doing exactly what it was told to do. Bugs are not necessarily examples of instructions being misexecuted. Often they happen because the interpreter followed instructions to the letter.

I discovered the source of the bug by using my favorite Visual Basic tool, which also appears in VB/DOS: the Immediate window, introduced in Chapter 5, "Definition and Declaration." As described elsewhere in this book, this window is in fact a command line interpreter. Using the CLI, you can break an operation in progress and quiz the interpreter regarding the status of the program and its individual variables.

When the VB/DOS application is operating in suspension and the code window is active, the line being executed when the program was stopped appears in the procedure window in brighter text. You can suspend the application by pressing Ctrl-Break. On some keyboards, the Break key doubles as the Pause key (although I've never seen it pause anything).

A *breakpoint* immediately suspends the program after it is executed.

After suspending execution with Ctrl-Break, you can set a *breakpoint* for the running application by indicating the instruction line to receive the breakpoint and pressing the F9 key. A breakpoint is an instruction line that temporarily forces execution of the program to be suspended immediately following execution of that line. Breakpoint lines are indicated in text listings by red lines.

To set the breakpoint for an instruction line, perform the following steps:

1. While the program is in suspension, indicate the instruction line to receive the breakpoint by placing the cursor within that line and pressing the F9 key.

2. When you run the program, execution stops after the breakpoint line as if there were a STOP statement following the line.

With the breakpoint having suspended the program, you can then use the Immediate window to quiz the current state of the program. It isn't a well-known fact, but you can use the Immediate window to execute small programs. As in the old BASIC interpreters, you can use colons to separate instructions typed to a single line within the CLI. You can then enter a small loop clause to a line, such as the following:

```
for b=1 to 15:?stat(b):next b
```

Here you can use abbreviated syntax and lowercase letters, and the `?` stands in place of the `PRINT` statement.

You also can use the Immediate window to resume execution at any procedure heading by typing that heading as an instruction line, as if it were a procedure call in the program. You can type the name of the `SUB` procedure into the immediate window using the CLI. You can also make it an expression that passes control to a `FUNCTION` procedure, or a GOTO or GOSUB statement that picks up execution at a specific line. Any of these can be used as "hooks" so you can begin a program, for the sake of testing, in the middle. Once the procedure containing the hook has completed execution, however, control is passed back to the immediate window, which is identified by VB/DOS as though it were the calling body of a program. Execution ceases as though the interpreter processed an `END` statement.

Another way to pass control to a specific statement is through the source code window containing that statement. When the application is "on break"—whether you pressed Ctrl-Break or the interpreter processed a `STOP` instruction—the instruction to be executed next appears in one of the source code windows, highlighted with bright text. You can highlight the instruction line you would like to execute next within that same procedure by placing the cursor on that line and selecting **S**et Next Statement… from the Code Editor's **D**ebug menu. The instruction you highlight must appear within the same window as the instruction VB/DOS was about to execute before the break. Otherwise, the interpreter will be confused as to the identity of which instruction it's executing.

Bugs are non-trappable because the interpreter cannot recognize them.

No debugging system is automatic, in the same way no spelling checker for your word processor can spot every possible error. For a spelling checker to be able to correct all errors, it would have to know the context in which the word you intended to spell should appear. One of the most commonly misspelled words I've found in editing other people's copy, for instance, is *you're*. It seems correct from *your* vantage point, but in the sentences "*Your* going too far," or "Why, *your* much thinner than you were," you can plainly see there are two misspelled words. A spelling checker cannot know that because the misspelled words are words, nonetheless.

This limitation is what differentiates a bug from an error in computing. If things do not proceed smoothly, a formal error would be generated and could possibly be trapped.

Keeping Watch O'er the Flock

One of the debugging features in Microsoft's "professional" programming environments that programmers greatly appreciate is the inclusion of *watchpoints* and *watch variables*. With the VB/DOS watch system, you can have the interpreter break the program's execution whenever a certain mathematical condition is true. This condition is not expressed within the program, but within a separate window of the Code Editor. The condition is written as an expression of comparison, just as though it were appearing beside IF in an IF-THEN clause. The break expression is never "seen" by the program, so it doesn't really know it's "being watched."

Here's one handy use for the watch system: Suppose someplace in your VB/DOS application you use some sort of a "progressive value," such as a loop that counts from 1 to 1000 or an axis coordinate value for a control being dragged over the form. You want to stop the program at a specific point in the progression and poll the Immediate window for the contents of specific variables. To do this, you can place an expression in the watchpoint list, stating the mathematical condition that must exist in order for the program to break.

There are two ways to enter a watchpoint into your current VB/DOS application. The following steps illustrate the conventional method:

1. From the Code Editor's **D**ebug menu, select **W**atchpoint.... A dialog box will appear.

2. Within this dialog is a text line, within which you can enter the expression that triggers execution to be suspended.
3. Click **OK**. The watchpoint will be entered into the Debug window.

Alternately, you can highlight an expression within the source code and select **D**ebug/**W**atchpoint. No dialog box will appear. Instead, the expression you highlighted automatically appears within the Debug window. You can view the contents of the Debug window at any time while execution is suspended, by selecting **D**ebug from the Code Editor's **W**indow menu.

A similar device of the Code Editor enables you to specify a certain watch variable whose value you want to monitor. By selecting **A**dd Watch from the Code Editor's **D**ebug menu, you can enter the name of an existing variable. While the application is being executed, the Debug window takes note of when the value or contents of that variable have changed, along with the name of the procedure that changed it.

Summary

An error is a fault in the processing of a program that suspends or terminates execution. Despite the negative connotation of the term, errors help you determine whether the logical structure of a procedure being developed is workable. Suspension or termination of a program's execution can be intercepted with a procedural error trap. The error trap branch is baited using the phrase `ON ERROR GOTO`. Within this error-trapping routine, you can use the internal variable `Err` to determine what error occurred, and you can use `ERROR$(ERR)` to generate a system-defined error message. The `RESUME` statement terminates an error-trapping routine. A bug is a failure on the part of the program to operate in the manner in which it is intended, although it might operate in the manner in which it is designed.

Values of certain variables within a running application can be monitored by enlisting them as watch variables within a list maintained in the Code Editor's Debug window. The application currently running within the interpreter control program might be forced to break when a mathematical condition, called the watchpoint, evaluates to be true. This watchpoint condition is evaluated separately by the interpreter whenever the value or contents of the enlisted watchpoint variable have changed.

Review Questions

Answers to Review Questions appear in Appendix B.

1. Would the instruction `LINE xbeg, ybeg, xend, yend` generate a bug or an error?
2. Would the instruction `circ = 2 * pi / r` for calculating the circumference of a circle generate a bug or an error?

Review Exercise

Program a routine or procedure for the file selector box SELECTOR.FRM that determines whether a filename exists before it sends the value of `targetfile$` to the application that invoked it. Use an error trap and the internal error variable `ERR`.

Part IX

Data Management

43

Data in Memory

In this chapter, you'll see how arrays are filled using lists of data contained entirely within the source code of the Visual Basic for MS-DOS program. Later, you'll see how elements of text can be transported between graphic objects using the VB/DOS clipboard.

The Way DATA Works

As you've seen in many of the previous examples, the reason for having array variables in some programs in the first place is so that they can contain small—not large—lists of data. Perhaps an array has a dozen or so elements, all of which retain their contents throughout the course of the program. You could use 12 statements of assignment to render values to this array, such as `ang(0) = 5 : ang(1) = 13 : ang(2) = 6`, and so on.

A more efficient way to work is to save the dozen values to a data file on disk, retrievable by means of an `OPEN` command. On the other hand, building an entire file for just 12 entries might be going to too much trouble. Besides, you would need to write a separate program just to save the 12 data entries to the file.

An even more efficient way is to embed the handful of elements within the source code of the program itself. In assembly language, data is frequently embedded in this way. Because BASIC was partly modeled after assembly language, early in BASIC's development an embedding statement was added to the language, as described in the following section.

DATA **Statement**

Syntax:

```
DATA element1[, element2. . . elementn]
```

where each *element* in the list can be a value, an expression that can be logically reduced to a real value, a variable which represents a value, a string enclosed within quotation marks, a concatenation of such string expressions, or a string variable.

The DATA statement serves to declare a series of data elements as being available for entry into any variable using the READ statement. The DATA statement does *not* assign any values or contents to variables. Instead, it adds elements to a list that is maintained by the VB/DOS interpreter, to be assigned later in the course of execution. The statement can appear only within module-level code.

Each element in the DATA statement is added to a concurrent list of entries being maintained by the interpreter. VB/DOS maintains only one such list at any time. The contents of this list can be assigned at will to any number of unit or array variables. Each successive DATA statement adds new data elements to the end of this list. Any number of elements can appear in a single DATA statement, and any number of DATA statements can appear within a module.

The READ statement assigns DATA elements from the list to specific variables, as described in the following section.

READ **Statement**

Syntax:

```
READ variable1[(subscript)][, variable2[(subscript)]]
  ...[, variablen[(subscript)]
```

The READ statement assigns the next available element of data declared by the DATA statement and pointed to by the internal list pointer of the VB/DOS interpreter to the listed *variables* in sequence. For each assignment made, the interpreter's internal pointer is incremented so that it points to the next available element in the DATA list if there is one. The statement generates an error if there are no more DATA elements available for assignment or if the form of the data currently pointed to by the interpreter's list manager differs from the form of the currently listed variable designated to receive the element.

Example

Here are some examples from previous chapters where you've seen the DATA and READ statements at work. In Chapter 38, "Manual Windowing," you saw an example of the DRAW statement using a "dynamic" routine that let the user enter draw commands from the keyboard and have them executed on the fly. A DATA statement is needed to list for the routine which draw commands are acceptable.

```
DIM cmd$(10)
DATA "B","N","D","E","F","G","H","L","R","U"
FOR no = 1 TO 10
    READ cmd$(no)
NEXT no
SCREEN 9
COLOR 15
stpr:
dr$ = INKEY$
IF dr$ = "" THEN GOTO stpr
FOR no = 1 TO 10
   IF dr$ = cmd$(no) THEN
        DRAW dr$
        EXIT FOR
   END IF
NEXT no
GOTO stpr
```

A loop clause assigns the 10 string elements to the string array `cmd$()`. You'll find that using a loop clause is the most common and convenient way to assign values to an array.

Example

In Chapter 37, "Bitmapped Plotting," I presented a SCREEN mode test program that required two small lists: the first containing the currently supported screen modes and another whose values corresponded directly to the first list, containing the maximum number of color registers supported for each screen mode.

```
DATA 1,16,2,2,7,16,8,16,9,64,10,9,11,256,12,256,13,256
DO
    READ mode, maxcolors
    SCREEN mode
    LOCATE 25, 1
    PRINT "Graphics mode"; mode
    FOR linecolor = 0 TO 320
        LINE (0, linecolor)-(320, linecolor), linecolor
          MOD maxcolors
    NEXT linecolor
stpr:
IF INKEY$ = "" THEN GOTO stpr
LOOP UNTIL mode = 13
```

Here the READ statement groups the elements in the single DATA statement into pairs. Each pair is read and assigned to *unit*, not array, variables. The DO-LOOP clause then operates on each pair of unit variables before replacing their values with the next pair of elements from the DATA list.

Notice the routine doesn't count just how many elements there are, as did the DRAW command routine. Instead, you know when you reach the end of the list because the last SCREEN mode supported is 13. You can therefore continue to read elements `UNTIL mode = 13`.

In loop clauses where the actual number of DATA elements is unknown, you can set the clause to look for a specific element. If, however, the last element in the DATA list appears several times in that list in identical form, you could set up a "dummy entry," such as the string "END OF DATA" for the final string entry or an unreasonable value for the final numeric entry. To prevent this dummy entry from being entered into the real array or unit variable, you can enter a conditional clause as follows:

```
READ element$
IF element$ = "END OF DATA" THEN
    EXIT SUB
ELSE
    item$(no) = element$
    no = no + 1
END IF
```

The entry is entered into the array only if it is meaningful—that is, as long as the manually entered tag "END OF DATA" has not been encountered.

Only one statement is provided for changing the location in memory of the DATA element pointer: RESTORE.

RESTORE **Statement**

Syntax:

`RESTORE [label]`

The RESTORE statement is used to move the interpreter's internal DATA pointer back to a new starting location. By itself, the RESTORE statement moves the pointer to the first data element listed in the module. The next READ statement then looks to the first data element of the first DATA statement. If *label* is specified, the RESTORE statement places the data pointer at the beginning of the first DATA statement following the stated line *label*. Execution does *not* branch to this label.

Checking the Clipboard

The VB/DOS interpreter maintains an internal device called the *clipboard*, whose primary purpose is to facilitate the easy transfer of textual data from one form or graphic object to another during runtime. The clipboard makes cut-and-paste possible. Following are the three methods VB/DOS supports for operating the `Clipboard.` system object.

`Clipboard.SETTEXT` **Method**

Syntax:

```
Clipboard.SETTEXT string$
```

The .SETTEXT method places the text currently referred to as string$ on the VB/DOS clipboard.

`Clipboard.GETTEXT()` **Method**

Syntax:

```
string$ = Clipboard.GETTEXT()
```

The `.GETTEXT` method acts in the manner of a function—it returns the current textual contents of the system clipboard within *`string$`*. The parentheses are added at the end of the method for the sake of compatibility with Visual Basic for Windows and for no other reason.

Clipboard.CLEAR **Method**

Syntax:

```
Clipboard.CLEAR
```

The .CLEAR method clears the current contents of the system clipboard.

Example

At one point during the development of the Expressor application, I added a clipboard method to place on the clipboard the number currently in the readout:

```
SUB EditCut_Click ()
Clipboard.SETTEXT readout.Caption
END SUB
```

Example

At any time, an instruction can be invoked that takes the text currently indicated by the user within a large text box and copies it to the system clipboard:

```
Clipboard.SETTEXT Text1.SelText
```

Now, if you want to make this operation an Edit-and-Cut operation rather than an Edit-and-Copy operation, you might want to add the following instruction:

```
Text1.SelText = ""
```

At some later point, if you want this clipped text inserted at the current cursor location, you can invoke the following:

```
Text1.SelText = Clipboard.GETTEXT()
```

Notice that the parentheses are left within the Get operations but omitted within the Set operations.

Summary

Short lists of data can be embedded within the source code of a VB/DOS application or module. The `DATA` statement is used, when forms are not active, to declare a short list of elements that can be read into unit or array variables later using the `READ` statement. VB/DOS maintains an internal pointer that keeps track, independently of the instruction currently being executed, of the current `DATA` element in the module's list. This pointer can be reset or moved using the `RESTORE` statement.

The VB/DOS clipboard is a system whose purpose is the transfer of text between graphic objects and forms. The `.SETTEXT` method for the `Clipboard.` object is used to acquire data from an object and place it on the system clipboard. Likewise, the `.GETTEXT` method is used to place data from the clipboard on a qualifying object. You use the `.CLEAR` method, naturally, to clear the clipboard of its contents.

Review Questions

Answers to Review Questions appear in Appendix B.

1. How many `READ` instructions are required within the body of the source code to enter 12 items of data declared within the `DATA` statement into an array variable?
2. If there are 36 `DATA` elements in a module and a loop clause is used to `READ` those elements into a list of three array variables, what should be the maximum value of the count variable in the loop clause?
3. If `Clipboard.` is a legitimate object, why does it not have its own `.Text` property?

44

Sequential Access

In this chapter, you examine the mechanism used by the BASIC programming language for storing user-created data to disk as files. This mechanism has changed little since the early 1970s, even with its inclusion in Visual Basic for MS-DOS. You see how DOS filenames are assigned to VB/DOS as ordinal numbers, which serve to represent data channels. These channels are opened and closed like the locks on a dam. When opened, data flows through the *stream*. In this chapter, you learn how to "turn the locks" and manage the stream.

The Hydrodynamics of Data Files

Most applications you will ever use create stored files for one purpose or another. BASIC programs themselves are files. A VB/DOS project or compiled application can be composed of several files. Yet up to this point, I haven't discussed how the VB/DOS application produces files *outside* of itself, in the manner and format specified within the program. It might seem unusual at first, but originally BASIC could not be programmed to produce files for the user other than its own source code file. The reason was not lack of foresight on the part of its designers, but the fact that operating systems used by relatively inexpensive computers of the mid-1960s stored memory on rotating drums so that the single program running at the time was *the* file. Only in the 1970s when programmers started to use BASIC on computers that had memory that was more *solid-state*—reliant more on electrical currents than on centrifugal force—was a BASIC program capable of being instructed to produce files.

A *database* is data stored structurally as records of related entries.

All applications that produce and utilize their own data files—regardless of the language they're programmed in—have their own *database.* A well-structured database includes a small portion of data that describes how the rest of the data relates to each other. The mechanics of BASIC data files were invented, for the most part, in 1970, at about the same time E.F. Codd was developing the concepts of modern databases for IBM. Because BASIC couldn't wait for Dr. Codd, the data file storage mechanism chosen for the language was somewhat blind to the structure and relationships between the elements of data being stored.

A *channel* is a logical device that maintains the flow of data between the interpreter and an output device.

In a sense, the data storage and retrieval mechanism for BASIC-produced files is little more than a verbally commanded tape recorder. For a sequential-access file (the subject of this chapter), each element of data is stored to disk in a stream, one datum after the other. This stream is referred to as a *channel,* which is a throwback term to the first file-maintaining small systems of the '70s. A channel is a logically interpreted device (not a tangible, physical entity) for maintaining the flow of data between the interpreter and an output device or storage unit.

The sequential-access mechanism works like this: A channel is opened with the `OPEN` statement, and this channel is rendered an ordinal number—for instance, `#1`. Each element of data is "printed" to this channel, one datum after the other, using the statement `PRINT #1`. No data concerning the physical makeup or construction of the file is included with this data. There's simply a bunch of raw numbers printed to magnetic media with the same technical consideration given to them that a typewriter gives the individual letters it types on a page.

A sequential-access data file is always read in the same way it was written—beginning-to-end, one datum after the other. When the file is created, the first 1,000 elements might be names of people, the second 1,000 might be their addresses, the third might be their cities of origin, and so on. These elements can be stored in this order using the PRINT # statement. So that the recalled data elements retain the same meaning and purpose in the program after they are loaded back into memory from disk, each element must be reloaded in exactly the order in which it was saved. So in this instance, the 1,000 names would be reloaded first, followed by the 1,000 addresses and the 1,000 cities. A program could not open the file and have it immediately pick out just the addresses. In fact, if you want just the addresses, after you open the file using the OPEN statement, you must read the 1,000 names anyway to get to the 1,000 addresses.

This might seem like an archaic manner in which to store data...and for many programmers, it is. However, assume you're writing a program that maintains several array variables to describe the main portion of data in memory—for instance, a vector-plotted drawing like you'd find in a CAD program. In such cases, the data is pertinent only in its entirety—half the number of vector plots in a drawing would result, no doubt, in a senseless drawing. In cases in which it is more convenient to dump the entire image of data from memory to disk in one lump, sequential-access techniques prove to be convenient. In cases in which an individual item of data is important itself—for instance, somebody's address in a list—sequential access is rather cumbersome. *Random-access* data storage is less cumbersome, although it is far more complex. I reserve discussion of that technique for the next chapter.

Example

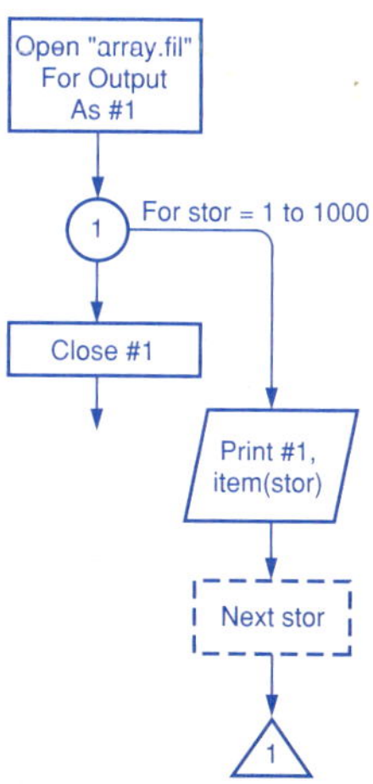

Here's how an array of 1,000 items is stored to disk using sequential access:

```
OPEN "array.fil" FOR OUTPUT AS #1
FOR stor = 1 TO 1000
    PRINT #1, item(stor)
NEXT stor
CLOSE #1
```

Here's pseudocode for the preceding procedure:

Open a storage file for the arrays generated
thus far, make this an output file for sequential
access, and give this file channel 1.
Count from 1 to 1,000, the maximum number of units in
the array.
Store the array value for this count to disk,
using channel 1.
Count the next item.
Close the channel.

Here you see the modern incarnation of the old BASIC ordinal file system. A channel is opened and given ordinal number 1. The `OPEN` statement links `#1` with the filename `array.fil`. As a result, anything that is sent through the channel using `PRINT #1` is written to that file. When the array is depleted, the channel is closed.

The `OPEN` statement is the primary statement behind all data file access operations.

OPEN **Statement**

Syntax:

```
OPEN filename$ [FOR mode] [ACCESS restriction] [locktype]
   AS [#]channel% [LEN = bytelength%]
```

The `OPEN` statement initiates a channel for the transfer of data between the VB/DOS interpreter and a physically stored file. The DOS filename of this file is specified as *`filename$`* and can contain the complete file storage path. The channel number associated with this file is expressed as *`channel%`* and can be any integer between 1 and 255. The choice of numbers here is completely arbitrary. A lower-numbered channel need not be opened previously before a higher number is chosen. After the `OPEN` statement is used to assign a channel number to a filename, any data transfer instruction that refers to this number affects the file attributed to the number by the `OPEN` statement. A pound sign before the channel number is optional to maintain syntax compatibility with earlier versions of BASIC.

The term represented by `mode` specifies the type of data transfer being established. This term can be stated as any of the following:

Sequential access:

`OUTPUT`	Opens a channel for sequential data output to the specified file, starting at the beginning of the file. If the file does not currently exist at the time of the `OPEN` statement's execution, the file is created. Otherwise, it is overwritten.
`APPEND`	Opens a channel for sequential data output to the specified file, beginning at the point just following the last datum entered into the existing file. If the file does not currently exist at the time of the `OPEN` statement's execution, the file is created. However, with `APPEND`, an existing file is never overwritten.
`INPUT`	Opens a channel for sequential data input to the specified file, in the order the data was output, starting with the beginning of the file.

Random access:

`RANDOM`	Opens a channel for data exchange using random-access mode. In this mode, data can be written to or read from a file at any specifiable point at any time. This is the default mode for channel initiation and is assumed if `mode` is omitted from the `OPEN` statement.

Binary access:

`BINARY`	Opens a channel for data exchange using binary file mode. In this mode, individual bytes of data—for instance, pixels in an image or characters in a document—can be written to or read from a file at any specifiable point at any time.

The optional parameter *restriction* following ACCESS can include either or both of the terms READ and WRITE, specifying any extra restrictions to be placed on file access, especially with regard to running the VB/DOS application over a network. The optional term *locktype* that follows is used to specify any access restrictions for clients attempting to open the same data file already opened by another client in the network. The term *locktype* can be stated as SHARED to allow any other client access to the open data file, LOCK READ to prevent every other client from reading the data file while it's open, or LOCK WRITE to prevent every other client from writing to the data file while it's open. These two terms are especially—and in many ways exclusively—helpful in networking environments, for use in "steering" a data file so that all clients in the network can obtain access to the most current version of the file, and no single client can override the changes made to that file by another client.

The term LEN = *bytelength%* is used in random access mode to establish the fixed character length, in bytes, of each element of data being exchanged between the interpreter and the data file. Random access uses fixed field lengths to establish the beginning and end of a data item within a file. By default, this length is set to 128 bytes. Sequential access, by contrast, relies on the program to know the sequence in which each item was stored to the file and to know in turn the field length of each item in the sequence. The methodology is that if the program knows in advance the precise contents of a file being recalled from disk—as it must with sequential access—it must know, as a result, the byte length of each item in that file. The term LEN = *bytelength%* is used optionally in sequential-access mode to establish the length of the internal memory buffer being used to house characters being exchanged between the interpreter and data file. By default, this length is set to 512 bytes.

Obviously, the OPEN statement is extremely complex, and it will probably require all of this and the following two chapters to explore every permutation of the statement. By stark contrast, the statement's counterpart on the reverse side of the channel control operation, CLOSE, is extremely simple.

CLOSE **Statement**

Syntax:

```
CLOSE [#]channel1%[, channel2%, . . . channeln%]
```

The CLOSE statement terminates access to the data files that have names that were attributed by the OPEN statement to the *channel%* numbers listed. Any read or write instructions following CLOSE pertaining to the channel numbers stated just previously within CLOSE generate errors. Access to files using those numbers can only be reinstated using an OPEN instruction. CLOSE cancels any association between the stated numbers and the filenames attributed to them by the OPEN instruction, so the numbers can be used again for any other filenames. Pound signs are optional before each channel number. If no channel numbers are specified, all open channels are closed.

Example

Suppose you have data in memory that contains the names of the 50 United States, along with each state's governor's name, total population, total measurement of land mass, and official state bird. Here's one way you can save all that data to disk using a sequential-access technique:

```
OPEN "50states.dta" FOR OUTPUT AS #2
FOR state = 1 TO 50
    PRINT #2, name$(state)
NEXT state
FOR state = 1 TO 50
    PRINT #2, pop(state)
NEXT state
FOR state = 1 TO 50
    PRINT #2, mass(state)
NEXT state
FOR state = 1 TO 50
    PRINT #2, bird$(state)
NEXT state
CLOSE #2
```

At some later date, when you start running the program and memory is clear, you load all that data back into memory using the following routine:

```
OPEN "50states.dta" FOR INPUT AS #3
FOR state = 1 TO 50
    INPUT #3, name$(state)
NEXT state
FOR state = 1 TO 50
    INPUT #3, pop(state)
NEXT state
FOR state = 1 TO 50
    INPUT #3, mass(state)
NEXT state
FOR state = 1 TO 50
    INPUT #3, bird$(state)
NEXT state
CLOSE #3
```

Your choice of numbers for both `OPEN` statements is not extremely important, as long as that choice remains constant throughout the data exchange process and doesn't conflict with any other existing open channel number. What must remain identical in both instances is the order data is stored and retrieved from the file. Using conventional sequential-access techniques, neither you nor the user, therefore, can access a data file like you can with, for instance, Structured Query Language—`SELECT * POPULATION FROM 50STATES...`. In other words, you can't contact a portion of data by the category it falls under; there are no provisions for categorization of data in sequential access. The VB/DOS interpreter therefore cannot know what data is being stored and retrieved. It can only keep track of where that data is. Using sequential access, you narrow the definition of *where* to *wherever the next datum resides.*

The preceding two routines were written more for ease of reading by human beings than for ease of interpretation by VB/DOS. The `OUTPUT` routine stores each list of 50 in sequence in its entirety before storing the next list. One good reason, perhaps, for dividing this sequence into individual loops is so that functions specific to the variables being stored can be easily placed and isolated. For instance, there are two numeric array variables in the preceding routines. If these variables are retrieved from text box fields in a form, however, the text from those boxes must be converted into numeric variables before it can be stored as values. The routines are converted as follows:

```
OPEN "50states.dta" FOR OUTPUT AS #2
FOR state = 1 TO 50
    PRINT #2, name$(state)
NEXT state
FOR state = 1 TO 50
    pop = VAL(pop$(state))
    PRINT #2, pop
NEXT state
FOR state = 1 TO 50
    mass = VAL(mass$(state))
    PRINT #2, mass
NEXT state
FOR state = 1 TO 50
    PRINT #2, bird$(state)
NEXT state
CLOSE #2
OPEN "50states.dta" FOR INPUT AS #3
FOR state = 1 TO 50
    INPUT #3, name$(state)
NEXT state
FOR state = 1 TO 50
    INPUT #3, pop
    pop$(state) = STR$(pop)
NEXT state
FOR state = 1 TO 50
    INPUT #3, mass
    mass$(state) = STR$(mass)
NEXT state
FOR state = 1 TO 50
    INPUT #3, bird$(state)
NEXT state
CLOSE #3
```

Notice how in both of the preceding routines, when writing the numeric values to disk and reading them from the disk, you did not need to specify the variable as an array. The values in the `INPUT` routine are restored first to simple numeric variables and then assigned to string arrays. VB/DOS does not keep track of the variable name associated with the data stored to disk, only the variable type. You can use a variable with a different name to restore data that was stored to disk. It is essential, however, that the variable you use is declared, either explicitly or informally, to be the same type as the one you used to store the data to disk.

The reason for this necessity is as follows: Each variable type has a different amount of bytes reserved for storage in memory. When you use the `PRINT #` statement (explained in detail in the next section), the contents of the data are printed digit-by-digit to a text file, in the same manner used by the `.PRINT` method for a *virtual terminal graphic object,* such as a "picture box." So, instead of saving an image of data to disk as it appears in memory, `PRINT #` saves the textual equivalent of that data. You can go into that file with a text editor such as Notepad, and the file appears with precisely the same contents it would have if the data were printed to a graphic object.

When reading this file back into memory, the interpreter has no idea what it sees at the moment. The only clue it has about what each character represents is the variable type of the `INPUT #` statement for the variable that is supposed to hold the converted value in memory. The interpreter determines the beginning and end of each printed element in the file by looking for its surrounding space characters. In the midst of an opening and closing space is an alphanumeric string that is extracted into memory. The interpreter then performs its own covert form of the `VAL()` function to convert this string back to a value if the variable type expressed in `INPUT #` is numeric. The results of this translation do not correspond with the data as it was printed to the file if the variable type expressed in `INPUT #` is not the same as it was in `PRINT #`. The interpreter will use the wrong number of bytes to store the value conversion.

Following are discussions of the two data storage and retrieval instructions.

PRINT

Statement

Syntax:

```
PRINT #channel%, expression1[{;¦,} expression2]
    [. . . {;¦,} expressionn]
```

where each *expression* can either be logically reduced to a numeric value or expressed as an alphanumeric concatenation of one or more elements of text.

The PRINT # statement prints the text of the values or contents of each expression in the list to a text file that acts as the data file attributed to the integer *channel%*. This channel number must have been opened previously with the OPEN statement for OUTPUT or APPEND and attributed to a specific filename found within the OPEN statement. PRINT # prints text to a file with this filename. The form of this text is exactly as it would appear if it were printed to a graphic object or to the printer, using the PRINT instruction.

> **CAUTION:** A pound sign *must* precede the channel% number so that the interpreter can better distinguish this statement from the PRINT instruction.

If a semicolon appears before an expression, printing of the expression to the file takes place immediately at the present character pointer position—thus canceling any carriage return or line feed before printing begins. If a comma appears before an expression, printing of the expression to the file takes place at the beginning of the next print zone. Because no text font is assumed for printing to a disk file—because you're not dealing with images or appearance specifically—a print zone begins every 14 characters.

The current character position within the file is maintained by the interpreter for each open channel until the CLOSE statement is executed for that channel, thus closing the file. Multiple PRINT # statements executed in sequence for the same channel number have their results appear within the file associated with that channel, in the same sequence.

INPUT # **Statement**

Syntax:

```
INPUT #channel%, variable1[, variable2, . . . variablen]
```

The `INPUT #` statement reads data from a textual data file whose *channel%* number was previously opened for `INPUT` by the `OPEN` statement and whose filename was previously specified within the `OPEN` statement. The pound sign is required to distinguish the `INPUT #` statement from the `INPUT` statement. Each textual element from the file is assigned to the variables in the `INPUT #` instruction's list, in sequence. If the variable being assigned a datum from the file is a numeric variable, the interpreter automatically attempts to convert the text string associated with that variable to a numeric value before assigning a value to the variable.

Example

Now that you know more about the nature of printing to a sequential-access file, you can modify the two `PRINT #` and `INPUT #` routines for greater efficiency, as follows:

```
OPEN "50states.dta" FOR OUTPUT AS #2
FOR state = 1 TO 50
    PRINT #2, name$(state);
    pop = VAL(pop$(state))
    mass = VAL(mass$(state))
    PRINT #2, pop, mass,
    PRINT #2, bird$(state)
NEXT state
CLOSE #2

OPEN "50states.dta" FOR INPUT AS #3
FOR state = 1 TO 50
    INPUT #3, name$(state); pop, mass, bird$(state)
    pop$(state) = STR$(pop)
    mass$(state) = STR$(mass)
NEXT state
CLOSE #3
```

A *record* is a logical grouping of related elements of data within a data file or database.

In both cases, you're using single loops to govern both the storage mechanism and the retrieval mechanism. In so doing, each item of information is interleaved into the others so that the data entries for each state appear on the same "line" within the text file. You can officially consider this grouping of related elements to be a *record*.

Example

The previous examples assume the program knows in advance how many records of related data will be entered into application memory. Suppose you were to extend the program, however, so that the application would store information about the individual counties or boroughs in each state. You really don't want to have to create 50 different array variables for the states. Instead, it would be more convenient for you to create two-dimensional array variables, of which the first dimension represents a state and the second dimension represents a county. You then let the data file decide for you, after the data is loaded into memory, how many counties each state has. Here are the storage and retrieval routines you might write for storing each county or borough's name, land area, and county seat:

```
OPEN "counties.dta" FOR OUTPUT AS #4
FOR state = 1 TO 50
    PRINT #4, counties(state)
    FOR lc = 1 TO counties(state)
        PRINT #4, cname$(state, lc), mass(state, lc),
          cseat$(state, lc)
    NEXT lc
NEXT state
OPEN "counties.dta" FOR INPUT AS #5
FOR state = 1 TO 50
    INPUT #5, counties(state)
    FOR lc = 1 TO counties(state)
        INPUT #5, cname$(state, lc), mass(state, lc),
          cseat$(state, lc)
    NEXT lc
NEXT state
```

In the preceding pair of routines, each state has a variable apportioned to it called `counties()` that keeps count of the number of counties or boroughs in the state. By looking at the `PRINT #4` routine, you can see that the number of counties per state is stored to disk *first.* Following that is a list of as many names, land masses, and bastions of power as there are counties in the state currently being counted. Because the `lc` loop counts only to the number of counties registered to be in the current state and then stops, you can be certain that in the "semi-cloned" `INPUT #5` routine, the loading loop "knows" in advance how many counties to load in memory before it initiates the loop. This number is always the first number in a county *cluster.* After the cluster is loaded, the file pointer points to the next number of counties automatically. You also can guarantee from the identical way you structured the saving and loading routines that `INPUT #5, counties(state)` always picks up the number of counties for the current state, and not a county name by mistake.

One of the dangers in using this method of storage is that, when reading character files into memory, the sequential-access loader treats commas and semicolons as delimiters. You can easily store the sequence of characters *Washington, D.C.* to disk using `PRINT #`, but the comma after the *n* will cause the interpreter to think *Washington* is the entire data field. What's worse, *D.C.* is likely to become the start of the next data field. It is likely that the District of Columbia will show up as a ZIP code, and all the fields that follow will be one datum off.

In a strange way, the cause of this problem is also the solution to it, as explained in the following section.

WRITE # — Statement

Syntax:

```
WRITE #channel%, expression1[, expression2
    . . , expressionn]
```

where each *expression* can either be logically reduced to a numeric value or expressed as an alphanumeric concatenation of one or more elements of text.

The `WRITE #` statement prints the text of the values or contents of each expression in the list to a text file that acts as the data file attributed to the integer *channel%*. This channel number must have been opened previously with the `OPEN` statement for `OUTPUT` or `APPEND` and attributed to a specific filename found within the `OPEN` statement. `WRITE #` prints text to a file with this filename. This text is in the form of an *ASCII-delimited* data file as used by the *mail merge* feature of many word processors. All elements are separated from each other by commas, and all alphanumeric strings are enclosed within quotation marks. Commas and any punctuation other than quotation marks themselves that are intended to appear within a string are enclosed within the quotation marks.

> **CAUTION:** A pound sign *must* precede the `channel%` number in the `WRITE #` statement. Commas are used within the `WRITE #` statement only to separate data items—they do not affect the "printing" position of that data in the text file generated by the interpreter. You *cannot* use semicolons as delimiters within `WRITE #`.

Sequential Data as Pages

A stored sequential-access file is, in essence, a printed page although VB/DOS maintains no height property for that page. VB/DOS does, however, maintain an optional column width, which is resettable by means of a statement, not a property.

WIDTH # **Statement**

Syntax:

```
WIDTH #channel%, columns%
```

The `WIDTH #` statement sets the "printing" width of a sequential-access file whose *channel%* is currently open by means of the `OPEN` statement. The setting is made to a specified number of *columns%* from 0 to 255. Once the interpreter has stored *columns%* number of characters to an open file, it automatically generates a carriage return and line feed character. "Printing"—or storage of entries to the file—then begins on the following line. If *columns%* is zero, no lines are assumed, and text is presumed to wrap around without carriage returns until its termination.

Assuming `WIDTH #` is set to a reasonable amount, you then have access to the `LINE INPUT #` statement.

`LINE INPUT #` **Statement**

Syntax:

`LINE INPUT #`*`channel%`*`,` *`string$`*

The `LINE INPUT #` statement reads a line of text from a sequential-access file and stores it in memory within the variable *string$*. A line of text in this instance is defined as a continuous stream of characters that end with a carriage return. This character is assumed to be the end-of-line character. If no such break occurs in the file or if `WIDTH #` is not used to specify the line width of the sequential data file, `LINE INPUT #` could be used to assign the entire textual contents of the data file to string variable *string$*.

Summary

All applications that use data in one form or another operate a database. A database management system maintains the categorical and relational information about elements of data. VB/DOS has no such system. It can only open channels for data and maintain their throughput and positioning in a file.

The appearance of a VB/DOS stored data file is a page, although one that seems to be "printed" to disk. In fact, the statement `PRINT #` is the primary statement for printing a sequential-access record to disk. You can open a channel with the `OPEN` statement. If the access mode is specified as `OUTPUT`, using sequential access, data can be "printed" to this file or "written" to this file with more descriptive delimiters using `WRITE #`.

The `WIDTH #` statement is used to specify the fixed length of all records being written to a sequential-access file. This is to help the interpreter determine where a record begins and ends. Once this distinction has been drawn, and all records within a data file are guaranteed to have the same length, the `LINE INPUT #` statement can be used to retrieve character data from those fixed-length records.

Review Questions

Answers to Review Questions appear in Appendix B.

1. What is the operational difference between the `PRINT #` statement and the `WRITE #` statement?
2. What is the operational difference between the `INPUT #` statement and the `LINE INPUT #` statement?

Review Exercises

1. Suppose you're writing an astronomy program in which the user catalogs the celestial objects she happens to view with her telescope. Write a routine that stores to disk all the objects the user has cataloged thus far, along with their celestial catalog names and observed magnitudes and brightnesses.
2. Suppose the astronomer sees planets, stars, galaxies, or other celestial phenomena. Given the fact that the description criteria for each category is different, but you don't have it all on-hand at the moment, write a routine that saves a sequential-access file for all objects observed in the skies thus far. Have the saving and loading routines differentiate between the celestial objects so that each time a new type of object is sighted, the individual content and structure of the object is chosen and utilized by the program.

45

Random Access

In this chapter, you witness the other primary method of storing and retrieving data as files in Visual Basic for MS-DOS—the random-access method. This method involves the storage of related data elements as records and the retrieval of each record by number, although not necessarily in sequence. You can pull one record out of a file at random, which is where the access method gets its name. You also see the binary-access method in action, in which data are stored and retrieved byte-by-byte into memory rather than datum-by-datum.

Yippie I/O

In the real world of file storage, people do not open up a cabinet and read word-for-word the contents of every file that falls before the one they're looking for. If that were so, people with last names beginning with Z would probably be the last to receive their tax refunds. Random-access file storage should perhaps be called *rational access* because each element of data has its own recognized place or location within the file, and the element can be called at any time by specifying that location.

You actually use the term *random access* often in your life, especially with regard to memory—as in RAM. In random-access memory, you can address, acquire, and store a byte of data by referring to its location—or in terms of memory, its address. When programming in assembly language, you address data by byte location. For arithmetic operations, certain elements of data often are copied into *registers*, which on paper appear to be variables. Registers are actually physical containers for values retrieved from memory. Oftentimes, a database manager will use a logical container (simulated in code) that will hold the values of data items retrieved from memory. Logical registers are used in many random-access data schemes. Logical registers are not variables, though, since they cannot be used for arithmetic evaluation purposes. In other words, the data contained within these registers must be *transferred* to variables.

Normally, in BASIC, a variable refers to a location in memory where the data reside or, in the case of an alphanumeric string, begin to reside. Many versions of BASIC, including VB/DOS, enable you to address this memory location directly with the `VARPTR` statement. If you use a brand-name expanded memory driver such as QEMM or BlueMAX, the physical location in memory of this variable's data can be shifted frequently without VB/DOS ever being notified. Most of these drivers employ what can best be called a "Data Relocation Program" for segments of data in which the data have grown too large for the segment.

The invocation of a VB/DOS variable is an example of random access, technically speaking. Such an invocation is merely an indirect way of referring to an element of memory by its address—except for the fact that in many modern systems, that address keeps changing. Notice that in the sequential data access technique, you actually employ random access anyway. You use sequential access to place all the data that had been stored on disk into memory, and from there you can access any element of it randomly. The subscript of the array into which you loaded the data serves as the address of that element—so you have random access whether or not you want it.

In the random-access data storage and retrieval technique, you're merely being more up-front about what technique you use to address data. The access takes place from the disk or stored file rather than from memory. You use the `PUT #` and `GET #` statements rather than `PRINT #` and `INPUT #` to retrieve and store, respectively, an element of data by its address. You therefore directly address the disk rather than the memory and save the VB/DOS application a bit of work.

Following is the PUT # statement used to write data to a random-access file, described in detail.

PUT # **Statement**

Syntax:

```
PUT #channel%, [location&], variable
```

The PUT # statement writes the contents of the specified *variable* to a random-access data file, previously opened with the statement OPEN...AS RANDOM or OPEN...AS BINARY, and whose *channel%* number is designated by that OPEN statement. The term *variable* cannot be replaced with an expression or a value. In the instance of the PUT # statement, only a variable can be explicitly stated. Only one variable can be included; the VB/DOS interpreter does not recognize lists of variables for this statement.

When using the random-access technique, if *location&* is stated, the *variable* contents are assumed to be written to the element position in the list numbered *location&* from the beginning of the file. If an element already exists at that position, it is replaced for the contents of *variable*. If *location&* is not stated, the comma that holds the place where *location&* would have been stated must remain to distinguish its purpose in this statement from that of *variable*.

The VB/DOS interpreter maintains a file pointer for each data file opened with the OPEN statement. This pointer registers the location where the next data element is written. In random access, if *location&* is omitted, writing takes place to the location currently being pointed to by the file pointer. After writing to a random- or binary-access file takes place, the file pointer registers the location just following the preceding write. Therefore, if a PUT # statement writes to some *location&* in the middle of an existing file, after the write the file pointer increments itself to the next location in the middle of that file. In other words, the default location of the file pointer when *location&* is not specified is not at the end of a random-access file in VB/DOS.

If the value of `location&` is beyond the value where any data has been written to the file, the contents of the data at locations previous to `location&` might be erroneous. It is legal, however, to specify a storage `location&` that is far greater than the number of elements in the file.

The length in stored bytes of each element is, by default, 128 bytes. You can respecify this length with the `LEN = length%` portion of the `OPEN` statement for that file. This is considered the field length of each element in the file. Each field can be from 1 to 32,767 bytes in length, and all fields within a random-access file have identical lengths. This many bytes are written to the file each time `PUT #` is executed, regardless of the byte length of the specified `variable`. An alphanumeric string cannot be longer than the number of bytes in the field length minus two, to account for a string descriptor value. Each time `PUT #` is executed, the number of bytes in the field length is added to that pointer to maintain that pointer's current absolute location.

When using the binary-access technique—when the data file is opened using `OPEN...AS BINARY`—the value of `location&`, when specified, represents the absolute byte number within the open file. This byte number acts as an absolute address. Elements of a binary-access file do not have identical lengths, so the `PUT #` statement writes exactly as many bytes to the binary-access file as are used to store the specified `variable` in memory. If `location&` is not specified, writing takes place at the next byte address in the sequence.

CAUTION: The binary-access method does not write descriptors to a file specifying the beginning and end of a variable's contents or value. It is therefore possible to accidentally (or purposefully) write bytes as data in the midst of a previously stored element, thus invalidating that element. Binary access should therefore be used only for nonrecord data, such as long textual documents and bitmapped images.

Figure 45.1 depicts the differences between random- and binary-access storage. In the top example, a random-access file has been opened with a field length of 16, specified within the `OPEN` statement using `LEN = 16` at the end. The values of two variables are stored to this file using `PUT #`. The first is a double-precision floating-point variable consuming eight bytes of memory, and the second is the string form of the filename CUOMO1.DTA, which is 10 characters long. With the random-access file, the eight-byte value is stored within a 16-byte field, leaving an excess of eight bytes. The 10-character string is then stored within another 16-byte field, with two characters included as a string descriptor, leaving an excess of four bytes.

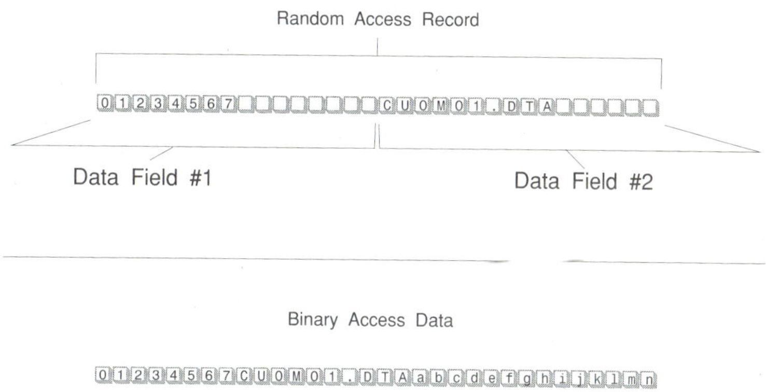

Figure 45.1. The two addressable data storage schemes.

In the bottom example of Figure 45.1, a binary-access file has been opened, and such files have no fixed field lengths. Here the same two variables are being stored to the file using the same `PUT #` statement. The eight-byte value is stored to eight bytes of the file, leaving the file pointer at the next byte. The ASCII values of the 10 characters in *CUOMO1.DTA* are stored immediately following the eight-byte value. The file pointer then rests at the byte just following the *A*.

Keep these two examples in mind as you read about the statement that reloads variables from a data file into memory: `GET #`.

GET

Statement

Syntax:

```
GET #channel%, [location&], variable
```

The `GET #` statement reads the contents of the specified *variable* from a random-access data file, previously opened with the statement `OPEN...AS RANDOM` or `OPEN...AS BINARY`, and whose *channel%* number is designated by that `OPEN` statement. The term *variable* cannot be replaced with an expression or a value. In the instance of the `GET #` statement, only a single variable can be explicitly stated by itself, not a list of variables.

When using the random-access technique, if *location&* is stated, the *variable* contents are assumed to be read from the element position in the list numbered *location&* from the beginning of the file. If *location&* is omitted and a comma holds the empty space where *location&* would have appeared, reading takes place at the location currently being pointed to by the file pointer. After reading from a random- or binary-access file, the file pointer registers the location just following the preceding read. Therefore, if a `GET #` statement reads from some *location&* in the middle of an existing file, after the read the file pointer increments itself to the next location in the middle of that file.

If the value of *location&* is beyond the location where any data have been written to the file, any value read from that nonexistent position is zero, and any string read from that position is null. It is legal, however, to specify a storage *location&* that is far greater than the number of elements in the file.

When using the binary-access technique to load a value into memory, the `GET #` statement reads exactly as many bytes to the binary-access file as are used to represent the specified value *variable* when it is loaded into memory. When loading an alphanumeric string and assigning its contents to a string variable in memory using binary access, the number of characters loaded into memory is exactly the number of characters currently belonging to that string variable. In other words, if contents have yet to be assigned to a string variable and its official contents are null (`string$ = ""`), a `GET #` statement does not load any characters into the specified string variable.

If `location&` is not specified, reading takes place at the next byte address in the sequence.

CAUTION: If the variable type stated within `GET #` is different from the type used when storing that variable to the binary-access file using `PUT #` earlier, the value or contents of the `GET #` variable are erroneous. It is therefore important that the instruction pattern of the binary-access loading routine be somewhat similar to that of the binary storage routine.

A *field* is any container for an element or item of data.

In some of the preceding descriptions, I've introduced the concept of *fields,* or regions of data. A field is any container for an element or item of data, whether it is any of the following:

A graphic object for the display of that datum

A region of memory reserved for that datum

A region of a file reserved for that datum

A *table* is a combination of data and data structures, such as field names and relations.

In true database management, a category of data—such as last name or amount owed—is addressed by its field name. VB/DOS has no native database manager (in the Professional Edition, one can be attached as an add-on library) although the random-access data files VB/DOS creates have field lengths that are fixed by the `OPEN` statement. These field lengths are not stored along with the data, however, but are determined within the source code. Because these field lengths are a necessary component for the structure of a formal database *table,* VB/DOS does not manage a formal database. A table is a stored database component consisting of data, along with the structure of that data, such as field names and relations.

Figure 45.2 shows the appearance of a random-access data document and how each field in that document appears within a column. This way each datum in the column consumes the same amount of space, regardless of its real length. With the interpreter knowing beforehand the length of each field in the document, it is easier for the interpreter to know where a datum begins and ends—no delimiters are necessary to inform the interpreter of the boundaries of a datum. The interpreter is therefore free to move back and forth through the data file, acquiring data from anyplace in the document randomly, as necessary. This is one more reason the technique is called random access.

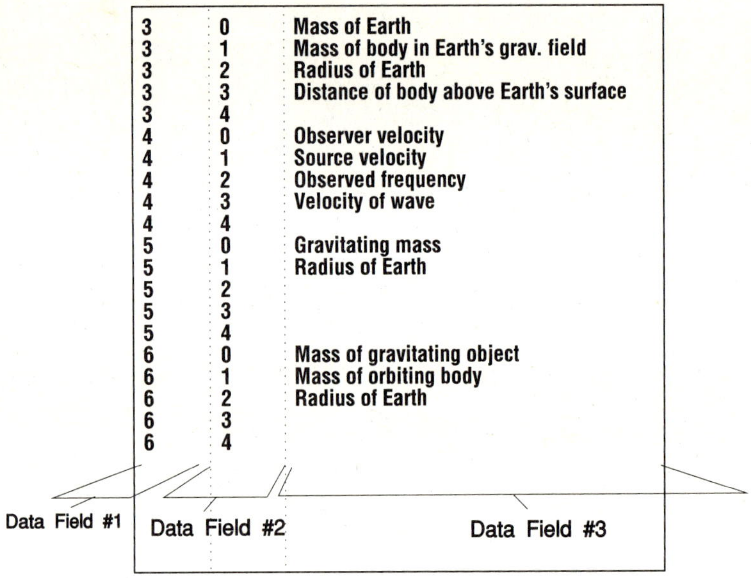

Figure 45.2. A properly fielded random-access data document.

One of the primary differences between the sequential- and random-access techniques is that random access is *bidirectional*—you can read to and write from the same channel. With sequential access, the mode `OUTPUT` or `INPUT` is specified first, setting the direction of the data stream in advance. With random access, there is no data stream; the file pointer is positioned wherever you want, and data is either sent to or acquired from that position. The file pointer then moves over one element, so it knows that a sequence exists. In random access, however, the sequence of data elements in a file does not govern how that data is accessed.

For instance, suppose the application has a form on the screen that contains fields for data about one of the 50 states. To acquire this data, the user types the two-letter postal abbreviation for a state into a field marked `Postal Abbr.`, which is a text box. The user then clicks a button marked `Reference`, and the application is then directed to acquire the rest of the data for that state from the file. In memory is a string array variable that acts as a sort of directory; within each element of the array is a postal abbreviation. If the abbreviation typed matches an abbreviation in the array, the array subscript value for that abbreviation is used to acquire the record of that state from a file.

Example

Here's how the procedure for determining which record is loaded might appear:

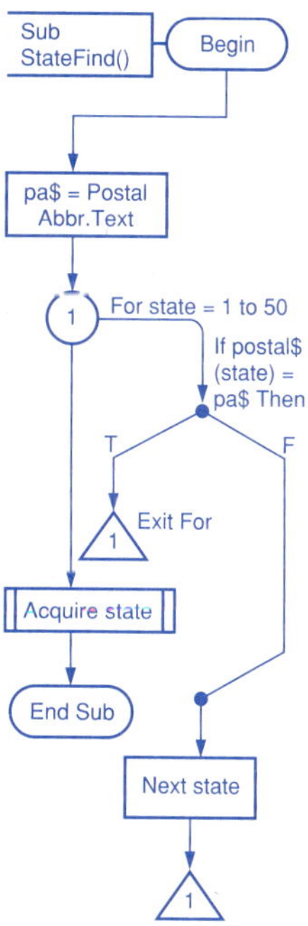


```
SUB StateFind ()
pa$ = PostalAbbr.Text
FOR state = 1 TO 50
    IF postal$(state) = pa$ THEN EXIT FOR
NEXT state
Acquire state
EXIT SUB
```

First, the contents of the postal abbreviation field are copied to string variable `pa$`. The loop clause then compares these contents to those within the array `postal$(state)` and continues to execute this comparison as long as the contents are *not* equivalent to each other. When they become equivalent, the loop is exited and control is passed to `SUB Acquire ()`, a procedure that loads data about the state into memory. Assume that earlier in the program the following instruction was executed:

```
OPEN "50STATES.DTA" FOR RANDOM AS #1 LEN = 48
```

As you move from procedure to procedure, channel #1 is still open. You can address the file for channel #1 using `SUB Acquire ()` as follows:

```
SUB Acquire (state AS INTEGER)
locat = (state - 1) * 4
GET #1, locat, name$(state)
StateName.Text = name$(state)
GET #1, , pop
pop$(state) = STR$(pop)
Population.Text = pop$(state)
```

```
GET #1, , mass
mass$(state) = STR$(mass)
LandMass.Text = mass$(state)
GET #1, , bird$(state)
Bird.Text = bird$(state)
END SUB
```

The first order of business is to determine where the record for this state starts. The way the example works thus far, there are four fields per record. When the first state's record (Alabama's, if you're proceeding alphabetically) was saved to the file 50STATES.DTA, the file pointer started at location 0. After all four elements of that record were saved, the pointer was at location 4 waiting for the next record to be saved. The pointer position is therefore at a location four times the value of the state being saved, minus 4. The formula

```
locat = (state - 1) * 4
```

thus returns the proper file pointer location for the state being loaded into memory.

The first element of the record is loaded into the string array variable `name$()` using `GET #` and specifying the starting file pointer location `locat` directly. From then on, each time an element is loaded, the pointer location is automatically incremented, so you don't need to specify a pointer location variable again for the rest of the loading procedure. In the preceding procedure, after each element is loaded into its appropriate string array variable, the text of that element is also displayed within the form on-screen.

Is This on the Record?

If you're comparing the choice of terms this book uses to discuss random access with the choice of terms in the manuals that were supplied with your copy of VB/DOS, you might be confused at the moment, and with good reason. To dispel the confusion, here's an explanation: The term *record* is used universally to describe a grouping of related elements of data. This is the technical definition of record subscribed to worldwide, especially by programmers of database management systems. Microsoft uses the term record only with respect to VB/DOS to describe an element of data being written to or read from a file—or what is still sometimes called a *datum*. This choice was probably made because the term record has been used historically—however incorrectly—by the originators of BASIC to describe a datum stored to a random-access file.

Because authors and publishers have a duty to describe the operations of more applications and interpreters than just VB/DOS, I chose to adhere to the universal definition of record rather than the specific definition. This way, each time you jump from one application's "world" to the next application's "world," you don't find yourself rewriting the dictionary.

Another reason I adhere to the universal definition of record is because VB/DOS has provisions for the creation of formal records for use in random-access files. This is done by invoking a TYPE clause at the module level. This clause contains the structure of a formal record—the grouping of related elements of data. You can then use PUT # to write a record of several elements of data to a disk file using just one variable.

Example

Here's how a TYPE clause might appear at the module level (the declarations section) of the 50 States program:

```
TYPE StateData
    name AS STRING * 24
    pop AS LONG
    mass AS LONG
    bird AS STRING * 16
END TYPE
COMMON SHARED StateRecord AS StateData
```

When declaring a string as in STRING * 24, you set the length of the declared string. Formal data records using "user-defined" composite variable types cannot include strings of variable length because a formal random-access record must have a fixed length for it to be recognized as a record. Array variables cannot be invoked within a TYPE clause. In the case of the revised 50 States program, you no longer need array variables because the record arrays are kept on disk now rather than in memory. The active record number is still kept in variable state. The value of state, however, is now also the value of the current file pointer location, assuming record number 0 is a null record.

Assume now that, someplace in the application, you invoke the following instructions:

```
RecLength = LEN(StateData)
OPEN "50STATES.DTA" FOR RANDOM AS #1 LEN = RecLength
```

Normally, the LEN() function is used to return the length of a string variable, but in this instance, the keyword LEN can also be used to return the byte length of a composite variable. In this case, RecLength is now 48, and that value is assigned as the length of the formal records accessed through channel #1. Your storage routine for a state's data might appear as follows:

```
StateRecord.name = StateName.Text
StateRecord.pop = VAL(Population.Text)
StateRecord.mass = VAL(LandMass.Text)
StateRecord.bird = Bird.Text
PUT #1, state, StateRecord
```

This is the entire storage routine. The contents of the currently displayed form are transferred to constituent variables invoked as properties of an object StateRecord. You can use object-oriented syntax to address these variables because they were previously included within a TYPE clause that attributed them to StateRecord as if that were an object. The values and contents of these variables having been set, StateRecord now contains a complete record for the state. It is stored to disk at location number state—translation from state number to location number does not need to take place.

You now can modify SUB Acquire () to work in the reverse:

```
SUB Acquire (state AS INTEGER)
GET #1, state, StateRecord
StateName.Text = name
Population.Text = STR$(pop)
LandMass.Text = STR$(mass)
Bird.Text = bird
END SUB
```

Once StateRecord is loaded into memory, the contents and values of its four constituent variables follow.

Summary

After opening a file in RANDOM access mode using the OPEN statement, data elements can be stored to and retrieved from a designated file at random from any location within the boundaries of the file, and at any time. Random access is bidirectional, whereas sequential access is unidirectional—either INPUT or OUTPUT/APPEND. Opening a file in BINARY access mode allows for the storage and retrieval of individual bytes from a file, rather than elements of data in the form of variables.

You can use the PUT # statement to write the value or contents of a single variable to a random-access file, either at a specified location within the file or at the point just following the last recorded writing to that file. You can use the GET # statement to retrieve data from a random-access file, from a specified location or just after the last location read from or written to.

A data element within a random-access file has a fixed field length, specified within the OPEN…AS RANDOM statement using the optional LEN term. If LEN is not included in the OPEN statement, the field length is set to 128 bytes. A record is a collection of related data elements. An entire record can be stored within this single field, as long as the constituent variables within that record have fixed field lengths themselves. The constituent variables of a record can be specified within a TYPE clause at the module level of the VB/DOS application.

Review Questions

Answers to Review Questions appear in Appendix B.

1. What is the maximum length of an alphanumeric string within a random-access data element?
2. Using the formal database model, if a set of records defined by a TYPE clause can be considered a table, a variable within the clause might be considered what?

3. What is the value returned by `LEN(Precinct)` if the `TYPE` clause is expressed as follows:

```
TYPE Precinct
    name AS STRING * 36
    seat AS STRING * 25
    latitude AS SINGLE
    longitude AS SINGLE
    PopRegistered AS LONG
END TYPE
```

46

Data File Attributes

In this chapter, you are introduced to the functions that you can use to retrieve data about a data file—or functions that return the attributes of that file. Later, you learn an alternative method for retrieving individual bytes from a stored data file in either sequential or binary access mode.

Now, Then, Let's See...Where Exactly Are We?

As you've seen demonstrated in the previous two chapters, the Visual Basic for MS-DOS interpreter maintains a file pointer for each open data channel. This pointer is a value in memory—not a variable—which registers the current location where an element of data is read from a file or is stored to a file. Because VB/DOS does not see stored data files as formal structures with stored field lengths, attributes, and relations, practically the only control you have over the data-transfer process is through this file pointer.

Perhaps the simplest file pointer control function to comprehend is the one that tells you whether you've reached the end of the proverbial rope: the `EOF()` function.

EOF() **Function**

Syntax:

```
variable% = EOF(channel%)
```

The `EOF()` function returns whether the file pointer for a specified `channel%` is currently within its boundaries. If the file pointer has reached the *E*nd *O*f the *F*ile, `EOF()` returns a Boolean value of true (–1). If there are still more data elements or bytes to be read within an open data file, `EOF()` returns false (0). The function works only on files that have a `channel%` opened previously with the `OPEN` statement and are currently considered open by the interpreter. The pound sign before `channel%` is omitted for this function.

Example

One common use of the `EOF()` function is in loading the contents of a sequential-access file into array variables in memory when the number of data elements within the file has not been determined. Here is an example routine that loads the contents of a sequential-access file of any length into an array variable, assuming that variable has been dimensioned for a high enough value:

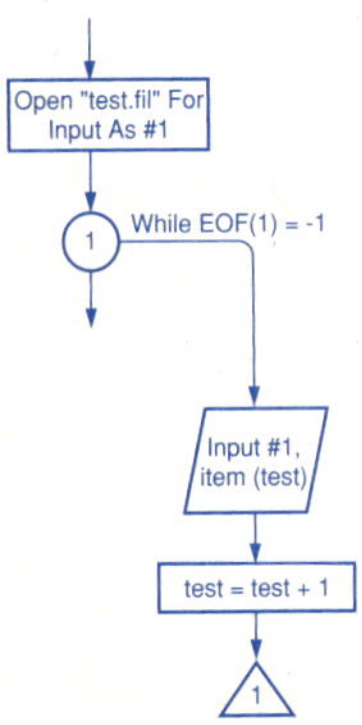


```
OPEN "test.fil" FOR INPUT AS #1
WHILE EOF(1) = -1
    INPUT #1, item(test)
    test = test + 1
WEND
```

You could have used a `FOR-NEXT` loop within the preceding routine, but only if you knew ahead of time or could specify indirectly within a variable the number of elements within the data file—because you'd have to count from `1` to `something%`. Here variable `test` is incremented manually, and the `WHILE-WEND` loop executes until the end-of-file register is set to true.

The VB/DOS interpreter maintains values for the last location written to or read from a data file, as well as the *next* location. These are not to be confused with each other.

LOC() **Function**

Syntax:

`location& = LOC(channel%)`

The `LOC()` function returns the location of the previous storage to or retrieval from an open data file, the *channel%* number of which is specified between the parentheses. For random-access files, the `LOC()` function returns the number of the previous data element or record, where 1 is the number of the first element in the file. For sequential-access files, `LOC()` returns a rounded value equivalent to the current byte location of the data pointer—not the element or record location—divided by 128. For binary-access files, `LOC()` returns the location of the byte previously written to or read from the data file. The pound sign before *channel%* is omitted for this function.

SEEK() **Function**

Syntax:

`location& = SEEK(channel%)`

The `SEEK()` function returns the location of the file pointer within an open data file, the *channel%* number of which is specified between the parentheses. This pointer location is where the next read or write operation takes place. For random-access files, `SEEK()` returns the number to be given the next data element written to or read from the data file. For sequential- and binary-access files, `SEEK()` returns the byte location where the next character of data is written to or read from the data file. The pound sign before *channel%* is omitted for this function.

Example

Suppose your application maintains a random-access data file. A record of related data elements within this file is grouped informally—without the aid of the TYPE clause. A cluster of individual elements, each with a small, fixed data length, comprises a record. You might have a procedure that, at some time, needs to know whether the current file pointer is in the midst of a record or at the beginning of one. You can use the following routine fragment to determine this state:

```
lc = SEEK(1)
IF lc / reclength = INT(lc / reclength) THEN
    ' Beginning of Record
    .
    .
    .
ELSE
    ' Midst of Record
    .
    .
    .
END IF
```

The total number of data elements within a complete random-access data file *must* be a multiple of the number of data elements in a complete record in that file. It therefore follows that if the record length does not evenly divide into the element location of the file pointer, the pointer must not be at the beginning of a new record.

You can use the SEEK # statement, which is related to the SEEK() function, to set the current location of the file pointer manually.

SEEK # **Statement**

Syntax:

```
SEEK [#]channel%, location&
```

The SEEK # statement sets the location of the pointer for a data file, where the next read or write operation takes place, to a specified *location&*. The data file is specified by its designated *channel%*, which is given to that file when it is opened using the OPEN statement. The value of *location&* can be specified as greater than the actual current length of the file. In such cases, the interpreter generates null values for all locations between the final location and the stated *location&*.

For random-access files, the value of *location&* is set to the data element number where a variable is to be written when PUT # is invoked next, or to the data element number where it is to be read when GET # is invoked next. For sequential- and binary-access files, the value of *location&* is set to the byte address of the next character to be written to or read from the data file. The pound sign before the *channel%* number is optional.

Example

Perhaps the most common use for the SEEK # statement is to set the current file pointer to element #1 of a file, as with the following instruction:

```
SEEK #1, 1
```

Data Process Control

A *buffer* is an area of memory where data are temporarily stored.

When storing information to a data file, that data usually waits within a data *buffer* before it actually is sent to disk. A buffer is a holding area in memory consisting of a fixed number of bytes, reserved for data that are to be sent to some device—often a disk file—at some later time, generally when the buffer is full.

The purpose of a buffer in this case is to speed writing operations to a file because writing to an address in memory is much faster than writing to a single location on a disk, and writing several data elements to a single location on a disk once is much faster than writing several data elements to several locations on that disk at different times. In sequential access, specifying the LEN = option in the OPEN statement sets the size of this buffer in memory; by default, it is set to 512 bytes, or half of a kilobyte.

Each open channel has its own memory buffer apportioned to it. Part of what the CLOSE instruction does is flush the memory buffer apportioned for the stated channel number. Until the CLOSE instruction is executed, the image of the data file that the VB/DOS interpreter sees cannot be equivalent to the image of the data file on the disk itself. Updates of the physical file on disk take place only when the buffer is full. After each update, the buffer is emptied. *Caching* in microcomputer hardware is similar to buffering in software, in that hard-coded registers are reserved for holding data that are to be transferred to another device. Because transferring data all at once is always faster than transferring one unit at a time, processing is noticeably expedited.

The only danger in batch-storing is that, in the event of a fatal error or a system crash, the logical image of the data in memory is lost and the non-updated physical image of the data remains. You can use the RESET statement at the end of a program, during an error-trapping routine, or before loading a new document file into memory to shut down data transfer officially and to make the physical data image equivalent to the logical image.

RESET **Statement**

Syntax:

```
RESET
```

The RESET statement shuts down all data-transfer processes by flushing the contents of all open data buffers to their apportioned OPEN files and closing all open channels without having to invoke CLOSE statements for those channels.

Following are the rest of VB/DOS's general file maintenance functions.

LOF() **Function**

Syntax:

```
length% = LOF(channel%)
```

The LOF() function returns the length in bytes of the open file whose *channel%* appears between the parentheses. The pound sign before *channel%* is omitted for this function.

FREEFILE **Function**

Syntax:

```
channel% = FREEFILE
```

The FREEFILE function returns the lowest-valued available unopened channel number, within the variable *channel%*. You can then use this variable within an OPEN statement that may follow. The FREEFILE function requires no parentheses.

FILEATTR() **Function**

Syntax:

```
setting% = FILEATTR(channel%, attribute%)
```

When *attribute%* is stated as 1, the FILEATTR() function returns a value that describes the data file access mode assigned to the specified data channel. This value can be any of the following:

1	Sequential INPUT
2	Sequential OUTPUT
4	RANDOM

8 Sequential APPEND

32 BINARY

When *attribute%* is stated as 2, the FILEATTR() function returns a value representing the file's handle or access number attributed to it by MS-DOS.

Unformatted Data Input

VB/DOS maintains one function (not a statement, mind you) for the acquisition of data from a file—any file—that might not necessarily be a file in one of the three regular VB/DOS formats. You can use this statement to acquire characters from a regular text file and convert those characters into usable data later.

INPUT$() **Function**

Syntax:

```
string$ = INPUT$(numchars%, [#]channel%)
```

The INPUT$() function is used to acquire raw data from a file, the data elements of which, if there are any, are not distinguished from each other in any way that is immediately recognizable by the VB/DOS interpreter. After the data are acquired, it is up to the VB/DOS application to interpret the data and find a purpose for them.

The function retrieves *numchars%* number of alphanumeric characters from a data file that has a *channel%* number apportioned to it by the OPEN statement for sequential INPUT or BINARY access. The current file pointer is moved to the byte following the last one read by INPUT$(). The string is retrieved and assigned to the string variable *string$*. Each byte in the retrieved string is treated as an alphanumeric character that can be converted to a value between 0 and 255 with the ASC() function. This function is not available for files opened for RANDOM access. The pound sign before *channel%* is optional for this function.

Example

Suppose you have a file selector box that contains a preview line, which shows the first 85 characters of a text file currently being highlighted within the file directory box. Here is a routine that displays the first line:

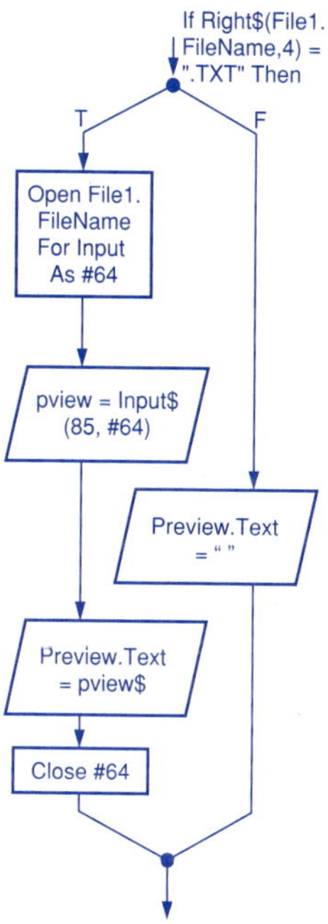


```
IF RIGHT$(File1.FileName, 4) = ".TXT" THEN
     OPEN File1.Filename FOR INPUT AS #64
     pview$ = INPUT$(85, #64)
     Preview.Text = pview$
     CLOSE #64
ELSE
     Preview.Text = ""
END IF
```

Here is the preceding routine written as pseudocode:

If the file currently being highlighted is a
  text file, then
   Open that file as a data file, give it channel
    number 64, and pretend it is a sequential-access
    input file.
   Retrieve the first 85 characters from channel #64.
   Place those characters within the preview text box.
   Close the channel because you need no more
    characters.
Otherwise,
   Clear the preview text box because you're not reading
    a conventional text file.
End of condition.

Summary

The `EOF()` function is used as a flag to determine whether the final element of a data file has been read. The `LOC()` function is used to return the file pointer location of the element that has just been read, whereas the `SEEK()` function is used to return the file pointer location of the element that is about to be read. You use the `SEEK #`

statement to position that pointer to a specific location. The file pointer location for a sequential- or binary-access file is a byte address within the data file, whereas the location for a random-access file is a data element number, regardless of the length of that element.

The `LOF()` function is used to return the length in bytes of an open file. The `FREEFILE` function is used to return the first available unopened file channel. You use the `FILEATTR()` function, for the most part, to determine the file-access mode attributed to an open channel.

The `INPUT$()` function is used for files that appear to be opened for sequential or binary access, for acquiring a specified number of characters from any file, whether or not it is a formal VB/DOS data file. This function bypasses the standard access techniques for sequential and binary access.

Review Questions

Answers to Review Questions appear in Appendix B.

Assume a text file is composed in its entirety of the following:

```
We hold these truths to be self-evident: that all men
  are created equal...
```

Only one space follows the colon, by the way. This file has been opened and given a channel number with the following instruction:

```
OPEN "CONSTITU.DTA" FOR INPUT AS #5 LEN = 512
```

1. What is the current value returned by `LOF(5)`?
2. What are the contents of `c$` after invoking the instruction `c$ = INPUT$(7, #5)`?
3. After invoking the preceding instruction, what is the value returned by `LOC(5)`?
4. What is the current value returned by `SEEK(5)`?
5. Suppose the instruction `SEEK #5, 32` is executed. What are the contents of `c$` now?
6. What are the contents of `c$` after executing the instruction `c$ = INPUT$(7, #1)`?

Part X

Appendixes

A

ASCII Code Chart

The following table lists the values that represent alphanumeric characters for the Visual Basic for MS-DOS interpreter. The table shows the character codes of the American Standard Code Information Interchange (ASCII).

Dec X_{10}	*Hex* X_{16}	*Binary* X_2	*ASCII Character*
000	00	0000 0000	null
001	01	0000 0001	☺
002	02	0000 0010	☻
003	03	0000 0011	♥
004	04	0000 0100	♦
005	05	0000 0101	♣
006	06	0000 0110	♠
007	07	0000 0111	•
008	08	0000 1000	◘
009	09	0000 1001	○
010	0A	0000 1010	◙
011	0B	0000 1011	♂
012	0C	0000 1100	♀
013	0D	0000 1101	♪
014	0E	0000 1110	♫

Dec X_{10}	*Hex* X_{16}	*Binary* X_2	*ASCII Character*
015	0F	0000 1111	☼
016	10	0001 0000	►
017	11	0001 0001	◄
018	12	0001 0010	↕
019	13	0001 0011	!!
020	14	0001 0100	¶
021	15	0001 0101	§
022	16	0001 0110	–
023	17	0001 0111	↨
024	18	0001 1000	↑
025	19	0001 1001	↓
026	1A	0001 1010	→
027	1B	0001 1011	←
028	1C	0001 1100	FS
029	1D	0001 1101	GS
030	1E	0001 1110	RS
031	1F	0001 1111	US
032	20	0010 0000	SP
033	21	0010 0001	!
034	22	0010 0010	"
035	23	0010 0011	#
036	24	0010 0100	$
037	25	0010 0101	%
038	26	0010 0110	&
039	27	0010 0111	'
040	28	0010 1000	(
041	29	0010 1001	)
042	2A	0010 1010	*
043	2B	0010 1011	+
044	2C	0010 1100	,
045	2D	0010 1101	-

Dec X_{10}	*Hex* X_{16}	*Binary* X_2	*ASCII Character*
046	2E	0010 1110	.
047	2F	0010 1111	/
048	30	0011 0000	0
049	31	0011 0001	1
050	32	0011 0010	2
051	33	0011 0011	3
052	34	0011 0100	4
053	35	0011 0101	5
054	36	0011 0110	6
055	37	0011 0111	7
056	38	0011 1000	8
057	39	0011 1001	9
058	3A	0011 1010	:
059	3B	0011 1011	;
060	3C	0011 1100	<
061	3D	0011 1101	=
062	3E	0011 1110	>
063	3F	0011 1111	?
064	40	0100 0000	@
065	41	0100 0001	A
066	42	0100 0010	B
067	43	0100 0011	C
068	44	0100 0100	D
069	45	0100 0101	E
070	46	0100 0110	F
071	47	0100 0111	G
072	48	0100 1000	H
073	49	0100 1001	I
074	4A	0100 1010	J
075	4B	0100 1011	K

continues

Dec X_{10}	*Hex* X_{16}	*Binary* X_2	*ASCII Character*
076	4C	0100 1100	L
077	4D	0100 1101	M
078	4E	0100 1110	N
079	4F	0100 1111	O
080	50	0101 0000	P
081	51	0101 0001	Q
082	52	0101 0010	R
083	53	0101 0011	S
084	54	0101 0100	T
085	55	0101 0101	U
086	56	0101 0110	V
087	57	0101 0111	W
088	58	0101 1000	X
089	59	0101 1001	Y
090	5A	0101 1010	Z
91	5B	0101 1011	[
092	5C	0101 1100	\
093	5D	0101 1101	]
094	5E	0101 1110	^
095	5F	0101 1111	–
096	60	0110 0000	`
097	61	0110 0001	a
098	62	0110 0010	b
099	63	0110 0011	c
100	64	0110 0100	d
101	65	0110 0101	e
102	66	0110 0110	f
103	67	0110 0111	g
104	68	0110 1000	h
105	69	0110 1001	i
106	6A	0110 1010	j

Dec X_{10}	*Hex* X_{16}	*Binary* X_2	*ASCII Character*
107	6B	0110 1011	k
108	6C	0110 1100	l
109	6D	0110 1101	m
110	6E	0110 1110	n
111	6F	0110 1111	o
112	70	0111 0000	p
113	71	0111 0001	q
114	72	0111 0010	r
115	73	0111 0011	s
116	74	0111 0100	t
117	75	0111 0101	u
118	76	0111 0110	v
119	77	0111 0111	w
120	78	0111 1000	x
121	79	0111 1001	y
122	7A	0111 1010	z
123	7B	0111 1011	{
124	7C	0111 1100	¦
125	7D	0111 1101	}
126	7E	0111 1110	~
127	7F	0111 1111	DEL
128	80	1000 0000	Ç
129	81	1000 0001	ü
130	82	1000 0010	é
131	83	1000 0011	â
132	84	1000 0100	ä
133	85	1000 0101	à
134	86	1000 0110	å
135	87	1000 0111	ç
136	88	1000 1000	ê

continues

Dec X_{10}	*Hex* X_{16}	*Binary* X_2	*ASCII Character*
137	89	1000 1001	ë
138	8A	1000 1010	è
139	8B	1000 1011	ï
140	8C	1000 1100	î
141	8D	1000 1101	ì
142	8E	1000 1110	Ä
143	8F	1000 1111	Å
144	90	1001 0000	É
145	91	1001 0001	æ
146	92	1001 0010	Æ
147	93	1001 0011	ô
148	94	1001 0100	ö
149	95	1001 0101	ò
150	96	1001 0110	û
151	97	1001 0111	ù
152	98	1001 1000	ÿ
153	99	1001 1001	Ö
154	9A	1001 1010	Ü
155	9B	1001 1011	¢
156	9C	1001 1100	£
157	9D	1001 1101	¥
158	9E	1001 1110	₧
159	9F	1001 1111	ƒ
160	A0	1010 0000	á
161	A1	1010 0001	í
162	A2	1010 0010	ó
163	A3	1010 0011	ú
164	A4	1010 0100	ñ
165	A5	1010 0101	Ñ
166	A6	1010 0110	ª
167	A7	1010 0111	º

Dec X_{10}	Hex X_{16}	Binary X_2	ASCII Character
168	A8	1010 1000	¿
169	A9	1010 1001	⌐
170	AA	1010 1010	¬
171	AB	1010 1011	½
172	AC	1010 1100	¼
173	AD	1010 1101	¡
174	AE	1010 1110	«
175	AF	1010 1111	»
176	B0	1011 0000	░
177	B1	1011 0001	▒
178	B2	1011 0010	▓
179	B3	1011 0011	│
180	B4	1011 0100	┤
181	B5	1011 0101	╡
182	B6	1011 0110	╢
183	B7	1011 0111	╖
184	B8	1011 1000	╕
185	B9	1011 1001	╣
186	BA	1011 1010	║
187	BB	1011 1011	╗
188	BC	1011 1100	╝
189	BD	1011 1101	╜
190	BE	1011 1110	╛
191	BF	1011 1111	┐
192	C0	1100 0000	└
193	C1	1100 0001	┴
194	C2	1100 0010	┬
195	C3	1100 0011	├
196	C4	1100 0100	─
197	C5	1100 0101	┼

continues

Dec X_{10}	*Hex* X_{16}	*Binary* X_2	*ASCII Character*
198	C6	1100 0110	
199	C7	1100 0111	╟
200	C8	1100 1000	╚
201	C9	1100 1001	╔
202	CA	1100 1010	╩
203	CB	1100 1011	╦
204	CC	1100 1100	╠
205	CD	1100 1101	═
206	CE	1100 1110	╬
207	CF	1100 1111	╧
208	D0	1101 0000	╨
209	D1	1101 0001	╤
210	D2	1101 0010	╥
211	D3	1101 0011	╙
212	D4	1101 0100	╘
213	D5	1101 0101	╒
214	D6	1101 0110	╓
215	D7	1101 0111	╫
216	D8	1101 1000	╪
217	D9	1101 1001	┘
218	DA	1101 1010	┌
219	DB	1101 1011	█
220	DC	1101 1100	▄
221	DD	1101 1101	▌
222	DE	1101 1110	▐
223	DF	1101 1111	▀
224	E0	1110 0000	α
225	E1	1110 0001	β
226	E2	1110 0010	Γ
227	E3	1110 0011	π
228	E4	1110 0100	Σ

Dec X_{10}	*Hex* X_{16}	*Binary* X_2	*ASCII Character*
229	E5	1110 0101	σ
230	E6	1110 0110	µ
231	E7	1110 0111	τ
232	E8	1110 1000	Φ
233	E9	1110 1001	θ
234	EA	1110 1010	Ω
235	EB	1110 1011	δ
236	EC	1110 1100	∞
237	ED	1110 1101	ø
238	EE	1110 1110	∈
239	EF	1110 1111	∩
240	F0	1110 0000	≡
241	F1	1111 0001	±
242	F2	1111 0010	≥
243	F3	1111 0011	≤
244	F4	1111 0100	⌠
245	F5	1111 0101	⌡
246	F6	1111 0110	÷
247	F7	1111 0111	≈
248	F8	1111 1000	°
249	F9	1111 1001	•
250	FA	1111 1010	·
251	FB	1111 1011	
252	FC	1111 1100	η
253	FD	1111 1101	^{2}
254	FE	1111 1110	■
255	FF	1111 1111	

The `_KeyPress` event is recognized whenever a standard character—not including function keys—is pressed on the keyboard. The returned value will be one of those listed in the preceding table.

B

Answers to Review Questions

The following are answers to the Review Questions at the end of each chapter. You can obtain answers to the Review Exercises by ordering this book's companion disk. See the disk offer page at the back of this book for more information.

Chapter 1

1. Because BASIC is designed to more closely approximate the language used by people, whereas a low-level language is designed to more closely approximate the logic of the computer.
2. An instruction
3. Machine language
4. The BIOS—the Basic Input/Output System of your computer.
5. Realistically speaking, a computer does not receive information. It can't be informed of anything because information implies the presence of a reasoning capability that the

computer does not have. The instruction does, however, inform the human reader that a symbolic reference or variable called *a* will be used to represent the numeral value 6, and it tells the person to think of *a* as being equal to 6—to replace *a* for 6 in his mind. The BASIC language thus performs a dual purpose: it informs the human reader while it instructs the computer. This is another reason why BASIC is considered a high-level language.

Chapter 2

1. A project
2. Buttons
3. An underscore character (_)
4. `_Click`. In other words, the term following the underscore character.
5. The Code Editor
6. Form Designer
7. .FRM, the extension given form modules

Chapter 3

1. `f = 6`
2. `INT(a + b + c)`
3. `good = 1`
4. 3
5. A subroutine

Chapter 4

1. Whenever you press a calculator key from 1 through 9, that digit appears in the display, moving any other digits before it to the left. The 0 key works in a similar manner, except that if the display already reads *0*, no digits are added. Because there was an exception, the 0 key was excluded from the control array. It could be included, although you would need to add a special conditional statement to the procedure, such as `SELECT CASE 0`, that would determine whether the key pressed is in fact the 0 key. The period or point key is not handled at all like a digit, so it should remain outside the control array.

2. In standard calculator notation, or *algebraic notation,* the user enters the mathematical function *before* entering the value to which that function pertains. As a result, when entering the expression `5 + 8 – 6`, the addition of 8 to 5 takes place when the user presses the *minus* key just before pressing 6. This makes algebraic notation a confusing procedure to implement. In Reverse Polish notation, the preceding expression would be entered as `5 Enter 8 Enter 6 –`. The function takes place at the time the user presses the function key. This makes it possible in VB/DOS for a procedure to be executed on pressing a command button that acts as the function key.

Chapter 5

1. A value

2. A statement

3. A statement or expression of assignment

4. 32

5. The sign of a value in memory consumes one bit, thus reducing its maximum absolute numeric value by a power of two. If one bit isn't being used to store the sign of the value, it can be used to store a digit, thus increasing the capacity of

that value by a power of two. Furthermore, you can imagine dividing the number of representable values in half, resulting in the negative side and the positive side. But you would be forgetting zero, which is a value that is neither negative nor positive. The number of representable values in a byte is always an even number, but 0 is one value and 1 is an odd number. It must therefore take space from one side or the other, negative or positive; computer designers chose the positive side. This is why a byte can represent –256 but not +256.

Chapter 6

1. A. `x = 47.2`
   B. `x = 3.333333`
   C. `x = 48`
2. A. `v = (3.1415927 / 3) * r ^ 2 * h`
   B. `P = F / (1 + i) ^ n`

Chapter 7

1. –1
2. –1
3. 0
4. –1
5. –1
6. 0
7. 0

Chapter 8

1. `Ardwight`

2. `94201`

3. `WallaceArdwight` (notice that no space separates the two)

4. `5151 Back o' the Bay Way`

5. `Oakland, CA  94201`

6. ```
   Wallace T. Ardwight
   5151 Back o' the Bay Way
   Oakland, CA  94201
   ```

7. ```
   Wallace T. Ardwight

   Oakland, CA  94201
   ```

8. `Mr. or Ms. Wallace T. Ardwight`

Chapter 9

1. Nebraska

2. A bishop

3. 400

4. `DIM Aspen() AS DOUBLE`

Chapter 10

1. The sixth power

2. Zero

3. No. Any number to the zeroth power is 1, and 1 divides into every integral (whole) number evenly.

Chapter 11

1. `DIM`
2. No. The `STATIC` statement preserves the values of the listed variables when the procedure is exited, for when the procedure is reentered. If the interpreter comes across `STATIC` for a second or third time, the previous values are recalled.
3. The `COMMON SHARED` statement declares variables that will have a global scope. They can be used anywhere and everywhere throughout the program. As a result, the statement need only be written once, at the beginning of the declarations section of the project's main module. Because you need only one `COMMON SHARED` statement per application, you don't need to name the values to which it refers—the variables for those values will not be redeclared within the application anyway.

Chapter 12

1. `CONST FALSE = 0`
2. Not really. `ERASE` is more handy for use in clearing the contents of static arrays. `ERASE` can be used, however, to erase both the contents and the bounds of dynamic arrays. In so doing, the statement clears memory without redimensioning the array. `REDIM` will erase the contents of a dynamic array although it allows you to respecify the bounds of the array. It doesn't erase those bounds.

Chapter 13

1. The `END SUB` statement closes a procedure, whereas the `EXIT SUB` statement forces an exit from that procedure before its `END SUB` statement is executed.
2. `END` by itself ends the entire program. No other statement does that.

Chapter 14

1. Absolutely not, even if the instruction is properly phrased. A metacommand will be executed by the VB/DOS interpreter although that isn't really an instruction in the VB/DOS programming language. As far as every other series of characters not preceded by a `$` is concerned, VB/DOS will ignore whatever's there up to the end of that program line.
2. A statement because there is no graphic object on the form that `PRINT` refers to. If there were a graphic object (an *anteced-ent*), it would appear before `PRINT` and be separated from it by a period. `PRINT` would then be used as a method.

Chapter 15

1. 15
2. 3
3. "Go"
4. 0
5. ""

Chapter 16

1. `FOR-NEXT`
2. `DO-LOOP UNTIL`
3. `DO WHILE-LOOP`

Chapter 17

1. The interpreter "errors out." Naturally, it generates a `RETURN without GOSUB` error.

2. Any form of `DO-LOOP` constructs using `WHILE c < 4` as a qualifier, or a `WHILE c < 4. . . WEND` loop.
3. Any form of `DO-LOOP` constructs using `UNTIL c = 4` as a qualifier.

Chapter 18

1. A graphical mode program
2. At the instruction immediately following the `INPUT` statement.
3. No place at all. The next instruction to be executed is determined by whether a graphical event performed by the user triggers any of the event procedures which might specify that event.

Chapter 19

1. The module-level code of the startup module.
2. After the interpreter clears and resets the workspace, absolutely nothing. No instructions are executed whatsoever. The project rests in limbo.
3. Either `Form2.SHOW` or `LOAD Form2`.

Chapter 20

1. A function in computing combines arithmetic functions to derive a single result value, whereas a statement merely changes the operative state of the program without returning a value. Because all instructions in VB/DOS are arithmetic operations in one form or another, the instruction that calls the `FUNCTION` routine must be mathematical in nature as well. Because this instruction is stated in the form of an equation and the equation contains an obvious result value

location, the instruction fulfills all the requirements of a function in computing. Thus, a call to a procedure that returns a value is a function. For that matter, all function procedures in computing—whether they are written in VB/DOS or assembly language—must be called by some body of the source code, so all functions are in turn *function calls.*

2. The `CALL` statement places a call to a procedure that is not considered a function because no value is returned. Values are passed to this `SUB` procedure, however, and those values are declared at the beginning of the `SUB` procedure within parentheses. In this book, I specified functions and function calls with parentheses, as in `LEN()`, even when I didn't state any parameters. Programmers do this to distinguish the role of the instruction as a function or function call. If you leave parentheses around the `SUB` (non-function) procedure call, you violate the syntax of functions. By *including* parentheses in the `CALL` syntax, you specify parameters using standard syntax not for the name of the `SUB` procedure but for the word `CALL` itself.

Chapter 21

1. A function of arithmetic is any operation that can be expressed symbolically and that changes the state or value of something. In trigonometry, for instance, a "true" function is any operation that can be solved logically as a single value for any one unit of time. A graph of such a function, therefore, can only show one point plotted for any vertical line along the graph. A VB/DOS function is representative of a low-level process within the interpreter. It represents an arithmetic function and logically "returns" an explicit value. It *simulates* an arithmetic function, although it cannot actually be calculating that function specifically.

2. Not in VB/DOS, as this instruction might in some other dialects of BASIC. In VB/DOS, the instruction reserves all variables of single or multiple letters beginning with the letters A through Z as being integer variables by default, unless stated otherwise.
3. Because the Timer control, the `_Timer` event, and the `TIMER()` function, for instance, can be confused with each other if not for the extra punctuation provided in this book.

Chapter 22

1. 3
2. 65
3. "z"
4. 65
5. 1600

Chapter 23

1. 3
2. –1
3. 1

Chapter 24

1. "When"
2. "events"
3. "n"
4. "the"
5. "When in, of, and around the course of human events"

Chapter 25

1. Yes. Both types can be included within a `TYPE-END TYPE` clause.
2. No. Although VB/DOS uses object-oriented syntax here, it does not use object-oriented *structure* in its composite variables.
3. Zero. The `DEF FN` clause is the only clause in VB/DOS where a variable can be declared with clause-level scope, the narrowest scope.
4. When an element of a composite variable is referenced, that reference takes the same place in an equation that a conventional variable normally takes.

Chapter 26

1. Between 0 and 1. Read the question carefully. The multiplication by 72 takes place *after* the randomization rather than during the randomization.
2. Most of the time you will be using the function as if it were written `RND(0)`. Omitting the parentheses along with the "dummy parameter" makes using this function a bit easier.
3. Yes, as long as that number is rounded to a short (two-byte) integer expression.

Chapter 27

1. No. If the form has not been loaded yet using the `LOAD` statement, the `.SHOW` method will perform that duty on behalf of `LOAD`.
2. Yes. `UNLOAD` only takes the form out of the workspace and out of memory.
3. In the object-oriented methodology, an object can be referred to as such only if it has the memory constructs associated with it that make the item *object*-ive. Those constructs do not

exist when the object is not in memory. Object-oriented syntax, therefore, cannot be used to refer to a nonexistent object. `LOAD` and `UNLOAD` are both non-object-oriented because the forms and graphic elements to which they refer do not exist in memory yet and do not have objective constructs associated with them.

Chapter 28

1. Alaska would be state #49, and Hawaii would be state #50, regardless of the `.Sorted` state of the list.
2. Guam will be the 11th item in the list because it has yet to be loaded into memory, and you're accounting for the State of Columbia.

Chapter 29

1. Yes. They will still be considered independent objects although they will be referenced using the same procedure.
2. No. A control is made part of a frame by creating it within the frame area. If it is created outside the frame, the VB/DOS interpreter always considers it to be outside the frame.
3. Visually it can, but logically a control cannot "half-belong" to a frame.
4. A scroll bar created as a result of setting the `.ScrollBars` property of a text box cannot be set to a minimum or maximum value.

Chapter 30

1. An input box
2. Modal

3. Because the program, by displaying a file selector box, evidently needs a filename for its process to continue, it generally is safer to suspend any other inputs to the program until such a filename is delivered.

Chapter 31

1. `Surname.Text`
2. `Group(1).TabIndex`
3. `BobTheBear.Tag`
4. `Screen.ActiveControl.Text`
5. `Source.Status.Text`
6. `Screen.ActiveForm.Status.Text`
7. `Source.Parent.Status.Text`

Chapter 32

1. Gray
2. Blue
3. `.Text`

Chapter 33

1. A menu bar is not a positionable object you can place on a form using a pointer. Therefore, you should not use a pointer graphically to invoke a menu bar within a form.
2. A dialog box follows the selection of this menu command.
3. The general procedures area of the form that contained the removed button and now contains the menu command.

Chapter 34

1. A drag operation leaves the dragged control where it is and carries a *copy* of the control. A move operation actually relocates the control to a new location.
2. Yes. The procedure responds only to drops into the region it inhabits, thus making it the target.
3. Coordinates are relative to the control and must be offset by means of additive arithmetic if they are to be made relative to the form or the screen.

Chapter 35

1. `"##%"`
2. `"****000.00"`
3. `"h AM/PM"`
4. `"##.##;(##.##);Unchanged"`
5. ```
   CHR$(34) + "by " + CHR$(34) + "h:mm AM/PM" + CHR$(34) +
     " tonight at the earliest." + CHR$(34)
   ```

Chapter 36

1. Regardless of how many lines of text you might see in a text box, the VB/DOS interpreter considers the contents of all text boxes as if they were written in one long, straight line.
2. At this point, the `.SelText` property would automatically be set to the contents of the selected characters in the text box. No equation is necessary.
   ```

Chapter 37

1. The entire screen is filled with the foreground color.

2. Once again, the entire screen is filled with the foreground color. When angles are specified in the `CIRCLE` statement, an arc is drawn, which is not an enclosed area. With no *bordercolor%* specified, the `PAINT` statement then draws directly over the arc because, by default, it doesn't recognize the arc's color register as a border.

3. No. This question is not rhetorical, although it might as well have been and it would have made its point well enough. In any event, graphics hardware over the years has been developed and redeveloped without its developers paying any attention to the standards set by Microsoft BASIC. When the hardware changes, so does the mathematics for maintaining the graphics array. For each new array supported, Microsoft adds another number to the list for its `SCREEN` statement. (Did you notice that support for `SCREEN 5` and `6` has been dropped?) When that happens, the way the default registers work changes, and `COLOR` is the statement that sets colors for the default registers.

Chapter 38

1. Yes. Because `POINT(0)` and `POINT(1)` return the x and y coordinates, respectively, of the last point plotted to the screen. The `PSET` statement is designed to do exactly that.

2. `(30, 0)`. Because the term `SCREEN` is specified along with `VIEW`, the physical screen coordinates remain as they were before `VIEW` was executed.

3. `(60, 0)`. Without the `SCREEN` keyword stated along with `VIEW`, the logical screen coordinates `(30, 0)` are moved 30 pixels to the right when the first pair of coordinates in the `VIEW` statement are `(30, 0)` as well. When you plot to `(60, 0)` from then on, you actually plot to the physical coordinates `(90, 0)`.

Chapter 39

1. Zero. After printing the line, the interpreter executes a carriage return with line feed, resetting the `LPOS(0)` value to 0.
2. 53. The semicolon stops the interpreter from resetting `LPOS(0)`. If you were to print anything else to the printer, the new text would appear just to the right of the exclamation point in the previous sentence.
3. 54. A tabulation is considered a single character by `LPOS(0)`, regardless of how many spaces it appears to consume.

Chapter 40

1. About 1:05.536
2. A. `_Timer`
   B. `TIMER`
   C. `TIMER()`

Chapter 41

1. The scan code values are not functionally additive. The BIOS doesn't think in decimal numbers. If there was any summing of the two, the result would be Boolean rather than decimal.
2. Most likely the first key pressed out of a sequence, no matter how closely together the sequence was pressed, will be the first key scanned. However, the lower BIOS values do take precedence.
3. You have to read this question carefully to be able to answer it logically. If you understand the problem logically, you understand something about the art and theory of programming. Mechanically speaking, one key takes precedence over the other. The faster the computer is at scanning, the more adept it is at determining which key came first—or *appearing*

to determine which key came first. The BIOS code at its lowest level scans for only one key at a time. At no time does it consider which came first because it never deals with two values at the lowest level. Thus, the computer's quick reflexes have nothing to do with which key will take precedence over the other.

4. By virtue of the scanning sequence, yes, one key higher up in the sequence will have "authority" over another. This is not a hierarchy by virtue of one key's assumed importance over another, however, just its sequence.

Chapter 42

1. An error. This is not the proper syntax for the `LINE` statement. A set of parentheses is missing.
2. A bug. The division operator in the instruction should be a multiplication operator, but the interpreter has no way of knowing your original intentions.

Chapter 43

1. One. The whole idea of using `DATA` and `READ` is so that statements of assignment can be minimized to one per list.
2. Twelve. Because there are 36 elements and three variables receiving them in the `READ` statement, the loop should be executed (36/3) times.
3. `Clipboard.` can be an object, but it is not a *control* by the official VB/DOS definition. It is only a holding point for textual data transfer. Therefore, methods apply to it but not properties.

Chapter 44

1. The PRINT # statement creates text on disk that has the same format as if the same text were printed to the screen or printer using the .PRINT method or PRINT statement. The WRITE # statement, by contrast, places all data entries within quotation marks and separates each entry with a comma for applications with "mail-merge" features to be able to import this data.
2. The INPUT # statement retrieves data entries from disk that have been saved using the PRINT # statement. These entries have the same length after the INPUT # is executed as they had after the PRINT # was executed. The LINE INPUT # statement inputs a string of characters—rather than an explicit entry—that is terminated by a carriage return.

Chapter 45

1. 32,765 bytes, which is the maximum length of the actual element minus two for the descriptor.
2. A field
3. 73 bytes

Chapter 46

1. 74
2. "We hold"
3. 7
4. 8
5. "We hold." The SEEK statement does not affect the contents of a string variable.
6. "these" with spaces around the word. The INPUT$ function starts inputting characters beginning at the current SEEK() position.

C

The History of BASIC

A computer used to be a thing that the human being, in the daily course of business, never even saw. In fact, the first business computers—as huge as they were—were largely invisible to the naked eye. If you were the principal buyer for a major industrial organization in 1956 and you made a major computer purchase for your company, you purchased one computer. You had your construction crew erect an entire building for the thing, or you devoted a whole floor of the office structure to it. Preferably this would be a lower floor because you wouldn't want your major purchase to fall through any of the upper floors, and besides, lower floors are easier to keep cool. Still, for the major part of your workday you probably never saw your computer. It spent nearly all day performing crucial office tasks in the background, such as adding numbers together.

If you were a computer operator in 1956, you probably were witness to a new revolution in computing in the making: laptop computers. For the most part, you sat on its lap instead of it on yours, but it was a revolution nonetheless. In this era, the best computing opportunity a scholar had was to enroll in a college lucky enough to have a computer.

At this time in history, the hub of the world computer network was Boston, Massachusetts. Surprisingly, this revolution began along one of the "surrounding nodes," in New Hampshire at Dartmouth College. In 1956, a man named John Kemeny—who later became president of Dartmouth—developed (at least to some extent) a concept for simplified computer programming. The idea was to represent the instructions that a computer uses to execute programs—what today is called *machine language*—with simplified, more easily implementable terms. The other idea was to be able to have one assembly language for several computers without having to account for variations in the models.

The project was called *Share Assembly Language.* The project was greatly expedited when Kemeny was given access to some computers—namely, an IBM 704 and some GEs. In 1956, Kemeny conceived a dialect for the Share language, which he called *DARSIMCO.* It sounds like it was named for a hardware store; in fact, if you consider a "hardware store" a way of implementing instructions that store values in a piece of hardware called the *accumulator,* then in fact it was. *Dar*tmouth *Sim*plified *Co*de took the major categories of assembly language at the time and, from those sets, created a generalized superset that could be reinterpreted and broken down later into the native machine language of a particular computer. The following is a program listing in DARSIMCO:

```
LDA A
FAD B
STO C
```

This DARSIMCO program took the contents of `A`, added to them the contents of `B`, and stored them in a register `C`. In other words, this program was `c = a + b`. Mind you, back then the word *program* referred specifically to the process that ran within the hardware of the computer; so an interpreted routine like the preceding one, which was translated by the computer into a program later, was called a *template.*

While Kemeny was busy at work refining assembly language, his colleague Thomas E. Kurtz, who directed the Kiewit Computation Center at Dartmouth, was refining algorithmic language. His project was to find a way to reduce algorithmic interpreted languages such as ALGOL to a subset that was still logically sound but that could fit on computers that had smaller memory. Then, releases of programming languages were given numbers taken from the year of their completion, so the current version of ALGOL during the time of this project was ALGOL 60. Perhaps in jest, Kurtz' reduction of this language was called "ALGOL 30" (at least it was a joke then), and the language was able to fit successfully onto 4K of memory.

If you've forgotten or have never studied the 1960s definition of the term *memory,* here's what the Dark Ages looked like. Back then, a huge drum dipped in a magnetic solution was set to rotate at 30 times per second. This drum was divided into sectors, not unlike the way a hard disk drive is divided today. Each sector contained a certain number of 30-bit *words*—a word then was like a *byte* today. Four thousand ninety-six of those 30-bit words, rotating at "break-neck" speed along a piece of ceramic, constituted *memory.* Still, this was slow. We're discussing memory using the Thomas Edison model of the phonograph.

In 1962, Kurtz, along with Dartmouth students Stephen Garland and Anthony Knapp, produced a 4K single-pass "ALGOL 30" compiler called the *Self-Contained ALGOL Processor*, or *SCALP*. By *self-contained,* I mean that the student who was busy trying to complete his homework for the day did not have to see the intermediate code for his program punched onto a spool of paper tape. Imagine for a moment being a Dartmouth student, busy compiling a major application such as one that, for instance, adds two numbers together. You gain access to one of the terminals, log yourself in, and make yourself comfortable for a very long stay. After entering your program, you literally see the representative code for it being punched by the computer as holes in a very large roll of paper tape. The equivalent of Norton Utilities for rescuing data in this era was a handy roll of cellophane tape.

That same year, on the other side of campus, John Kemeny, along with Sidney Marshall, was still busy refining assembly language. The two had gone so far as to represent arithmetic operators as symbols, so addition was now a legitimate plus sign. Still, there was no English-language syntax in this language—that was Kurtz' department. In Kemeny and Marshall's *Dartmouth Oversimplified Programming Experiment* (*DOPE*), the program `c = a + b` was represented by the following:

```
7 + A B C
```

The 7 in this case referred to a *line number,* which was in itself a revolutionary accomplishment.

When Kemeny and Kurtz decided finally to combine their talents in 1964, their goal was to merge the two projects—the oversimplified assembly language with the truncated algorithmic language. They received a grant from the National Science Foundation, and they were soon at work on a "little" GE-225 computer attached to a storage device for memory called a Datanet-30. Their partners were Michael Busch and John McGeachie, who deserve credit for developing the operating system portion of the project that would be called *Beginners' All-purpose Symbolic Instruction Code.*

All-Purpose Defined

The original definition of *all-purpose* in computing was not what you might think. One of the brilliant ideas shared among this team of four was to integrate the operating system of the computer with the program language. These program engineers imagined that one day people (students) would use computers in much the way people use telephones—more to the point, *public* telephones. They would walk up to a terminal, say HELLO, punch in a program, have it be compiled and functional without having to get out the cellophane tape, tell the terminal GOODBYE, and then walk off and go play some tennis. So HELLO and GOODBYE were two of the primary commands in the first edition of BASIC, completed May 1, 1964.

An all-purpose computer would act as the terminal, the compiler, the program language, the operating system (or *monitor program* as it was called then) and, for all intents and purposes, the environment. Busch and McGeachie for this reason developed the commands NEW, OLD, RUN, SAVE, and LIST. It was largely their idea to distinguish monitor commands from program instructions by preceding all instructions with their line number. This way, if the monitor saw a line with a number on it, it would not process that line right away, but instead count it as part of the interpreted program being entered by the student.

The beauty of the RUN command at that time was that the entire compilation and execution process became automated. There were no batch-processing commands for the student to redundantly execute, and no paper tape spools to wind back up. The student merely entered the program and typed `RUN`. After waiting a short period of time (measured in thumb twiddles), the program executed, and the results displayed right there on the terminal screen rather than having the student wait for one of the people in the back room to come out with a ream of paper.

In the merging of assembly-language syntax with English-language syntax, Kemeny and Kurtz accomplished this: Each BASIC instruction in the 1964 edition was divided into three elements: the instruction number, the operation, and the operand. In the instruction `10 PRINT C`, you easily can spot the three elements of the instruction. This is the way of thinking Kemeny brought to the language. Yet there were also program constructs with contexts that were greater than just the preceding instruction; there were groups of instructions that could be clustered and that had pertinence to each other. Linguistic structures—paragraphs, methods, and algorithms—comprise the way of thinking Kurtz brought to the language.

In the first edition of BASIC, all function instructions were identifiable because they were three letters long and had parentheses. They were restricted to three letters (`SIN`, `COS`, `RND`, `INT`) because on the GE-225, a word was 20 bits long and a character was six bits long. A single word was used to represent a function; therefore, three characters would fit with a two-bit excess.

The second edition of BASIC was released in October, 1964. This edition marked the premiere appearance of the `INPUT` statement, which prompted the user for input. The original programmers of BASIC thought their language would not need to be conversational; the only conversation necessary would be between the user and the monitor. The user entered a program, the monitor processed it, and that was the interaction. The concept of user interaction with the program was added to the language, if you can believe this, as a result of user suggestion.

When array variables were added to the language for the third edition in 1966, the designers considered changing the name of BASIC to MATRIX. Most likely, the designers kept the original name because General Electric was trying to market the language to new customers and didn't want to have to change the campaign in midstream. GE wrote an independent operating system for the GE-635 edition of BASIC, which was the fourth edition released in 1967. This system was called the *DTSS operating system,* which accessed individual files by ordinal number. This is why in the fifth edition of BASIC, released in 1970, the `OPEN #1` and `CLOSE #1` commands were used to look into the contents of data files. Although practically no one uses DTSS today, the ordinal numbers remain as an integral part of the data access portion of the language.

After Kemeny and Kurtz

The man largely responsible for the idea that BASIC should be a modular programming language, and perhaps should drop this dependence on line numbers and the `GOTO` statement, was Stephen Garland. Garland was an associate of Kemeny and Kurtz who, on his own and with permission, produced his own edition called *SBASIC* in 1976. Gone were the `GOTO` and `GOSUB` statements; in their place were more modern function calls and more developed clause structures, such as the first recorded instance of the `SELECT CASE` clause.

The preceding few paragraphs were presented for the benefit of those of you who were under the impression that Microsoft invented BASIC. Indeed, Microsoft has taken charge of the language ever since William Gates and Paul Allen developed the first BASIC interpreter for microcomputers in 1975 for the Altair 8800 kit computer.

Yet I felt it proper in this context to give credit and pay tribute to a group of people who unknowingly launched what could best be described as a renaissance of logical thought among laypeople. We have a tendency today to credit the mouse with being the implement that brought computers out of the basement of offices and into our lives. If we stop there, we have not cultivated this 20/20 hindsight for which we give ourselves so much credit. In large part, it was John Kemeny and Thomas Kurtz who, one early morning in the outskirts of what was then the only network of computing, initiated the computing process which has, at long last, brought us together in this context, in this place of business, to work and, to some degree, to play as we do today. It was they who made computers visible to the naked eye.

D

Complete Source Code Listings of Major Applications

The Expressor

Project name: EXPRESOR.MAK
Constituent file: EXPRESOR.FRM

Object Type	*Property*	*Setting*
Form	.Left	13
	.Top	2
	.Width	65
	.Height	20
	.Caption	Expressor
	.BorderStyle	1 - Fixed Single
	.BackColor	9 - Bright Blue
Label	.Left	2
	.Top	1
	.Width	53
	.Height	2
	.CtlName	Readout

Object Type	*Property*	*Setting*
	.Caption	0
	.BackColor	9 - Bright Blue
	.ForeColor	15 - Bright White
Button	.Left	56
	.Top	1
	.Width	5
	.Height	2
	.CtlName	EditCut
	.Caption	Cut
	.BackColor	1 - Blue

Control Array	*Property*	*Setting*
Label	.Left	2
	.Top	3
	.Width	34
	.Height	1
	.CtlName	ParamText
	.Caption	(blank)
	.Index	0
	.BackColor	15 - Bright White
	.ForeColor	0 - Black
	.BorderStyle	0 - None
	.Left	2
	.Top	4
	.Index	1
	.Left	2
	.Top	5
	.Index	2
	.Left	2
	.Top	6
	.Index	3
	.Left	2
	.Top	7
	.Index	4

Control Array	*Property*	*Setting*
Text box	.Left	37
	.Top	3
	.Width	18
	.Height	1
	.CtlName	Param
	.Caption	0
	.BackColor	11 - Bright Cyan
	.ForeColor	0 - Black
	.Index	0
	.Left	37
	.Top	4
	.Index	1
	.Left	37
	.Top	5
	.Index	2
	.Left	37
	.Top	6
	.Index	3
	.Left	37
	.Top	7
	.Index	4
Button	.Left	57
	.Top	3
	.Width	4
	.Height	1
	.CtlName	StoreBank
	.BackColor	1 - Blue
	.Index	0
	.Left	57
	.Top	4
	.Index	1

continues

Control Array	*Property*	*Setting*
	.Left	57
	.Top	5
	.Index	2
	.Left	57
	.Top	6
	.Index	3
	.Left	57
	.Top	7
	.Index	4
List box	.Left	2
	.Top	9
	.Width	38
	.Height	1
	.CtlName	CalcList
	.BackColor	9 - Bright Blue
	.ForeColor	15 - Bright White
	.Sorted	False
Button	.Left	2
	.Top	14
	.Width	37
	.Height	3
	.CtlName	ApplyFormula
	.Caption	Display
	.BackColor	1 - Blue
Button	.Left	41
	.Top	12
	.Width	4
	.Height	3
	.CtlName	ClearEntry
	.Caption	CE
	.BackColor	1 - Blue

Control Array	*Property*	*Setting*
Button	.Left	41
	.Top	15
	.Width	4
	.Height	2
	.CtlName	ClearAll
	.Caption	C
	.BackColor	1 - Blue
Button	.Left	46
	.Top	13
	.Width	3
	.Height	2
	.CtlName	ButtonPos
	.Caption	1
	.BackColor	1 - Blue
	.Index	1
	.Left	49
	.Top	13
	.Caption	2
	.Index	2
	.Left	52
	.Top	13
	.Caption	3
	.Index	3
	.Left	46
	.Top	11
	.Caption	4
	.Index	4
	.Left	49
	.Top	11
	.Caption	5
	.Index	5

continues

Control Array	*Property*	*Setting*
	.Left	52
	.Top	11
	.Caption	6
	.Index	6
	.Left	46
	.Top	9
	.Caption	7
	.Index	7
	.Left	49
	.Top	9
	.Caption	8
	.Index	8
	.Left	52
	.Top	9
	.Caption	9
	.Index	9
Button	.Left	46
	.Top	15
	.Width	6
	.Height	2
	.CtlName	Button0
	.Caption	0
	.BackColor	1 - Blue
Button	.Left	52
	.Top	15
	.Width	3
	.Height	2
	.CtlName	ButtonPoint
	.Caption	.
	.BackColor	1 - Blue

Control Array	*Property*	*Setting*
Button	.Left	56
	.Top	9
	.Width	5
	.Height	1
	.CtlName	Percent
	.Caption	%
	.BackColor	1 - Blue
Button	.Left	56
	.Top	10
	.Width	5
	.Height	1
	.CtlName	DividedBy
	.Caption	/
	.BackColor	1 - Blue
Button	.Left	56
	.Top	11
	.Width	5
	.Height	1
	.CtlName	Times
	.Caption	X
	.BackColor	1 - Blue
Button	.Left	56
	.Top	12
	.Width	5
	.Height	1
	.CtlName	Minus
	.Caption	-
	.BackColor	1 - Blue
Button	.Left	56
	.Top	14
	.Width	5
	.Height	3
	.CtlName	Enter
	.Caption	Enter
	.BackColor	1 - Blue

```
DECLARE SUB assess_readout ()
DECLARE SUB ClearAll_Click ()
DECLARE FUNCTION surf_area_rccyl! (r!, h!)
DECLARE FUNCTION volume_rccyl! (r!, h!)
DECLARE FUNCTION zone_sphere! (r!, h!)
DECLARE FUNCTION force_att! (me!, mb!, r!, y!)
DECLARE FUNCTION dopp_shift! (vo!, vs!, fo!, c!)
DECLARE SUB Clear_Params ()
DIM SHARED label$(15, 4), p(4)
DIM SHARED readout_value AS SINGLE, combine_value AS SINGLE,
➥ solution AS SINGLE
DIM SHARED ready AS INTEGER
CONST PI = 3.1415927#
CONST GRAV = 6.6732E-11

SUB ApplyFormula_Click ()
FOR in = 0 TO 4
p(in) = VAL(param(in).text)
NEXT in
ndx = CalcList.ListIndex + 1
IF ndx = -1 THEN GOTO The_end
ON ndx GOTO f1, f2, f3, f4, f5
GOTO display_result
f1:
solution = surf_area_rccyl(p(0), p(1))
GOTO display_result
f2:
solution = volume_rccyl(p(0), p(1))
GOTO display_result
f3:
solution = zone_sphere(p(0), p(1))
GOTO display_result
f4:
solution = force_att(p(0), p(1), p(2), p(3))
GOTO display_result
f5:
solution = dopp_shift(p(0), p(1), p(2), p(3))
display_result:
readout.caption = STR$(solution)
The_end:
END SUB
```

```
SUB assess_readout ()
readout_value = VAL(readout.caption)
END SUB
SUB Button0_Click (Index AS INTEGER)
IF ready > 0 THEN
    IF ready < 20 THEN
        readout.caption = readout.caption + "0"
        ready = ready + 1
    END IF
END IF
assess_readout
END SUB
SUB ButtonPos_Click (Index AS INTEGER)
IF ready > 0 THEN
    IF ready < 20 THEN
        readout.caption = readout.caption +
          RIGHT$(STR$(Index), 1)
        ready = ready + 1
    END IF
ELSE
    readout.caption = RIGHT$(STR$(Index), 1)
    ready = 1
END IF
assess_readout
END SUB
SUB Button_Point_Click (Index AS INTEGER)
STATIC point_lock AS INTEGER
IF point_lock = 0 AND ready < 20 THEN
    readout.caption = readout.caption + "."
    point_lock = 1
    ready = ready + 1
END IF
assess_readout
END SUB
SUB CalcList_Click ()
FOR n = 0 TO 4
    ParamText(n).caption = label$(CalcList.ListIndex, n)
NEXT n
Clear_Params
END SUB
SUB ClearAll_Click ()
readout.caption = "0"
```

```
readout_value = 0
combine_value = 0
ready = 0
END SUB
SUB ClearEntry_Click ()
readout.caption = "0"
readout_value = 0
ready = 0
END SUB
SUB Clear_Params ()
FOR pl = 0 TO 4
param(pl).text = ""
NEXT pl
ClearAll_Click
END SUB
SUB DividedBy_Click ()
assess_readout
IF readout_value <> 0 AND combine_value <> 0 THEN
    readout_value = readout_value / combine_value
END IF
combine_value = readout_value
readout.caption = STR$(readout_value)
ready = 0
END SUB
FUNCTION dopp_shift (vo, vs, fo, c)
dopp_shift = ((c + vo) / (c - vs)) * fo
END FUNCTION
SUB EditCut_Click ()
Clipboard.SETTEXT readout.caption
END SUB
SUB Enter_Click ()
assess_readout
readout_value = readout_value + combine_value
combine_value = readout_value
readout.caption = STR$(readout_value)
ready = 0
END SUB
FUNCTION force_att (me, mb, r, y)
force_att = -GRAV * ((me * mb) / ((r + y) ^ 2))
END FUNCTION
SUB Form_Load ()
CalcList.ADDITEM "Surface Area of RC Cylinder"
```

```
CalcList.ADDITEM "Volume of RC Cylinder"
CalcList.ADDITEM "Zone Area of Sphere"
CalcList.ADDITEM "Force of Earth/Body Attraction"
CalcList.ADDITEM "Doppler Shift Transmitted Freq."
label$(0, 0) = "Radius of right circular cylinder"
label$(0, 1) = "Height of cylinder"
label$(1, 0) = "Radius of right circular cylinder"
label$(1, 1) = "Height of cylinder"
label$(2, 0) = "Radius of sphere"
label$(2, 1) = "Height of zone"
label$(3, 0) = "Mass of Earth"
label$(3, 1) = "Mass of body in Earth's grav. field"
label$(3, 2) = "Radius of Earth"
label$(3, 3) = "Distance of body above Earth's surface"
label$(4, 0) = "Observer velocity"
label$(4, 1) = "Source velocity"
label$(4, 2) = "Observed frequency"
label$(4, 3) = "Velocity of wave"
END SUB
SUB Minus_Click ()
assess_readout
readout_value = readout_value - combine_value
combine_value = readout_value
readout.caption = STR$(readout_value)
ready = 0
END SUB
SUB Percent_Click ()
readout_value = readout_value / 100
readout.caption = STR$(readout_value)
ready = 0
END SUB
SUB StoreBank_Click (Index AS INTEGER)
param(Index).text = readout.caption
ready = 0
END SUB
FUNCTION surf_area_rccyl (r, h)
surf_area_rccyl = (2 * PI) * r * h
END FUNCTION
SUB Times_Click ()
assess_readout
readout_value = readout_value * combine_value
combine_value = readout_value
```

```
readout.caption = STR$(readout_value)
ready = 0
END SUB
FUNCTION volume_rccyl (r, h)
volume_rccyl = PI * (r ^ 2) * h
END FUNCTION
FUNCTION zone_sphere (r, h)
zone_sphere = 2 * PI * r * h
END FUNCTION
```

NameForm Mark IV Mailing List Manager

Project name: NAMEFRM4.MAK
Constituent files: NAMEFRM4.FRM, SELECTOR.FRM

NAMEFRM4.FRM

Object Type	*Property*	*Setting*
Form	.Left	3
	.Top	2
	.Width	74
	.Height	19
	.FormName	NameForm
	.Caption	NameForm Mark IV

Menu	*Control Name*	*Caption*
	File	&File
	FileOpen	..&Open
	FileSort	..&Sort
	separator1	..
	FileSaveMerge	..Save as &Mail Merge
	FileTrim	..&Trim
	Edit	&Edit
	EditCopy	----Cop&y
	EditClear	----Clea&r
	Record	&Record
	RecordInsert	----&Insert
	RecordDelete	----&Delete
	Display	&Display

Menu	*Control Name*	*Caption*
	DisplayFirst	----&First Name First
	DisplayLast	----&Last Name First
	GoToRecord	&GoTo

Object Type	*Property*	*Setting*
Text box	.Left	10
	.Top	1
	.Width	24
	.Height	3
	.CtlName	LastName
	.Caption	(blank)
Text box	.Left	40
	.Top	1
	.Width	17
	.Height	3
	.CtlName	FirstName
	.Caption	(blank)
Text box	.Left	63
	.Top	1
	.Width	5
	.Height	3
	.CtlName	MidInit
	.Caption	(blank)
Text box	.Left	10
	.Top	4
	.Width	58
	.Height	3
	.CtlName	CompanyName
	.Caption	(blank)
Text box	.Left	10
	.Top	7
	.Width	58
	.Height	3
	.CtlName	Address
	.Caption	(blank)

continues

Object Type	*Property*	*Setting*
Text box	`.Left`	`10`
	`.Top`	`10`
	`.Width`	`27`
	`.Height`	`3`
	`.CtlName`	`City`
	`.Caption`	(blank)
Text box	`.Left`	`45`
	`.Top`	`10`
	`.Width`	`7`
	`.Height`	`3`
	`.CtlName`	`State`
	`.Caption`	(blank)
Text box	`.Left`	`57`
	`.Top`	`10`
	`.Width`	`11`
	`.Height`	`3`
	`.CtlName`	`Zip`
	`.Caption`	(blank)
Label	`.Left`	`4`
	`.Top`	`1`
	`.Width`	`6`
	`.Height`	`2`
	`.Caption`	`Name`
	`.Alignment`	`1 - Right Justify`
Label	`.Left`	`34`
	`.Top`	`1`
	`.Width`	`6`
	`.Height`	`1`
	`.Caption`	`First`
	`.Alignment`	`1 - Right Justify`
Label	`.Left`	`59`
	`.Top`	`1`
	`.Width`	`4`
	`.Height`	`1`
	`.Caption`	`M.I.`
	`.Alignment`	`1 - Right Justify`

Object Type	*Property*	*Setting*
Label	.Left	2
	.Top	4
	.Width	7
	.Height	2
	.Caption	Company Name
	.Alignment	1 - Right Justify
Label	.Left	2
	.Top	7
	.Width	7
	.Height	1
	.Caption	Address
	.Alignment	1 - Right Justify
Label	.Left	5
	.Top	10
	.Width	5
	.Height	1
	.Caption	City
	.Alignment	1 - Right Justify
Label	.Left	40
	.Top	10
	.Width	5
	.Height	1
	.Caption	State
	.Alignment	1 - Right Justify
Label	.Left	52
	.Top	10
	.Width	5
	.Height	1
	.Caption	Zip
	.Alignment	1 - Right Justify
Label	.Left	50
	.Top	14
	.Width	17
	.Height	1
	.CtlName	Register

continues

Object Type	*Property*	*Setting*
	.Caption	Record #
	.Alignment	1 - Right Justify
Scroll bar	.Left	70
	.Top	0
	.Width	1
	.Height	16
	.CtlName	RecordShown
	.Min	1
	.Max	1
	.LargeChange	10
	.Value	1
Check box	.Left	7
	.Top	14
	.Width	27
	.Height	1
	.CtlName	MidName
	.Caption	Middle Name Prominent
	.Value	0
Button	.Left	35
	.Top	14
	.Width	11
	.Height	1
	.CtlName	Add
	.Caption	Add
	.Enabled	False

```
DECLARE SUB ShowRecord ()
DECLARE SUB ClearForm ()
DECLARE SUB LoadFile ()
DECLARE FUNCTION Envelope$ (rec AS INTEGER, order AS INTEGER)
'$FORM Selector
DECLARE SUB RecordShown_Change ()
DECLARE SUB AssessFilename ()
OPTION BASE 1
DIM SHARED LstName$(1000), FrstName$(1000), MdInit$(1000),
➥ CompanyNam$(1000), Adress$(1000),
Cty$(1000), Stat$(1000), Zp$(1000)
```

```
DIM SHARED RecordNo AS INTEGER
DIM lastline AS INTEGER, lhght AS INTEGER, llft AS INTEGER,
➥ lastmark AS INTEGER
DIM RecordNo AS INTEGER, MaxRecord AS INTEGER
DIM sortarray() AS INTEGER
COMMON SHARED targetfile$, pattern$, prmpt$
COMMON SHARED cancl AS INTEGER
TYPE NameRecord
    LastName AS STRING * 30
    FirstName AS STRING * 20
    MidInit AS STRING * 3
    CompanyName AS STRING * 50
    Address AS STRING * 50
    City AS STRING * 20
    State AS STRING * 5
    Zip AS STRING * 10
    MidProm AS INTEGER
END TYPE
COMMON SHARED CurRecord AS NameRecord

SUB Address_Change ()
CurRecord.Address = Address.Text
END SUB
SUB Add_Click ()
PUT #1, RecordNo, CurRecord
RecordNo = RecordNo + 1
MaxRecord = MaxRecord + 1
ClearForm
CurRecord.FirstName = "~*End"
PUT #1, MaxRecord + 1, CurRecord
RecordShown.Max = RecordShown.Max + 1
RecordShown.Value = RecordNo
IF RecordNo = MaxRecord THEN
    CurRecord.FirstName = ""
    PUT #1, RecordNo, CurRecord
END IF
ShowRecord
END SUB
SUB City_Change ()
CurRecord.City = City.Text
END SUB
SUB ClearForm ()
FirstName.Text = ""
```

```
LastName.Text = ""
MidInit.Text = ""
CompanyName.Text = ""
Address.Text = ""
City.Text = ""
State.Text = ""
Zip.Text = ""
MidName.Value = 0
END SUB
SUB CompanyName_Change ()
CurRecord.CompanyName = CompanyName.Text
END SUB
SUB DisplayFirst_Click ()
c$ = Envelope$(RecordNo, 1)
MSGBOX c$, 0, "Preview"
END SUB
SUB DisplayLast_Click ()
c$ = Envelope$(RecordNo, 0)
MSGBOX c$, 0, "Preview"
END SUB
SUB EditClear_Click ()
ClearForm
END SUB
SUB EditCopy_Click ()
c$ = Envelope$(RecordNo, 1)
Clipboard.SETTEXT c$
END SUB
FUNCTION Envelope$ (rec AS INTEGER, order AS INTEGER)
GET #1, rec, CurRecord
IF ASC(LEFT$(CurRecord.MidInit, 1)) <> 0 THEN
    Separator$ = " " + RTRIM$(CurRecord.MidInit) + " "
ELSE
    Separator$ = " "
END IF
IF order = 1 THEN
    IF MidName.Value = 0 THEN
        FullName$ = RTRIM$(CurRecord.FirstName) + Separator$ +
          RTRIM$(CurRecord.LastName)
    ELSE
        FullName$ = RTRIM$(CurRecord.MidInit) + " " +
          RTRIM$(CurRecord.FirstName) + " " +
            RTRIM$(CurRecord.LastName)
    END IF
```

```
ELSE
    IF MidName.Value = 0 THEN
       FullName$ = RTRIM$(CurRecord.LastName) + ", " +
         RTRIM$(CurRecord.FirstName) + Separator$
    ELSE
       FullName$ = RTRIM$(CurRecord.LastName) + ", " +
         Separator$ + RTRIM$(CurRecord.FirstName)
    END IF
END IF
WorkPlace$ = RTRIM$(CurRecord.CompanyName)
StreetAddress$ = RTRIM$(CurRecord.Address)
Residence$ = RTRIM$(CurRecord.City) + ", " +
  RTRIM$(CurRecord.State) + "  " +
RTRIM$(CurRecord.Zip)
  Next_Line$ = CHR$(13) + CHR$(10)
Envelope$ = FullName$ + Next_Line$ + WorkPlace$ + Next_Line$ +
  StreetAddress$ + Next_Line$ + Residence$
END FUNCTION
SUB FileOpen_Click ()
prmpt$ = "Choose a file to open:"
pattern$ = "*.nfm"
Selector.SHOW 1
filename$ = targetfile$
IF cancl = 1 THEN EXIT SUB
cancl = 0
CLOSE #1
LoadFile
END SUB
SUB FileSaveMerge_Click ()
prmpt$ = "Name of mail merge file:"
pattern$ = "*.mrg"
Selector.SHOW 1
IF cancl = 1 THEN EXIT SUB
filename$ = targetfile$
OPEN filename$ FOR OUTPUT AS #2
FOR ConvRec = 1 TO MaxRecord
    GET #1, ConvRec, CurRecord
```

```
    WRITE #2, RTRIM$(CurRecord.LastName),
      RTRIM$(CurRecord.FirstName),
      RTRIM$(CurRecord.MidInit),
      RTRIM$(CurRecord.CompanyName),
      RTRIM$(CurRecord.Address),
      RTRIM$(CurRecord.City),
      RTRIM$(CurRecord.State),
      RTRIM$(CurRecord.Zip),
      CurRecord.MidProm
NEXT ConvRec
CLOSE #2
ShowRecord
END SUB
SUB FileSort_Click ()
DIM j AS INTEGER, k AS INTEGER, l AS INTEGER, t AS INTEGER,
 seed AS INTEGER
REDIM sortarray(MaxRecord)
tmp = RecordNo
RecordNo = MaxRecord
IF ASC(LEFT$(LastName.Text, 1)) > 0 THEN
    PUT #1, RecordNo, CurRecord
END IF
FOR seed = 1 TO MaxRecord
    sortarray(seed) = seed
NEXT seed
DO
    l = l + 1
    IF l = MaxRecord THEN EXIT DO
    j = l
    FOR k = j + 1 TO MaxRecord - 1
        IF Envelope$(k, 0) <= Envelope$(j, 0) THEN
            j = k
        END IF
    NEXT k
    IF l <> j THEN
        t = sortarray(j)
        sortarray(j) = sortarray(l)
        sortarray(l) = t
    END IF
LOOP
OPEN "~temp.fil" FOR RANDOM AS #2 LEN = 190
FOR replac = 1 TO MaxRecord - 1
```

```
    GET #1, sortarray(replac), CurRecord
    PUT #2, replac, CurRecord
NEXT replac
CLOSE #2, #1
KILL filename$
NAME "~temp.fil" AS filename$
OPEN filename$ FOR RANDOM AS #1 LEN = 190
RecordNo = sortarray(tmp)
ShowRecord
END SUB
SUB FileTrim_Click ()
OPEN "~temp.fil" FOR RANDOM AS #2 LEN = 190
plc = 1
tmp = RecordNo
DO
    GET #1, plc, CurRecord
    PUT #2, plc, CurRecord
LOOP UNTIL CurRecord.FirstName = "~*End"
CLOSE #2, #1
KILL filename$
NAME "~temp.fil" AS filename$
OPEN filename$ FOR RANDOM AS #1 LEN = 190
RecordNo = tmp
ShowRecord
END SUB
SUB FirstName_Change ()
CurRecord.FirstName = FirstName.Text
END SUB
SUB Form_Load ()
filename$ = "NAMES.NFM"
LoadFile
END SUB
SUB GoToRecord_Click ()
recno$ = INPUTBOX$("Go to which record number?", "Go To. . .")
RecordNo = VAL(recno$)
RecordShown.Value = RecordNo
ShowRecord
END SUB
SUB LastName_Change ()
CurRecord.LastName = LastName.Text
END SUB
SUB LoadFile ()
```

```
OPEN filename$ FOR RANDOM AS #1 LEN = 190
IF LOF(1) > 190 THEN
    DO
        GET #1, MaxRecord + 1, CurRecord
        MaxRecord = MaxRecord + 1
    LOOP UNTIL CurRecord.FirstName = "~*End" OR MaxRecord >
    ➥ LOF(1) / 190
ELSE
    CurRecord.FirstName = "~*End"
    PUT #1, 2, CurRecord
    CurRecord.MidProm = 0
    CurRecord.FirstName = ""
    PUT #1, 1, CurRecord
    MaxRecord = 1
END IF
titl$ = "NameForm Mark IV - [" + UCASE$(filename$) + "]"
NameForm.Caption = titl$
RecordNo = 1
RecordShown.Max = MaxRecord
RecordShown.Value = 1
IF RecordNo < MaxRecord THEN
    Add.Enabled = 0
ELSE
    Add.Enabled = -1
END IF
ShowRecord
END SUB
SUB MidInit_Change ()
CurRecord.MidInit = MidInit.Text
END SUB
SUB MidName_Click ()
CurRecord.MidProm = MidName.Value
END SUB
SUB RecordDelete_Click ()
IF RecordNo < MaxRecord THEN
    FOR mve = RecordNo TO MaxRecord
        GET #1, mve + 1, CurRecord
        PUT #1, mve, CurRecord
    NEXT mve
END IF
ClearForm
IF RecordNo = MaxRecord THEN
```

```
    RecordNo = RecordNo - 1
END IF
IF MaxRecord > 1 THEN
    MaxRecord = MaxRecord - 1
    RecordShown.Max = RecordShown.Max - 1
ELSE
    PUT #1, 1, CurRecord
END IF
ShowRecord
END SUB
SUB RecordInsert_Click ()
FOR mve = MaxRecord + 1 TO RecordNo STEP -1
    GET #1, mve, CurRecord
    PUT #1, mve + 1, CurRecord
NEXT mve
ClearForm
PUT #1, RecordNo, CurRecord
MaxRecord = MaxRecord + 1
RecordShown.Max = RecordShown.Max + 1
END SUB
SUB RecordShown_Change ()
PUT #1, RecordNo, CurRecord
RecordNo = RecordShown.Value
IF RecordNo < MaxRecord THEN
    Add.Enabled = 0
ELSE
    Add.Enabled = -1
END IF
ShowRecord
END SUB
SUB RecordShown_GotFocus ()
hght = (250 + RecordShown.Top) * (RecordShown.Height /
➥ RecordShown.Max)
lft = RecordShown.Left - 200
NameForm.DrawMode = 7
linmark = RecordShown.Value
NameForm.CurrentX = NameForm.Width - 1000
NameForm.CurrentY = linmark - 250
NameForm.PRINT RecordShown.Value; " ";
cx = NameForm.CurrentX
LINE (cx, linmark)-(NameForm.Width - 1000, linmark),
➥ RGB(255, 255, 0)
```

```
NameForm.DrawMode = 13
lastline = NameForm.CurrentY
lastmark = linmark
llft = lft
END SUB
SUB RecordShown_LostFocus ()
NameForm.DrawMode = 7
NameForm.FontName = "Helv"
NameForm.FontSize = 8
NameForm.Line (llft, 250)-(llft, lhght), RGB(0, 0, 255)
NameForm.CurrentX = NameForm.Width - 1000
NameForm.CurrentY = linmark - 250
NameForm.PRINT RecordShown.Value; " "
cx = NameForm.CurrentX
LINE (cx, lastline)-(NameForm.Width - 1000, lastline),
➥ RGB(0, 0, 255)
NameForm.DrawMode = 13
END SUB
SUB ShowRecord ()
GET #1, RecordNo, CurRecord
Reg$ = "Record #" + STR$(RecordNo) + " of " + STR$(MaxRecord)
Register.Caption = Reg$
LastName.Text = RTRIM$(CurRecord.LastName)
FirstName.Text = RTRIM$(CurRecord.FirstName)
MidInit.Text = RTRIM$(CurRecord.MidInit)
CompanyName.Text = RTRIM$(CurRecord.CompanyName)
Address.Text = RTRIM$(CurRecord.Address)
City.Text = RTRIM$(CurRecord.City)
State.Text = RTRIM$(CurRecord.State)
Zip.Text = RTRIM$(CurRecord.Zip)
MidName.Value = CurRecord.MidProm
END SUB
SUB State_Change ()
CurRecord.State = State.Text
END SUB
SUB Zip_Change ()
CurRecord.Zip = Zip.Text
END SUB
```

SELECTOR.FRM

Object Type	*Property*	*Setting*
Form	.Left	16
	.Top	3
	.Width	50
	.Height	17
	.FormName	Selector
	.Caption	(blank)
	.BorderStyle	3
Drive	.Left	3
	.Top	2
	.Width	18
	.Height	1
	.CtlName	Drive1
	.BackColor	14 - Yellow
Directory	.Left	3
	.Top	4
	.Width	18
	.Height	8
	.CtlName	Dir1
File list	.Left	23
	.Top	4
	.Width	21
	.Height	7
	.CtlName	File1
Text box	.Left	23
	.Top	2
	.Width	21
	.Height	1
	.CtlName	Filename
	.Text	(blank)
	.BackColor	15 - Bright White
Label	.Left	23
	.Top	1
	.Width	21
	.Height	1
	.Caption	Filename:

Object type	*Property*	*Setting*
Button	.Left	23
	.Top	13
	.Width	12
	.Height	1
	.CtlName	OK
	.Caption	OK
	.BackColor	10 - Bright Green
Button	.Left	34
	.Top	13
	.Width	12
	.Height	1
	.CtlName	Cancel
	.Caption	Cancel
	.BackColor	12 - Bright Red

```
DECLARE SUB File1_Click ()
DECLARE SUB OK_Click ()

SUB Cancel_Click ()
cancl = 1
TargetFile$ = ""
UNLOAD Selector
END SUB
SUB Dir1_Change ()
File1.Path = Dir1.Path
File1_Click
END SUB
SUB Drive1_Change ()
Dir1.Path = Drive1.Drive
CHDRIVE Drive1.Drive
END SUB
SUB File1_Click ()
Filename.Text = File1.Filename
END SUB
SUB File1_DblClick ()
OK_Click
END SUB
SUB Form_Load ()
```

```
IF Pattern$ = "" THEN
    File1.Pattern = "*.*"
ELSE
    File1.Pattern = Pattern$
END IF
Filename.Text = File1.Pattern
cancl = 0
IF prmpt$ = "" THEN
    Prompt.Caption = "Filename:"
ELSE
    Prompt.Caption = prmpt$
END IF
END SUB
SUB OK_Click ()
pth$ = Dir1.Path
IF File1.Filename = "" THEN
    fil$ = Filename.Text
ELSE
    fil$ = File1.Filename
END IF
IF RIGHT$(pth$, 1) = "\" THEN
    Filename.Text = pth$ + fil$
ELSE
    Filename.Text = pth$ + "\" + fil$
END IF
TargetFile$ = Filename.Text
UNLOAD Selector
END SUB
```

Glossary

algorithm Any real-world process having inherent objects and elements, however tangible, that can be represented by linguistic or numeric code, and having procedures that can be simulated using terms acquainted with logic.

alphanumeric Having the quality of containing either letters or digits, or both.

antecedent The graphic object referred to by a property or method, generally written following the period that separates it from the graphic object with which it is associated.

application An operational program or set of cooperative programs within the computer environment having a work product that is a specific document or set of documents.

argument A value or variable used within a function or formula. This term is often synonymous with *parameter*.

array A list or set of related values or alphanumeric contents, collectively referred to by a common term.

ASCII The American Standard Code for Information Interchange. This is the most widely used code for transmission and storage of alphanumeric data in a bitwise form within or between computers.

binary Representable using as many as two digits. This term also refers to the base 2 numeral system.

binary access A method of storing data to and retrieving it from a device, whereby the structure of the data is not a factor, and data is interpreted only as single bits, bytes, or characters.

binary operator A symbol that represents a mathematical function combining, comparing, or equating two values.

binary state The minimum unit of value in a computer, which can be described as either true (–1 or 1, depending on the interpreter) or false (0).

bit Short for *binary digit,* which is the elementary unit of value within a computer, representing a logical state of true (1 or ON) or false (0 or OFF). Mechanically, it represents the presence of electrical current.

bitmap A group of related values which, when represented on-screen as pixels rather than characters, forms an image.

blit Short for *block transfer,* it is an instantaneous relocation of a grouping of memory contents from one region to another.

Boolean operator A term used to represent the comparison of one binary value to another, the intent being to derive a single binary value as a result.

branching To direct the interpreter to suspend execution of the normal sequence of instructions and resume the sequence at some other specified point in the program.

break A suspension of the operating state of the program.

breakpoint An instruction line temporarily scheduled to force execution of the program to be suspended immediately following the execution of that line.

buffer A holding area in memory consisting of a fixed number of bytes, reserved for data that is to be sent to some device—often a disk file—at some later time, generally when the buffer is full.

bug The result of any process that fails to perform in the manner for which it is intended or designed, although which cannot be detected automatically by the interpreter or compiler. Thus, by its nature, a bug allows logical program execution to continue along a potentially disastrous course.

button A control or graphic object used for passing directives or commands to the program.

byte The primary memory storage unit for all forms of data in a computer system, composed of eight binary digits (bits).

caption A non-editable element of text appearing within a form or graphic object.

channel A logically interpreted device (not a tangible, physical entity) for maintaining the flow of data between the interpreter and an output device or storage unit.

check box A graphic control used to represent an on/off or true/false state, the setting of which is chosen by the user.

child An object or element belonging to, or residing within, a greater *parent* element.

clause **1.** A compound instruction that contains one or more subordinate instructions and is distributed in a single group over more than one line. **2.** Any set of instructions, the execution of which is dependent on the value of a variable in a mathematical expression.

clipboard The logical device maintained by Visual Basic for MS-DOS, which retains an element of text being transferred between forms or graphic objects.

combo box A control that enables a user to choose an item from a list or type a choice that may not appear on that list.

compiler A program that takes high-level source code and breaks that code into its most primary logical components, resulting in a machine code executable file that requires no pre-interpretation by any other program.

composite variable A container for multiple numeral, string, or other composite variables, addressed together as one unit using a single, arbitrarily defined term and invoked within an instruction using object-oriented syntax.

concatenation The process of joining elements of data together, especially with respect to strings.

condition **1.** The test of whether an instruction will be executed. **2.** A mathematical test, stated in the form of an expression, used to determine the order of execution of the program.

constant A term that stands in place of a value in an expression, having its value set only once.

context The "understanding" the interpreter has of which variables and functions of a procedure pertain only to that procedure, which values and variables are exchanged between this procedure and the one that called it, and which variables and functions pertain to the program as a whole. In other words, the relative degree to which one component of a program pertains to the rest of that program.

control A graphic object placed on a form specifically for purposes of data acquisition and display, in a manner that easily can be made familiar to the user.

control array A set of similar, related controls in a form that are referenced together as a group, and the operation of which is jointly defined by a single procedure in the source code.

cross-modular variable A variable declared at the module level, whose scope extends between the various modules in the project but does not extend to any procedures in the project.

cursor A marker indicating the point within a document or textually oriented control where new characters appear after they are typed; also called the *caret.*

data The carrier(s) of information within a computer.

database Any stored group of data elements containing the structure by which those elements are related to each other.

decimal A number that can be represented using as many as 10 digits. The term also refers to the base 10 numeral system.

declaration **1.** The first statement in a program to assign a legitimate value to a variable. **2.** An instruction that introduces a procedure or process and defines the context of that process.

default The state of an object, device, or memory construct that is presumed beforehand if no instructions to alter that state have been processed.

delimiter A character of punctuation used to distinguish elements of an expression from each other or to separate them from each other.

dialog box A window having the purpose of obtaining at least one element of user input. It is often abbreviated as *dialog*.

document The primary data product of an application as it is represented in memory.

drag To move an image of a graphic control using the mouse, when forms are active.

dynamic array An array whose length in elements can be set or changed on demand.

environment The logical and often graphical facilities one program provides another for easier, more efficient operation.

equation A statement of equality that assigns a value—whether it is a numeral or an arithmetically derived value—to a variable.

error The result of any process that fails to perform in the manner it is intended or designed, and which, by its nature or in the interest of preventing disaster, prevents logical program execution from continuing.

event A unit of user input, utilizing any of the available devices attached to the computer system, which triggers the execution of a procedure in response.

event procedure A portion of a form module that is executed once a graphical event is recognized by the system.

executable file A file recognized by MS-DOS as being composed of instructions to the CPU, and not data.

expression **1.** An arithmetic comparison between two values, the result of which is expressed logically as a binary state. **2.** One or more values or variables arithmetically joined by functions or functional operators. **3.** An assignment of value to a variable with another value, variable, or another expression.

field Any container for an element or item of data, whether it is a graphic object for the display of that datum, a region of memory reserved for that datum, or a region of a file reserved for that datum.

floating-point The storage format for a possibly fractional value, having its decimal point position stored in memory as a separate value.

focus The state of a graphic object indicated on-screen by a hazy rectangle, which designates that the control is active or awaiting input from the user.

form The Input/Output window for Visual Basic for MS-DOS applications and the container for graphic objects that act as controls.

formula An algebraic expression of equality that states the relationships between qualities, quantities, or other such values, whether they are known or unknown.

frame A subdivision of a form that divides groupings of elements, such as options, from groups in other frames and elsewhere on the form.

function An arithmetic operation performed on a value, variable, or expression, the result of which is returned in a single variable.

global Extending in scope or context to all parts of an application.

graphic device Any mechanical or logical unit having the purpose of displaying data as both characters and images.

graphic object A data structure that can be represented visually and behaves to some degree as a device that receives user input and displays result data.

graphics array The method for interpreting graphic images to be displayed on-screen as a map of binary code.

handle The accession number given a logical device by the operating system or environment, used to identify that device within the program.

hexadecimal A number that can be represented using as many as 16 digits. This term also refers to the base 16 numeral system.

high-level language A computing language that is designed to be more interpretable by humans, and that is generally reinterpreted into low-level machine code.

icon A functionally symbolic representation of a form, window, device, or application.

image The visual interpretation of a segment of values in memory.

index The value represented by a subscript of an array.

information Any symbol or message that is meaningful to people.

instruction Any complete directive made within a program, composed of a keyword and any parameters, terms, or delimiters associated with that directive.

integer Any whole number that has no fractional value.

integrity The measure of the logical correspondence between data and the information it is intended to represent.

internal variable A variable whose name is recognized by the interpreter as a keyword, and whose purpose has been defined beforehand by the interpreter.

interpreter Any program that receives a set of compound, high-level instructions from the programmer and instantly translates them into more rudimentary instructions that are easier for the computer to understand and execute.

iteration One repeated cycle of execution of the instructions in a loop clause or any repetitious body of instructions.

keyword A term having its use reserved for instructions. It cannot be used for variables or labels.

label A non-instruction written on a line by itself and succeeded by a colon, designating a branching point.

library A set of process names that are treated as procedure names by Visual Basic for MS-DOS, but which are actually calls to processes within an executable file outside of Visual Basic for MS-DOS, that can be linked to or compiled with the Visual Basic for MS-DOS application.

list box A control that allows one or more items to be chosen from a list, often a scrollable list.

local The minimum scope of a variable or composite structure, which limits its references to the confines of a single procedure.

logical context A program structure that simulates an electronic device for the sake of any routine that directs data to it for output.

logical reduction The act of obtaining the solution value to an expression by reducing the elements of that expression through arithmetic combination.

loop A sequence of instructions that are executed repetitively either for a specified count or until a condition is evaluated true.

low-level language A set of computing symbols that is designed to be readily interpretable more by the computer than by the human programmer.

map A large block of code in memory whose contents numerically encode in another form the contents of some other block—generally a larger one—or the contents of the screen.

maximize To bring a reduced icon back into the workspace as the form or window associated with that icon.

memory map A database table in memory specifically for the operating system's use, which regulates the storage of object code, of intermediate Visual Basic for MS-DOS p-code, and of variable values and contents.

menu bar The area of a form or window below the title bar where categorical command or directive choices are listed.

meta-application A single task formed by the cooperation of several application components working in conjunction within the same environment.

method An instruction that directs the interpreter to perform a programmed action on a graphic object.

minimize To reduce a form or window to its associated icon temporarily, thus suspending its primary execution.

modal An attribute of a window that suspends the operability of every other window until it is exited.

modular variable A variable declared at the module level, whose scope does not extend to procedures within that module.

module The core component of a Visual Basic for MS-DOS application, comprising routines and procedures, and possibly comprising form contents and properties, stored within a single file.

module-level code That portion of the source code in a module that exists outside of the framework of a formal procedure.

multitasking The planned or scheduled cooperation of multiple programs within a single computer system, with the capability for single elements of data to be recognized by those multiple programs during the same session.

nest The special indentation of typesetting optionally given to a set of dependent instructions within a clause.

object In object-oriented syntax, a data structure that combines the contents and attributes of the data, along with the encoded form of its function.

object code A file on disk or in memory composed of CPU instructions that are not symbolized in any way for human interpretation. Also called *machine code.*

octal Numbers that can be represented using as many as eight digits. This term also refers to the base 8 numeral system.

operator A symbol that represents a mathematical function combining, comparing, or equating two values.

option dot A control, generally one of a set of such controls, used to represent the user's single choice of all the elements within a collected set.

parameter A value or variable passed to a procedure from outside that procedure.

parent The greater object or element with which another object or element is associated.

phrase Any functional combination of terms within an instruction or routine.

pixel The minimum unit of measurement or plotting in the physical screen coordinate system.

pointer[1] The logical device operated by the mouse, used for indicating elements on-screen.

pointer[2] **1.** A value that represents the location in memory where a value or contents of a variable are stored. **2.** Any logical value that represents the location or position where another value can be obtained.

precision Refers to the number of bytes used to represent a variable's value.

procedure The component of a Visual Basic for MS-DOS application whose purpose is to logically describe or model at least one task or mathematical function, passing its results to some other component.

program The symbolic form of a task, or any computing process that is described logically in a uniformly interpretable code.

project All the files that collectively comprise a Visual Basic for MS-DOS application.

property An attribute of a graphic object that is addressable by name using object-oriented syntax and can be described by a value or term.

random access A mode for storing data to and retrieving it from a device, either physical or logical, whereby data can be written to or read from a region or file at any specifiable point, at any time.

record A logical grouping of related elements of data within a data file or database.

relation The mathematics that symbolically join two or more elements or fields of a database.

RGB Refers to a method of mixing red, green, and blue colors optically.

routine Any arbitrarily bounded sequence of instructions within a body of source code.

runtime The period in which instructions within the source code of the program are executing.

scope The extent to which the reference of a variable is applied across the various divisions of the source code of a program.

scroll bar A sliding graphic device having the purpose of representing a value within a minimum and maximum range.

sequential access A mode for storing data to and retrieving data from a physical device in an absolute, specifiable sequence.

setting A term that represents the state, appearance, or some aspect of a graphic object.

source code The written text of a program in its native language.

startup module The module within a project slated to begin execution first.

statement An instruction that specifies a change or deviation in the operating status of the program.

static Used to describe a variable or structure local to a procedure, having its value or contents maintained by the interpreter on exiting that procedure, for use when the procedure is entered again.

static array An array whose size in elements is fixed throughout the execution of the application.

string A sequence of any number of bytes that are interpreted jointly as text or alphanumeric characters.

subordinate module One whose procedures are called by the main startup module.

subroutine A set of instructions within a procedure that is executable repetitively, is callable by name, and at whose end forces a branch back to the instruction just past the one that called it.

subscript An integral value or variable within an array variable that represents the place or position of a value in the array's list or table.

syntax The arrangement of terms within an instruction or clause.

tab sequence The arbitrarily designated order of graphic objects within a form, representing the sequence in which the focus passes through those objects during runtime, when the user presses the Tab key.

table A stored database component consisting of data, along with the structure of that data, such as field names and relations.

tag Refers to the alias name arbitrarily given to a graphic object.

title bar The uppermost bar of a form or window, which generally contains the title of that window.

variable An arbitrarily named term that represents a unit of data in memory that can be altered by the program.

viewport A rectangular subdivision of a graphics screen, to which graphic output is restricted.

virtual terminal Any graphic object capable of receiving input and output in the manner of a standard computer terminal.

watchpoint A program line designated by the programmer to send an extra signal to a special window, containing the value or contents of a specific variable being watched.

window **1.** The graphical rectangular container for all subordinate graphic elements in an application containing forms. **2.** A portion of the graphics screen that logically displays a different magnification of the physical graphics array.

workspace The area of the screen where forms and Visual Basic for MS-DOS tools reside—but may not necessarily appear—during an application's runtime.

Index

Symbols

A

B

C

D

E

J–K

L

M

N

O

P

Q–R

S

T

W

X-Z

Free Catalog!

Mail us this registration form today, and we'll send you a free catalog featuring Que's complete line of best-selling books.

Name of Book ______

Name ______

Title ______

Phone ( ) ______

Company ______

Address ______

City ______

State ______ ZIP ______

Please check the appropriate answers:

1. Where did you buy your Que book?
   - ☐ Bookstore (name: ______)
   - ☐ Computer store (name: ______)
   - ☐ Catalog (name: ______)
   - ☐ Direct from Que
   - ☐ Other: ______

2. How many computer books do you buy a year?
   - ☐ 1 or less
   - ☐ 2-5
   - ☐ 6-10
   - ☐ More than 10

3. How many Que books do you own?
   - ☐ 1
   - ☐ 2-5
   - ☐ 6-10
   - ☐ More than 10

4. How long have you been using this software?
   - ☐ Less than 6 months
   - ☐ 6 months to 1 year
   - ☐ 1-3 years
   - ☐ More than 3 years

5. What influenced your purchase of this Que book?
   - ☐ Personal recommendation
   - ☐ Advertisement
   - ☐ In-store display
   - ☐ Price
   - ☐ Que catalog
   - ☐ Que mailing
   - ☐ Que's reputation
   - ☐ Other: ______

6. How would you rate the overall content of the book?
   - ☐ Very good
   - ☐ Good
   - ☐ Satisfactory
   - ☐ Poor

7. What do you like *best* about this Que book?

   ______

   ______

8. What do you like *least* about this Que book?

   ______

   ______

9. Did you buy this book with your personal funds?
   - ☐ Yes ☐ No

10. Please feel free to list any other comments you may have about this Que book.

    ______

    ______

    ______

QUE

Order Your Que Books Today!

Name ______

Title ______

Company ______

City ______

State ______ ZIP ______

Phone No. ( ) ______

Method of Payment:

Check ☐ (Please enclose in envelope.)

Charge My: VISA ☐ MasterCard ☐

American Express ☐

Charge # ______

Expiration Date ______

Order No.	Title	Qty.	Price	Total

You can **FAX** your order to **1-317-573-2583.** Or call **1-800-428-5331, ext. ORDR** to order direct.
Please add $2.50 per title for shipping and handling.

Subtotal	
Shipping & Handling	
Total	

QUE

NO POSTAGE
NECESSARY
IF MAILED
IN THE
UNITED STATES

BUSINESS REPLY MAIL
First Class Permit No. 9918 Indianapolis, IN

Postage will be paid by addressee

que®

11711 N. College
Carmel, IN 46032